INTRODUCTORY PSYCHOLOGY

Sir Wilfred Grenfell—a splendid embodiment of those fundamental principles of human psychology that are set forth in this book. A man of high courage, boundless energy, and unquenchable faith in his fellow men, he has left upon the northland an imprint of his self-sacrificing and winsome personality that will endure as long as the sun. (Read about Dr. Grenfell's life on pages 469-470.)

Introductory Psychology

LAWRENCE A. AVERILL, Ph.D.

HEAD OF THE DEPARTMENT OF PSYCHOLOGY

WORCESTER STATE TEACHERS COLLEGE

WORCESTER, MASSACHUSETTS

New York · THE MACMILLAN COMPANY · *1949*

FOREWORD

To the Teacher

In the present situation in which man finds himself on the earth, it is not enough that youth shall be schooled merely in science and in the formal subjects of the curriculum. The years of the immediate future will put considerable strain upon the personalities and characters of men as they seek to redeem a world that has developed an unfortunately one-sided technological civilization. Of equal importance at least with the training of youth in the formal and the material in our culture must needs also be the development of the sane and rational mind and of keen insight into personal values and potentialities, and the comprehension of some of the more significant motives and principles that underlie human behavior as it manifests itself in the individual and in the mass. It will prove a disastrous mistake if we allow youth, facing as it does the problems and the challenge of living in a world of mighty physical force and of powerful man-made machines, to be handicapped in achieving its place by failure of the schools to lay the secure foundations of an enduring mental health. On no other basis than this may the operation and control of tomorrow's world be safely left to the rising generation.

The single purpose of this elementary textbook in psychology is to provide beginning students with a highly practical and helpful introduction to the important contributions which psychology has to offer the adolescent in ordering and conducting his life. In a very real sense, the adolescent lives simultaneously the life of a student, the life of a family member, the life of a budding thinker, the life of a toiler in the workaday world, the life of an individual-by-himself, and the life of a participating member of the social group. In the belief that elementary psychology can be presented in such a way as to aid the young person to know himself better and to adjust more satisfyingly in each of these categories of experience, this book has been prepared.

The author professes no cramping allegiance to any particular school or viewpoint in psychology. Beginners in any field ordinarily have scant interest in moot questions and theories of interpretation, and those who write textbooks for them should be guided accordingly. The science of psychology is notably fecund in theories and points of view, and the author has striven to avoid any semblance of indoctrinating elementary students into any particular system or pattern of psychological thought. Indeed, he has refrained so far as possible from devoting any attention whatever to partisan considerations.

The viewpoint maintained throughout is that of the mental hygienist. Developed from this angle, applied psychology has for the adolescent a timely and dynamic message. The rapidly increasing number of schools in the United States that are offering work in adjustment problems and personality development testifies to the strong feeling of need that exists for a practical and usable psychology at this very important level.

The book, with its exercises and problems, is calculated to provide all the requirements for a complete elementary course. The subject matter has been carefully adapted to the experience and the capacity of the students for whom it was prepared. Anecdotal materials, diagrams, and illustrations have been chosen for their appeal to young people and for their power to captivate their interest as well as to fix the inherent lesson. Teaching aids and suggestions may be made points of departure for much fascinating adventure by youthful questers in the psychological terrain. Simple but interesting and valuable experiments are provided for each chapter. At the ends of the chapters will be found references which have been selected not from the conventional textbooks in psychology—which are apt to make rather forbidding reading for elementary students —but for the most part from the world's great classic and contemporary literature—fiction, biography, adventure, poetry, drama. They furnish a most stimulating backdrop against which the panorama of living psychology is enacted.

To the Student

In the course of your progress along the educational pathway which you have been following, you have adventured into many fields of human knowledge. You have studied some of the great masterpieces of literature. You have explored the richness of our English language and have developed skill in written and oral speech. You have developed facility in handling numbers and symbols in arithmetic, algebra, geometry, and perhaps trigonometry. You have thought after them the great thoughts of physicists, chemists, biologists, zoologists in your laboratory work in science. You have drawn aside the dusty curtain of the past and have stood beside Darius, Pericles, the Caesars, Charlemagne, Elizabeth, Washington, Bonaparte, Victoria. You have delved into the cultures of Orientals and Occidentals; of Moslems, Hindus, Christians, Jews. You have learned about geographical regions; about the production and distribution of commodities; about commerce in the world's

far-flung traffic lanes. You have studied Spanish and French—
perhaps also Latin, Italian, German.

These represent some of the many fascinating fields of
knowledge into which you have ventured.

It is now time for you to begin to learn more about yourself as an individual, more about living adequately and satisfyingly in this extremely complex world in which you find
yourself.

A great Teacher once asked the question: "What shall it
profit a man, if he shall gain the whole world, and lose his
own soul?" Surely the mere mastery of facts, the mere achieving of information in all the broad fields of human knowledge
and experience, can hardly make anybody an interesting and
effective individual. One who would fit harmoniously into
his world must learn much about the psychology of *himself*.

In this book, you will be studying about the psychology of
you, and of your friends and associates. As an adventurer in
living, you can undertake no greater or more vital task than
that of learning to understand yourself better.

What do you want of life? How will the habits you are
forming aid or hinder you in your quest? How powerful is
the role which your mental attitudes will be playing as you
proceed? How can you learn to study economically as new
problems confront you from day to day? Can you detect the
difference between true fatigue and the treacherous pseudo
fatigue? What is the role which your feelings and your emotions are playing in regulating your conduct and motivating
you onward? What is sound thinking, and what is wish-thinking, and how will they affect your achievements? Can you
detect propaganda, and steer your course serenely and intelligently among the pressure groups that will assail you on every
hand?

How are you meeting the obstacles in your everyday experience that would thwart and discourage you? What thinking are you doing about your vocation and your place in tomorrow's world? What are the secrets of building a character that will bring lasting satisfactions? Have you learned how to live happily with yourself and with others? What sort of personality are you fashioning to carry you through the years? Are you constructing the blueprints of a healthy mind?

Here are questions of prime importance to every individual as he prepares to take his place in the world of work and of achievement. You will find it challenging in the extreme to attempt to answer them. True, your pursuit of these questions will be quite different from the conventional work units you have done in literature, in the social studies, in mathematics and the sciences. It will be, however, certainly no less stimulating, and the values yielded will be no less momentous.

Here's wishing you a pleasant journey as you explore widely this new field of the *psychology of you!* When you have completed the journey, you will find that you have in your possession many valuable and lasting mementos of the trip that we shall have taken together.

Forward!

Acknowledgments

Grateful acknowledgment for permission to reproduce copyrighted material is herewith made to the American Medical Association; to the American Psychological Association; to Farrar and Rinehart; to Henry Holt and Company; to Houghton Mifflin Company; to Fred E. Inbau and to the Williams and Wilkins Company; to the C. H. Stoelting Company; to the *New York Herald Tribune;* to the *New York Times;* and to Nixon Waterman.

The author desires also to express his appreciation to Miss Mary Brightman, of the Worcester (Massachusetts) Public Library; to Mrs. Elizabeth Webb and Mrs. Earl Pulsifer, of the Wiscasset (Maine) Public Library; to the staff of the Portland (Maine) Public Library for invaluable assistance in connection with the bibliographical materials; and finally, to his wife, Esther C. Averill, without whose discriminating and resourceful co-operation this book could never have been written.

LAWRENCE A. AVERILL

CONTENTS

WHAT'S AHEAD IN CHAPTER 1

What Do You Want to Make You Happy?

Silas Marner, in George Eliot's story of the same name, wanted only one thing—his gold. At least, that is what he thought for a long time.

Evening after evening, he would draw his curtains closely so that no prying eyes might see, pull forth from its hiding place his well-filled chest, and pass his fingers greedily, gloatingly, through the mass of yellow coins within it.

Silas had not always been a miser: time was when he had been as fine and generous as his neighbors. But evil days had fallen upon him, soured him to all human sympathies, and made him a hard man. If you have read the story, you know how the influence of Eppie, a little waif who came to live with him, finally succeeded in extricating Silas from his shell and softening him into a kindly old man.

Alexander the Great, King of Macedon and conqueror of the world, from earliest boyhood wanted power, domination. "My father will leave nothing for me to do!" he exclaimed in disappointment after one of Philip's notable military successes.

But events subsequently proved that there was plenty left for the son to accomplish. A king before he was twenty years old, Alexander set forth on a career of fiery conquest that brought under Macedonian sway Greeks, Persians, Egyptians, Scythians. "Sighing for more worlds to conquer," as he is said to have done, he led his hosts even to the gates of distant India. Before the close of his brief life (he died at thirty-three) his name was written high among the greatest conquerors of all time. Consumed by an almost fanatical thirst for domination, Alexander was foremost among the world's early tyrants.

Tom Belford lives with his parents on Cedar Avenue. That is to say, he does when he isn't off somewhere with Ted Perry and Joe Splaine and Bill Barton and the rest of the "bunch." This group of boys wants nothing more than to be together. The classes at South High being over for the day, Tom and his friends may be seen any afternoon in a huddle somewhere planning how to spend the next few hours. Some days they play ball on the athletic field; some days they take long hikes out of town and back; some days they go to the movies; some days they just fool, hang around, indulge in the craziest kind of horse play.

Often it is suppertime before Tom appears on Cedar Avenue, tired—yes, but contented with the good companionship the day has brought. In the evening, he is likely to monopolize the family telephone, chatting with the same Ted and Joe and Bill!

Sometimes Tom's mother grumbles a bit. "You'd think," she remarks dryly, "that you boys would get sick and tired of each other, the way you're always together and always telephoning!"

But the boys never do!

All of Us Have Wants, Wise or Unwise

Silas Marner, Alexander the Great, and Tom Belford are all alike in one respect: they are all motivated by strong wants of one sort or another. With Marner, it is money, treasure;

with Alexander, it is authority, dominion; with young Belford, it is companionship, good fellowship. You and I—and everybody else in the world—are no different from these three, and no different from one another, for we, too, each have wants, drives, appetites that motivate us in the things we do. Some of our wants are of doubtful or negative value, like Marner's and Alexander's; some of them are of real worth and comfort, like Tom Belford's. Regardless, however, of their wisdom or their unwisdom, we all have plenty of wants.

✶ ✶ ✶

In this chapter you will be thinking about a large number of these wants of ours by which we are driven day after day, year after year, and throughout all our lives. You will learn to understand better some of your own aspirations and yearnings, and why they seem so important to you. You will find out also how to gauge and judge your wants wisely.

Fig. 1. What fundamental human wants are these young people satisfying? How do you satisfy these same wants?

1. OUR HUMAN WANTS

You are now setting out upon an exploration of one of the most fascinating of subjects—*psychology,* the science of the human mind and of human behavior. Before you begin to read this first chapter on human wants, transfer the following chart to a sheet of paper and make as many entries in both columns as you can:

AS I SEE IT

Things I Want Very Much	Things I Strongly Do Not Want
1.	1.
2.	2.
3.	3.
4.	4.
5. etc.	5. etc.

You will certainly have no difficulty in filling in this table. Everybody can think of innumerable things he wants, as well as of plenty of things he doesn't want!

ANIMAL AND HUMAN WANTS

An animal's wants are mostly physical. Animals live pretty largely on a physical level. Though their wants are strong, they are not numerous; they may be included in the single category of *comfort,* or *freedom from pain.* Specifically, animal wants comprise food, drink, warmth or coolness, sleep and rest, activity or inactivity, mating, protection of the young, the stoppage of pain, freedom from restraint, and the continuance of what is comfortable. These wants are so simple and

5

elementary that we may consider them to be entirely *instinctive* (inborn or natural) requiring no mental direction or control.

The daily round of the animal—domestic or wild—is thus principally limited to the seeking and devouring of food when hungry and of drink when thirsty; to the seeking of warmth when cold and of coolness when hot; of rest when tired and of sleep at the usual rhythmic time for sleep; of activity when rested; of inactivity when fatigued or when satiated with food; and of a mate when the mating rhythm becomes ascendant. When all these things, in turn or in season, are experienced, the animal is comfortable and satisfied; if they are denied, it is restless, uncomfortable, and sometimes dangerous.

It is probable that animals in general are not motivated by any conscious purpose similar to what drives human beings. Their daily lives are regulated principally by *physiological* (physical) urges, and it is not necessary to go beyond these to explain their behavior. Even in such apparently human traits as affection, loyalty, and vanity, which some animals display, it is not impossible to discover that instinctive wants, such as food, comfort, and freedom from pain or annoyance, are at their root. Who shall say, for example, that the intelligent-appearing dog, as he capers or wags his tail or looks fondly at his master, is doing more than display an instinctive physical response to the individual who means for him food, shelter, comfort, and freedom from pain?

Man, too, has physical wants. Now you may go again through these lower physical wants which we have enumerated and apply them in exactly the same way to human beings. So far as our physical wants are concerned we are no different from animals ourselves. We, too, want comfort and freedom from pain. We want food, drink, warmth and coldness, rest and sleep, activity and inactivity, and ultimately families of our own. We covet, like them, release from pain and the continuance of what is physically pleasant and agreeable. From this point of view, we are all animals, endowed by the Creator with strong physical wants that are instinctive, invariable for all, and relatively unchangeable for a lifetime.

HIGHER-LEVEL WANTS IN HUMAN BEINGS

But man's mental wants are greater. Man is infinitely more than an animal! His wants are not limited, like the animal's, to the satisfaction of a half dozen or so elementary physiological *drives* (wants or motives). Man is forever separated from the animal series by his possession of a rational mind. Being so endowed, man also possesses the strong drive to use his mind, to find for himself means of self-expression, or of developing and enlarging his *ego,* of making his *self* felt, of influencing the present scene, of bending the world to his will, of bringing his intellect to bear upon his surroundings and fitting them to his desires.

Man's desire to express himself. Every normal human being is activated by this powerful want—the desire for self-expression. This higher-level want is as instinctive as is the lower-level one of comfort and freedom from pain; the latter, which man holds in common with the animal, is of a lower and more elementary order; the former, which he holds alone of all the animals, is (or ought to be) of a higher order.

The self-expressional drive manifests itself in innumerable ways. We shall attempt in this section to combine the various forms of the self-expressive instinct into six wants, which we shall call higher human wants. Do not forget as we discuss them individually, however, that each is but a form of a single instinctive want: each is merely a channel through which one's self strives to find ways of making itself felt in its own particular environment.

SIX HIGHER HUMAN WANTS

Before starting out, it will be helpful to you in your own thinking to prepare a sheet of data to indicate some of the ways in which you yourself find self-expression. Use the form below:

WAYS IN WHICH I FIND SELF-EXPRESSION

1. Membership in the High School Athletic Club
2. Earning money on Saturdays to buy extra things I want
3.
4.
5. etc.

(There are ways innumerable. Think them up!)

Desire for companionship starts early. One of the interesting ways in which our self-expressive want finds opportunity to satisfy itself is through our intimate association with other selves. Almost as soon as the baby begins to be conscious of himself as an individual, he is conscious also of other individuals around him, and he finds comfort and satisfaction in being much in their company. Left alone for very long, he grows ill at ease, fretful, and perhaps fearful. When with the other members of the family, he blossoms out and expresses his ego in the group.

By the time a boy gets to be eight or nine years of age, he in all probability belongs to some "gang" of chums, and in the bosom of that gang he will have abundant opportunity to make his personality felt. Girls, too, commonly move in "sets" or "crowds." Throughout elementary and high school years, children continue to belong to social groups of congenial companions, to clubs, societies, and other organizations in which they may find rich channels for self-expression.

All normal grown-ups crave it, too. This strong appetite for companionship is not ordinarily lost when adulthood comes. Witness the sewing circles and the community clubs, the men's clubs and the women's clubs, the service clubs and the trade and fraternal organizations to which men and women continue to adhere most of their lives. In these groups they find opportunity for self-investment: for leadership, for fol-lowership, for committee work, for program making, for contest conducting, or for such other types of activity as they may be individually equipped to carry on. In performing these functions in and for the group, people derive strong satis-faction of the general want of self-expression.

Incidentally, one's character is ennobled by the opportunities he finds in these groups for making and holding close friends, for experiencing sympathy and affection, for developing loyal-ties, for obeying rules and regulations, and for championing his particular organization before any and all challengers that may arise. Thus, while affording us the channels we instinctively crave for expressing ourselves, the social groups to which we belong in turn make us better people. Tramps, wanderers, hermits, and other solitary persons must, from this point of view, be considered to be abnormal. Their social natures have either never developed or else—and more likely —they have been for some reason stifled or denied.

Another fundamental want: security. From the lowliest earthworm that burrows in the ground to find safety, to the master of finance who seeks to buttress himself by his wealth and possessions, every living creature instinctively seeks for security in order that his self may have the fullest opportunity to perpetuate and express itself. Recent world-wide movements for old-age security have resulted from a long line of efforts on the part of humanity to guarantee to men and women their peace of mind. Among these movements have been the estab-lishment of life insurance, property insurance, annuities, accident and liability insurance, job insurance, hospital insurance, and pensions, all of which have been designed to promote a reassuring feeling of security in the minds of men and women as they move through life. No one who is continually harassed by fears for his own future can make the best of the opportunities that come his way.

Security through our possessions. So it is that the urge to express ourselves drives us early and late to earn, to amass, to possess, to own. We see evidence of this profound drive in the child who delights in *his* toys, *his* bicycle, *his* things. "Mine! Mine!" becomes an early cry in life, and unless it is carefully controlled children often come to be selfish and thoughtless, hoarding their belongings for themselves and refusing to share them with others.

It may be a far cry from the trinkets that the small child clutches to himself to the rich possessions of the man of money; but the same sense of security comforts both the child and the man. All of us find among our strongest motives those concerned with winning a livelihood, with "saving for a rainy day," with building a bank account, and with accumulating goods and chattels of one kind and another. Our possessions give us a flattering sense of security, no matter what may come, and in amassing them we experience abundant opportunity to match our wits against those of others and to demonstrate the effectiveness of our skills, abilities, and ideas. The success we achieve in the process of *getting* satisfies and flatters our ego.

The business man, the laborer, the professional man, the captain of industry—all are driven alike by this urge for success and security as measured by one's possessions. To own a home of one's own, to have some money in the bank or in securities, to have an automobile, a yacht, a camp at the shore, a home in the country—these things spell for us security and also provide evidence to others of our personal ability and of our success in life.

Security through our friends and family. Still another form which the passion for security takes is the wish to be accepted and approved by our friends and contemporaries. We experience much satisfaction in the consciousness that we are secure in the love of our relatives and the confidence and respect of our friends. There is perhaps nothing more tragic in anybody's life than a broken home—broken by death, or by separation, or by disharmony and strife. As long as one has confidence that his home will resist all attacks upon it, and that the members of his family are loyal and devoted, he can face the world with a stout heart. Let his faith in his home go, and his security is gone; with security gone, he may become a wanderer, an embittered and disillusioned cynic, a delinquent. No wonder the family is referred to so often by *sociologists* (social scientists who study group living) as the backbone of the nation!

Beyond the walls of home, we crave also the respect and even the admiration of our friends. To retain this respect, we obey the laws, keep ourselves wholesome and interesting, play the role of good neighbor, take part in community and civic activities, participate in the social life around us, are philanthropic, sympathetic, civic-minded. He who is indifferent to these things forfeits the respect and confidence of his neighbors and is in danger of losing his sense of security. In striving to be the reliable friend, the good neighbor, the intelligent citizen, one finds plenty of opportunity to use his mental powers and to demonstrate his originality and the validity of his ego. Can you see how on a still broader basis—that of the citizen of a nation—we all crave security?

Another strong want: to dominate. It is a strong human trait to wish to control, to be the master, to dominate. This drive for mastery may be positive and constructive, or it **may** be negative and destructive.

Whenever and wherever one individual or group is pitted in rivalry against some other individual or group, the self-expressive urge to dominate is shown in operation. Scholastic

Photo by Meisel for Monkmeyer

Fig. 2. How do the members of a school band achieve self-expression through music?

competition and interclass and interschool athletic and other contests are good examples of this drive at the school level. Striving to have the largest collection of stamps, or to perfect one's curve in baseball, or to swim the farthest, or to skate the most smoothly, or to run the fastest are other common examples from the life of young people. To "lick the bully," to win the prize, to tame the colt, to trap the mink, to hit the target, to win the contest, to solve the puzzle—these achieve-ments represent the successful investment of the youthful self in overcoming obstacles.

Winning our way, fighting for principle and the right, championing good causes, overcoming temptation, and com-pelling the world to "sit up and take notice" are further forms which the urge to dominate takes as both young and old bring their personalities to bear upon the environment around them.

Men and nations alike have always sought domination of other men or other peoples. See if you can get together a good number of instances from history to show this tendency in human beings. Use this form:

SOME HISTORICAL EXAMPLES OF THE WILL TO DOMINATE

1. The strong rivalry among the city-states of ancient Hellas
2. Roman conquest under the Caesars
3.
4.
5. etc.
(Keep right on down to the twentieth century.)

Social rivalry. It would be difficult to overestimate the im-portance which this urge for domination in all its numerous branches plays in human *psychology* (here, behavior). In the social sphere, it lies behind the efforts we all put forth to achieve rank, or position, or repute; to compel the respect and confidence of our associates; to have our opinions sought out, our ideas accepted, our standards and principles known; to be singled out from others, to be yielded preference or preced-ence, to enjoy popularity, be a "regular feller."

Economic rivalry. In the economic world and the world of business, the urge to dominate expresses itself in the enjoy-ment of building up an enterprise, of controlling a corporation, of being a power in the financial world, of surpassing or outdoing one's competitors. It has operated unquestionably in the building up of the great private fortunes in this and in all other countries. It is easy to imagine the thrill experienced by any man who finds his ideas prevailing in a practical, dollars-and-cents way and who experiences in the amassing of his fortune a far-flung opportunity for self-expression.

Political and professional rivalry. In the realm of politics, this desire to control is behind the activities of the man who aspires to a position of authority, to a place in the party councils, to the carving out of a long-time political career that may eventually result in high and exalted office. In the professional realm, too, it motivates men and women to undergo years of arduous preparation for a career, to carry research into new territory, to blaze new trails in science, and to pit their own abilities and resources against those of other workers in allied fields, thus impressing their ego indelibly upon the professional world about them.

Domination in its grosser forms. In exaggerated form the self-expressive instinct shows itself negatively in the urge to dominate found in the great tyrants and autocrats of history, with their conquests and their purges and their massacres and their cruelties. Among the rank and file of folks, it is found in bullying, cheating, lying, swindling; in cut-throat competition in the business world; in the exploitation of the poor, or the weak, or the innocent; in the formation of trusts and corners; in the development of rackets and underworld activities.

Negatively also, the urge to dominate leads to wars and to conquests of other nations and peoples. Oftentimes concealed beneath the pretense of liberating oppressed races, or of finding essential markets or raw materials or colonies is another reason. Most wars of conquest have turned out to be wars for domination and for the elevation of the "superior" race. In conducting such a war to a successful termination, the aggressive country finds flattering opportunity to express its courage and its intelligence.

Desire for new scenes, new experiences. There is something of the hobo and the gypsy in us all; we tire of sameness and monotony, in large part, probably, because in an unchanging environment there is little opportunity to bring one's personality to bear upon the circumstances that surround him. Self-expression demands a variable, disuniform environment in which one's originality and resourcefulness may be continually challenged. Man is at best a profoundly restless creature; whatever is static irks him: he likes to be on the go, to find the novel, to visit new scenes, to see new faces. This has always been true of the race.

Here is an instinctive form of activity that is often opposed to the urges for security and domination. Security and domination necessitate ordinarily that we shall "stay put," that we shall become rooted in a single environment and impress ourselves upon it continuously; consequently we may find it necessary to resist to a considerable degree the urge to change. Most of us cannot afford to "take to the road," to be gypsies, to live like the Bedouins of the desert, although undoubtedly these unconventional people find opportunity for security and domination through the control of the environment in which they live.

Common ways of satisfying this want. About the only ways open to us who live in settled communities to satisfy our demand for change are occasional trips to new places and scenes: an annual visit to the seashore, the mountains, the country, or the "old home town"; a spring fishing trip or a fall hunting trip; a week-end automobile tour. By these means we often find it possible to invest our talents and our personalities in novel experiences.

Through reading travel books or adventure and mystery tales, or through romantic stories unfolded before us on the silver screen, we may also satisfy to a considerable degree this inner demand for variety and change. There is always, of course, the danger that too much of this sort of thing will make us dissatisfied with things as they are, and fill our heads with empty notions of personal adventure that cannot be carried out.

For the most part—and it is best so—we are compelled to satisfy our urge for self-expression by staying at home and doing the day's work and the day-by-day tasks. Security, mastery, and domination come rather from continuity than from change. "The rolling stone gathers no moss!"

The desire to use our minds actively.   Have you ever tried to make your mind a complete blank? It is an impossible thing to do, for our minds hasten on and on incessantly. Only when the blood supply to the brain is lessened in sleep does our mental activity cease. Even the tiny babe lying in his crib follows inquisitively with his eyes the moving patterns of shadow and sunlight on the wall, or the colored ball dangled before him. The five-year-old asks interminable "why" questions, almost driving his elders to distraction trying to answer his persistent queries. Curiosity drives the child to make collections, learn new games and riddles, catch the firefly, steal the robin's eggs from the nest, skate where the ice is thin. In all these and hosts of other ways he finds self-expression. Possessed of a curious mind, he turns his mental gymnastics upon every conceivable object or process in his environment.

Life for all of us is what it is because we have naturally active minds and are intrigued by everything around us. We find delight in reading and thinking about myriads of situations, and in occupying our minds, even during resting hours, with books, newspapers, magazines, puzzles, games, conversations, radio programs, movies, lectures, zoos, fairs, circuses, exhibitions. We carry on running mental comments about what we are doing, what our friends are doing or saying, what we see and hear, the weather, the stock market, the landscape, and hosts of other objects and events that pass under our observation. We employ our insatiable minds in thinking about past, present, and future; in fanciful imagining and air-castle building; in planning, reasoning, worrying, hoping, dreaming, criticizing, evaluating ourselves and others.

There is no limit to the range of action which our minds encompass. Geared for exercise, they snatch at every situation that offers material for reflection or speculation.

This incessant mental activity that characterizes all of us is one of the most interesting *phenomena* (observable facts or events) to watch. See if you can tap some of your own mental processes as illustrations, using this form for noting them down:

WAYS IN WHICH I USE MY MIND ACTIVELY

1. Holding up my end of a conversation.
2. Thinking up illustrations for this exercise!
3.
4.
5. etc.
(How mentally alert and active are you, anyway? This list will show!)

Creativeness is especially satisfying. On the higher creative levels, the urge to be mentally active expresses itself in writing books, in editing periodicals, in painting and sketching, in drawing architectural plans, in composing music, in projecting new enterprises, in exploring new territory, in inventing new devices, and in carrying on scores of other productive forms of activity. The creative minds of a nation, at work in the arts and sciences, in government and politics, in business and finance, in education and planning for the future, are its most priceless human resources.

The desire for self-perpetuation. The instinctive drive for self-expression finds one of its strongest outlets in the ardent desire of the ego for immortality. Many of the religions of the world emphasize the certainty of a hereafter in which one's opportunities for self-expression will be unlimited. Mankind has always been fascinated by this prospect. Quite apart from its religious aspect, however, this urge for self-perpetuation finds common expression through two other outlets: first, in the opportunity which the rearing of children provides; and second, in the opportunity afforded by the material bequests which one leaves behind him.

Perpetuation through children. In his children one sees himself reborn, and through them he can visualize the continuation of his own personality through succeeding generations. This accounts not only for the pride which most parents experience in their offspring, but also for the care they take to "bring them up in the way they should go," so that the parental self may find worthy and flattering reflection in them. Conversely, it accounts, too, for the extreme chagrin and feeling of frustration which parents commonly feel when their children turn out badly.

Unquestionably one of the strongest regulators of society is the unceasing endeavor of parents to provide for their children, to sacrifice for them, and to ensure for them, if possible, easier and happier lives than they themselves have been permitted to enjoy. Even though it sometimes happens that excessive anxiety results in spoiling the child, or in destroying his initiative and dwarfing his character, the activating purpose of the parent is clearly to smooth out the rugged way for his child and thus provide him with a better chance to make good in life than he himself had.

Perpetuation through leaving property. The other means of self-perpetuation lies in the passing down of one's material possessions—the fruit of his labor and industry—to posterity. It is seen most strikingly, of course, in the bequests of the people of great wealth who leave legacies to endow or support institutions of learning, to promote scientific or social research, to found libraries, to stimulate the arts. Some of the great fortunes that were amassed in our own country during the expanding nineteenth century have been thus given back to the people through the insatiable urge of men to extend their influence beyond the years of their actual life and work. One need but mention the benefits to society which have been made possible through such funds as the Carnegie Foundation, the Rockefeller Foundation, and the Commonwealth Fund, to give evidence of this strong hope for earthly immortality, which springs eternal in the breast of mortals.

Less conspicuously, the strength of this same urge for self-expression through self-perpetuation may be exemplified in the efforts of men and women around us everywhere so to order their affairs that they may leave behind them as much property as possible to pass down to their children.

HOW PSYCHOLOGISTS WORK

Animals make excellent subjects for scientific investigation into the strength of drives or wants. One of the first and still commonly used pieces of apparatus for studying drive in animals is the *puzzle box*. It consists of a wire compartment, having a door with a fairly simple fastening. The experimental animal, a cat for example, is confined in the box, from which it can escape only if and when it reaches through the wire bars and releases the catch.

The motive or want which activates it to escape may be either desire for freedom or desire to get the food which lies just beyond reach; or it may be a combination of the two drives. So strong are these desires that the animal will thrash about actively until it succeeds, often quite by accident at first, in clawing up the latch.

Figure 3 is a sketch of a puzzle box. Note that the spring attached to the door causes it to swing open automatically as soon as the catch is released. This same kind of apparatus is used also in studying rate of learning in the animal; during early trials the animal takes much longer than during later ones to escape or to reach the food outside.

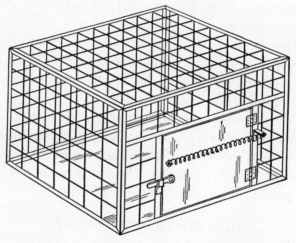

Fig. 3. Puzzle box, a device used in studying animal drives.

Another and somewhat more elaborate piece of equipment for studying the strength of drives in animals is the *obstruction box*. This consists of an entrance compartment, leading into a grid chamber which in turn leads either into the food compartment or to freedom. The only way of escape into the food compartment or to the outside is through the grid chamber, the floor of which is composed of metal bars connected with an electric current of known and variable power. When the animal ventures upon the floor of the grid, he receives a fairly strong shock. The power of the drive for food or for escape may be measured either by the amount of punishment the animal is willing to take in order to reach the goal or by keeping count of the number of times he will persist in his attempts to cross the electrified metal. Figure 4 shows the floor plan of a typical obstruction box.

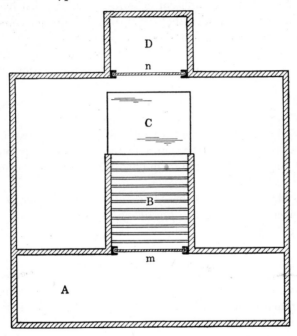

Fig. 4. Obstruction box. A: *Entrance compartment with door* m, *operated at will by the experimenter.* B: *Metal grid with electric connection.* C: *Plate which, when the animal's weight is upon it, causes the door* n *to open.* D: *Food or escape compartment.*

TO HELP YOU LEARN

Questions to Ask Yourself

1. On the basis of the urge for security, how can you account for the fact that most studies of delinquent children that have been made in our great cities show that the delinquents come from broken homes or inadequate homes?

2. How might the urge for self-expression through security and domination conflict with the urge for self-expression through change? Can you cite examples?

3. How strong a role does our acceptance by our associates and friends play in giving us a feeling of security?

4. Try making your mind a blank for a period of two or three minutes or so. What is the nature of the ideas that pop into it, in spite of your efforts to keep them out? Why cannot one completely exclude such ideas?

5. In what way or ways has your study of this chapter given you new understanding of the *psychology of you?* Mention specific evidence.

Working with Psychology

1. Try the following bit of real scientific observation, using either a pet animal or some animal at the zoo as your subject of study: Watch the animal carefully for a short time (if possible, on several different occasions) and make a catalogue of its obvious wants as indicated by its behavior. Compare them with those of human beings.

2. See what information you can find in the library about some one of the great philanthropic foundations, like those of Carnegie and Rockefeller. Be prepared in class to describe some of the important humanitarian work which the foundation carries on, and to give an opinion as to whether the government would subsidize work of this nature if the foundation did not.

3. As civilization becomes more complex, our human wants mul-

tiply. Conversely, the more primitive a people, the fewer and simpler are its wants. Select for a little study from this point of view a representative from each of three cultural levels in human history, for example, the American Indian, the feudal baron, and the contemporary John Doe, and contrast the wants of the three types of individuals. Keep in mind both the fundamental wants and the incidental or luxury wants at each level.

4. Read again carefully the Declaration of Independence of the American colonists, especially the opening and closing sentences of the immortal document:

> We hold these truths to be self-evident, that all men are created equal, that they are endowed by their Creator with certain inalienable rights, that among these are Life, Liberty and the pursuit of Happiness. . . . And for the support of this declaration, with a firm reliance on the protection of Divine Providence, we mutually pledge to each other our Lives, our Fortunes and our sacred Honor.

Try to visualize exactly what those "inalienable rights" are, to whose perpetuation our forefathers were willing to pledge themselves so unreservedly. How are these rights related to our human wants?

What Others Say

1. In Adventure:

Danger Is My Business by John D. Craig. A true narrative depicting the lure of pyramid climbing, of hunting tigers in India, of stalking jungle animals, of salvaging treasures from the hulls of sunken ships on shoals and reefs.

2. In Biography:

Benjamin Franklin by Carl Van Doren. The fascinating and absorbing story of a great American whose keen and active mind was insatiable in its analytical and creative penetration into the fields of philosophy, science, and social intercourse.

3. In Fiction:

A Lantern in Her Hand by Bess Streeter Aldrich. The story of a young woman of courage and bright dreams, who found those dreams to be always somewhere in the future, yet who pressed on indomitably to their fulfillment.

The Man Without a Country by Edward Everett Hale. A powerful tale of an American, who, exiled from his native land because he held his citizenship too lightly, and doomed to wander an outcast over the earth, experiences the bitterest regrets for his youthful folly and yearns to his dying day for home and flag and country again.

4. In Poetry:

Excelsior by Henry W. Longfellow. An allegorical portrayal of the power of ideals to drive a young man forward and upward against heavy odds.

Sea Fever by John Masefield. The strong fascination which the sea has for almost everybody is expressed in the swift-moving lines. A seafaring man, far from his beloved ocean, yearns for the scenes which the poet pictures so vividly.

5. In Drama:

The Little Foxes by Lillian Hellman. The length to which avaricious and covetous people will go in order to enrich themselves is skillfully portrayed in this drama, in which schemers do not hesitate to victimize even their own closest relatives, if need be, to gain their own ends.

WHAT'S AHEAD IN CHAPTER 2

Could We Get Along Without Habits?

Thomas De Quincey did not write his notable book, *Confessions of an English Opium Eater,* from fancy: far from it! He was himself a slave to the opium habit for many years, having started it in the first place as a means of ridding himself of the vexatious and severe pains from neuralgia which he suffered as a student in 1804, during his second year at Oxford.

Though he was partly able to shake off the habit in later years, he was never entirely free from its clutches. In the *Confessions* he has left a classic document describing vividly his struggles with the monster that shackled him. It is a gruesome, lurid, and dramatic tale of what slavery to a vicious habit can mean for a person who allows himself to fall into it.

Old Scrooge, the unregenerate villain in Dickens' *Christmas Carol,* is pictured by Dickens as "a squeezing, wrenching, grasping, scraping, clutching, covetous old sinner. Hard and sharp as flint, from which no steel had ever struck out generous fire; secret and self-contained, and solitary as an oyster. The cold within him froze his old features, nipped his pointed nose, shrivelled his cheeks, stiffened his gait; made his eyes red, his thin lips blue; and spoke out shrewdly in his grating voice. A frosty rime was on his head, and his eyebrows, and his wiry chin. He carried his own temperature always about with him; he iced his office in the dog-days; and didn't thaw it one degree at Christmas."

Could any word picture of a man enslaved by his own callous meanness be more striking than the one Dickens has painted? Creature of a lifetime of habit, Old Scrooge could only be softened and humanized by some supernatural power such as that wielded by the nightmare of his awful dream.

Belle Amingdon had a brand-new typewriter. It was a birthday present from her uncle.

"Now," exclaimed Belle enthusiastically, running her fingers over the shiny new machine, "I shall be able to typewrite all my themes for Miss Brackett!"

This is the way the opening paragraph of Belle's next theme, entitled "My Trip to Washington," looked when Belle had got it all typed out:

```
    i Was thirteen yeard old whenmy fatger de-
cided to takemother andme  to washington For a
little trip? zIt was vacationweekat school.  so
itwas easy for me toget away/ wE wereto go by
traun, and whenthe day came wewere all ay thr
station brightand warlyȼ in spiteof father8s
misgivingx.. #it Would befunnyif you twq ladiez
tooj solong primpinh anddolling up that wemissed
the traon, wouldn8t/it, hehad askes. Well. wedid
primp somr.buteven dad had  toadmit  that wewere
in plengy oftime.
```

Do you think there was something "out of kilter" on Belle's typewriter that made it behave so? If not, what *was* wrong? (Belle decided to write her theme in long hand, after all!)

Habits May Be Either Good or Bad

Here are three striking examples of the important role played by habit. De Quincey and Old Scrooge were both in its grip so tightly that in the former case emancipation never completely occurred, and in the latter, only an unnerving experience in the depth of night could break its hold.

In the case of Belle Amingdon, on the other hand, it was a lack of adequate habits that made her work poor. Any individual is bound to be clumsy and futile when he attempts to perform some physical or motor task for which he has had no proper training. After Belle uses her typewriter for a few months, if she really practices upon it with determination, she will become quite as much the master of it as was opium the master of De Quincey and meanness, of Old Scrooge. Habits you see, work both ways—for good as well as for bad.

✓ ✓ ✓

In this chapter, you will see that you are after all largely a creature of habit—and everybody else, too. You will discover that every individual is a combination of good habits and bad. You will learn how habits are formed and, perhaps most important of all, how they may be broken if one really wants to break them. You will find out also that habits make for limitations in people and in nations.

Photo by Ralph F. Morris for F. P. G.

Fig. 5. These boys have developed many beneficial habits. They must have good health habits to be strong and to co-ordinate their muscles. They must be mentally alert. Can you name at least ten habits which every skillful player must have formed?

2. OUR HABITS

Before proceeding with your study of the chapter, prepare as full a list as you can of your own personal habits—good and bad. Use this form for recording and classifying them:

SOME OF MY HABITS

Name of Habit	How I Came to Form It	Advantage of It	Disadvantage of It
1. Brushing my teeth	Home training	Keeps my mouth and teeth clean	
2. Saying "they's" instead of "there are"	Careless imitation		Makes a bad impression when I'm talking
3.			
4.			
5. etc.			

How many of your habits can you identify? Once you start listing them, you will be nothing short of amazed at their number and range! Some of them—let us hope most of them—you will find extremely beneficial; others of them you will probably conclude are of doubtful value to you.

WE ARE ALL SLAVES!

An idle boast. We like to boast about our independence and our freedom as individuals to do as we please. Actually, however, we are not free at all, but are slaves to our habits, good and bad as well. There are few things that we do, say, or think in the course of the day that were not done, said, or thought in just about the same way the day before, and that will not be done, said, and thought without much variation tomorrow and the next day. Life comes to be for all of us an existence in which we are necessarily bound and held by habit. "Habit is a cable that we cannot break" is an old maxim which remains perpetually true. By its twisted strands we are tied fast to things-as-they-were; to cut the cable and free ourselves from our habits is all but impossible.

Maybe you had always supposed that only elderly people were creatures of habit, and that young people were still their own masters. Only to a limited extent is this true. "You can't teach an old dog new tricks"—at least, it is much harder to do so; but once even a young dog has been taught a trick it is not easy to break him of it. Almost from the very first day of our lives we are forming habits; every day we continue to practice them; long before we reach high school hundreds of habits have fastened themselves upon us, and they will continue to control us during the rest of our lives.

The only difference between the habits of the elderly person and those of the younger one lies in the fact that forming them and breaking them is ordinarily a bit easier for the young person. This is partly because he has not repeated his habits so many times, and partly, as we shall see later in this section, because his nervous system is more plastic.

We are slaves when we rise. Observe your own behavior during the course of any ordinary day, and you will have plenty of proof of the power your habits are already exerting over you, even though you are still in your teens. You get up at the habitual hour; you dress in the habitual manner—even putting the same foot into your stocking first; dressing the same foot first; buttoning buttons, tying knots, parting and combing your hair, washing your hands and face, brushing your teeth—always in the same way. Try some morning inserting your other arm first into your coat sleeve, buttoning a button with the wrong hand, tying a bow or a four-in-hand on somebody else, combing your hair with the other hand, or otherwise attempting to interfere with a habit previously formed, and see how awkward and uncomfortable you feel!

At the breakfast table, you sit in the accustomed place, carry on the same small talk with the family, use knife, fork, and spoon habitually, butter your bread and raise your coffee cup always with the accustomed hand. Habitually, too, you either tilt your knife against your plate or lay it horizontally across the plate when you are not using it; you prefer your coffee to be of the usual sweetness and your cereal of the usual kind; you eat the articles of food in the usual order, at the usual rate, and with the usual satisfaction. Later you start to school at the usual hour; carry your books in the usual way; even walk on the usual side of the street, with the usual gait (any of your friends will recognize you at a distance by the way you walk), your head up or down, your pace quick or slow, just as you always do.

Slaves all the rest of the day. In school, you attend the usual classes; use habitually grammatical (or ungrammatical!) forms in your speech; pitch your voice at the usual level; handle your books, pen, paper, ruler, and eraser in the usual manner and with the usual hand; write in the usual way; sit in the usual position, with the usual posture; laugh or smile with the same expression of face; stammer and hesitate when you are uncertain; speak boldly and confidently when you are sure; participate in or avoid participation in the day's work; study as much or as little as is your wont; display your customary degree of politeness, co-operativeness, and interest, or their opposites; and in general exhibit to your world the same personality everybody is familiar with as *you*.

If you will carry this analysis through the after-school and evening hours, you will understand still more clearly how your habits are already stamping themselves firmly into your whole personality. As a matter of fact, you are so absurdly like yourself every minute of every day, because of your habitual ways of acting, speaking, and thinking, that not one of your friends ever mistakes you for somebody else!

HABITS ARE INEVITABLE

It's just as well, too. Habits, then, seem to be inevitable: there appears to be no way of escaping them. And it is well that this is the case, for if we were compelled to start each new morning with a clean slate, so far as our habits of yesterday were concerned, we should never get anything done. If, for example, we had to learn all over again each day how to tie a knot, or button a button, there would be no time left to do anything worth while. (Do you recall what a struggle you had, when you were five years old, every time you tried to button a button or tie a knot?)

By equipping us with the capacity to form habits and to retain them after we have formed them, nature has made it possible for us to devote the major portion of our lives to the accomplishment of our long-time purposes without having to attend to the more automatic functions that habit can better take care of.

Why not become slaves to the good? If, as the adage has it, we are creatures of habit, it is evident that we should desire to be creatures of good habits rather than of bad. Take so simple a thing as the matter of our speech. There is all the difference in the world, even from a dollars-and-cents point of view, between habitually good speech and habitually bad speech. The time you and I consume in learning to use our mother tongue correctly is time most profitably spent. The easy thing, of course, is to use slipshod speech habits, to be careless and ungrammatical in our speaking and writing, to substitute slang and speech barbarisms for real language, to clip off the final syllable or the final *g,* to be satisfied with a harsh, unpleasant voice, to be slack in both enunciation and pronunciation.

Of two young candidates for a job, other things being half-way equal, the employer is bound to favor the applicant who has learned good habits of speech. From the standpoint of politeness, refinement, and culture, too, as well as from the utilitarian viewpoint, it pays to cultivate acceptable speech habits. Our speech, whether we are aware of it or not, is constantly branding us as educated or uneducated, as cultured or uncultured, as courteous or discourteous.

Why not avoid being slaves to the bad?   One could say the same things about our habits of posture. There is just as much difference between good posture and bad posture as there is between good speech and poor speech. It takes a little effort to form the habit of standing erect and facing the world with square shoulders and unwavering eye—certainly more effort than it does to form the habit of slouching and looking down at one's feet! Do you sit erect, walk easily and naturally, and stand on two feet? Or do you lounge in a chair as if you had no spine, half stand with the support of a desk or a chair or the side of the wall, and walk as though you were six separate pieces strapped loosely together?

So with scores and scores of other habits: it is important to form those that will make us more successful, more happy, more self-reliant, more healthy, wealthy, and wise; it is important to avoid forming those that cannot be expected to further us along the pathways mentioned. Though it is inevitable that we shall become creatures of habit, it is not inevitable that the habits which master us shall be the most desirable ones; we shall have to look sharply to it that they are not habits that will interfere with rather than promote our best welfare.

WHY WE CAN FORM HABITS SO EASILY

Only the baby is really free. The only people who are not creatures of habit are very young babies. They have formed almost no habits; they are bound by no past experiences; they face the future without any handicap or any advantage of habit. At birth they are somewhat like a mass of clay which can be shaped in any form desired by the potter. But they begin to form habits almost as soon as they are born, and by the time they are old enough to toddle about by themselves, they already show the fast hold of habit upon them.

Some psychologists believe that in the first two or three years of life are formed those fundamental habits that will play a large part in determining what sort of individual a child is likely to become when he grows up. During the early years every child certainly does lay the foundation of honesty or dishonesty, co-operativeness or non-co-operativeness, controlled or uncontrolled temper, thoughtfulness or selfishness; and whatever experience he has in later years will tend only to confirm him in one direction or the other.

The baby's nerve pathways are unlinked. We said in the preceding paragraph that the newborn child may be compared to a mass of potter's clay, so easily molded is it into this pattern or that. Of course you realize that the human nervous system is a very complex mechanism, in no way actually resembling a lump of clay. It is made up of thousands of millions of nerve cells and nerve fibers, every one of which may by training and practice be linked with hundreds of others. Once a group of nerve structures has been linked up, it tends to stay linked up thereafter and to make the repetition of the original behavior nearly inevitable whenever conditions are the same again.

Suppose, for example, the baby screams and kicks when its

mother leaves the room, and immediately the mother comes hastening back. An entire nerve unit, comprising the nerves in the eyes, the nerves in the brain, the nerves in the vocal cords, and the nerves in the muscles of the chest and arms and legs, is connected up as a result of the baby's screaming and kicking at the same time that the mother leaves. Another set of nerves is linked up as a result of the discontinuance of the screaming-kicking activity and the appearance of the smil-ing-cooing activity at the same time that the mother re-enters the room.

The next time the mother leaves the room, the same unpleas-ant behavior will show itself again; and when she returns, it will again be replaced by more pleasing behavior. Breaking up the screaming-kicking habit, once it has been allowed to ap-pear, will require much firmness and a good deal of will power on the part of the mother. Here is a very simple illus-tration of the way in which habits are formed in the first place.

PLASTICITY OF THE NERVOUS SYSTEM

Why we can form habits. The distinctive characteristic of our nervous system that makes it possible for us to form habits is its plasticity. So receptive is it to the environmental forces that play upon it, that nearly everybody can train himself or be trained to do almost anything. Thus, one learns to speak, read, and write; to comprehend and use numbers; to dance, swim, play tennis; to drive an automobile, knit a sweater, play a piano; to eat politely, maintain good posture, keep himself clean and healthy; to save his money, avoid quarrels, and champion the downtrodden.

One can learn that two and two make four, five, or nine-teen; that honesty is the best or the worst policy; that the United States comprises 48 states, or 148, or 1048; that Chicago is east of San Francisco or west of it: all that is necessary is to *practice the habit*—regardless of whether it is right or wrong.

Youth is especially favored. This amazing plasticity of our nervous system is the basis of all habit formation. Because of it we can choose between skilled muscles and clumsy muscles, accurate speech and inaccurate speech, an inquiring mind and a sluggish mind. We can learn to speak English, Chinese, Greek, or Sanskrit. We can learn to sing, paint, and act; to fence, wrestle, and shoot; to show or conceal our emotions; to be ambitious or lazy; to be optimistic or pessimistic.

And the most significant thing about it all is this: that the younger the individual is, the more plastic is his nervous system and the easier it is for him to form whatever habits he will. There is practically no limit to what any young person of normal intelligence may do or become if he learns early the importance of the habits which he is forming and discovers how to direct them toward the achievement of his life goals.

WHY WE CAN BREAK HABITS

Our nervous systems are alterable, too. The human nervous system is not only plastic—easily molded: it is also modifiable—easily remolded. Undesirable habits may be easily built up; they may also, especially in youth, be easily broken down and replaced with better ones. Herein lies the foundation for our hope of doing better tomorrow, of "turning over a new leaf." After defeat one may turn about and seize victory; from being a slave to injurious habits one may convert himself into a servant of useful habits that will aid him in reaching his objectives.

Always a second chance! The world is full of people who have made mistakes, yet who have been strong-willed enough to reform their habits, to make their nervous systems their allies instead of their enemies. There is always a second chance, perhaps even a third or a tenth chance, for anybody who learns that, although bad habits may enslave us, their shackles may be broken if we determine to break them.

Do not make the mistake of supposing that, if your language is faulty, or your tongue is unruly, or your mind is frequently occupied by unworthy thoughts, you cannot make things otherwise if you are willing to face about and practice more advantageous habits. The test of a man's character is not how perfect his habits were from the start, but rather how well he succeeded in shaping them toward desirable ends.

HOW OUR HABITS HELP US

They save us time. How long it takes for a two-year-old to express a simple idea! How unsteady he is upon his feet as he plays about the room! How awkward he is in trying to button a button or carry his food to his mouth! His habits are not yet well formed; his performance is slow and uncertain. By and by, after he has become more skilled through practice, he will be able to accomplish in an instant what now requires long minutes to do or what cannot be done yet at all.

When he is seven or eight, he will be able to spring out of bed and jump into his clothes in a jiffy; tie his shoelaces and button his coat almost on the run; wash his face and hands, slick down his hair, come bounding down the stairs, and be eating his breakfast before you can say much more than "Jack Robinson!" It is no longer a slow, laborious process to do all these acts of skill; thanks to the great timesaver, Habit, they can be dispatched in short order.

So with all of us—young and old. It takes time and persistence to learn any skillful act: for example, shaving, braiding hair, tying a necktie, sewing, knitting, writing, typing, shuffling a pack of cards, pitching a curve. But after all the motions have been mastered, we find it possible to do all these and a thousand other routine tasks quickly and effectively. In the workaday world, too, the skilled mechanic and the skilled carpenter and the skilled factory worker are skilled because through long practice of specific habits they have reached the plane where their work is done with speed and accuracy. Likewise, in the realm of the fine and practical arts, deft fingers become skilled through practice; and deft fingers are always fast-moving fingers.

They make us more exact. The novice in any sort of performance not only takes too much time but also makes a good many mistakes that mar his work. Observe yourself, or somebody else, in the early stages of learning to typewrite or to play a musical instrument, and you will have plenty of proof of this fact. It often seems in the early stages of practicing a skill as if one is more often wrong than right, and he wonders, often in despair, whether he will ever improve. Watching the performance of an expert, he marvels at the precision of every move. Yet precision is almost inevitable for anyone who persists in the practice of an art. The world ordinarily has plenty of room for the skilled individual, especially if his skill lies in a field in which there is a market for effective and economical performance. Habit may be our master, but it enables us in turn to become masters!

They keep us from tiring too quickly. There is perhaps no more tired person than the one who has just finished his first day of apprenticeship in any field in which it is necessary for him to learn new and unfamiliar physical acts. The process of linking up new nerve pathways, to which we referred above, is one that seems to result in a good deal of fatigue, especially in the early stages of practice. As the days go by, however, and as practice proceeds, one's performance becomes a little more smooth and less tiring.

It appears that the new nerve pathways that one is trying

to form offer at first rather high resistance, but that this resistance is rapidly lowered under persistent practice. Early resistance is transformed into later *facilitation* (lowering of resistance), and the skill becomes easier and easier to perform. Thus it is that the experienced bricklayer, painter, cabinetmaker, stenographer, clerk, cook, or housekeeper may find himself or herself almost as fresh and fit at the close of the day's work as at the beginning. All thanks for the boon of habit, which helps us to perform skills smoothly and effectively.

They free our minds from routine. The story goes that a centipede was once asked by a curious observer on which foot he started off when he walked. The centipede became so confused by the query that he fell over, helpless, and was unable to walk at all.

This fable illustrates well the value of habit in freeing the mind from attention to routine activities and allowing it to concern itself with the higher processes of learning and reasoning. How much mental work could one ever get done if he had to think constantly about the physical act every time he put one foot down, every time he put the other one down, every time he spoke a word, or wrote a letter of the alphabet, or touched a key, or made a stitch! All his waking life would be devoted to the carrying out of routine, mechanical movements; there would be no time left for his brain to pay attention to the important things of life, to those which require thought.

Nature has done us a great service in so constructing our nervous system that the routine acts of daily living are largely self-operating. When we walk or talk or write or use a more specialized skill, our muscles turn out the desired product mechanically: our brain is left free to think, to organize ideas, to weigh facts.

Using the form below, try classifying some of your own habits in terms of the four benefits just discussed.

HOW MY HABITS PROVE THEIR WORTH

These Save My Time	These Make Me More Accurate	These Keep Me from Tiring Quickly	These Free My Mind from Routine
1. Getting dressed in the morning	Using my dictionary	Using my typewriter	Knowing how to spell and punctuate
2.			
3.			
4.			
5. etc.			

(Fill in each column. Don't be surprised if you think of more than five!)

HOW HABIT MAY IMPEDE PROGRESS

But habits may be dangerous, too. In a sense, neither an individual nor a society nor a nation can keep progressing unless conduct is kept from becoming too unvaried. One reason why older people tend to become conservative, while younger ones are more radical is because of the inflexibility in the habits of the former, and their relative plasticity in the latter. The price one pays for growing up is, in part, the loss of plasticity. Old ways and old traditions become more and more virtuous; progress slows down and civilization becomes static.

Progress depends upon willingness to adopt new ways. As soon as a nation becomes hidebound by custom and tradition, it ceases to be young and progressive. Perhaps the well-known example of nineteenth-century China, with its age-old veneration of the past, best illustrates the stagnating power of habit on a national scale. The same thing is illustrated in any individual who grows set in his ways, or who looks to the past instead of to the future, or who becomes content with things-as-they-were.

Youth, fortunately, is progressive by nature. Young people ought to make every effort to remain progressive. They should be unwilling to become what William James called "mere walking bundles of habits." Every young person should keep an open mind and a forward look.

JAMES'S LAWS OF HABIT FORMATION

A famous psychologist, William James, many years ago formulated several rules to guide anyone in the formation of a habit. These rules have become classic, and rightly so. Here are the principal ones:

Begin the new habit with determination. Unless one really means business when he starts to break an old habit or to form a new one, he will never be successful. The mere admission that a habit is a poor one amounts to nothing at all: it is necessary to go at its uprooting with determination. Old nerve pathways will continue to operate as long as we make no decisive effort to break them up and fashion new ones. Hence, such a thing as a public pledge, or a wager with one-self, or a calm and confident declaration to one's friends, is a good way to launch the new habit.

See that no exceptions are allowed to occur. The mere launching of a new habit is not enough. There will follow days and days in which the temptation to lapse back into the old pattern will assail you. This will be the acid test of whether or not you are succeeding. Once you have turned your back upon the old habit, there must be no compromise with the enemy. When he assails you, put him again and again to rout by throwing the new habit in his teeth. He will gnash and bluster and try hard to reassemble his legions for a new attack. Do not be dismayed: he cannot win if you maintain your ground. By and by he will withdraw his forces completely and leave you victorious.

Seize the first opportunity to practice the new habit. The trouble with most people, even though they are really serious in their desire to uproot a poor habit, is that they delay acting upon their resolution. The days and the years go by, and nothing is done about it further than to talk about the need for reformation. The actual attack is always postponed, and in the meantime the old habit becomes, through continuing practice of it, more and more thoroughly entrenched in the nervous system. Do not make the mistake, as so many do, of deciding to wait until New Year's to make your resolution to reform! Not only is there no time like the present to attack habit patterns: the present is the *only* time to act.

A FAMOUS QUOTATION FROM WILLIAM JAMES

The following is one of the most noted passages ever written about habits. It is well worth reading more than once:

Could the young but realize how soon they will become mere walking bundles of habits, they would give more heed to their conduct while in the plastic state. We are spinning our own fates, good or evil, and never to be undone. Every smallest stroke of virtue or of vice leaves its never so little scar. The drunken Rip Van Winkle, in Jefferson's play, excuses himself from every fresh dereliction by saying, "I won't count this time!" Well! He may not count it, and a kind Heaven may not count it; but it is being counted none the less. Down among his nerve cells and fibers the molecules are counting it, registering and storing it up to be used against him when the next temptation comes. Nothing we ever do is, in strict scientific literalness, wiped out.

Habit is the enormous flywheel of society, its most precious conservative agent. It alone is what keeps us all within the bounds of ordinance and saves the children of fortune from the envious uprisings of the poor. It alone prevents the hardest and most repulsive walks of life from being deserted by those brought up to tread therein. It keeps the fisherman and the deckhand at sea during the winter; it holds the miner in his darkness, and nails the countryman to his log cabin and his lonely farm through all the months of snow; it protects us from invasion by the natives of the desert and the frozen zone. It dooms us all to fight out the battle of life upon the lines of our nurture or our early choice, and to make the best of a pursuit that disagrees, because there is no other for which we are fitted, and it is too late to begin again. . . . It is well for the world that in most of us, by the age of thirty, the character has set like plaster, and will never soften again.

—William James, *The Principles of Psychology*, Vol. I, Chapter 4. (Quoted by permission of Henry Holt and Company.)

TWO WELL-KNOWN CASE HISTORIES

Tom Mallett usually has to be called by his mother two or three times in the morning before he can bring himself to wake up and climb out of bed. The result is that, quite often, Tom is tardy for his first high school class. Nobody blames Mrs. Mallett for Tom's laziness, for she invariably calls him at seven-thirty on school mornings, usually adding this warning: "You know, Son, you'll be late again if you don't scamper up out of that bed right away!" But Tom never "scampers" until a second or third summons! Tom admits that he ought to form the habit of rising promptly when he is first called, but that is all he ever does about it!

Even a New Year's resolution, which he made somewhat half-heartedly during Christmas vacation a year ago, has failed to help matters any. When the second day of January came around, the same old story was repeated. Mrs. Mallett called her son at seven-thirty, as usual. Nothing happened! At seven-thirty-five she called him again. Still nothing happened! At seven-forty-five the summons was repeated, with this addition: "Where's that New Year's resolution of yours, Son?" Grumblingly, Tom got out of bed, still sleepy and groggy. "I didn't say I'd get up the very first day!" he growled. "I meant, I'd do it sometimes!"

It is now more than a year later, and Tom is a dignified senior. But Mrs. Mallett still has a daily tug-of-war to get her son up in the morning!

Do you think Tom will *ever* form the habit?

And then there is the case of an inveterate smoker whom I used to know. During Christmas week, one year, he resolved that after January first he would smoke no more. On the evening of December thirty-first he smoked excessively, even for him, reflecting gloomily that it would be the last time.

Next evening he sat disconsolately at home, lamenting the hardness of his lot, when suddenly an idea struck him. "Look here!" he exclaimed. "I didn't say anything about not smoking on January first: what I said was that after *January first I'd quit smoking!" Again he smoked several packs of cigarettes before retiring.*

The man is smoking yet! And no wonder!

Do you see how this smoker and Tom Mallett resemble each other?

Use the form below for listing some of the habit patterns which hold people back, either individually or as a group, and which make for personal or social stagnation:

REASONS WHY SOME HABITS LIMIT PEOPLE

Habit Pattern	Kind of Limitation
1. Reading only the newspaper	Failure to broaden one's views as much as by a variety of good reading
2. Keeping ancient laws on the statute books	Lack of progress in legislation and law enforcement
3.	
4.	
5. etc.	

(Here is a chance for you to do some real sleuthing.)

A FORWARD LOOK

In this chapter we have been discussing the formation of habits. We have observed that the fact that we have a nervous system is basically the reason why we are able to develop new skills, new responses, new ways of doing things. This same nervous apparatus makes possible not only the forming and the re-forming of habits, but it also underlies all of those mainsprings to action—our human wants—about which we learned in the first chapter. We may anticipate also the conclusion that the operation of this nervous mechanism makes it possible for us to study, to pay attention, to learn, to remember, to do our daily tasks, to experience feeling and emotion, and to adjust ourselves to the obstacles of one sort or another that beset our pathway.

Of such profound significance is this inner mechanism that regulates all our thinking, feeling, and doing, that you will find it profitable to turn aside in Chapter 3 to become somewhat familiar with the marvelous machinery which drives us all.

HOW PSYCHOLOGISTS WORK

One interesting way in which psychologists have studied the formation of habit is to set a person at work on a perplexing manual task and then to note the diminishing amount of time and error until perfection is reached.

One of the problems used in such experiments is learning to take apart some sort of mechanical puzzle. At the start the subject knows nothing about the particular puzzle presented to him. He has never tried to solve it before. The experimenter passes it to him, instructs him to take it apart as quickly as he can, and then immediately starts a stop watch to time him. Figure 6 illustrates a typical puzzle. The task is to separate the two links in the quickest possible time. Figure 7 is a common type of stop watch used.

At first the subject is likely to make a large number of random, useless movements, because he does not know where to begin or to what point to direct his attention. Fumbling at it for some time—maybe for several minutes—he gets nowhere. The links still are meshed together and resist all attempts to separate them. It looks to the performer as though the task

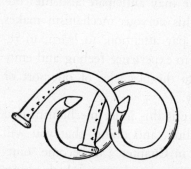 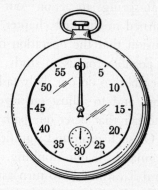

Fig. 6. Link puzzle for studying the formation of habits.   Fig. 7. Stop watch used in timing each performance.

could not be accomplished at all. He pulls and twists and jerks and fumes and exclaims over it for some time. Then, all of a sudden, and without any apparent cause, the links fall apart in his hands. The experimenter notes the time which has elapsed since the subject first started; then he rejoins the links (the subject being instructed not to watch him) and passes them again to the learner with the instruction to take them apart a second time.

The second performance may not be much better than the first: indeed, it may even take the subject longer! Not having any insight from his first attempt, he is no more able to perform the task than he was before. Again, accident comes to his aid and the links fall apart. By and by, as trial succeeds trial, the subject begins to get ideas that help. He observes, for example, that only when he holds the two links in one exact position is it possible to separate them, that pulling and straining are no help, that a little narrowing or flattening of one link and a little widening of the other link provide the only route over which the two can be passed in order to become separated.

As a result of these successive hints the subject becomes, after many attempts, so skilled in manipulating the links that he can take them apart with his eyes shut and without any random or waste effort. Meantime the experimenter has kept a careful record of the time spent during each attempt, and now, after complete skill has been achieved, is able to graph a curve to indicate the picture of his subject's progress in learning the

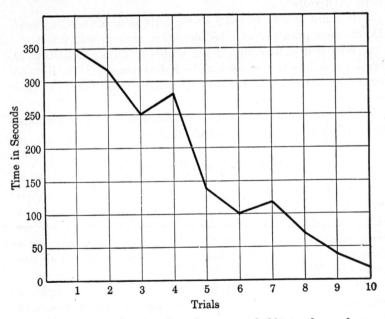

Fig. 8. Graph showing how fast a new habit was learned.

new habits. Figure 8 represents such a curve of learning new motor habits by a student who used the links shown in Figure 6.

TO HELP YOU LEARN

Questions to Ask Yourself

1. If we are slaves to habit, how is it possible for anybody ever to be original, or to be a reformer, or to make a new invention, or ever to do anything different from the old way?

2. Do you think that your fundamental habits are very different today from what they were a year ago? Two years ago? Does it seem to you likely that they will be much different two years from now? Ten years?

3. Is it just as easy to learn wrong facts as to learn right ones? Do the same principles of habit formation apply in both cases?

4. Why is it so necessary, if one wishes to form a new habit or break an old one, to start off with high determination? To allow no exceptions to occur? To begin the new habit today instead of next week?

5. Is it ever possible to break an old habit without forming some new one in its place? Explain and illustrate.

Working with Psychology

1. Decide upon some vexing habit of yours which you particularly want to break, like uncontrolled temper or slouchy posture. Pay special attention to the habit during the next few weeks and see what progress you can really make in overcoming it. Keeping a diary over the period, with a line or two every day about your success or failure, will be very helpful.

2. Make a collection during the next week of all the examples of ungrammatical speech that you note in yourself and in those with whom you converse. Classify the errors you find under appropriate

headings. You might entitle your record sheet: Some Slipshod Habits of Speech. You should, of course, adopt some unobtrusive way of recording the ungrammatical forms, so that nobody will be subjected to any embarrassment. An investigation of this sort has to be conducted with extreme caution, so that nobody except the investigator is aware of what is going on.

3. Do this experiment at the dining table at home. (You'd better not try it when you are at somebody else's table, nor when your mother happens to have guests!) During the entire meal, handle everything with the unaccustomed hand. Give your right hand a complete vacation by using your left hand every time to raise food to your mouth with fork or spoon, to pass dishes, to butter your bread, to stir your beverage. Reflect during and after the meal upon the amazing degree to which you are a slave to your right (or left) hand.

4. Make a little survey of household gadgets, mechanical appliances, furnishings, equipment, and machines to determine the extent to which all these things are designed by manufacturers for use by right-handed people. See if you can discover anything in your schoolroom or school building that indicates the same consideration for right-handed pupils and teachers. If you are right-handed, you will be amazed at the number of examples you find. Ask several left-handed people how they have adjusted themselves to a right-handed world.

What Others Say

1. In Essay:

Wake Up and Live by Dorothea Brande. The author maintains that one of the things that keep people from achieving their best is slavery to routine. She suggests deliberately putting yourself into new situations so that you must adjust yourself to them.

The Importance of Living by Lin Yutang. Taking a typically Oriental view of life, the author glorifies leisure—even indolence— as underlying happiness, comfort, and lasting satisfaction. He distinguishes three leading American vices: efficiency, punctuality, and the passion for success.

Art of Being a Person by George R. Wells. Assuming, like Lin Yutang, that happiness is the most important thing in life, this author insists that it is to be achieved principally through learning how to live skillfully and artistically every day and all the time.

2. In Fiction:

Teeftallow by Thomas S. Stribling. A striking and serious portrayal of the characteristic bigotry, ignorance, and superstition of the folks who live in a Southern hill town. The effects of narrow conventionality and provincialism upon ambition and character are shown.

3. In Poetry:

Elegy Written in a Country Churchyard by Thomas Gray. A sympathetic appreciation of the humdrum toil of earlier villagers who now lie in the churchyard, unheralded and unsung, yet whose faithful and devoted performance of the unlovely routine tasks of life gained for them an immortality far more noble than that aspired to by those who seek for fame and honor.

4. In Drama:

Tobacco Road by Erskine Caldwell. A picture of the hopeless vassalage of a degraded poor white family living in a shack on barren Georgia soil. The tentacles of habit completely enslave the family.

Marco's Millions by Eugene O'Neill. A glamorous, fantastic tale of Marco Polo, who passes through distant lands seeking always for material gain and running so true to form, as the action proceeds, that even the love of a beautiful Chinese princess is insufficient to turn him aside from his ingrained lust for wealth.

Do We Need Our Senses, Brains, Muscles?

In the year 1811, when he was but three years old, Louis Braille met with a misfortune that darkened his whole subsequent life. One day when his father, a harness maker of Coupray, near Paris, had stepped out of the shop, Louis got hold of a sharp awl and began playing with it. Placing the point against a strip of shiny leather, he raised the wooden mallet and brought it down upon the awl handle, as he had seen his father do. The instrument glanced away from the leather and plunged into Louis's eye. A few days later his other eye became infected from the wound. In spite of all that his frantic parents could do, within a month Louis Braille was permanently and totally blind.

Years later, when he was in a school for the blind in Paris, laboriously trying to "read" the impressions made by large letters, Louis got the idea of making a simplified dot alphabet for the blind. By originating a different grouping of dots for each letter in the alphabet, and by bunching them into an area so small that a blind person could feel all of them simultaneously with the tip of his finger, Braille invented a new language that was to bring hope to hundreds of thousands of sightless boys and girls, and men and women.

A hundred years later, in 1929, Louis Braille's countrymen unveiled a statue of him in the little village where he had been born. Many blind people, who had come to Coupray for the event, pressed about the effigy and passed their sensitive finger tips reverently over the stone face of their benefactor.

On the 13th of September, 1848, in Cavendish, Vermont, Phineas P. Gage, foreman of a gang of workmen, was covering over with an iron bar a charge of gunpowder in a hole drilled in a ledge. Carelessly he allowed the bar to strike the charge of powder. In the deafening explosion that followed, the bar was driven obliquely upward through his head and high into the air, so that it fell several rods away, smeared with blood and brains. This notable "Crowbar Case," as it is known to psychologists, would have been forgotten along with thousands of other accidents had it not been for the amazing fact that Phineas Gage lived more than twelve years after the occurrence which should, by all rational odds, have killed him instantly. A yawning hole measuring two by three and a half inches had been torn through his skull, and shreds of brain hung upon his hair. The physician who attended him was able, while probing for fragments, to pass his two forefingers through the two openings, so that they met inside his head.

But though Phineas Gage survived, and worked for many years afterwards, he never regained his former mental powers and control. He was fitful, irreverent, grossly profane, extremely obstinate, changeable. His emotions passed quite out of bounds. His mind became that of a child. Toward the end of his life he was frequently seized with fits and convulsions, in one of which he eventually died. His skull and the bar that passed through it were sent to the Warren Anatomical Museum, at Harvard University, for preservation.

Born in Minneapolis in 1897, Earl Reinhold Carlson sustained at birth a brain paralysis (victims of such birth injuries are commonly known as *spastics*). Unable to control or coordinate any of his muscles, for years he could not walk, talk, or even bring food to his mouth. All his muscular expressions were explosive; he was painfully awkward and graceless in every move he made. Few people expected he would ever be anything more than a helpless, unlettered, and stupid cripple.

By dint of heartbreaking determination, however, and with the help of many sympathetic and kindly people, the little paralyzed boy forced himself to go to school and to learn. Possessed of a keen mind, he fought for years and years against all but overwhelming odds—fought his way through school, to the University of Minnesota, to Princeton, and then to Yale Medical School, from which he eventually graduated triumphantly. Throughout all the weary, trying years, Earl Carlson had never faltered in his self-discipline and in his determination to win through.

Obsessed with the dream of devoting his medical skill and insight to the aid of cripples like himself, Dr. Carlson has been able to see his ambition realized in a remarkable way. Having first established a clinic for spastics at the New York Neurological Institute, he has subsequently founded institutions of his own on Long Island and in Florida, has aided in setting up similar clinical centers in many places in the United States, and has lectured widely in this country and in South America before medical bodies. He is a leading practitioner in the treatment of the very handicaps from which he himself suffered, and which he magnificently overcame.

Receiving, Comprehending, Responding

The importance of the three related processes that constitute our conscious mental life is plainly exemplified in the stories of these three handicapped individuals.

We could never become aware of what is going on around us without sense organs to bring us the information. Because Louis Braille was blind, he was necessarily limited in the

knowledge he could receive. We could never comprehend and
tie together all the information that pours in upon us if we
had no brain to supervise the process. Because Phineas Gage
suffered an accident that destroyed vast areas of his brain, he
became a child again, both emotionally and mentally. We
could never put our ideas into action if we did not have responsive muscles in back and shoulders, arms and legs, hands
and feet, and in our vocal organs. Because Earl Carlson sustained an injury to that area of the brain which controls the
muscles, he could not manage his locomotive organs, his
speech organs, or any of the rest of his muscular apparatus.
Only by reason of years of agonizing determination could he
succeed eventually in building up new nerve pathways from
his brain to his muscles.

✓ ✓ ✓

In this chapter you will come to appreciate more clearly, perhaps, than you ever have before, the miracle of mind! You
will learn about the brain and the gateways that lead into it;
about the magnificently complex system of communication
which holds together all its parts; and about the elaborate
traffic routes along which its myriads of executive orders are
transmitted to every part of the body, and into the world outside. You will find out also something about the methods
which psychologists employ in studying the performance and
the mental output of the marvelous organ we call the brain.

Photo by Brown Brothers

Fig. 9. "The Boyhood of Sir Walter Raleigh" by Millais. The dreamy look in young Walter's eyes reveals how his inner world of ideas is influenced by the fascinating tales which he hears from seafaring men.

3. SCIENTIFIC BASIS OF PSYCHOLOGY

Before beginning the study of the chapter, you will find it helpful to list a number of objective situations and the corresponding mental responses which we are likely to make to them. Use a form such as the one below for the purpose:

SOME EXAMPLES OF WHAT THE BRAIN DOES

In This Situation	The Brain Does This
1. The passing of an airplane over-head	1. Identifies, classifies, labels
2.	2.
3.	3.
4.	4.
5. etc.	5. etc.

We become aware, of course, of the external material world around us because our sense organs are attracted to it and take it in. Try to include in the list above some situations that arouse senses other than your eyes, together with the corresponding reactions that your mind makes to each.

OUR TWO WORLDS

The outside and the inside worlds. The world outside is obvious enough to anybody. It has houses and streets and people; it has flowers and trees and animals; it has books and newspapers and radios; it has countries and continents and hemispheres; it has color and size and depth; it has land and water and sky, automobiles and railways and ships and planes, tables and desks and chairs, and myriads more of things and conditions that can be sensed by anybody.

But there is another world—an inner, or mental, world—
that is quite different from the outer one. Instead of houses
and animals and books and continents and stars and airplanes,
this inner world is a world of ideas, of thoughts, of wants, of
habits and memories, of feeling and emotion, of character and
personality. Nevertheless, these latter are mysterious reproduc-
tions of the objective world of things that exists around us on
every side; they are extraordinary copies of reality as we sense
it in the world outside our bodies; they are inexplicable reactions somewhere within us to the experiences and events that
make up living.

An amazing transfer! Do you see that house over there?
Of course, you do: everyone sees it. It is white, with brown
trimmings, has two stories, a garage attached, a broad lawn
with flower beds in front. It is a part of the outer world.

Now, close your eyes. Do you still see the house? Of course
not; yet, yes—you can still see it in your mind's eye! But it is
no longer a part of the outer world: it is a part of your own
personal inner world. It exists not objectively, but subjec-
tively. A portion of the outer world has been transferred in
some mystifying way into your own inner world, and you
recognize the resulting idea as a likeness of the object for
which it stands.

Our inner world of ideas. Turn to the picture on page 273
and read the caption. Then pause for a minute or two to
reflect upon the ideas that Rodin, the sculptor who created
this statue, meant "The Thinker" to convey to us. Man opposed by fate, man perplexed by the obstacles that spring up in
his pathway toward the light, man "stumped," baffled, helpless; but, more than this, man stopping to think his way grop-
ingly forward, man refusing to be thrust back into savagery,
man searching his mind for some glimmer to light him onward! Here is the message of "The Thinker."

Notice, now, that all the ideas that come into your mind as you reflect about Rodin's statue are inner arousals that have no objectivity, at least with the exception of the sight of the picture that set them off. These ideas are a part of your inner world, just as the mental picture of the house was a fragment of it. This inner world of thought and feeling is vast and unlimited, vaster far than the objective world of things outside.

From the simple act of glancing at a statue, trains of thought may be set in motion that carry one across the entire universe of space and across the entire reach of time. Thus, in observing Rodin's statue, one might find the following ideas succeeding one another in his mind: savage man could think little; fossil remains of savage men have been found in widely separated parts of the earth; by the power of his mind, man has raised himself above all the animals; by thinking, he has conquered the earth and the sea and the sky; by thinking, he has found ways to hurl his voice around the globe; by thinking, he has puzzled out the secrets of the solar universe and discovered the laws that govern its operation; man's mind will one day win the victory over disease, pestilence, even perhaps war.

A great mystery.   Here is one of the greatest mysteries in the world! How is it possible for things in the outside world to reach the human brain and set it into action? How is it possible for one idea to suggest other and yet other ideas, until the whole range of human experience is embraced? What is the nature of this strange and mighty inner world in which we live, and by what means is it created and maintained?

Fascinating questions, these!

And questions whose answers psychologists are interested in seeking out. How the outside world is brought inside; how we use the information thus afforded in building our systems of ideas; what we do as a result; why we do what we do—with these challenging queries we shall be concerned in every chapter in this book.

WHAT OUR SENSE ORGANS DO FOR US

Gateways to the inner world. Standing at the external boundaries of our bodies, on the frontier, as it were, between the outer and the inner world, are our sense organs: our eyes, our ears, and our skin senses particularly. Constructed of highly sensitive kinds of tissue, these organs act as the gateways through which the objects, events, and conditions in the world outside are admitted into our inner world of ideas and feelings and purposes. Without them as intermediaries, our minds could never be reached, and we should be utterly without consciousness and intelligence.

To be born even with one sense lacking, such as vision, would mean to face life with a severe handicap. To be born both blind and deaf would be a misfortune practically insurmountable; and to be born blind, deaf, and lacking in a sense of touch would mean that the individual would be compelled to go through life a helpless *idiot* (feeble-minded person of the lowest type) who could make almost no contacts with the outside world.

The eye gate. The eye responds to waves of light and of color. The daylight world, we are told by the *physicists* (scientists who study the principles of matter and motion), is crisscrossed with these waves.

Each color of the *spectrum* (natural arrangement of the colors in order of wave length) has a different *wave length* from every other. Those at the red end are longest; those at the violet end are shortest. Figure 10 illustrates wave length and wave *amplitude,* the former determining the color and the latter the intensity of the light.

Through its very delicate nerve structure, the human eye

is able to register all the different color *stimuli* (environmental agents that arouse a sense organ) as well as, of course, *achromatic* (colorless) stimuli such as ordinary daylight pro-

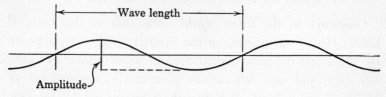

Fig. 10. Light wave. The length of a light wave is determined by the horizontal distance between a given point on one wave and the corresponding point on the next. The shortest visible waves are about 400 millionths of a millimeter; the longest are about twice as long, or 800 millionths of a millimeter. The vertical distance from the crest to the base of the wave, known as the amplitude, determines the intensity of the light.

duces. The eye is helpless in unilluminated darkness because there are no light waves to be reflected from objects into it.

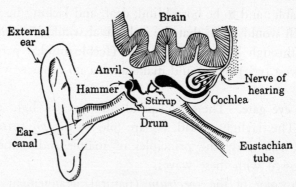

Fig. 11. Parts of the human ear. The three bones named, from their shapes, hammer, anvil, and stirrup are in the middle ear. The cochlea, shaped like a shell, is in the internal ear.

The ear gate.   The ear responds to a different kind of stimulus: the sound wave. Sound waves are thrown off by vibrating bodies that have been set into activity by internal or external force. The waves vary enormously in the rates at which they vibrate, those producing the lowest audible tones vibrating about 20 times per second, and those producing the highest audible tones vibrating more than 20,000 times a second.

Sound waves vary also in the speed at which they travel, depending upon the medium through which they are transmitted.

Waves that vibrate regularly and smoothly are called musical; those that vibrate irregularly produce nonmusical sound, or noise. To both types of sound waves the human ear is adjusted, and it is able, by means of sensitive nerve endings within it, to pick them up and cause them to be transmitted to the brain, where they register consciously either as tones or noises. Figure 11 is a sketch showing the important parts of the ear.

The skin gate. The skin is a tissue containing several distinctly different kinds of sense organs. One type is sensitive to touch, and is found universally over the skin area. It gives

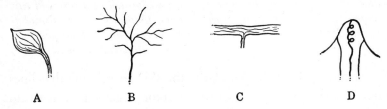

A   B   C   D

Fig. 12. Principal skin sense organs. A: Organ of cold. B: Organ of pain. C: Organ of warmth. D: Organ of touch. These lie embedded in or below the skin. Each picks up its particular kind of stimulus and sends it along toward the central nervous system.

us information about the smoothness or roughness, the size and shape, the wetness or dryness of objects that we handle or feel.

Another type of skin organ reacts to coldness; another, to warmth and heat. Still another, lying deep, is sensitive to surface pain, and carries warning sensations from the piercings, bruises, distortions, and the like, that frequently occur in accidents. Figure 12 includes sketches of each of these four different kinds of skin *receptors* (organs which receive stimuli).

The skin that covers the tongue has embedded within it a peculiar kind of sense organ, the *taste buds,* which enable us to recognize sweet, sour, bitter, and salt, and their various combinations. Figure 13 is a sketch of one of these innumerable buds.

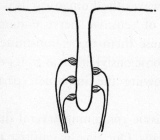 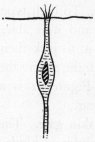

Fig. 13. Taste organ. The saliva collects in the groove of each bud and stimulates the nerves, which carry the sensation to the brain. Can you see why dry food is tasteless?

Fig. 14. Olfactory organ. Cells like this project from the skin of each nostril as a series of tiny hairs. Odorous vapors stimulate the organs and set up the reaction called smell.

The gate of smell. Similarly, the skin membrane that lines our nostrils contains sensitive receptor organs that react to odorous gases that are thrown into the air—for example, by food or flowers—and by their aid we are enabled to enjoy pleasant or savory smells and to receive warning when dangerous vapors are escaping around us. Since there is an open passageway from the back of the throat up into the nostrils, many of the "taste" flavors we get from foods are in reality smell sensations that have traveled up this pathway. Figure 14 is a sketch to indicate the general appearance and structure of one of the nerves making up the *olfactory sense organ.*

The gate of muscular strain and tension. Deep within our bodies also are sensory organs that give us additional information from our muscles, tendons, and joints. Every muscle is supplied with these sensitive organs. We are, through the messages they initiate, able to feel strain and tension when we use our muscles, as well as to feel tiredness and soreness from them when they have been overexerted.

The gate of balance. Each inner ear contains a sensory structure consisting of three *semicircular canals,* which inform us about the momentary equilibrium, or balance, of our bodies and the degree of leaning present at any given instant. This sense—known as the *static* or *vestibular sense*—is of special importance to the aviator, who needs to be as sensitive as is humanly possible to the changing positions of his body while he is in the air.

The gateways of pain and comfort. Every internal organ, such as the stomach, the lungs, and the heart, is also supplied with sensory nervous structures that inform us of comfort or of discomfort within it. Through the messages thus received, we are able to take steps to secure needed relief when our bodies are not functioning normally. Through them, also, we are encouraged to maintain our activities and habits in the customary manner so long as the sensory information brought in to the brain is reassuring.

Through all these sensory gateways—many of them at the exterior of the body, some of them within it—we receive information from the outer world concerning material objects and from the inner world concerning organic operation and state of being. Outposts on every frontier, these sensory receiving organs afford an easy access to the brain within, carrying to it information from every department and area of human experience. Marvelous, indeed, are these gateways that mediate between the world without and the world within!

Limitations of our sense organs. It should be pointed out in passing, however, that despite the readiness of our sense organs to receive stimuli and cause them to be transmitted to the brain, each receptor is definitely limited in the range of stimuli that it can accommodate. While it is true that our eyes, for example, can respond to light and color stimuli all the way from the red end of the spectrum to the violet end, and all the way from the whites through the grays to black, there are innumerable waves—the *infrareds* (waves longer than those of visible light) and the *ultraviolets* (waves shorter than those of visible light)—to which they are not sensitive.

Similarly, our ears, while they record faithfully sounds and tones from the lowest bass to the highest treble, are not sensitive to sound waves that vibrate less than 20 nor more than 20,000 times a second. In other words, beyond the reach of eyes and ears and other senses, we must suppose that there is a vast universe of light, color, and tone far above our poor human powers to experience it. If our sense organs were stripped of these limitations, we should undoubtedly be able to hear, with Milton, the music of the "sphery chimes" as the planets turn in their orbits, or see with Alice and Peter Pan, at least in fancy, all the invisible gnomes and elfins that people the forests and fields!

The ultimate purpose of the sense organs is to take up sensory information in the form of stimuli and to transpose it from mechanical or electrical energy into nervous current, so that it can be relayed to the brain and nervous system.

THE CENTRAL NERVOUS SYSTEM

The great seat of consciousness. The brain, the chief organ of the central nervous system, is locked away safely within the bony casket of the skull. It is the great seat of consciousness, of judgment, of thinking, of will. Structurally, it is an irregular organ, consisting of an upper portion called the *cerebrum;* an intermediate portion called the *cerebellum;* and a lower portion called the *medulla oblongata.*

The cerebrum. The upper section of the brain—the cerebrum—is really a mass of billions of nerve cells and connecting fibers arranged in highly complex patterns. The cells lie thickest along the outer rim of the cerebrum, forming the *cortex.* The intercommunicating fibers lie beneath the cells. In some manner, not very well understood by scientists, the cortical cells are able to receive the incoming nerve currents sent into them from the sense organs, to sort them into the proper brain areas for interpretation, to co-ordinate their meaning, and to make us conscious of their significance. They are able to plan and execute appropriate response to the information received, to use the material actively in thinking and weighing, and to retain the information in varying degrees of clarity.

We see, for example, markings on a page, and we immediately recognize words and become conscious of their significance; we sense the vibrating of sound waves against our eardrums, and immediately we recognize the voice of a friend speaking and perceive the meaning of what he is saying. In like manner, each of the other receptor organs makes us aware of objects, events, and conditions in the world around us, and of what they mean or stand for.

Of all the mysteries of science, there is none greater than the electrochemical mystery of the human brain!

Localization of control in the cerebrum. As will be seen in Figure 15, some areas of the brain preside over specific functions and abilities. Thus, the brain center for seeing is located in the *posterior* (rear) part of the cerebrum; the center for hearing is located near the middle. Injury to or destruction of these areas brings about temporary or permanent loss of vision and of hearing, respectively.

Experimentation indicates, however, that the brain has marvelous power to adapt itself to new conditions. Even when a function is impaired or lost through destruction or injury to that part of the brain that controls it, other parts of the brain have been found able to take over, and to develop new centers for controlling the old function. There are, of course, definite limitations in this capacity of the brain to restore de-

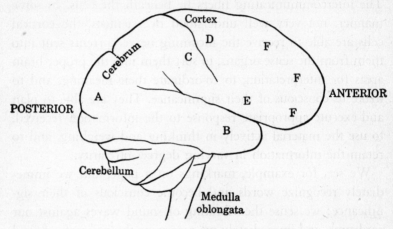

Fig. 15. The human brain. A: *Center for vision.* B: *Center for hearing.* C: *Center for bodily sensations.* D: *Center for sending out motor responses.* E: *Center for speech.* FFF: *Vast association area.*

stroyed functions. For example, if that area in the posterior section which is the seat of vision is destroyed, the victim is left permanently and incurably blind, since no other part of his brain can assume control over the highly specialized function of vision.

The cerebrum is not only the largest part, but it is also the most important part of the brain. Within its labyrinthine nerve cells and fibers all our conscious life is centered and controlled. Deprive a man of his cerebrum, and you will make him unable longer to see and hear; to think, speak, remember; or to do any other of those complex acts which we ordinarily associate with the human intellect and will.

The cerebellum and medulla. The cerebellum, located below and to the back of the cerebrum, is concerned largely with the co-ordination of our muscles in acts of skill, and with the maintenance of our body balance and equilibrium.

The medulla oblongata, still lower down at the base of the brain, is a nerve center controlling certain of our vital organic processes, notably breathing and the circulation of the blood.

The spinal cord. The spinal cord may be looked upon as an assembly of complex nerve lines. Some of these lines carry incoming messages from the sense organs upward toward the brain; others of them bring back outgoing *impulses* (messages from the brain) to the muscles. The former are called *sensory* or *afferent nerves,* and they occupy the posterior half of the spinal cord; the latter are known as *motor* or *efferent nerves,* and occupy the *anterior* (front) side of the cord. The sensory nerves bridge the gap between the sense organs and the brain; the motor nerves bridge the gap between the brain and the muscles. There are millions of both kinds of them within the spinal cord. There are other millions of them that run up to the brain and downward to the muscles, but which are located completely outside of the cord.

The spinal cord is, then, in effect, a vast two-way thoroughfare, or a mighty two-way telegraph cable, bringing information in to headquarters and causing executive orders to be brought out. Housed safely within the bony spinal column, this thoroughfare—this trunk cable—is protected from injury along its entire extent, just as the overarching brain from which it emerges is protected by the enclosing skull.

Taken together, the spinal cord and the brain comprise what is called the *central nervous system.* All parts of this system are interconnected by communicating fibers, so that it is a highly integrated unit. The central nervous system is the great regulative and adjustive apparatus of our organisms. Without it, we could sense nothing, understand nothing, make no response in either thought, word, or deed.

The responding mechanism. The outgoing executive orders dispatched from the brain and cord go, as we have said, to our muscles—to the muscles of speech, the muscles of locomotion, the muscles that make possible manual skill and dexterity. These, together with all the other muscles and glands in our bodies, make up what is appropriately called the *responding mechanism.* The complete response begins when the brain classifies and interprets the ideas aroused in it by incoming sensory information and makes decisions regarding those ideas; it is finished when we have responded to them with whatever language or other motor expression is appropriate to the situation.

Thus, to the words we hear from a companion, we respond with language; to the felt need to know the definition of an unfamiliar word, we respond by going to the dictionary, turning its pages, locating the word, and reading the definition; to the cry of "Fire!" we respond by jumping up, running, exclaiming, and so forth; to the awareness that all eyes are turned upon us, we respond by flushing and stammering, by showing off, or by rising to the occasion.

Simple or reflex response. Into every muscle in the body, motor nerves from the brain or cord proceed. When impulses are passed along these into a muscle or a group of muscles, the latter react and produce motion or adjustment calculated to fit the need of the moment. This muscular response may occur at the lowest level of the nervous system—the *reflex level*—or it may occur at the highest level—the *cortical* or *brain level*.

Figure 16 illustrates response at the reflex level, called *reflex action.* This type of response is controlled by the spinal cord. You will observe from a study of the diagram that the incoming stimulus reaches the cord by means of the sensory nerve, but that instead of traveling upward within the cord to the brain, the message is switched directly across from the sensory (posterior) side to the motor (anterior) side at the same level. The adjusting response thus goes out directly and by the shortest route to the appropriate responding muscle or muscles.

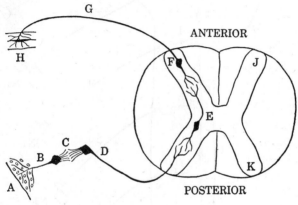

Fig. 16. Diagram illustrating reflex action. A: Sense organ, such as one in the skin. B: Sensory or afferent nerve fiber. C: Synapse, or point of junction of two nerves. D: Another sensory nerve fiber. E: Nerve lying wholly within the spinal cord and serving to relay incoming sensory information to the appropriate outgoing motor nerve. F: Motor or efferent nerve cell. G: Motor nerve fiber. H: Muscle. J: One of the two anterior horns of the spinal cord. K: One of the two posterior horns.

This sort of direct response occurs, for example, when you jerk your hand hastily away from a hot stove which you have inadvertently touched. In such a situation, it would be extremely uncomfortable if the information had first to travel all the way up to the brain and be there interpreted and analyzed before a withdrawing motor response could be shot back into the arm muscle! Reflex action is protective and immediate.

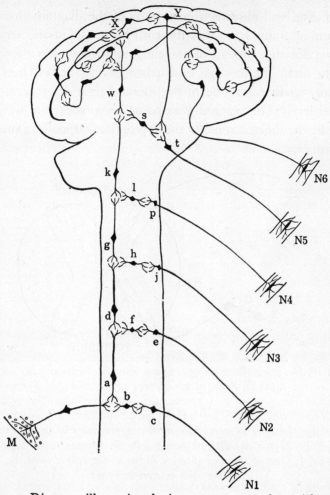

Fig. 17. Diagram illustrating brain response, together with reflex response at various levels of the cord. M: Sense organ, such as one in the skin. a, d, g, k, w: Sensory or afferent nerves carrying impulses up to the brain. X, Y: Cortical or cerebral cells for associating and for sending out adjustive reactions to muscles. c, e, j, p, t: Motor or efferent nerves running outward from the central nervous system to the muscles. b, f, h, l, s: Nerves lying within the spinal cord and connecting the sensory side with the motor side. N1, N2, N3, N4, N5, N6: Muscles.

Higher level or brain response. But it is not enough merely to jerk your hand away from the hot surface. You will need to do something *cerebral* (intelligent) about the resulting burn. *Brain level response,* as illustrated in Figure 17, becomes therefore necessary. After the spinal cord center has taken matters into its own hands and has caused you to jerk away your hand, your brain will determine what corrective or adjustive action needs to be made. Shortly, perhaps, you will decide to go to the first-aid cabinet for sterilizing medication, and bandaging. Your spinal cord could never of itself set in order this complex sort of reaction. And it certainly could never put the experience into language describing the occurrence to your friend! Only the higher thinking and interpreting centers of the cerebrum could do these things.

In these two levels of the central nervous system all our responses are initiated and carried through. Those that are protective, simple, immediate, are taken care of within the spinal cord as reflexes; those that are ideational, willed, planned, reasoned, are prepared in and projected from the brain.

THE AUXILIARY NERVOUS SYSTEM

Deep within our bodies is going on, of course, other muscular action that does not commonly rise to the level of conscious experience at all. The importance of a smoothly running inner body machine, operating, on the whole, without our attention, is quite obvious. Before you read further in the chapter, try to identify several internal processes that thus proceed automatically, day and night. Use the form at the top of page 72 for recording them.

Every regulative process that goes on within our physical organisms is, in the last analysis, muscular. Muscles in the walls of the stomach and intestines provide the energy used in digesting the food we eat; muscles in the walls of the veins

THINGS THAT GO ON AUTOMATICALLY INSIDE OUR BODIES

When This Happens:	Nerves and Muscles Cause This to Take Place:
1. Food is taken into the stomach	1. Gastric juice is discharged into it and the stomach muscles agitate the food.
2.	
3.	
4.	
5. etc.	

(You should be able to think of a half dozen or more items for this table.)

and arteries control the size of the vessels, and so regulate the amount of blood that is, at any given instant, being pumped through them; muscles in our lungs and chest regulate our breathing. It goes without saying that if the central nervous system had to maintain supervision over all these and other internal processes, we should have no time for learning and thinking and using our brain in all the higher ways; we should be compelled to expend all our nervous power in the regulation of the internal mechanisms of the body.

To free the higher centers from the routine supervisory work over the various organic processes, nature has developed an auxiliary nervous system, called the *autonomic nervous system.*

Lying completely outside of the central nervous system, the autonomic system sends its fibers outward to the heart, liver, stomach, intestines, and glands, and keeps each of them performing its accustomed work twenty-four hours of the day. While the autonomic system is connected by intermediate fibers to the central nervous system—so that in an emergency the brain and higher centers can be brought into action—the former is relatively automatic in its operation. Only rarely is

its control over the physiological processes of the body inter-
fered with.

Thus, we really have two nervous systems: one that presides
over our higher thought processes and our reflex actions; and
one that presides over the more purely organic and regulative
functions of the body machine.

THE METHODS USED IN STUDYING PSYCHOLOGY

The method of observation.   Students of psychology commonly make use of many different methods in their search for
information about mental life and behavior. We shall mention
but three of them.

The first method is that of observation of others. All of us
use this method naïvely when we study the actions or evaluate
the emotions of those around us. We are called upon constantly to "size up" somebody, to try to read his mind, to decide
what his reactions are likely to be. We use the method of observation whenever we note a person's gestures, his flushing or
paling, his manner of speaking, his self-control or his lack of
control. This is at once the easiest, the most popular, and the
least accurate method of studying human beings.

The method of introspection.   The second method is the
method of introspection. When one uses this method, he turns
his analytical attention inward upon his own behavior and
motives. What color does he like best? What is his feeling about
capital punishment? What emotion is aroused in him by a
sunset? by a falsehood? by snakes? by the weather? What
is his attitude toward Socialists? toward optimism? toward
tipping?

These are obviously matters which only the individual himself can observe with any degree of exactness. Nobody can read
another's mind or know his values or his goals or his motives
but himself. But even the method of introspection is seldom

used accurately, since it is extremely difficult to look into one's own mind and study its operation reliably.

The method of experimentation. The third method—the method of experimentation—is the most laborious and the most nearly exact of all. By its means it is possible to set up a controlled, standard situation, and to observe the effects of it upon the behavior of the subject being studied. If, for example, it should be desired to find out the rapidity with which mental fatigue develops under different conditions of work or of distraction, it would be possible to construct an experiment in which a continuous amount of work of known difficulty was carried on, while the distractions were varied from day to day, or from hour to hour. By repeating this experiment under identical conditions upon great numbers of people, it would be possible for the psychologist to reach valid conclusions that might be presumed to apply universally whenever the conditions were identical.

As youthful psychologists, you will be called upon to make considerable use of all three of these methods—observation, introspection, and experimentation—in carrying out the assignments of the succeeding chapters of this book.

THE FIELDS OF PSYCHOLOGY

Inasmuch as the science of psychology deals with human behavior and the human mind, it is apparent from the outset that it must work in many fields and that it must contribute to many areas of life.

One of these important fields is that of *adolescent psychology,* which deals with the interests, activities, and motives of youth. You will find it helpful at this point, since you are yourself an adolescent individual, to identify some of the more common traits and characteristics of present-day youth. Use the following table to record your results:

HIGH LIGHTS IN THE PSYCHOLOGY OF ADOLESCENCE

Youth Today Is Interested in These Things	As Shown by the Following Observations
1. Fads in dress	1. High school boys (or girls) are wearing ....
2.	2.
3.	3.
4.	4.
5. etc.	5. etc.

(If your class really "gets going" on this topic, you will need more than one sheet of paper to record all the ideas!)

Some of the areas of psychology. We shall make only the briefest mention of the fields of psychology here. *Child psychology* deals with child behavior and mental development. Another field—*educational psychology*—is concerned with the complex subject of learning and teaching, and deals with the laws underlying learning. Another—the *psychology of advertising*—is concerned with the problems involved in the sale of commodities over the counter and through the medium of the advertising page. Still another field—*personnel selection*—deals with various tests, inventories, and practices which help to choose those applicants for jobs who will be likely to succeed best in them; while another—*social psychology*—is concerned with investigating the motives that lie back of group movements, such as political parties, mobs, and wars.

Other fields of psychology include *animal psychology, racial psychology, national psychology, individual psychology, genetic psychology* (the psychology of inheritance), and *general psychology*.

Our concern with these fields. In this book we shall invade all or most of these different areas of psychology, selecting from each of them those ideas and principles that are of most significance for the young person who is striving better to understand himself and the world in which he lives. In the fascinating journey which you are now making in this absorbingly interesting field, the author trusts and believes that you will have many profitable and interesting adventures.

Now that you comprehend something of the miracle of the brain and of the nervous system, you will better understand the scientific basis of the principles of practical psychology which follow in the other chapters of this book. Certainly in no aspect of your experience does your brain mechanism come into more obvious operation than it does when you sit down to study. To the subject of how to study, then, we turn our attention in Chapter 4.

HOW PSYCHOLOGISTS WORK

Scientists who study the brain and nervous system are called *neurologists*. They are primarily interested in the structure of the nervous system, and in its diseases and disorders. One very fruitful method of studying the relationship of nervous structures to the physical body consists of investigating changes that take place in the brain following the destruction of sensory gateways into it, or of motor pathways out of it. By making post-mortem examinations of the brains of people who have met with crippling accidents, or who have been in other striking ways physically abnormal, neurologists have learned much about the intimate connection between brain and body.

One of the most remarkable of such examinations was made of the brain of Laura Bridgman, by Dr. H. H. Donaldson, a noted brain *anatomist* (scientist who studies bodily structure).

Born in Hanover, New Hampshire, Laura Bridgman suffered at the age of two years a severe attack of scarlet fever. When she recovered, it was found that the disease had completely destroyed her hearing, had left her totally blind in her left eye and nearly so in her right, and had practically obliterated her senses of smell and of taste. Some rudimentary vision remained for a time in her right eye, but that, too, completely faded out by the time she was eight years of age. She was then placed in an institution for the blind, where she learned to read by the sense of touch, and to converse with the sign manual. Her progress was rapid. She studied geography, algebra, and history, and learned to do needlework, housework, and letter writing. In due time she herself became a teacher of the blind, deaf, and dumb.

When Laura Bridgman died, at the age of sixty, her family consented to have the brain of this famous woman dissected and studied, in order that scientists might test out certain theories with regard to the relationship between the sensory gateways and the brain. To Dr. H. H. Donaldson the task was entrusted. Here was the brain of a perfectly healthy woman who had lived an active and surprisingly happy life in spite of being deaf, blind, and mute for more than half a century. What would the examination show to be true of those areas of her brain connected with the senses of sight, of hearing, and of smell and taste, all of which she had been early deprived of?

Minute examination of the brain revealed that its weight was only slightly under the average, and that in only one particular was it definitely an abnormal organ. When Dr. Donaldson explored the terminal areas of the nerves of vision and hearing, of smell and taste, he found them to be poorly developed. In fact, the nerve terminations of the nose and eyes were either completely destroyed or highly disorganized. There was great destruction also of the middle ear and of the nerves connected with the organ of taste.

Most striking of all were the findings relative to the brain areas connected with the incoming nerves of sight. Since the right eye had remained partially sensitive for some time after

the left eye had become completely blind, the dramatic finding was made that that portion of the brain connected with
the former was considerably more developed than that connected with the latter. Here was conclusive evidence of the fact,
which scientists had surmised before, that specific areas of the
brain exercise control over specific sensory functions, and that
when for any reason a given area of the brain fails to receive
any stimulation from its arousing sensory gateway, it will
degenerate.

Miss Bridgman was not only blind and deaf; she was also a
mute, since she had developed no speech patterns. Careful

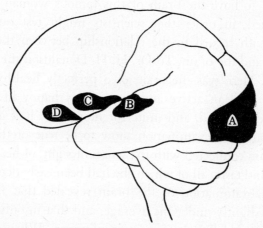

*Fig. 18. Diagram showing the "blacked out" area of Laura Bridg-
man's brain. A: Visual area. B: Auditory area. C: Olfactory area.
D: Gustatory area.*

study of those areas in her brain that would normally be
associated with articulate speech showed similarly defective
development, together with actual deterioration. Thus did science demonstrate not only that sensory interpretative areas in
the brain of a blind person remain undeveloped, but also that
motor areas that normally control definite muscle groups are

likewise undeveloped in the brain of a person suffering from a paralysis of any such group.

Dr. Donaldson's examination of the Laura Bridgman brain was made in 1889. It was one of the first scientific anatomical brain examinations ever reported. While, as we have already stated, later research demonstrates the fact that unaffected parts of the brain may under some conditions succeed in taking over functions normally controlled by affected parts, still Dr. Donaldson's original confirmation of the theory regarding definite cerebral areas remains unassailed.

TO HELP YOU LEARN

QUESTIONS TO ASK YOURSELF

1. Many animals are possessed of the same organic structures as you and I are. In what profound ways, however, are animals inferior to human beings?

2. In the last analysis, where do we get the ideas that crowd into our minds every minute of every waking hour of every day?

3. Do you know how Helen Keller, who became totally blind and deaf when she was nineteen months old, succeeded in spite of her handicap in mastering the physical world about her?

4. Assuming that each of the following structures in an individual could be painlessly severed, without in any way disturbing or injuring any other part of the organism, what responses would it be impossible for the victim to make?

The cerebrum
The cerebellum
The medulla
The spinal cord
The autonomic nervous system

5. Which of the three methods commonly used by psychologists to study human behavior do most people use naïvely? What are

some of the obvious advantages of the method? What are some of its greatest weaknesses?

WORKING WITH PSYCHOLOGY

1. Do the following experiment. Embedded within the skin are two very interesting kinds of sense organs—the organs of cold, and the organs of warmth. They lie quite near together, but singly, throughout the entire covering of our bodies. It is easy to locate them with a blunt-pointed metal stylus (a moderate-sized nail will do). Thoroughly cool the stylus by immersing it for a few minutes in cold water, or by laying it against a piece of ice. Then, before it has time to be warmed by the surrounding atmosphere, set the blunt point of the stylus down in an exploratory way upon several successive points on the skin, pressing it down only enough to barely indent the surface. When you touch one of the cold organs, you will feel an intensely cold sensation from it.

In a similar way, heat the stylus by immersing it for a few moments in very warm (not hot) water, and then search out with its point some of the warm sense organs on your skin. You will experience a suffusing sensation of warmth whenever you touch one of them. For both explorations, use a small area of skin (about a half-inch square) on the back of your left wrist. When hundreds of these cold organs are stimulated by cold air or cold water, our bodies feel cold; when they are stimulated by warm air or water, they feel warm. Ordinarily the cold organs respond only to cold stimulation, and the warm ones only to warm.

2. You have probably observed that when you have a head cold you do not experience such keen taste sensations as customarily. Much of the satisfaction we derive from food comes from its savory smell, and we are disappointed in the "flat taste" food has when we have a cold. The reason for a partial loss of taste at such times is an interesting one. A great deal of the flavor of food is, strange to say, contributed by its smell. Since the organs sensitive to smell lie far up in the nasal cavity, and since when one has a head cold this cavity is blocked at both ends, the odor thrown off by food cannot readily reach them. Prepare small half-inch cubes of raw potato, raw carrot or turnip, and raw onion. Then, after blindfolding yourself, let some member of your family place one of the

cubes in your mouth. Chew it actively and note how tardily you are able to identify it. You may even fail completely to differentiate the three flavors. Taste and smell are one and inseparable. Even the same general area of the brain, as you noted in the sketch of Laura Bridgeman's brain, is the interpretative center for both functions.

3. Prepare five "letters" of different weights by placing in identical envelopes varying numbers of sheets of heavy paper, cardboard, or other convenient filling. After the envelopes are ready, imagine that each is to be sent in the mails. "Heft" each one carefully and discriminatingly, and try to decide how many ounces it weighs. You have done this same sort of thing frequently when, in the absence of a letter scale, you have reached a judgment as to whether double postage would be necessary on a somewhat bulky letter. Note on each envelope its guessed weight. Afterwards, weigh each one on a scale in order to check the accuracy of your judgment. Touch organs in your hands, and strain organs in your arm muscles co-operate in helping you arrive at a judgment of weight. You will find it interesting to "heft" other objects—both light and heavy—and to estimate their weight from the amount of skin pressure and muscle strain you experience in handling them.

4. Try the following bit of introspection. Imagine a solid wooden cube three inches by three inches by three inches, painted red on all six of its faces. Saw the cube up, in imagination, into small one-inch cubes. How many cubes do you now have? How many of them are red on all six sides? How many are red on five sides? On four sides? On three sides? On two sides? On one side? How many have no red on any side? As you work at the problem, try to observe how your mind operates. For example, do you see vivid images of the blocks? Do you see the red sides? Do your lips, tongue, and throat seem almost to be producing a kind of inaudible "inner speech" as you think about the problem? Do your fingers tend to point, or gesticulate, or make diagrams and patterns in the air? Do you feel your hands separating, piling over, or otherwise arranging the blocks? Do you close your eyes to "see" more clearly? Do you purse your lips, wrinkle your brows, or make other facial or bodily adjustments as you proceed? Do you punctuate your work with running inner comments about the reasonableness of various moves, hypotheses, and conclusions?

As you reflect upon your mental and motor processes occurring in this situation, you will be achieving something of the experience which psychologists undergo when they use the method of introspection to study the fascinating operation of mental life.

WHAT OTHERS SAY

1. In General Psychology:

An Introduction to Psychology by J. J. B. Morgan and A. R. Gilliland. A very readable, scientific discussion of the chief topics in general psychology. This book is intended primarily for people of high school age.

Psychology and Life by Floyd L. Ruch. While this is a college text in general psychology, you will find much of its content easily understandable. Well written, interesting, and stimulating.

Psychology by Robert S. Woodworth. A standard college text in psychology. You will find it a bit difficult in places, but it will amply reward your efforts in trying to dig out its meaning. It is decidedly, however, not an elementary text.

2. In Problems of Adolescent Psychology and Personality:

Adolescence: A Study in the Teen Years by Lawrence A. Averill. A college text, but by no means beyond the abilities of high school students. It deals with the problems of growing up, with conflicts and misunderstandings, with the interests and ambitions and ideals of youth.

People Are Important by Floyd L. Ruch, G. N. Mackenzie, and Margaret McClean. An interesting study of the drives, emotions, learning, and living of young people. It is designed for high school students and is interestingly written about real people in school.

A Girl Grows Up by Ruth Fedder. An especially valuable book for high school girls to read and think about. It deals with a number of real problems that confront every girl in the process of growing up and of adjusting to others around her.

Boy Grows Up by Harry McKowan and Marion LeBron. A book as good for high school boys to read and ponder as is Miss Fedder's book for girls. A practical and realistic treatment of many of the problems every high school boy must solve.

Is Studying Hard or Easy for You?

Roald Amundsen had so convinced people of his profound study and knowledge of the sea that he was chosen, at twenty-five, to go as mate on a ship that was making an expedition to the Antarctic. Returning after this first voyage, he began immediately to make plans for an independent scientific expedition of his own to the frozen Northland.

His whole subsequent career was dominated by the insatiable desire to learn more and more about the uncharted regions of the earth. He spent a lifetime studying from nature's interesting book. He learned that the North Magnetic Pole has no stationary position. He discovered the northwest passage from the Atlantic to the Pacific. Turning his efforts to the opposite end of the earth's axis he made a brilliant dash over mountains and perilous glaciers to the South Pole. Still later, he made the first air flight over the North Pole, from Spitzbergen to Alaska.

"Whatever I have accomplished in exploration," he wrote, "has been the result of lifelong planning, painstaking preparation, and the hardest kind of conscientious work."

A great many people have tried to imagine what Paradise might be like. André Maurois, in his book *The Art of Living,* affirms that for him such a land of bliss is not a place where angels play upon golden harps all day and sing songs of adoration. Rather, the best heaven Maurois can imagine is a sort of wonderful study room in which he would be able to write everlastingly upon some extraordinary novel that had no end. In the planning and writing of this masterpiece he would be inspired by a keenness of power and a depth of insight that had had no parallel in his earthly experience as a writer of literature.

Sophomore Mary Moller, whom I used to watch with some fascination while she "studied" at home in the evening, developed a truly Mary Moller technique in doing her lesson. First, she sat down on one foot in a rocking chair, started the chair off at its maximum speed—about fifty, I judge—sighed, looked at the clock, and then proceeded to read half aloud and in a dismal, monotonous voice the entire assignment from the beginning of, let us say, the sack of Rome by the Gauls, until the sack had been completed.

This unhappy process over, Mary then stopped her chair, changed to the other foot, sighed, looked at the clock, resumed speed, and waded a second time through the assignment, getting Rome sacked for a second time by the Gauls. Then the whole thing was repeated for a third time, and after the third sack Mary laid aside her history textbook and turned to her French!

Is it any wonder that Mary Moller got D in Ancient History at the end of the term?

Are You like Amundsen, or like Mary?

Roald Amundsen studies magnetic fields, glacial drifts, ocean currents, polar icecaps—and becomes a master in his science. André Maurois studies language, literary style, creative writing—and becomes a master in his art. Sophomore Mary Moller "studies" the history of mighty empires—Egypt,

Assyria, Persia, Greece, Rome—recorded in pages teaming with dramatic revelation—and gets a D!

There is surely something wrong—either with ancient history or with Sophomore Mary Moller! Which is it?

✓ ✓ ✓

In this chapter you will read something—not too flattering, either—about the study habits of many people; you will learn how to avoid the common pitfalls, in which students frequently get mired; and, best of all, you will find out how to develop study habits that will make learning and remembering come much more easily to you.

Fig. 19. Sir Francis Bacon embodied the insatiable thirst for knowledge of the Renaissance period. He "took all knowledge to be his province" and very nearly mastered the learning of his day. Have you read his essay entitled "Of Studies"?

86

4. HOW TO STUDY

Before you start this chapter about studying, copy on a sheet of paper the following form and list on it as many things as you can think of that make students waste time during a study period.

HOW STUDENTS WASTE TIME DURING STUDY HOURS

1. Going to find out from somebody else what is to be done next in the assignment or unit.
2. Strolling aimlessly about the room to note what others are doing.
3.
4.
5. etc.

Unless you and your classmates are quite different from most students, you should have no difficulty in finding plenty of entries for this exercise!

THE IMPORTANCE OF LEARNING HOW TO STUDY

The major part of your present school work involves some form of study. The courses offered in your school have been built up through the years to provide students with the essential knowledge for successful living. This knowledge you will have to secure principally by the study of books—books of geography and history, of government and economics, of science and the arts, of language and literature; books of reference, such as encyclopedias, almanacs, indexes, and guides. Nothing could be more helpful to you than to learn as early as possible in your student life how to study textbooks and reference books so as to get the most out of them, and how to do so most easily and economically. Your high school work is principally that of studying and learning. Why not learn how to make the best possible job of it?

THE GREAT AMERICAN STUDY HALL

Getting ready to start to commence to begin! It is 11:10 in the study hall. Miss K——, the teacher in charge, is busy at her desk preparing some lessons. From forty to a hundred pupils are distributed about the room. The gong has just sounded, and everybody faces a fifty-minute period for study. Now a sizable amount of studying can be done in fifty minutes; a sizable amount of time and effort may also be wasted in those same fifty minutes! Much will depend on whether the time is used for *studying,* or whether it is used in *getting ready to start to commence to begin!*

Notice Jack Gordon in the end seat over there. Jack has three books stacked up at his left awaiting his attention; he means to get right to work on them, too. But see what happens. He pulls off his literature book from the top of the pile and, with his head resting on one hand, thumbs the pages of the assignment with the other. A picture catches his eye, and he pauses to gaze at it. This done, he leisurely turns to the beginning of his assignment and counts up the pages that will have to be read. Then he looks over at the clock and is intrigued for a minute or two by watching a fly circling around and around it. Before he can bring his eyes back to his book, he notices that Tom Messer is on his way to look up a word in the dictionary.

The dictionary corner calls! The dictionary corner always makes an interesting place of rendezvous for pupils who are socially minded, and so Jack strolls over to it and holds a whispered conversation with Tom about—oh, it may be next week's game, or next month's, or it may be about anything else under the sun. On his way back to his desk five minutes later, Jack feels suddenly very thirsty, and off he heads for the bubbler in the corridor outside the door. Re-entering the study hall, he all but runs into Bill Pote, who is also overtaken by thirst, and the two pause to exchange whispered pleasantries.

So does the pencil sharpener!   Back in the room now, Jack returns to his seat and again finds the place in his literature book; he would settle down at last to do some studying if the thought did not suddenly occur to him that he ought to get out pencil and notebook and make a few notes as he reads. Examining the pencil lead critically, he decides it needs to be pointed, so away he heads for the pencil sharpener in the front of the room. Returning to his desk, he finds the place again and starts to read.

Other pressing matters call.   Suddenly a frown spreads over his face, and he turns a few pages backward and then a few more forward. "Exactly where *is* the assignment, anyway? Seems as if I read *this* yesterday. Or *did* I? Maybe I'd better make sure: I can't afford to waste time doing the wrong pages. I'd better ask Joe; Joe always knows." Off to a conference with Joe he saunters, away on the opposite side of the room. Joe supplies the needed information, and Jack proceeds back to his seat, pausing only a couple of times to look over the shoulder of this and that pupil to see what progress *they* are making.

Time flies!   "Wonder what time it's getting to be? I've only got fifty minutes before the gong. What! Not ten minutes of twelve? Only ten minutes left! I've got to get busy! Why do they have these study periods so short, anyway? What do they expect a fellow can do in ten minutes?"

How about it?   Do you think any pupils in your own school go about their studying in the rambling, half-hearted way Jack does? Honestly, now—*do you yourself?* When you get out into the business world and turn all your efforts toward making fame and fortune, do you suppose you will get very far toward your goal if you take so abominably long to *get ready to start to commence to begin?* You can be reasonably sure that you will go about the business of living and getting a living with just about the same determination and efficiency with which you go about the business of getting an education.

SOME HELPFUL STUDY HINTS

Intend to learn! Settling down to work promptly, however, important though it is, is not the only thing needful if you are to get good returns from your studying. There are other rules which people who have lessons to master have always found helpful. One of them is: Settle down to your studying with the full expectation that you are going to *learn*. The attitude with which you attack your work is of the first importance.

Look out for such ideas as these that may come sneaking into your head:

I'm not much of a student, I guess, anyway.

I guess my head is pretty thick.

I'm sort of "dumb," anyway.

I'm not so keen about working: all I want is my diploma. I'll show the world afterwards!

Somehow, lessons don't make much sense to me!

It's hard for me to collect my thoughts.

I never could really settle down to a book.

Joe and Tom and Bet can get *their* lessons easy; *I* can't! I can never seem to have the right answers, the way they do!

I'm too easygoing to make much of a scholar.

It's not much use for me to try to learn lessons from books!

Beware such silly attitudes as these. They are the worst kind of poison for any student!

The first rule in good study is: *Intend to learn!* Go at it with the fullest determination to master what you tackle. For the silly attitude of half-heartedness and defeatism, substitute the more sensible one of expectation and self-confidence, and you will be amazed at the results you get from an hour's study. Nobody ever gets far in any undertaking unless he believes in himself.

Look carefully for the meaning. Merely putting in your time in reading a textbook assignment does not guarantee that you will *understand* what you have read. It is easy to let your eyes move automatically to and fro across the lines and down a page and to find when you have reached the bottom that you have comprehended little or nothing. The trouble is, of course, that you are permitting your *attention* to go to something different from what your *eyes* are recording for you. You must be constantly on your guard to keep your wits about you and really *study,* not to let your thoughts go wool-gathering.

You may take it for granted that the books used in your school have been chosen, in large part at least, because they are written in language that can be comprehended by the average run of students. If you fail to grasp the meaning of the material in them, the fault must rest at your own door. You are failing to force yourself to comprehend. You are not taking this matter of study seriously. You are trifling with one of our greatest human capacities—that of controlling one's mind and focusing it upon the work at hand. You cannot afford to weaken your mind by self-indulgence. Go at your work with the full purpose of centering your complete attention upon it and digging out the meaning.

Keep your mind actively on your work. Studying is much more than reading. Suppose you are in the midst of a very exciting story; the plot is simple, and you know how it is going to turn out in the end. Your thoughts are carried along by the author's use of suspense; you do not have to employ any reasoning power; you do not have to look for deep meanings and relationships; you do not have to relate new knowledge to old: all you have to do is remain in a passive state and let the author do the planning and draw the conclusions.

Studying, on the other hand, is a wholly different process. Your mental attitude must now be active, dynamic, interpretative. You are dealing not with plot and action, but with facts and relationships. The story interest is lacking, and there is nothing to pull your thoughts along to a climax, as there is in a narrative. When you study, it is not enough merely to let the words of the book run passively through your mind: your mental attitude must be one of critical questioning. You should find yourself keeping up a running mental comment on what you read. Questions and inner remarks like these should always be present in your mind while you are studying:

Do I understand just what it is the author is driving at?
What does this paragraph mean?
Can I put this thought into my own words?
Does what the author is saying agree with my own experience or opinion? If not, is he right, or am I?
Where have I met these same ideas before?
I don't quite see the sense of that statement; oh yes, *now* I do! *This* is what it means. . . .
How does this thought tie in with what we were talking about yesterday, or last week, or last term?
Wonder what that word means, anyway? I'll have to look it up.
What's important, and what's unimportant in all this?

Is this the way *your* mind behaves while you study?
In every kind of study process you must keep yourself alert, critical, insistent that you *understand;* you must always be

awake to the need of working over what you study and impressing it meaningfully upon your mind. Then, when class
time comes, or when the occasion arises for demonstrating
your knowledge, you will have little difficulty in recalling
what you have studied. The reason why many a student finds
himself unable to talk intelligently about something that he
is supposed to have studied and mastered is that he did not
really *study* it at all: he simply read it over passively and expected it to be, by some miraculous process, indelibly photographed upon his brain. What you *learn* from books, or from
anything else for that matter, even from the movies and
from radio programs, comes only with effort and with an
active mental attitude.

Use the method of recall, not repetition. Sometimes a student makes the mistake, in studying a lesson, of using the
method of *repetition,* that is, of reading over the complete
assignment from beginning to end—once, twice, three times,
and then calling the lesson learned! Such passive going back
and forth over an assignment is poor strategy for any student,
since it does not insure that what is read will really stick in the
mind.

To make sure that what you study will sink in, it is essential
to use, instead of the method of repetition, the method of *recall.* This method requires simply that after you have completed your study of a chapter, or a section, or a unit, you put
the book aside and proceed to recall in your own words what
it is you have been studying. By so doing you will not only
pay better attention in the first place to the reading of the
material, knowing that you are going to check yourself on it
after you have finished, but you will also be giving yourself
practice in translating the author's language into your own.
His language is naturally a bit bookish and professional; yours
must be your own. His purpose is to convey his thoughts to

you; yours is to restate what he has said and to do it in terms of everyday meaning.

After all, your teachers are not interested in what an author says: what they are interested in is whether you can get the drift of what you read, and whether you can make it so much a part of yourself that you can talk about it intelligently and with assurance. Mary Moller never did anything like that. Her ideas were vague and jumbled, and no wonder!

Get a bird's-eye view first.   As a bird flies, he does not take in every detail of the landscape below him, but rather he gets only a rough, preliminary idea of it. Your first passage through an assignment should give you the bird's-eye view rather than the detailed, microscopic one. Skim through the assignment first in order to get your bearings, to note big ideas, to find what the general trend of the lesson is.

Suppose, for example, your lesson is to investigate the Industrial Revolution in America, to which some twenty pages in the various history books available are devoted. Thumb first through the pages for the main idea or ideas: the profound effect of machines upon the simple kind of living which Washington and Jefferson had foreseen for the young republic; the genius of certain English and American inventors; the beginnings of great industries; the effects of better transportation and communication upon trade and commerce. These are the principal topics discussed by the authors.

Now set to work methodically to master the details supporting these principal ideas. In other words, having received some notion of the skeleton of the assignment, proceed to clothe the skeleton with flesh and blood.

Try to understand how the inventions of the early nineteenth century helped to transform our nation from an agricultural to an industrial one; how the Napoleonic Wars had reduced the supply of English goods in the country and had set the stage for the rapid development of American manufacturing; how the cotton gin and the carding machine and the weaving machine and the sewing machine ushered in a gigantic new age; how the growth of the iron and steel industry brought about a tremendous increase in manufacturing and building; how steamboats and railroads carried the new goods to every corner of the land and beyond the seas; how the telegraph and the cable served to bring the people of this continent as well as of the rest of the world more closely together and made it easier for them to make known their wants and to sell their commodities.

All these are the details—the flesh and blood which complete the skeleton of the Industrial Revolution. But do not attempt to master the fine points for an assignment until you have determined upon the three or four big, general ideas that they illustrate. Systematic and piecemeal study is essential, but it is of first importance that one shall have in mind at the outset a clear idea of what it is he is studying about.

Work vigorously, not lackadaisically. A lazy, half-hearted worker never gets very far in anything. Indolence over books is especially unproductive of results. We have referred already in this chapter to the type of student who finds it so desperately hard to *get ready to start to commence to begin*. There are a good many students who find it even harder to *continue to proceed to persist in keeping going!* Nobody has much use for an idler. Mental work, it has often been shown in the psychological laboratory, is most effective when it goes forward at as rapid a pace as the pupil can maintain. Slowing down the mental pace seems to encourage the brain to break away from the task at hand and turn to distracting ideas.

If you want to get the best returns from the study, follow the mariner's maxim: *Full speed ahead!* Slowing down your mental machinery makes it easy to drift and hard to reach the port whither you are headed. It is just as easy to form the habit of working vigorously as that of avoiding exertion. When you go at your studying, go at it with a will, and keep up your zeal until the task is completed.

Photo by Brown Brothers

Fig. 20. Could these medical students earn their doctor's degrees without concentrated effort over a period of years? In great research laboratories such as this, scientists often devote their lives to the study of microbes and their control. What diseases have already yielded their secrets to research workers?

MAKING OUTLINES

Many students find that if they take the trouble to make outlines of their assignments as they study them, they will understand and remember them better. Somehow, the very act of outlining a section of material forces one to keep the active mental attitude we have discussed above. When you make your outline, however, be careful not merely to copy down a few random sentences from the book. Try first to *grasp the meaning of what you are reading,* and secondly to *boil that meaning down in your own language.* It is a good plan to ferret out the author's principal ideas and write them down as your main headings, and then to put underneath them such subtopics as may be needed to cover the material.

An outline, to be of any use, must be so clearly and logically made that, even though it is necessarily brief, it will serve to bring back to your mind when you read it again the main points of the assignment. Outline making, in other words, requires constant mental sifting and winnowing and weighing in order to get down to essential facts and meanings.

Prepare a good notebook outline of the preceding section of this chapter, entitled, "Some Helpful Study Hints." Use the following form:

AN EXAMPLE OF GOOD OUTLINING AS A HELP TO STUDY

The Author's Main Ideas	The Author's Supporting Ideas
1.	1.
2.	2.
3.	3.
4.	4.
5. etc.	5. etc.

This will be a real test of your ability to pick the essential thought of an author and to recognize how he develops or illustrates his main ideas through supporting or secondary material. Make the numbers on the right correspond with those on the left. If you find more than one supporting idea for each main one, label them *a* and *b*.

TAKING NOTES

Notetaking from occasional class lectures and discussions will also help the student to remember what he learns. But what monstrosities masquerade in our schools under the name of "notebooks"! Often about all they contain is a hodgepodge of ungrammatical snatches and meaningless phrases that are of no help to the student later on. And the margins! One might conclude from looking through almost any high school notebook—or even many college notebooks—that the owners must be preparing themselves during their classes to become cartoonists or artists!

Ordinarily, it is a safe bet that when a teacher prepares a lecture for his class, what he has to say is worth paying attention to and recording. A student can hardly retain very much from a teacher's discussion when, instead of trying earnestly to turn it into written form in his notebook, he busies himself absent-mindedly with decorating the margins with all conceivable sorts of sketches and hieroglyphics!

MAKING ALL POSSIBLE USE OF WHAT YOU LEARN

Only in so far as you make use of what you learn will it ever do you any good. Our minds are not a series of pigeonholes or filing cabinets into which we drop this and that bit of unassorted information, and from which we may later take out the facts exactly as we learned them! Instead, our minds have a way of discarding what is unused and of fusing together into a dynamic whole what is actually made use of from day to day. Since this is the case, you should take care to use your new information whenever and wherever you can.

Talk about what you learn; think about it and try to apply it to new situations; work it over and relate it to old information; keep all your knowledge and information mixed together. Don't make the mistake of supposing that what you learn in school is to be promptly forgotten after you have passed an examination upon it; rather, form the habit of reviewing it mentally, of keeping it fresh in mind, of making it a part of your mental stock in trade. Like a good store manager, be unwilling to carry useless stock on your shelves: see that it *moves!* Avoid making your mind into a sort of encyclopedia or dictionary: keep your mental content in solution, so that each new bit added will find its proper place in the mass.

To convince yourself that you are (or are *not*) putting to use some of the important things you have recently learned in various units of school work (units in social science, mathematics, language, literature, and so forth), see what you can do with the following exercise:

TO PROVE THAT I AM USING MY KNOWLEDGE AS I GET IT

Principle or Idea Learned	Subject Unit in Which I Learned It	How I Am Making Use of My New Knowledge
1. The law of supply and demand.	"Commodities," in economics.	I explained to my mother why prices of foods out of season are so high.
2. Not all newspaper material is of equal worth to a reader.	"How news is collected," in sociology.	I am reading our daily paper with better discrimination and understanding.
3.		
4.		
5. etc.		

Unless you can fill in many illustrations, you'll have to admit that you're not so good at study—and that would be bad!

PHYSICAL CONDITIONS ARE IMPORTANT

It goes without saying that in order to study most effectively, your physical surroundings and your physical condition should be wisely regulated. You should rule out distractions as far as possible and leave a clear track in your mind for the material being studied.

The following principles are excellent ones to observe when you have any studying to be done:

(1) Select a reasonably quiet room.

(2) Sit in a straight chair, not an upholstered one. (Why?)

(3) Work at the accustomed side of the table, in the accustomed part of the room, and so forth. (How will this help?)

(4) Avoid studying while lying down on a sofa, couch, or bed.

(5) Sit erect and go at your task with determination.

(6) Keep a little tension in your back and shoulders.

(7) Be sure that the light doesn't glare in your eyes and that it is bright enough to give clear impressions without being so strong as to be uncomfortable.

(8) Keep the thermometer not much higher than 68° F.

(9) Avoid studying immediately after a full meal. Give your stomach a chance, for half an hour or so, to get digestion well under way.

(10) Be sure your eyes are not being strained. Have glasses fitted if you need them.

(11) Stop working before you get tired out.

(12) An hour's work under full steam will yield far better returns than three hours of dillydallying.

HOW PSYCHOLOGISTS WORK

Although we have stated rather emphatically in the preceding section that concentrated study demands that quiet be maintained and that there be nothing in the surroundings that will interfere with keeping the mind focused on the task at hand, it must be admitted that there is experimental evidence justifying the presence of competing stimuli.

It is, of course, apparent that if the strength of a competing stimulus becomes sufficiently great, the book (that is, the study stimulus) will be completely disregarded and attention will be given to the distracting agent. But psychologists have been able to demonstrate that a certain amount of competition helps rather than hinders studying. The following table indicates some of the experimental results achieved from measuring the effects of distraction upon performance of various kinds of work:

SOME RESULTS FROM THE LABORATORY

Type of Work	Effects of Distractions
Comparing weights	Increased efficiency
Writing longhand	Greater effort put forth, as indicated by increased pressure upon the pencil
Memorizing new material	Lessened efficiency
Recalling the memorized material	Increased efficiency
Typewriting	No change in efficiency, but more energy used up

It looks from the above table as though efficiency does not necessarily suffer under conditions of distraction, but that since more energy is often required to hold one to the task, fatigue may come more quickly.

That this is the case was clearly indicated in the typing experiment, performed by Laird. On the days when the typists worked in soundproof rooms, which the outside noises could not penetrate, while performance was no better, the energy cost was less than was the case on days when the insulated partitions were removed and the usual office distractions and noises were allowed to reach the subjects who were participating in the experiment. The *metabolic index* (a measure showing energy changes in a person by comparing the oxygen intake with the carbon dioxide discharge) showed conclusively that under conditions of competing stimuli more oxygen was consumed and more carbon dioxide thrown off, and consequently more energy was used up.

Thus, we may conclude that the cost of needless distraction in terms of wear and tear upon the organism is considerable, and that while one may "grit his teeth" and persist in his attention to the work in hand, there is bound to be a continuous drain upon his system that will tire him out and reduce his efficiency after a while.

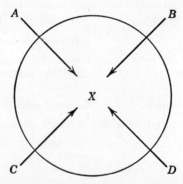

Fig. 21. Diagram indicating how distractions interfere with studying. The student wishes to keep his mind upon X, the lesson material he is studying. Competing stimuli might include A, the annoyance caused by a person's walking noisily about the room or house; B, the awareness of a conversation going on near by; C, the distracting hodgepodge issuing from a loud speaker; D, the consciousness that somebody is telephoning in the room. What will happen to the ideas represented by X if ideas A, B, C, or D are allowed by the student to hold his conscious attention?

Other experiments have shown that, while strong distraction possesses the disadvantages mentioned above, mild stimulation of the sense organs by the habitual conditions of the work environment is actually beneficial to learning and study. Were you to put yourself in a vacuum and attempt to study, you would soon find that the unaccounted *stillness* would distract. Put yourself in an ordinary human situation, on the other hand, with a mild degree of moving about, of rustling papers, of customary voices, and the like, and you will find that your mind will be stimulated favorably to hold to its course. It seems almost as though our nervous systems demand a bit of challenge to keep them functioning at their best.

A good rule for efficient mental activity is, then, to see to it that there is no needless, unusual distraction, but to expect and accustom yourself to the ordinary competing stimuli that necessarily exist around you. The good student is not annoyed by these stimuli; rather, he is challenged by them to do his most efficient work.

TO HELP YOU LEARN

QUESTIONS TO ASK YOURSELF

1. Why is it so important to *intend* to learn when one goes at his studying? How would a student come out who intended *not* to learn?

2. Have you ever had the experience of following with your eyes down a whole page in a book and then suddenly realizing that you had comprehended nothing of what you had "read"? How do you explain it? What is the moral?

3. Can you state in your own words the difference between an active mental attitude and a passive one while the process of studying is going on?

4. What new things have you learned from your work on this chapter that ought to help you to study more effectively than heretofore?

5. If, as seems to be the case, noise and confusion in the immediate vicinity of a brain worker cause fatigue to overtake him prematurely, can you make out an argument in favor of the compulsory reduction or elimination of needless noise in our cities? Do you know of any communities that are attempting to control this source of annoyance and inefficiency?

WORKING WITH PSYCHOLOGY

1. During the next study period, try to force yourself to work a little more vigorously than you have ordinarily been doing. Notice whether you accomplish more than customarily, and whether, even though you work harder, things come more easily.

2. Do this experiment. Select some paragraph of moderate length in one of your textbooks in the social sciences, and study it with the active mental attitude explained in this chapter. Note down afterwards what kind of comments and queries you made as you proceeded. Now select another paragraph of similar length and difficulty, and read it over with a passive mental attitude. Compare your comprehension of this paragraph with the other.

3. Do this experiment. During one of your next study hours make a survey of the study habits of several other students whom you can observe out of the corner of your eye. Note whether they are prompt or tardy in getting settled down to work, whether or not they seem able to resist simple distractions, and whether they appear reasonably absorbed in what they are doing, or whether their minds go woolgathering a good deal. (Be sure to select for your observation students from some other class than your own: otherwise, those whom you watch may be also watching you for the same purpose and everybody will then appear to everybody else to be a doubtful bet as a student!)

4. Keeping in mind all the important principles of effective study which you have noted in this chapter, try rating your own efficiency at studying your assignments during the coming week. Use the following scale, applying it independently to each day's study of literature, social sciences, mathematics, languages, and so forth:

Very Efficiently	Fairly Efficiently	Rather Inefficiently	Very Inefficiently

Place a check mark at that point on the scale which you believe represents your true performance. You may find that you study some subjects more efficiently than you do others. Try to account for the varying positions of the check marks.

WHAT OTHERS SAY

1. In Fiction:

Arrowsmith by Sinclair Lewis. The vivid story of a doctor who devotes himself and his energies to research, to scientific experimentation, and to a wide country practice. Some of the problems that confront medical practitioners in modern society are set forth.

2. In Essay:

The Turning Point of My Career by Archibald J. Cronin (*Reader's Digest*, May 1941). How the dogged stick-to-itiveness of a Scotch Highlander, digging at his bog, taught Archibald Cronin a timely lesson in literary perseverance, eventuating in *Hatter's Castle*.

Our Teen-Age Edisons by John D. Greene (*American Magazine*, July 1941). A striking account of how thirty thousand high school students, enrolled in high school scientific clubs promoted by the American Institute, are making the most amazing contributions to our applied science.

How to Increase Your Brain Power by Donald A. Laird. In this popularly written book, a well-known psychologist tells you many interesting things about your mind, and shows how you can vastly improve your ability to study, memorize, reason, and otherwise use your mental powers to the limit of their capacity.

Managing Yourself by Milton Wright. An unusually readable, popularly written book, which includes many excellent and practical suggestions for the improvement of work and study habits.

3. In Poetry:

Old John Henry by James Whitcomb Riley. The homely portrait of a plain countryman who

> . . . does his best, and when his best's bad,
> He don't fret none, nor he don't get sad—
> He simply 'lows it's the best he had.

4. In Drama:

What a Life by Clifford Goldsmith. The humorous and lively adventures of Henry Aldrich, a high school student who just cannot get book learning through his head, and who in consequence runs into all sorts of trials and tribulations at school.

WHAT'S AHEAD IN CHAPTER 5

Are You an Optimist or a Pessimist?

If you have read Browning's poem, *Pippa Passes*, you remember the little slave girl, Pippa. Pippa served her mistress faithfully three hundred sixty-four days in the year. On the three hundred sixty-fifth day she had a holiday and could do anything she wished. Grateful and happy for her brief day of freedom, Pippa passed up and down through the streets of Rome singing the refrain:

> God's in his heaven:
> All's right with the world.

Pippa was clearly an optimist.

In Dickens' *Nicholas Nickleby* there is another notable character, Mr. Mantalini. Unlike Pippa's attitude, Mr. Mantalini's outlook toward the scene around him was a decidedly mournful one. He was always giving expression to his inner gloom with the cynical reflection: "The world is going to the demnition bow-wows!"

Exactly what the "demnition bow-wows" might be Mr. Mantalini never explained, but it is clear that he did not mean that all was right with the world! The fate of the world, it appears, depends upon the peculiar slant or attitude of the person expressing the judgment. From Mr. Mantalini's sour standpoint, its fate is not to be a pleasant one!

Do you know anyone like Mr. Mantalini?

On a beautiful spring morning—as fair a day as ever dawned —Mr. White walked briskly down his front steps and started down the street to catch the 8:10 bus for his office. He whistled as he walked. Three houses away, whom should he meet but Mr. Black, likewise on his way to the bus. Mr. Black's face wore its habitual scowl, and he was *not* whistling.

"Good morning, Black!" called his neighbor cheerily, falling into step with him. "Beautiful morning, isn't it?"

Black returned the greeting sourly. "Yes," he admitted, grudgingly, "but it's going to rain before night!"

Our Attitudes Are Often Permanent

In the somber opinion of altogether too many people there is always rain just around the corner, "rain" of course being interpreted as misfortune, ill luck, or catastrophe of some kind or other. Worse still, these pessimistic attitudes cling tenaciously to those who harbor them.

Mr. Mantalini's cynicism is not of the moment, we may be sure, but rather is a chronic state with him. Likewise, the dour Mr. Black is a dyed-in-the-wool gloom dispenser. It may be that Mr. White purposely and with malice aforethought called out a cheery morning greeting to his neighbor, just to make sure that it was the same old Mr. Black of yesterday, and last week, and, indeed, last year!

Chronic or habitual viewpoints, such as Pippa's optimism and Mr. Mantalini's pessimism, are termed *attitudes*.

✓ ✓ ✓

In this chapter you will discover many other attitudes that people have and why they have them. You will learn how to judge whether *your* attitudes will help you to be happy and successful, and if not, how you can improve them.

Fig. 22. We get many of our attitudes from our associates. Do you choose your friends carefully?

5. OUR MENTAL ATTITUDES

Before beginning this chapter, think for a moment about your own attitudes regarding vocations. For this purpose divide a sheet of paper into two columns, labeling them as follows:

MY PRESENT VOCATIONAL ATTITUDES

Vocations That I Feel Sure I Would Like	Vocations That I Feel Sure I Would Not Like
1.	1.
2.	2.
3.	3.
4.	4.
5. etc.	5. etc.

Make just as long a list of vocations as you can think of. It will be interesting to list them in the order of their appeal to you (in the left-hand column) and of their distastefulness to you (in the right-hand column).

SOME OF OUR DOMINANT ATTITUDES

Attitudes toward the world of work. Undoubtedly you have already done a good deal of thinking about the vocation you would like to enter when you have finished your schooling. In the process, you have probably formed certain strong vocational inclinations and certain equally strong vocational disinclinations. Many of your ideas may be without much basis, either from the standpoint of information about the occupations or of self-evaluation and fitness for them. Still, your attitudes are *there,* justifiable or unjustifiable.

In recent years many junior and senior high schools have

been offering guidance courses for their students, trying to help them to develop informed attitudes toward vocations. Too many young people, who have not the necessary qualifications for probable success in certain professions, form an early emotional interest in entering medicine, or law, or engineering as a career, forgetting that there are actually almost 600 major occupations in the United States, and more than 20,000 specific kinds of jobs. It is highly unfortunate for any young person to close his eyes persistently to this or that occupation in which he might make good, in order to nourish a childhood interest in some other occupation for which he has little aptitude. On the other hand, when one does pick out a vocation with intelligence, it is the finest thing in the world for him to develop strongly favorable attitudes toward it.

Attitudes toward "stick-to-itiveness."   In preparing for a vocation, you should not lose sight of the importance of developing attitudes of industry and persistence in your work. The world is filled with people who have the false notion that it "owes them a living," or that their work is unappreciated, or that it is clever to shirk and loaf and do as little as possible on the job, or that it is old-fashioned to work with one's might and to do one's best. The people who arrive are not often the shirkers and the self-pitiers and the chiselers; they are the "stick-to-itivists" and the persisters. It may be "smart" to be slothful and indolent, but it is not clever. Early attitudes which a person develops toward his work stay with him long, and they forecast pretty accurately his future achievements.

Attitudes toward thrift and prudence.   For the spendthrift and the prodigal, society has never had much respect. On the other hand, for the individual who has learned how to spend his money sensibly and to save methodically for a rainy day, society has always had the greatest respect. Everybody desires to have certain things. (In Chapter 1 we have already discussed many of the things people want.) The only self-respecting way by which you may hope some day to have them is to *earn* them.

Most of us are not born with silver spoons in our mouths; in most cases, however, we are born with brains, and muscles, and the capacity to work. If, along with those, we develop attitudes of thrift and economy, most of us will have little trouble in eventually earning for ourselves the things we want. It may require years before we get them, but it is a far more healthy attitude of mind to be confident and determined that our work will win them by and by than it is to adopt either the attitude that "there isn't any use trying," or that "only the rich get there," or that it is justifiable to use shady methods or short-cut roads to bring us to our objectives. Jails, prisons, penitentiaries, reformatories, and even cemeteries harbor many who failed to use legitimate means of getting what they wanted.

Attitudes toward custom and tradition. Few human attitudes are stronger than those which people have toward tradition and convention. On a form like that on page 112 list as many instances as you can, from history, literature, and the current news, of the departure of individuals from the traditional and conventional in conduct. Indicate what was, or is, the verdict of the social group in each case.

From the earliest years of life we are continually instructed in the proper attitudes toward the family, the church, the school, the community, the nation. We are taught the customary thing, the appropriate thing, the *expected* thing in conduct. We learn to wear clothing adapted to the season, to the time of day, to the occasion; to raise the hat, give precedence to ladies, keep to the right, salute the flag; to be quiet in church, obey the law, honor the dead, respect our elders, obey our parents, revere our motherland. Men develop mascu-

INSTANCES OF DEPARTURE FROM THE TRADITIONAL

Historical, Literary, or Contemporaneous Examples	Convention or Tradition Violated	The Verdict of the Social Group
1. Benedict Arnold's treason	Loyalty to country	Shunned by those to whom he escaped
2.		
3.		
4.		
5. etc.		

(The departure may not always be harmful, nor the verdict just, but there is no defense against social disapproval.)

linity and aggressiveness; women covet femininity, wear attractive clothing, dress according to the fashion.

So one might go on indefinitely to enumerate conventions and customs and traditions which people ordinarily respect and with which they are usually anxious to conform. Such attitudes hold over all of us the power of habit, and are no more readily changed or broken. And when some ignorant, or malicious, or freethinking individual breaks the conventions, we tend to reward him with sharp criticism and disfavor. Sometimes, of course, society becomes so hidebound in its worship of tradition and custom and convention that all progress is halted until some radical reformer dares to challenge the old and set up the new.

The negative type of "reform," flaunted by the sensation seeker—young or old—who "stumps" for nudist colonies, trial marriages, atheism, two-hundred-dollars-a-month-for-everybody, and all other unconventional innovations is not, of course, to be mentioned in the same breath with true reform. The day of the sensationalist is deservedly brief, for he has no realistic and permanent program to offer in place of the tradition he seeks to destroy.

Attitudes toward our country and flag. Particularly strong among us are those attitudes that are linked with the sentiment of patriotism. External evidences that a man is patriotic include his coming to attention when the colors pass and rising to his feet when the national anthem is played. But there are many less obvious ways in which people demonstrate their patriotic attitudes. See if you can think of more than ten such ways:

WAYS OF SHOWING PATRIOTIC ATTITUDES

1. Obeying the laws of the land	6.
2.	7.
3.	8.
4.	9.
5.	10. etc.

(Patriotism goes much deeper than mere external conformity. It is in large measure an inner feeling of appreciation.)

> Breathes there the man, with soul so dead,
> Who never to himself hath said,
> This is my own, my native land!

This penetrating query of the poet suggests at once the strong hold that patriotism and love of country have upon every normal person. The flag of one's homeland signifies for all time the debt one owes to the land of his birth, or of his adoption, and when he raises his hand in salute to it he acknowledges eloquently the love and respect he feels within.

The nationalistic spirit is very strong among most peoples of the earth. In considerable measure it is behind most wars that arise between nations. Loyalty to the flag has nearly always involved the will to compel respect for it. From him who is a traitor to his country, the extreme penalty is usually exacted. Next to the Deity, the homeland is ordinarily held most precious and sacred, and when it is endangered by enemies from within or without, the loyal citizen is ready to sacrifice everything for its defense, even to the shedding of his blood.

Citizens of a democracy, such as our own, owe their allegiance, not to any individual tyrant, autocrat, or dictator, but rather to the nation itself. No matter how much an American may be in personal disagreement with any specific policy or activity of his country, if he is a true citizen, his loyalty and faith never swerve. He may do all within his power legally to attempt to bring about modification of the existing situation; beyond that he may not go. By being zealous to cast his vote, zealous to see the right, and zealous to help others to see, the good citizen is a strong, constructive force in helping to guide the destiny of his country along the higher pathways. There is never in the true patriot's mind the slightest doubt regarding his attitude toward his country.

Attitudes toward other peoples. It is not alone in time of war that our attitudes toward other peoples become pronounced. Under ordinary conditions of peace we show our prejudices against this country or in favor of that. The old Romans referred to the peoples who lived outside the sacred confines as "barbarians." To this day it is an unfortunate characteristic of most nationals to think of their own people as good, right, superior, and worthy, and to think of foreigners as bad, wrong, inferior, or unworthy. Hence we develop nationalistic feelings of superiority and tend to scoff at the virtues of other peoples. Not only is my race unquestionably the superior race, but my country is unquestionably the superior country, and its ideals and philosophies are the superior ideals and philosophies. Along with our prejudices against the peoples of other lands, we develop prejudiced attitudes also against their particular political ideologies, and will have none of them. We may even go so far as to prohibit study of them in our schools.

These national prejudices are good and bad for a people.

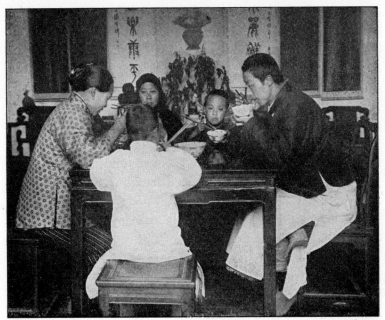

Photo by Burton Holmes for Ewing Galloway

Fig. 23. Is your attitude toward this Chinese family one of tolerance and friendliness? Can you see the best in other races and nations at the same time that you feel patriotism toward your own country?

To the degree that they deepen one's love for his country and persuade him to identify with it all his hopes, faith, and powers, they are good; to the extent, on the other hand, that they persuade him to close his eyes to the good points in all people, and confirm him in an ignorant and smug hostility toward them, they are bad. If the millennium ever dawns on this earth, it will be chiefly perhaps because people everywhere will have come to appreciate one another and to understand that fundamentally they are the same. Even under millennial conditions, however, you and I and everybody else in our country would still pledge to one another, as did her immortal founders, our lives, our fortunes, and our sacred honor. In other words, the attitude of the true patriot will always be strongly biased toward his own people and his own nation.

Attitudes toward the present scene.   A very large group of our attitudes are those which we develop with regard to the thousand and one conditions, events, and activities of life as it goes on about us. Thus, all of us have our own peculiar slant or bias about, for example, such items as current radio broadcasts; the political party in power; foreign relations; socialization of medicine; government control of utilities; intoxicating liquors; women in industry; war; "entangling alliances"; gambling; Sunday observance; law and order; crime prevention; "the butcher, the baker, the candlestick maker"; "rich men, poor men, beggar men, thieves."

There is, in short, no topic of present-day interest or discussion about which we do not maintain our own individual attitudes, and to these attitudes, often highly prejudiced and uninformed, we tend to cling tenaciously. So thoroughly committed are we to them that we usually feel ourselves called upon to defend them with considerable emotion and to become propagandists for them among our friends. We can hardly take part very long in any general conversation without discovering numerous strong opinions, "hunches," slants, prejudices, among our friends and associates.

Before reading further, prepare on a sheet of paper the form on page 117; then check yourself on each item you list, entering a *1* if your attitude is very strong; *2* if it is moderately strong; *3* if it is somewhat indifferent.

Attitudes toward morality and religion.   "Do right!" is an adage as old as civilization itself. One of the prime tasks of every parent is so to regulate the experiences that his child has that the latter may build up within himself strong attitudes in favor of what is right and moral. The attitude toward right and wrong is a highly important thing in conduct, and every

SOME OF MY ATTITUDES TOWARD THE CURRENT SCENE

Item in the Current Scene	My Attitude Ratings
1. Capital punishment	2
2.	
3.	
4.	
5. etc.	

(List as many items as you can, covering what people are talking about, what you read in the magazines, what you hear over the radio, and so forth.)

parent knows that it is impossible to begin too early to lay the foundations of morality in his offspring.

Fundamental moral codes do not change much in a dozen generations, nor in a thousand years. True, it may have been wrong in colonial Massachusetts to go visiting one's friends on the Sabbath Day, and in the Victorian Age for girls to engage publicly in athletics. Restrictions like these, however, have been only incidental to the persistence of primary and basal moral standards, which have remained approximately the same since Adam.

Any person who aspires to a respected and honorable place among his fellows will find it necessary first of all to adopt the moral attitudes that are approved and accepted, and to order his life accordingly. Once one has adopted them, it becomes relatively impossible for him to do, think, or will in a manner contrary to his code. In the same way, the immoral individual who has built up wholly different attitudes can only do, think, and will in accord with his peculiar moral slant.

It perhaps does not need to be added that we adopt our religious attitudes early, and that they ordinarily exert strong influence over our lives and conduct. We school ourselves to become God-fearing or God-denying; to be reverent or irreverent; faithful or faithless; we grow up with the Protestant attitude, or the Catholic, or the Jewish; with the Baptist, or the Presbyterian, or the Episcopalian. The influence which our religious attitudes exert over us has been illustrated, on the positive side, by the sacrifice and the enthusiasm of people of faith in all ages and at all times; and, on the negative, by the religious wars and persecutions and pogroms by which peoples of fanatical persuasions have disfigured the pages of history. There are perhaps no stronger attitudes than those centering in religion and morality.

Attitudes toward ourselves. Do you take yourself seriously or lightly? Are you in earnest about your education, or only in jest? Are you ambitious, or satisfied with your present state? Are you helpful, sympathetic, enterprising, intellectually thirsty, persistent? Or are you selfish and lackadaisical? These are questions the answers to which will indicate to you rather clearly the nature of some of the attitudes that you hold toward yourself. It is not a bad plan for all of us to examine occasionally our attitudes toward these personal adjustments. Sometimes we are surprised to find what strongly unhealthy slants are making their appearance in our make-up. Ridding ourselves of them will require real effort and attention.

WHERE DO WE GET OUR ATTITUDES

From our training. There are many sources from which we acquire our partialities and our prejudices. We shall refer here to only a few of the most common ones. First of all, our attitudes reflect the training we receive—training in the home, in the school, in the church. If you will check back through the principal attitudes which we have been discussing in this chapter, you will notice how much every one of them depends upon the formal or the informal training we got as children. Each of these three great social organizations—the home, the school, and the church—holds its prime function to be the

training of the young in the proper habits and attitudes. Where
would be our honesty, our loyalty, our fair-mindedness, our
morality, but for the shaping influences of these three major
institutions?

From our friends and associates.   In part we are what we
are because our friends have made us so. From them we
"catch" many of our prejudices, our likes and dislikes, and
our outlooks on life. If they are sincere, hopeful, ambitious,
and fearless, we tend to be the same; if they are deceitful,
cynical, lazy, and cowardly, we shall be influenced in the same
direction. Our attitudes are contracted from those with whom
we associate just as inevitably as are measles or whooping
cough, with this significant difference: we get over the measles,
whereas our attitudes become chronic and rarely relax their
hold upon us.

In this connection, we should not discount the influence over
our attitudes exerted by the wider culture group to which we
belong. If we count ourselves among the rich, we tend to look
down on the poor; if we belong to the ranks of the laborer, we
shall probably look askance at the capitalist; if we deem ourselves well educated, we are inclined to scorn the illiterate; if
we trace our American ancestry back to the early settlers, we
shall most likely boast of our blue blood. City folks make fun
of country folks, while farmers ridicule the ignorance of city
dwellers. Bostonians, New Yorkers, and Chicagoans adhere
to their respective culture patterns. These human slants and
prejudices are inevitable, and most of us find it a real struggle
to break away from them and become tolerant, sympathetic,
and cosmopolitan.

From what we read.   One of the most powerful sources of
our attitudes, opinions, and prejudices is what we read. Surrounded by thousands of new books every year; bombarded
by headlines and press dispatches from every quarter of the

globe; indoctrinated by magazines and digests; beset by the opinions of columnists, editorial writers, and commentators; swayed by the cartoonist and the reviewer and the analyst, what wonder is it that we derive many of our mental attitudes and mind-sets from the printed page!

From what we hear. Through our ears, as well as through our eyes, comes much of the powerful stimulation that shapes our attitudes and opinions. Within a single generation the auditory methods of appeal have been infinitely broadened by the radio. During all the waking hours, as well as during most of those ordinarily reserved for sleep, we are subject to the persuasive appeal of the broadcasters whom we may contact instantly by the twirling of a knob. Propaganda of all sorts penetrates the four walls of our homes, and we listen indiscriminately to political speeches, sales talks, beauty hints, news interpretations, and religious services. Thus has come within our orbit a powerful new social force, extending in all directions the older and more limited auditory channels of persuasion, represented by the stump speaker, the soapbox orator, the lecturer, and the agitator. Nobody can yet calculate the effect upon our ideas, our opinions, and our sense of values which the broadcasters will ultimately exert. There is no question but that it will be profound.

From the movies. Because the motion-picture industry furnishes every one of the 40,000 movie theaters in the United States with daily or weekly releases on every conceivable subject, and presents on the silver screen the typical movie standards of life, this huge industry must be charged with the responsibility of having created and popularized among us many innovations in opinion and in conduct. It is inevitable that upwards of seventy-five millions of people—those who comprise the average weekly movie-going audience in America—cannot escape looking at life and its problems through glasses that have been colored by the makers of this popular form of entertainment.

From propaganda and pressure groups. Regardless of whether one has a new kind of shaving cream to be put on the market, or a new piece of legislation to be enacted, he relies principally upon some form of propaganda to arouse support among the people. Advertising and lobbying are powerful means of creating popular opinion. Billboards, trade journals, educational films, slogans, Blank-for-Congress clubs, lapel buttons, and scores of other devices are made use of constantly by various pressure groups to create desired attitudes and opinions in you and me. To steer a sane and rational course through all these bombardments requires a cautious eye and a keen brain on the part of the helmsman.

MOST ATTITUDES INVOLVE STRONG FEELING

For the most part our attitudes are not only fixed, like habits, but are also strongly tinged with emotion. We find ourselves feeling favorably or unfavorably, for example, about foreigners, alcohol, capital punishment, or the unions, and we often wax exceedingly warm in our conversations about them. We react cordially to the political party to which we belong and frigidly to the opposing party. We accept our friends, our school, our community, but reject our enemies, the rival school, the competing community; and we do both with warmth and enthusiasm.

Our attitudes toward these and innumerable other situations are strong, emotionally tinged, often prejudiced, and enduring. Because of their emotional content, our attitudes exert profound influence over our lives and conduct, determining much of our behavior and coloring much of our thinking. You are *you* quite as much because of the consistency of your mental attitudes as because of your habits; your mates and associates interpret and accept you in the light of your individual slant upon life and its diverse activities.

CAN OUR ATTITUDES BE CHANGED?

Yes, attitudes, like habits, can be changed. The very fact that we find ourselves assailed by all the forms of propaganda suggested in the above paragraphs indicates that people are known to be changeable, and that they may be won to this, that, or the other cause, if only the appeal is skillful enough. Time, too, becomes a modifier of our attitudes; as we grow older and gain more experience, we are sometimes amazed at the changes that come in our outlooks and our sense of values, perhaps even in our ideas of right and wrong. The important thing for us all, on the one hand, is to recognize which of our attitudes are prejudiced and narrow, and to be zealous in uprooting them; and, on the other hand, to strive to cultivate from the beginning those mental attitudes which will contribute the most toward making us happy ourselves, toward making us considerate of others, and toward keeping us open to calm and rational conviction in every field and in all directions.

HOW PSYCHOLOGISTS WORK

A number of interesting investigations have been made by scientists to find out the extent to which our mental attitudes may be modified by various influences. One agency that has lent itself readily to such inquiry is the moving picture. Here is, unquestionably, a powerful force in the modern social scene —powerful and universal alike, since almost everybody falls under its influence.

In one piece of research, carried on by a scientist named Thurstone, 240 school children were each given a list of the names of many different varieties of criminals and asked to rank them in the order of their badness, from the most bad to the least bad. The list included such law-breaking types as the following: bootlegger, kidnaper, gangster, gambler, and bank robber. The results of all the pupil judgments were pooled and an attitude scale constructed in which the type of criminal which was thought to be the worst of all stood at the top and the least harmful type at the bottom. Gangsters were found to rate highest, tramps lowest, and gamblers about midway between these two extremes.

Sometime later, these same 240 children were shown a motion picture entitled "Street of Chance," which disclosed many of the evils of gambling in a most dramatic manner. Subsequently, when asked to rate again the original list of criminals in order of their badness, these children were found to have moved gambling up to a position much higher on the scale. Thus objective evidence that people's attitudes are noticeably altered by moving pictures was obtained.

In a somewhat similar study, made by Peterson and Thurstone, a group of high school students was asked to rate the Chinese people on a scale of ten. A rating of ten meant that a student had a most unfavorable attitude toward them, while a rating of one indicated that his attitude was highly favorable. Next day the students saw the film "Son of the Gods," an absorbing story of Chinese life, with a real Chinese hero. Subsequent re-ranking of their attitudes toward the Chinese showed that, whereas before seeing the film the majority of the students had been quite unfavorably disposed toward the Chinese, rating them not much better than seven, the majority were now quite favorably inclined toward them and ranked them better than five.

To determine whether or not this change in attitude brought about by the film was permanent, a group of these same students was asked, more than a year and a half later, to rank the Chinese again on the same scale they had used originally. Sixty-two per cent of the change in attitude was found to persist. Thus again, evidence was discovered to demonstrate the fact that moving pictures are highly instrumental in changing and in molding people's attitudes.

TO HELP YOU LEARN

QUESTIONS TO ASK YOURSELF

1. What part do our feelings and emotions seem to play in our attitudes? Can you illustrate from some of your own personal attitudes?

2. Do you think the world would be better off if people did not form pronounced mental attitudes about anything? Defend your opinion.

3. Can you detect any actual change that is taking place in your own personal attitude toward any part of the present scene? If so, can you account for this evolution?

4. How has this chapter given you a better understanding of human attitudes? Show by some concrete example that it actually has done so.

5. In what way or ways has your study of this chapter helped you to understand yourself and your own attitudes a little better than before? Be specific.

WORKING WITH PSYCHOLOGY

1. Collect from among your friends or acquaintances, or from reading, examples of prejudiced attitudes, strong personal opinions, "hunches," slants, and the like. Try to determine how much logic there may be behind each of them, and to what extent they are apparently illogical. (If you observe that you yourself have any prejudices, try to account for their source; try also to decide how to correct them.)

2. Select a school subject for which you have a strong liking and which is popular among the other students in your school also. Then do a bit of personal research into the matter of how the instructor succeeds in creating favorable attitudes toward it in his pupils. Consider, among other things, his own enthusiasm for his subject, his personality, and his ability to arouse interest.

3. You can scarcely walk past a bank window without observing in it some placard or poster designed to persuade people of the importance of thrift, of the wisdom of opening a savings account, and the like. Bring in to class several examples of propaganda efforts made by advertisers, broadcasters, business houses, or editorial writers, to create favorable mental attitudes toward this or that product, person, event, or activity.

4. Determine upon some pressure group (an agency of propaganda designed to enforce its will) and investigate its aims, its method of appeal, and the results which it appears to be achieving. One example of such a pressure group might be a congressional lobby; another might be a group of students.

What Others Say

1. In Fiction:

Nicholas Nickleby by Charles Dickens. The fortunes of a high-principled youth are cast against the sordid background of cheap English boarding schools with such skill and cleverness that public opinion is aroused against these institutions and reform demanded.

Main Street by Sinclair Lewis. Going to live in Gopher Prairie after her marriage to Dr. Kennicott, Carol Kennicott finds the people among whom she is set down dull, mediocre, complacent, self-satisfied. Despite her efforts to improve them, she meets with little success. Main Street in Gopher Prairie is portrayed as typical of small-town American life everywhere.

2. In Biography:

Grandma Called It Carnal by Bertha Damon. The author portrays the severely critical attitudes of a New England woman of the last century who looked with strong disfavor upon every form of comfort and indulgence that the innovations of the day were making possible, yet who found much happiness in life.

3. In Sociology:

Press and World Affairs by Robert W. Desmond. This revelation of the fine art of news gathering, together with the dramatic role played by propaganda in the news, will fascinate you and help you better to evaluate newspapers.

War Propaganda and the United States by Harold Lavine and James Wechsler. A highly interesting account of the use of propaganda in connection with the Second World War, showing how national attitudes are created and nurtured.

Mein Kampf (*My Struggle*) by Adolf Hitler. One of the most amazing specimens of fixed and uncompromising attitudes to be found in any language. A book that has created social and political and nationalistic attitudes in millions of Germans disillusioned by the First World War.

4. In Drama:

The Wingless Victory by Maxwell Anderson. A sea captain of 1800, returning to Salem a wealthy man after seven years at sea, finds that the townspeople will not accept his wife, a Malay princess, whom he brings back from the Orient with him. The magnificent self-sacrifice of the Malay wife, when she comprehends the situation that develops, shows a depth of character that puts the Puritans to shame. Rarely has the interracial problem been more forcibly presented on the stage.

Can You Keep Your Mind from Wandering?

Miss Helen Stoner, in "The Adventure of the Speckled Band," had a piece of railway ticket in her left hand and seven spatters of mud on the left sleeve of her jacket. Noting these facts, Sherlock Holmes deduced that the lady had come up to London by train, that she had started early in a dogcart and had traveled along muddy roads to reach the station.

A character who, in the words of Christopher Morley, "has endeared himself to three generations and is well on his way to delighting a fourth," Holmes was able to unravel one after another of the baffling crimes that were tossed into his lap for solution. Chiefly responsible for his skill was an analytic mind that could pay unwavering attention to the problem at hand in all its details. Perhaps nobody in fiction better exemplifies this faculty of profound attention then does the amazing Sherlock.

To belong to the secretarial staff of the late Joseph Pulitzer, genius of American journalism, was a job that demanded the most exacting powers of observation and application. Possessed of the keenest and most penetrating sort of mind himself, Pulitzer—blind for half a lifetime—demanded of his staff the sharpest kind of eyes and the deepest kind of perception. One of Pulitzer's secretaries, Mr. Alleyne Ireland, has described in his book, "An Adventure with a Genius," the exacting requirements of the great Pulitzer, who had to depend upon others for his visual interpretations, and who "rebuilt his life with the eyesight and brains of other men."

"Never think that anything is too small to be of interest!" he exclaimed to Ireland. "Describe every cloud, every shadow, every tree, every house, every dress, every wrinkle on a face, everything, everything!"

"Strike two!"

An exciting moment for Washington High—and for Franklin High, too! It was the last half of the ninth inning, with Washington at bat and the score standing 6 to 5 in favor of Franklin. Bob Towner was at third, and Joe Grundy at second. If Pat Cronin could only make a smashing hit, in this sudden turn of fortune, he could bring in Bob and Joe and then that cup that Washington was defending could stand for another twelvemonth on Coach Donovan's trophy shelf in the gym. Do you suppose that Bob and Joe were not on the alert to steal, and that Pat did not keep his eyes glued to the pitcher—or that there was a single inattentive player or spectator that afternoon on field or bleachers!

Concentration Is Essential to Success

The ability to keep one's mind focused upon the most significant happening or idea of the moment is of prime importance to everybody. Whether, like Sherlock Holmes, one is intent upon searching out clues and theories; whether, like Alleyne Ireland, one is charged with observing and reporting upon the world about him; or whether, like the cup defenders of Washington High, one is watching narrowly all the moves of a closely contested game—the same fundamental thing is always true: keenness of attention is the first essential in successful performance. For the person who cannot keep his mind fixed upon the problem at hand, the chances of winning out in any field are slight indeed.

✓ ✓ ✓

In this chapter you will learn how inevitably we are at the mercy of hundreds of unimportant or irrelevant ideas and events which besiege our minds continually for attention. You will discover why it is impossible to shut out certain of these stimuli; how we must all discipline ourselves to give important ideas priority; how it is possible to keep attention from wandering; why we can sometimes do more than one thing at a time. You will learn also some important rules that will help you to improve your own habits of concentration.

Photo by Free-Lance Photographers Guild

Fig. 24. Is there any place in a football game for foggy minds and inattention?

6. PAYING ATTENTION

Before you begin your study of the chapter, copy the following form on a sheet of paper and indicate some of the things to which you have paid attention today:

THINGS THAT HAVE HELD MY ATTENTION TODAY

People	Ideas	Happenings and Events	Things
1. Mr. Andrews at assembly	1. Shakespeare's *Macbeth*	1. Fire drill this morning	1. Headlines in the newspaper
2.	2.	2.	2.
3.	3.	3.	3.
4.	4.	4.	4.
5. etc.	5. etc.	5. etc.	5. etc.

Since our minds are never completely blank, except when we are asleep, it follows that we must be paying attention to something or other every moment of our waking lives. You will find it extremely interesting to be an eavesdropper upon your own mind and to observe how one thing after another flashes into it!

CONTINUOUS MENTAL BOMBARDMENT

A thousand things demand attention. As you sit at your desk trying to concentrate on the lesson you intend to study, you may or may not find it easy to control your mind. If all you had to do when you settled down with your work was to snap on some mental switch and allow the material in the books to flow into your brain, much like an electric current, studying would be an easy matter!

But things are not so simple as that! Your lesson is only one of hundreds of objects and situations, every one of which is clamoring for attention at the same time. The clock on the wall, the students around you, the hissing of the radiator, the flapping of a curtain, the movements of the teacher, the distant whistle of a locomotive, a trolley car grinding past—all these things are bombarding your mind for attention.

And as if that were not enough, there are a thousand and one ideas within yourself that are angling for attention also: the game tomorrow, the movie you saw last night, what you are going to have for dinner, the trip you will take over the week end, what to do tomorrow, what you did yesterday, the story you have been reading, what you want to be later on, what grades you will get on the next report! These and innumerable other thoughts tend to flit through your mind incessantly when you try to pay attention to your studies.

External and internal stimuli. Psychologists have adopted the term *stimulus* to apply to any object, condition, idea, or situation, either internal or external, that draws our attention. Thus, the clock, the students, the radiator, the curtain, the teacher, the whistle, the trolley car, are all *external stimuli;* similarly, your thoughts about the game, the movie, the dinner, the trip, what you did or are planning to do, the story, your vocation, your grades, are *internal stimuli.* Since there is no limit to the number of things that will mar our attention, we are necessarily at the mercy of thousands, perhaps millions, of stimuli every moment of our lives.

THE PURPOSE OF ATTENTION

Our power to focus our attention. Fortunately, however, we are not entirely helpless in the midst of these bombarding stimuli, for we are endowed with the capacity to select, within limits, those stimuli to which we will to give our attention for the time being, and by the same token to neglect all the others that may be competing at the moment for our consideration. We call this capacity *attention*. The purpose of attention is to enlarge one stimulus or group of stimuli and at the same time reduce to the vanishing point the appeal made by all other present stimuli.

Attention is thus not unlike your camera which, after you have focused carefully upon the central object, produces a picture in which the central object stands out sharply, while the background objects are blurred and indistinct. So it is that psychologists often speak of the *focus* as contrasted with the *margin* of attention, meaning by the former the idea to which we attend for the moment, and by the latter the other ideas that are automatically relegated to the background or fringe of consciousness. The *focal idea* is the selected idea; the *marginal ideas* are the neglected ones.

Is it worth the struggle? Your power to pay attention to your studying—to go back to the illustration with which we began this chapter—gives you the ability to select the lesson material as the focal idea and to neglect all the irrelevant stimuli, such as the clock, the surrounding people, and your own inner ideas about yesterday's events or tomorrow's. It may be a tough struggle for you, or for any of us, and we may find the ignored or neglected ideas breaking through into consciousness in spite of all our efforts to exclude them; but if we persevere we shall be much more successful than we shall if we throw up our hands and permit our minds to become a sort of free parade ground for whatever stimuli happen to make the strongest appeal at the moment.

ATTENTION PAVES THE WAY FOR PERCEPTION

Meaning is the important thing. The mere turning of attention upon a stimulus does not, of course, guarantee that we shall understand the stimulus. If it did, the infant would comprehend the meaning of the conversation going on between the adults in the nursery, or would understand the operation of the law of gravity when he drops his doll or his rattle on the floor. All attention can do is to focus the sense organs and the mind upon specific stimuli.

The meaning which these stimuli arouse in consciousness will depend upon the past experience which we have had with those particular stimuli and which, in some marvelous way, our nervous system has been able to retain. This background of related past experience throws itself around the present incoming stimuli and gives them meaning for us. The process of bringing past experience to bear upon a present stimulus in order to interpret it is called *perception*. When we *perceive* we interpret the meaning of a stimulus.

Prepare a form like the following, and enter upon it several

WHY CERTAIN THINGS ACQUIRE MEANING FOR ME

Stimulus	Source or Sources in Past Experience from Which I Have Derived Meaning for the Stimulus
1. The word *patriotism*	1. Study of history and civics Listening to orators and speakers Reading books, poems, and articles Seeing parades and memorial services Studying about the flag Hearing about heroes and sacrifice
2. 78% on a test paper	2.
3.	3.
4.	4.
5. etc.	5. etc.

(Use concrete as well as abstract stimuli.)

examples to show how your interpretative background of past experience makes it possible for you to perceive (that is, understand) each of them.

How experience helps everyone. The infant cannot perceive the meaning of a conversation because he has no background of interpretation; and it will be a laborious process to build up such a background. For the same reason the infant cannot perceive the operation of the law of gravity in a falling toy; and he will not be able to do so for some years. He will not be able to interpret any stimulus, such as spoken or written language, gestures, honesty, love, shape, color, duration of time, extent of space, a typewriter, an aquarium, or any other concrete or abstract stimulus, until, through accumulating experience with these things, he succeeds in building up an interpretative background.

Once an individual has succeeded in amassing such a background, the myriads of stimuli that bombard him continually will nearly all fit into the recognized scheme of things. Until his background is filled in with such contact and experience, however, he will necessarily look out upon the world of objects, people, and events around him with mystification and uncertainty. We have all reached our present state of comfortable and reassuring familiarity with our surroundings through this inevitable process of increasing our background through experience.

Building up experience. Attention necessarily pays an indispensable part in experience building. If stimuli did not strike upon our sense organs, and so give us vivid impressions, and if we could not select out and pay attention to some of these impressions and at the same time neglect others, we should be helpless to find any order and unity in our surroundings. As it is, we can direct our minds upon this or that group of stimuli, or upon this or that idea sequence, and so start up the process of perception and establish meaning for the stimuli.

How we learn to make short cuts. As the child becomes more proficient in interpreting experience, he will be able to make many short cuts in perception. That is to say, it will not be necessary for him to bother to gather up all possible stimuli from a given object or situation: a single cue will usually be sufficient to arouse the interpretative background. Thus, a word or a gesture may come to signify for him the approach of his dinner; a light pat-pat on the floor will arouse his expectation of seeing a playful dog bound in; a heavy step on the stair will mean the coming of the individual who chirrups at him, tosses him up in the air, and carries him about sprawlingly in his arms.

The same with grown-ups: a word, a name, a gesture, a tone of voice, a color, a darkening sky, the honking of a horn, the ringing of a telephone bell, an odor from the kitchen, a photograph, a sudden pain from the region of the appendix, a souvenir, an envelope, a strain of music—each provides us with a cue that sets off specifically whatever interpretative background of past experience we may individually have amassed. Our attention often requires but a simple cue to set in motion highly complex memories and ideas.

On a form like the one on page 137 indicate the interpretative background set off by a number of cues such as the illustrations given.

INVOLUNTARY ATTENTION

If suddenly a light bulb should fall crashing from the fixture to the floor, if a blinding flash of lightning should set up a glare at the window, if a sudden twinge of indigestion should draw you up erect—there is no question but that you would pay attention to these stimuli. Even though you might

WHAT CUES MAY LEAD INTO

The Cue Stimulus	Ideas Aroused By It
1. Picture of Washington's Mount Vernon	1. Revolutionary War "First in war, first in peace," etc. Martha Washington Location in Virginia Love of home The gentleman farmer Life in the eighteenth century
2. A few strains from Dvorak's "Humoresque"	2.
3. Sir Walter Raleigh	3.
4. An isosceles triangle	4.
5. etc.	5. etc.

(What long trains of thought are set off by every familiar cue!)

be deep in study, or lost in an absorbing story, or otherwise strongly responsive to focal ideas, the forcing into consciousness of such powerful stimuli as these would drive out the material you were attending to and replace it with something quite different.

Thus, no matter how earnestly we may try to select out the most worth-while stimuli of the moment, we appear to be at the mercy of certain types of strong occurrences that somehow have the right of way to our brain. Attention thus drawn to stimuli that cannot be ignored is called *involuntary attention;* it is attention we cannot help giving because the nature of the stimulus is too overpowering. We may receive such stimuli through eye, ear, nostril, tongue, skin, or any other sense organ; or the stimulus may be a striking idea that suddenly pops into the mind and takes possession of it for the time being.

The following classifications include some of the stimuli capable of arousing involuntary attention:

(1) *Change or motion.* An object that is moving or undergoing change easily attracts our attention; for example, an electric sign that flashes on and off, a rotating barber's pole.

(2) *Suddenness or intensity.* Any stimulus that bursts upon us without warning likewise compels us to heed it; for example, a clap of thunder, a cry of "Fire!"

(3) *Color.* As between colorless and colored stimuli, the latter will tend to catch the eye sooner; for example, a red light, a colored advertisement.

(4) *Uniqueness.* Objects that are disproportionately large or small, grotesque, or in unusual positions compel us to attend to them; for example, a man eight feet tall or four feet tall, "screaming" newspaper headlines, a distorted facial expression, a "steeple jack" at work high in the air.

(5) *Imitative example.* Our attention tends to be drawn to what other people about us are doing; for example, we look up in the air when others are looking up, yawn when a near-by person yawns, pull ourselves up into better posture when somebody else does so.

To such stimuli as these there is no immediate alternative in most cases except to attend. The stimuli themselves become dominant, taking the selective function entirely out of our own hands. Advertisers, publicity seekers, "stunt" performers, and the like make constant use of one or another of these *factors of advantage* to compel our minds to attend involuntarily to their products or acts. Sometimes a teacher, by raising his voice, or by lowering it, or by suddenly rising or sitting, or by his gestures, or by moving about the room, or by stepping to the blackboard, draws from his pupils at least a momentary focus of involuntary attention.

Make a list of as many as possible of the stimuli to which you have paid involuntary attention since you awoke this morning. Use some such form as the one at the top of page 139.

THINGS TO WHICH I HAVE PAID INVOLUNTARY ATTENTION

Stimulus	Reason for Involuntary Attention
1. The sound of my alarm clock	Suddenness, intensity
2.	
3.	
4.	
5. etc.	

(There must have been dozens of such stimuli. Can you think of fifteen?)

VOLUNTARY ATTENTION

Everybody has to resist distraction. By an act of will we can ordinarily free our minds from the attention imposed by involuntary stimuli. We may be distracted by the bell, or the noise, or the color, but we usually have the final word as to whether we shall continue to pay attention to it or whether we shall pull away from it and resume attending to our lesson or whatever task it is we are engaged upon. Attention which we thus direct upon a stimulus or a situation because we *will* to keep it in mind is called *voluntary attention* (from Latin: *volo,* I will).

One pays voluntary attention because he feels it his duty, or his responsibility, or in line with his best interests. The carpenter attends to his saw, the mason to his trowel, the miner to his pick, the teacher to his teaching, the student to his books, the chef to his cooking, the maid to her housekeeping— all because such tasks are an expected part of the day's work, and because ultimately one's security and peace of mind depend upon routine and faithful performance of the tasks to which one is committed.

Many distasteful things have to be done. Our capacity to pay voluntary attention makes it possible for us to do not only the required or expected thing, but also to do the distasteful.

Much of the work of the world cannot, by any stretch of the imagination, be considered in itself interesting and appealing to those who perform it. Digging sewers, mopping floors, washing dishes, practicing scales, and studying uninteresting material in books—these are activities that are essential, though they commonly lack fascination. The faithfulness with which we discharge essential tasks is a good barometer of our character.

After all, civilization depends in the last analysis upon such traits as perseverance, earnestness, and devotion, and every time you or I concentrate upon the needful tasks—even though they may be distasteful or even annoying in themselves—we nourish these essential traits in our personality. Character is not fashioned and civilization is not advanced by the mere attending to stimuli that are loud, or bright, or changing, or novel; but rather by the heeding of those things that are constructive, worth while, and essentially of use or benefit to ourselves and others.

List on a form like the one below as many as possible of the stimuli to which you have paid voluntary attention since you awoke this morning. When you start to think back, you may find your list much longer (or shorter!) than you thought possible.

THINGS TO WHICH I HAVE PAID VOLUNTARY ATTENTION

Stimulus	Reason for Voluntary Attention
1. Stopping at the market with Mother's order	Duty, responsibility
2.	
3.	
4.	
5. etc.	
(Let's hope there have been some, at least!)	

HOW OUR ATTENTION FLUCTUATES

Our thoughts flow on like a stream. William James likened consciousness to a stream with wave succeeding wave as one idea follows another into the focus of attention. If we try to stop this mental stream and compel one idea to remain focused, we find it impossible; the mind seeks restlessly to go on and on. The best we can do is to keep bringing the focal idea back by an act of will. A single, unchanging stimulus simply will not stay focused for more than a second or two: the mind either keeps voluntarily bringing it back or else keeps searching for some new phase or aspect of it, thus transforming it into a changing stimulus.

So, when one is deeply engrossed in a problem, or a book, or any other object to which he is paying attention, he is concentrating, of course, upon one thing; but his mind is attacking it from various successive angles, now focusing upon this phase, now upon that, and often even darting aside for a second to some wholly unrelated stimulus that happens to be in the margin of consciousness.

Variation holds our attention. We never have any difficulty in keeping our attention fixed upon a changing landscape, or upon a story or movie that has plenty of action; but we do have difficulty in keeping it fixed on a single isolated object or upon a story without action. Books, dramas, conversations, lectures, yes, and even lessons may be so monotonous and lifeless as to lull us to sleep. If *you* would be interesting to people, you, too, must look to the challenge which you offer to their minds when you are with them.

We can't attend to one thing for long. Have you ever tried keeping your mind riveted upon the same stimulus for some time, to see what happened? Laboratory students in psychology sometimes try the experiment of *fixating* (directing the eyes

upon) a small object—like the figure *12* on the face of a clock
—and holding their minds upon it for two minutes; or trying
to do so, for they invariably find that they cannot pay continuous attention to the *12* for more than a couple of seconds
or so. Oh, yes, they may keep their *eyes* faithfully riveted
upon the stimulus: that is easy enough; but they cannot hold
down their *thoughts* very long! Here is the way one student
recorded what went on in his mind during the two minutes
of the experiment:

Twelve—that's simple enough—twelve—hear it tick—almost see
the hand move—round face—oh, no! twelve! I must pay attention
to the *twelve*—wonder if it's been a minute yet?—time goes so—
oh, yes! twelve! This is really silly—my eyes haven't moved—a fly
crawling over the face of the—oh, twelve! twelve o'clock—it isn't,
though: it's twenty past two—no, no!—I mustn't let that *twelve* get
away from me—twelve—twelve—that's the head of Minerva above
it on the—here, though—twelve!—I must—

TO HOW MANY THINGS CAN WE ATTEND AT ONCE?

We attend to but one at a given instant.   Only one idea can
be sharply in the focus of attention at once. But because, as
we noted above, our minds shuttle back and forth so rapidly
from one thing to another, it is easy to see how we can pay
attention to two or even three or four things at the same time
if they come through different sense organs or if they are all
of such a nature that they can maintain their clearness by
intermittent focus.

Thus one can read the musical score of a piece as he plays it,
and at the same time understand the conversation of a friend.
At one instant the score is in focus; at the next instant the
words being spoken by the friend are in focus. Enough of
the meaning of each is "photographed" during the instant of
focus to hold over while a bit of the other is being "photo-

graphed" in the next instant, and the two series of stimuli can be kept running along together without much if any loss of meaning.

We can do several things at once!   Most of us do not find it too hard to listen to a lecture and take notes at the same time; to telephone and jot down important items as we talk; to operate a typewriter and read shorthand notes as we write them; to read a book and enjoy music from the radio simultaneously. It sometimes happens, though, that we momentarily allow the mind to follow the trail of one stimulus a second too long and thus lose something of the other simultaneous stimulus. Both stimuli may then be interrupted disastrously. You have certainly experienced this when you have focused upon the notes you were making during a class or at a lecture and have lost for a time the trend of the teacher's or speaker's remarks.

There is one other condition under which we may do several things at the same time. Witness, for example, the stunt musician who has his instruments so placed that he can play the tune simultaneously on piano, harmonica, guitar, and drum. Basically a complex act like this is possible because each element in it has been reduced to a habit; and habits, as we know, require little or no mental supervision. It is possible for the mind to shuttle back and forth between a larger number of habitual acts or skills than of acts which depend upon semicontinuous attention.

You can talk and walk easily enough, because walking no longer requires focal attention; you can stir a batter and read a recipe at the same time because the stirring movements carry themselves along; you can crochet or knit while listening to the radio because needlework is more or less automatic. You can watch a movie, listen to the dialogue, beat time with your foot, chew gum(!), blow your nose with one hand and

paw over the contents of your bag for a pencil with the other—
and you can do all these things simultaneously, partly because
some of them have become automatic through habit and
partly because your mind has that shuttling capacity we have
discussed. Of course, it should not be necessary to say that we
pay attention best and most economically when there are the
fewest competing stimuli to challenge us.

DISCIPLINING OUR MINDS

In a former chapter we remarked how readily some students allow their thoughts to be taken away from their lessons
by every wind that blows. From the discussion in the present
chapter it is easy to understand how important it is—since
theoretically we are at the mercy of hundreds of stimuli at the
same time—to train ourselves to neglect the irrelevant or inconsequential and focus upon the essential. Those that are so
powerful or unique that they pull our attention to themselves
involuntarily are, of course, difficult or impossible to ignore.
But we can in most cases and at most times so regulate our
surroundings as to reduce stimuli of this sort to the vanishing
point.

Most of the things that are apt to play havoc with our attention, however, are not the bizarre or spectacular things, but
rather the simplest things, like people talking or moving about,
the temperature of the room, outside noises, passers-by, and
perhaps most common of all, our own vagrant thoughts that
keep intruding themselves and diverting attention away from
our work. To eliminate these things is sometimes a difficult
task, but the success we achieve will be largely the measure
of our earnestness and determination in ignoring them. Persistence is the only pathway along which we may hope to
reach those intellectual goals which we should have set for
ourselves.

THE ATTITUDE OF ATTENTION

We pay attention with our muscles! Some very interesting experiments in the psychological laboratory have shown that we pay the best attention when we put ourselves under slight muscular tension. That is to say, if we have mental work to do, we should not slouch down in an easy chair, or lie indolently on a sofa, or otherwise seek to get into a position of profound physical comfort. Such positions tend to promote mental lethargy and sleep rather than mental alertness and vigor.

The experiments show unquestionably that the maintenance of an alert, upright posture, with the muscles of the whole body, especially those of the hands, arms, and shoulders, just a trifle tense rather than relaxed, promotes efficient and economical mental work. It appears that we pay the best attention not only when our minds are intent upon the work at hand but also when our bodies are set for intense application. We pay attention with our muscles quite as much as we do with our nervous system!

Try this out in your own studying. See if your accomplishments during the time when you are half asleep physically can compare in effectiveness with those achieved when you are muscularly set in the attitude of attention.

SOME RULES FOR IMPROVING ATTENTION

Seek the widest possible experience. "The world is so full of a number of things," says Stevenson, "I'm sure we should all be as happy as kings." True enough; but unless you observe these things, attend to them, put your attention upon them, they will never mean anything to you, and the world might just as well be empty. Make as wide a contact with things as you can. Develop a mental curiosity, an intellectual thirst for new information, new ideas, new meanings. These restless, insatiable minds of ours need to be fed continuously with ever new experiences.

Try to get the meaning of each stimulus. The act of attention can bring a stimulus into focus, but only perception can interpret it and make it meaningful to you. Try to read meaning into your experiences. Make it a practice consciously to bring to bear on each new situation as it comes along the interpretative background of old experiences.

Cultivate the art of voluntary attention. The modern world is so filled with tumult and noise and visual appeal that our attention is kept more or less at the mercy of the advertiser, the showman, the tabloid, the broadcaster, and the propagandist. Steady attention to the simple and the commonplace is increasingly hard. Do not be victimized by the pull of the factors of advantage; learn to keep an even keel through them and to sail steadfastly toward your mental goal, keeping your attention upon the essential, the expected, the worth while. People who jump at the crack of each propagandist's whip have little stability and less perseverance.

Be faithful to the humdrum. The little things of life count up. Character is achieved quite as much through faithful discharge of the homely, everyday tasks as of the spectacular. Much of the world's work is necessarily prosaic and humdrum, and much of your work and mine will always be of that sort. We ought to learn to realize that attention to those things that may be in themselves monotonous and unstimulating is of the utmost importance, for by this means we *form the habit of paying attention,* and once the habit is formed it will always benefit us. By accepting the daily round as inevitable routine and following it with a will, we shall not only find present satisfaction but we shall save ourselves from future disillusionment and resentment.

Avoid needless distraction.   It is no sin to be distracted by the events taking place about us; it is, however, a sin to *stay* distracted. It is important for us all to learn to bring our attention back promptly to the work in hand after it has been interrupted and fastened on something inconsequential in spite of ourselves. Form the habit of seeking out a reasonably quiet place when you have mental work to do, so that the number of competing external stimuli will be reduced to the minimum. When you have thus cleared the immediate environment of stimuli that might distract, you will find it infinitely easier to keep the important task in focus.

Make many of your responses automatic.   As we observed in our discussion of habit, those acts which we learn, through practice, to perform automatically do not thenceforth require conscious attention, and the mind is left free to devote itself to the higher mental processes. The person who must continue all his life to "hunt and pick" the keys on his typewriter, or to figure out laboriously the notes on a musical score, or to puzzle over correct spellings and punctuations in his letter writing will always be placing needless demands upon his powers of attention. Through proper drill and practice all such things as these should be made automatic early in life.

Put a little tension into attention!   Remember that attention at its best is a positive, aggressive mental attitude; it requires the expenditure of real muscular energy to keep the body alert. Refrain from slouching, sprawling, and lolling when you have mental work to be done. Flabby muscles go well with sleep but poorly with all kinds of work. Learn to put a little tension into your attention!

HOW PSYCHOLOGISTS WORK

In order to pay attention to a stimulus and perceive its meaning all of us are dependent, first of all, upon our sense organs (our eyes, ears, skin, nostrils, tongue, and so forth). None of us could ever get any information about objects or events in the outside world if it were not for the fact that we all possess at least some of these gateways to the mind. Figure 25 and Figure 11 are sketches of the most important of these organs—the eye and the ear.

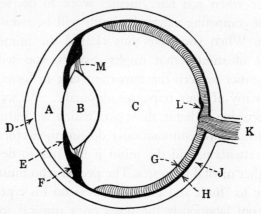

Fig. 25. Parts of the human eye. A: *Aqueous humor, or fluid.* B: *Crystalline lens.* C: *Vitreous humor, or jelly.* D: *Cornea.* E: *Iris.* F: *Ciliary muscle.* G: *Retina.* H: *Chorioid coat.* J: *Sclerotic coat.* K: *Optic nerve.* L: *Macula lutea, or yellow spot.* M: *Suspensory ligaments.*

All sense organs are designed by nature to pick up the mechanical energy thrown off by the objects and conditions around us and transform it into nervous energy that is flashed along nerve pathways to the brain, where it is interpreted.

It follows from this, of course, that if a person were born blind and deaf, he could never receive any information from the visual and auditory stimuli around him. You have read about the noted Helen Keller who, since before she was two years old, has been severely handicapped because of blindness and deafness. Fortunately she had a wonderful teacher, Miss

Sullivan, who taught her to substitute her sense of touch for the two important senses she lacked. By this means she learned to read and even graduated from college with distinction.

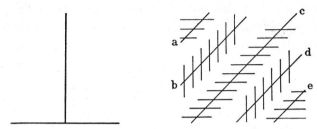

Fig. 26 and 27. The vertical line appears to be longer than the horizontal base line. Actually, both are exactly the same length. The lines a, b, c, d, e do not appear to be parallel, but they actually are. Can you explain these two illusions? What has Figure 27 to do with our sense of perspective?

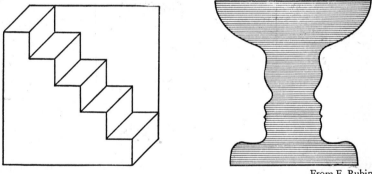

From E. Rubin

Fig. 28 and 29. At one moment, as you fixate the stairs, you seem to be looking down at them from above; at the next moment you seem to be looking up at them from beneath. Is Figure 29 a vase, or is it something else? At one moment it appears to be a vase; at the next, two human faces. Can you make Figures 28 and 29 alternate as you pay attention to them?

Indispensable as our sense organs are, however, they are sometimes deceived by the stimuli that reach them, and consequently we make wrong interpretations of the things around

us. Psychologists give the name *illusions* to falsely interpreted
stimuli. Misinterpreted sensory impressions are by no means
uncommon. Figures 26 and 27 illustrate two illusions.

Besides the fact that our sense organs may be actually deceived, our attention to a stimulus is bound to fluctuate, as
we have already noticed in this chapter; so that at one instant

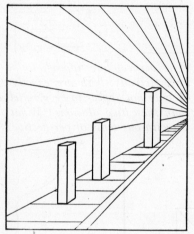

From Morgan, *Psychology,* Farrar and Rinehart

Fig. 30. Which post appears to be the tallest?
Actually, they are all the same height.

we perceive one aspect of a stimulus, while at the next instant
we perceive a different aspect of it, or sense it from a different
angle. Figures 28 and 29 are examples of illusions that are the
results of fluctuating attention.

Still another peculiarity that accounts for illusions is the
fact that sometimes we bring to bear the wrong interpretative
background of past experience upon the present sensory stimulus, or else we misapply this background. Figure 30 is a striking
example of such misinterpretation. We have become so accustomed to associate converging lines with distance in space

that even on a flat drawing objects of identical size may appear to be quite different.

It is important for everybody to realize that sometimes "things are not what they seem," since we may see them incorrectly, or interpret them falsely, or make only a partial interpretation of them. Artists make such skillful use of this phenomenon of illusion in their portrayal of perspective that we see depth on a flat canvas. Architects use illusion in projecting lines; novelty manufacturers use it in constructing puzzles. We are victims of the peculiarities of illusion when we misinterpret what somebody is saying, or misread what somebody has written, or misjudge distance, time, direction, or sequence. False interpretation of events, of signals, of the details of an accident may lead us into much grief. It is essential that we understand this liability to error through the false interpretation of stimuli.

TO HELP YOU LEARN

QUESTIONS TO ASK YOURSELF

1. Which is more at the mercy of the bombarding stimuli that clamor for attention: a year-old child or a sixteen-year-old high school student? Why?

2. Can you explain the aptness of the famous saying: "Genius is but the power of sustained attention"? Show how this power applies to the work of a man like Edison, or of a woman like Madame Curie.

3. In what ways do the various teachers in your high school arouse voluntary attention in their students? Involuntary attention? Which type do you think they prefer you to pay most of the time? Why?

4. Why does a year-old child, when learning to walk, pay such

earnest and careful attention to his feet, his balance, the floor, a near-by chair, the outstretched hands of his father?

5. Can you explain the importance of the attitude of attention? Of what elements is it composed?

WORKING WITH PSYCHOLOGY

1. Look through the current numbers of several magazines which carry a great many advertisements and note which strike your eye most quickly and draw your attention involuntarily to them. Cut out the ten best advertisements from the standpoint of their attention-getting value, rate them on a scale from 1 to 10 (1 for the best and 10 for the poorest), and write down on each one the characteristic that makes the advertisement catch your eye.

2. Now select from the same magazines ten advertisements which have poor attention-getting value in that they do not strike you in the face when the page is turned. Make specific suggestions for improving them so that they would compete for attention with the advertisements which you selected for the preceding problem. In the case of one of the poorest, try your hand at actually rewriting, rearranging, or otherwise revising it so that its appeal is unmistakable.

3. As you pass along the streets in the business part of your town or city, take note of the various advertising devices, such as billboards, posters, and neon signs, which the various merchants use to reach the attention of their prospective customers. You could make a very interesting analysis of your findings on some such form as the following:

Nature of Business	Attention-Getting Device	Quality That Compels Attention
1. Theatre	Alternating lights	Change, novelty
2. Barber shop	Barber's pole	Color, change
3. etc., etc.		

4. Make a survey of a dozen or more occupations which you know something about, either from acquaintanceship with persons engaged in them or from your reading, with the purpose of deter-

mining the importance of the worker's ability to pay profound attention. One good instance would be that of the surgeon making the incision for an appendix operation; another would be that of the automobile mechanic looking for trouble in a dead motor; still another would be that of the telegraph operator reading a code message as it comes over the wire. This survey should reveal to you the frequent life-or-death importance of being able to focus the mind intently upon a stimulus.

WHAT OTHERS SAY

1. In Fiction:

Oblomov by Ivan A. Goncharov. A Russian classic, portraying the fatal consequences of indolence and indecision upon the character and the destiny of a man who is incapable of definite action and sustained effort.

Doctor Mallory by Alan Hart. The tale of a medical practitioner in a small West Coast fishing village. Committed to the highest ideals, he consecrates his life to doing battle against disease, poverty, and ignorance among his people.

2. In Essay:

Give Yourself Background by Frank F. Bond. An interesting discussion of valuable ways of enriching the mind through attention to such agencies as libraries, radio, newspapers, moving pictures. Popularly written and extremely helpful to anybody wishing to develop mental power.

The Life of the Bee by Maurice Maeterlinck. A classic story of the science, drama, and mystery of the hive, portraying the amazing singleness of purpose of every member of the swarm—worker, male, larva, nymph, princess, and queen alike. A most fascinating romance.

3. In Drama

The Ghost Train by Arnold Ridley. You'll have no difficulty in paying attention to this mystery thriller, with its rumrunners, its roaring train, its scythe of death, its whistles and signal bells, and its huddled passengers. A "crinkling, creeping mystery," it holds involuntary attention to the very bursting point.

It Pays to Advertise by Walter Hackett and Roi C. Megrue. In this boisterous farce you will follow the achievements of the son of a millionaire soap-king, who puts his own soap on the market under the catchy name, "Number Thirteen Soap—Unlucky For Dirt." He cleans up magnificently, thanks to the help of a live-wire advertising booster who knows how to direct popular attention toward the new soap.

4. In Poetry:

Uncle Gabe's White Folks by Thomas N. Page. This poem narrates the faithful waiting of an old colored servant and his wife for the return of the long-absent young "marster." Uncle Gabe is proud of the fact that his "ole ooman" has the house always clean and ready for him.

WHAT'S AHEAD IN CHAPTER 7

Have You a Good Memory—or a Poor One?

Many years before he became President of the United States, and while he was still a very young man, William Howard Taft found himself one evening at a picnic in the country. Among those present was a young woman wearing what appeared to be a strangely flashing jewel on her dress. Though he did not know her, young Taft at length walked over to where the woman was sitting, begging that she would tell him what jewel it was that flashed on and off, as though to signal admirers to her side. As mystified as her questioner, the young woman investigated and found that a firefly had lighted upon her dress and was flashing intermittently in the evening dusk.

Half a lifetime later, the same woman, now gray with the years, was among a group of enthusiasts who were moving up slowly in a receiving line to greet the President of the United States. "I wonder if he will remember me?" mused the woman. "He never saw me but that once." Pausing but for a second or two as the mists of memory cleared, the President reached out and grasped her hand. "Well, well, well!" he exclaimed. "If it isn't the firefly girl!"

"But where could *you* hear it—where could you possibly hear it, Mr. Knightly?" cried Miss Bates (in Jane Austen's *Emma*). "For it is not five minutes since I received Mrs. Cole's note—no, it cannot be more than five—or at least ten—for I

had just got my bonnet and spencer on, just ready to go out—
I was only going out to speak to Patty again about the pork—
Jane was standing in the passage—were not you, Jane—for my
mother was afraid we had not any salting-pan large enough.
So I said I would go down and see, and Jane said: 'Shall I go
down instead? for I think you have a little cold, and Patty
has been washing the kitchen.' 'Oh, my dear,' said I—well, and
just then the note came. . . ."

SCENE 1: At Freddie's Home. Time: 8:00 A.M.

Mrs. Barring: Be sure to stop at your grandmother's when
you come home this afternoon, and get your umbrella you
forgot the other night.

Freddie: Yes, Mother, I'll stop for it.

SCENE 2: At School. Time: 10:00 A.M.

Miss Parker: What did we learn yesterday about Cassius,
Fred?

Freddie: (pausing awkwardly) I—forget, Miss Parker. Wasn't
he—er—er. . . .

SCENE 3: In the School Cafeteria. Time: 12:45 P.M.

1st Student: We'll practice after school tonight, fellows. Did
you all bring your gloves?

Students: (in unison) Sure! We all brought 'em!

Freddie: (disappointed) Er—I forgot to bring mine.

SCENE 4: Same as 1. Time: 6:00 P.M.

Mrs. Barring: Where's that umbrella, Fred?

Freddie: (embarrassed) Er—I—forgot it.

Mr. Barring: (impatiently) You'll forget what your name is
and where you live some fine day! By the way, where'd you
put that pen of mine you were using last night? I've needed
it a dozen times today.

Freddie: (uncertainly) Er—I forget, Dad. What was I doing
with it, anyway?

Memories Can Be Improved

There are almost as many different kinds of memory as there are different kinds of people. Some memories, like President Taft's, retain people's faces or names for a long time; others forget them quickly. Some memories are like Miss Bates's, retaining needless details which they grind out much as a phonograph reproduces from a record. Some memories, like Freddie Barring's, are a good deal like sieves that allow almost everything to sift through them: others hold materials with surprisingly little loss. However unreliable one's memory may be, it can be strengthened by using a few simple principles of psychology.

✓ ✓ ✓

In this chapter you will learn how to build up a reliable memory by using sane and sensible principles of psychology; you will discover that a certain amount of forgetting is wholesome and to be desired; you will find out also how excessive and needless forgetting can be stopped. Incidentally, you will probably conclude that while simple *mnemonic devices,* or memory props, may be occasionally helpful, they are sometimes quite misleading and confusing.

Fig. 31. Here are the experts in one "Information Please" program—John Kieran, Elmer Davis, Dorothy Parker, and Franklin P. Adams. They have trained their minds to remember innumerable facts in many different fields. How do they retain so much of what they read, see, and hear?

7. HOW TO REMEMBER

Before you start work on the chapter, test your memory on the following identification test:

A FIVE-MINUTE MEMORY TEST

Identify each of these:

PERSONS	EVENTS	PLACES	LITERARY WORKS
Euripedes	Opening of the first railroad	St. Helena	*Cotter's Saturday Night*
Charlemagne	Battle of the Wilderness	Harper's Ferry	*The Bluebird*
Van Gogh	Stanley finds Livingstone	Nauvoo	*Vanity Fair*
Victor Herbert	Assassination of Archduke Ferdinand	Reykjavik	*Merry Wives of Windsor*
Amelia Earhart	Opening of Tutankhamen's Tomb	Chemin des Dames	*Forsyte Saga*

Of course, nobody can possibly remember all the people, events, and places he has heard about, nor all the books he has ever read. Still, all of us ought to remember a great deal of what we experienced yesterday, and last week, and last year! Otherwise, our minds are in danger of becoming little better than sieves!

REMEMBERING IS NOT THE SAME AS MEMORIZING

A bad start and no ending! Mr. True's class in American History had just reported for recitation. It was the second day of the course. The day before Mr. True had assigned a brief introductory unit of study in the text and source books.

"Well, Tom," began Mr. True, "What did *you* learn about American history?"

Tom, never known as a fluent speaker, arose to his feet and proceeded to speak several well-constructed sentences! Both Mr. True and the class opened their mouths. They opened them still wider when, abruptly coming to a halt in the middle of a sentence, Tom sat down!

"Why, Tom—" gasped Mr. True. "That was unusually good —excellent! Why, though, didn't you finish that last sentence you began?"

"That's as far as I got, Mr. True," replied Tom, flushed with triumph that he had started off so well.

Mr. True opened the textbook and glanced mechanically at it. Then a light broke across his face: Tom had memorized the first page of the assignment, which left off where *he* left off— in the middle of a sentence—and the boy had evidently not had time to turn the page and complete it!

Lots of people make the same mistake. Unfortunately, far too many students make the mistake Tom was making: they confuse *remembering* with *memorizing*. Although, as we shall see in later paragraphs, verbatim learning, or learning by heart (called *rote memorizing*) has its place, it has little place in studying an ordinary lesson unit. The purpose of studying materials in history, as in most of the other subjects you have in school, is to remember certain important or out- standing facts, not to reproduce phonographically an author's words! Your chief concern must be to grasp meanings and ideas, to understand relationships, to relate effects to their causes. Your interest is not in the parrotlike rehearsal of the particular language in which these details are set down.

A pretty good indication of your knowledge of how to study is the skill you develop in interpreting an author's words and in translating them into your own, so that you can store up their meaning in your own brain and recall it when you wish to do so. This is real *remembering*.

LIMITATIONS OF ROTE MEMORIZING

Some things have to be learned by heart. Before proceeding in our discussion of how to remember, we pause merely

Photo by Marjory Collins for F. P. G.

Fig. 32. These drama club members are rehearsing their annual spring play. What is the difference between the kind of remembering they must use and the kind needed in preparing for an ordinary class recitation?

long enough to remark that of course learning by rote has to be practiced sometimes. We need to memorize, for example, arithmetic tables, rules of grammar and syntax, recipes, songs, hymns, poetry, quotations, and occasional declamations. Actors have to learn by rote their parts in plays or pageants; waitresses, the items on the bill of fare; store clerks, the prices of hundreds of articles they sell; clergymen, the various rituals of the church; lawyers, testimonies, rulings, and legal findings; physicians, the difficult names of diseases and medicines.

Transfer the following form to a sheet of paper, and enter upon it as many items as possible. How many of these selections can you still repeat from memory?

THINGS I HAVE LEARNED BY HEART

1. "The quality of mercy is not strained."
2. The Athenian Boy's Oath
3. "The Star-Spangled Banner"
4.
5. etc.

(You'll be surprised at how many things you *have* memorized! Or perhaps, how few!)

Otherwise avoid rote learning. Beyond the specific rote materials mentioned, verbatim learning has small place. It is especially to be avoided in the ordinary routine of study. While occasionally you may come upon a brief passage that is particularly well expressed and worth committing to memory, as, for example, a beautiful piece of English or a notable quotation from literature, and while occasionally there are specific events or facts that need to be remembered in exact series, for the most part you will find little need for verbatim memorizing.

Rote learning is slow and laborious for most people. It puts a premium on parrotlike, phonographic study of materials and discounts study for meaning and content. It squanders time and effort. It is the way of the timid, slavish mind, not the way of the bold, reflective mind.

ADVANTAGES OF LOGICAL REMEMBERING

Using your own words. Logical remembering is the kind that plays the principal role in the learning process. It requires that one shall ignore the language form in which facts are presented and seek after the ideas the language conveys. If, for example, you have followed the discussion about rote memorizing in the paragraphs above, you could not now, probably, reproduce many if indeed any of the actual phrases of the author; you could, however, summarize what he has said. Possibly you would state the meaning of rote memorizing, as he outlined it, in some such language as the following: "Rote memorizing is learning word for word what is given in print. It is helpful sometimes, as when you want to remember a poem or a quotation, but it is a slow process and doesn't make you do much, if any, real thinking for yourself."

You can save yourself time. It is easy to see how economical the logical method is. It ordinarily requires but a single thoughtful reading, or maybe two, after which one can rephrase what he has read and remember it without much effort. If you had attempted to memorize the paragraphs referred to, you would have had to devote an hour or more to the task, and then you would probably have forgotten most of it by tomorrow!

Other advantages. Here are some of the principal advantages of logical remembering:

(1) It requires less time.

(2) It is more interesting.

(3) It is more natural to read for ideas than it is to read for words.

(4) It stimulates us to put facts read into the language we shall be called upon to use later.

(5) It requires us to keep the interpretative background in a

changeable state so that each new idea can be assimilated properly into the total mass.

(6) It encourages an active mind and a reflective attitude.

By relying upon the logical method of remembering, we are applying most of the important principles of effective studying that were previously discussed: we put ourselves in the attitude of intending to learn; we strive to grasp meanings; we maintain the active attitude; we employ the method of recall rather than the method of repetition; we get an initial bird's-eye view of a unit of material; and finally we make ourselves use what we learn.

If for any reason you have been heretofore confusing remembering with rote memorizing, it will be the part of wisdom henceforth to devote more energy to the logical study and interpretation of lesson materials.

HOW TO DEVELOP A GOOD LOGICAL MEMORY

It must be admitted at the outset that certain people have better memories than others; they are born that way. Some have excellent memories for names; some, for faces; some, for ideas; some, for mathematical formulas; some, for historical facts; some, for musical scores, and so on. Notwithstanding these varying innate abilities, there is no real justification for our sitting back and excusing our blunders or our ignorance on the ground that we forgot, or that we have a poor memory. Except for the weak-minded and for some very aged people, all of us can remember well enough the things we need to remember if we will but observe a few simple rules. To a discussion of these we shall now turn.

Learn to pay attention. What do you think of Mr. Blair?

Mr. Barton: Mr. Blair, let me introduce my friend, Jim Courtney. Mr. Courtney, meet Mr. Blair.

Mr. Blair: Pleased to meet you, I'm sure, Mr.—er—Mr.—er—

Mr. Barton: Courtney.

Mr. Courtney: Hello, Mr. Blair. I'm glad to meet you.

Mr. Barton: (some time later in the evening) Well, Blair, what do you think of my friend Jim?

Mr. Blair: Seems a fine chap, Barton. Er—what did you say his name was? Er—my memory's kind of poor, I guess.

Mr. Barton: Courtney—Jim Courtney—a prince of a fellow, too.

Mr. Blair: (still later in the evening) Mr. Brown, let me introduce a friend of Barton's. Brown, this is—er—er—

Mr. Courtney: (coming obligingly to the rescue) Courtney's my name.

Maybe you have been similarly embarrassed yourself. Five minutes after you were introduced to a person, whose name you distinctly heard, you couldn't for the life of you tell his name from Adam!

If it were not so exasperating, it would be downright funny to realize how easy it is for us to forget the simple things that we ought to remember and want to remember. Such a sieve-like memory, which lets everything through it, is as unnecessary as it is annoying. The first thing to do to plug up the leaks is to *learn to pay attention* to the things we want to remember.

The trouble with Mr. Blair, as with numberless other people of his stamp, is that he doesn't really focus his mind on the name of the person to whom he is being introduced. Either he is preoccupied with the physical appearance or the reputation of the stranger, or he is wondering whether he himself is making a favorable impression, or else his thoughts have actually gone woolgathering! Consequently, when the name of the person is mentioned, his attention does not fix itself tenaciously upon it. As we know, we can pay conscious attention to but one thing at a time, and it is therefore seldom possible to be thinking about something else at the instant when a stranger's name is being spoken and to remember it afterwards.

If you would have a good memory, train yourself to fix your attention upon those people and events and ideas which you will later wish to recall. If it is the name of a person, listen intently to it, repeat it audibly as you greet him, and try hard to fasten it indelibly in your mind. If it is a news item, or a date, or a conversation, or an argument, or a point in a lesson, or whatever it is, put your mind intently upon it *while it is taking place*. You will find after a bit that your mind is no longer like a sieve. Memory is, after all, two thirds—or maybe nine tenths—attention; improving it is therefore principally a problem of improving attention. Things cannot be recalled unless they were originally impressed sharply and deeply upon the brain.

Form many associations. Our minds are so constituted that the various things we learn do not remain isolated from each other in the brain. Things that belong together because they are in some way related tend, through the laws of association, to cluster together. Thus, what you know about leather, about the canine family, about the Renaissance, about quadratic equations, is in some marvelous way retained in the brain in great memory masses, each distinct and complete; and every new fact that you learn about any of these items tends naturally to associate itself in your mind with the proper idea group.

But this process of association of a new fact with the material already known about the subject is not entirely automatic. It needs a little help on your part. As you learn a new fact, try consciously to tie it up with the other related facts you already know.

Suppose, for example, that you come across in your study of literature a statement something like the following:

So remarkable were the achievements of Shakespeare and other contemporaneous writers, and indeed so extraordinary were the physical and geographic expansions of the day as the great navigators pushed forward colonization and discovery, that the term "Elizabethan Age" has been applied to the sixteenth century.

Force your mind immediately to do a little logical associating of the facts and events of Elizabeth's England and Elizabeth's world. Recall, for example, that:

(1) Elizabeth was the daughter of Henry VIII and Anne Boleyn.

(2) Philip II of Spain sought Elizabeth's hand in marriage.

(3) Sir Walter Raleigh, one of Elizabeth's favorites, established the first English colony in America on Roanoke Island.

(4) Spenser wrote *The Faerie Queene* with the stated purpose of extolling Elizabeth's virtues.

(5) Spenser and Shakespeare were contemporaries.

(6) Shakespeare wrote *A Midsummer Night's Dream* for Elizabeth's amusement.

(7) Sir Francis Drake circumnavigated the globe during Elizabeth's reign.

(8) Other bold sailors were venturing to the far corners of the earth.

By making this associative effort, you will not only better appreciate the aptness of the term "Elizabethan Age" as applied to the sixteenth century in England, but you will find it easy to remember most of the important events and activities of the period.

Form the habit of trying consciously to fit all your incoming knowledge and ideas into their respective backgrounds. There is no more important principle of remembering than the one which stresses the importance of forming many and rich associations. It makes no difference whether the material to be associated is historical or literary or scientific; the important thing is to associate the things that belong together. Then, when you find it necessary to recall an item, you will have so many ideas pulling at it that it will be a simple matter to draw it back into consciousness.

Learn to organize material logically.   Remembering is immensely aided, too, by careful organization of the materials we study. If, for example, you were to attempt to learn the history of the American Revolution by casually reading two hundred pages from some source book or books, you would find that your understanding of the significance of this war in the history of our country would be pretty meager.

Suppose, on the other hand, you take the time and make the effort to think out and organize the facts of the Revolution in terms of, say, causes, events, and wider social implications. Your resulting outline would perhaps look something like this:

THE AMERICAN REVOLUTION

(1) Causes
> Navigation Acts
> Smuggling
> Writs of Assistance
> Sugar Act
> Stamp Act
> Taxation without representation
> Temper of George III
> Etc., etc.

(2) Events
> Boston Tea Party
> Minutemen
> Lexington and Concord
> Second Continental Congress
> Bunker Hill
> British driven from Boston

The war in Long Island and New Jersey
French aid under Lafayette
Howe and the Battle of Brandywine
Valley Forge
John Paul Jones's capture of the "Serapis"
Surrender of Cornwallis
Etc., etc.

(3) Wider Social Implications
Popular opinion in England regarding the King's policy
Whigs and Tories
Sympathy of other nations with the colonists
Parallel revolutionary movements in other countries
Reconstruction and the "Critical Period"
Etc., etc.

You will find it very helpful in bolstering up your memory if you will be careful to organize what you study in some such logical and systematic form. In so doing you force yourself to think actively about what you are reading, instead of being content with the mere passive mechanical intake of words.

Maintain a positive attitude. Lessons studied under a feeling of compulsion not only come hard but also evaporate shortly into thin air and are forgotten. Lessons studied, on the other hand, with pleasurableness and interest come easily and last long. Teachers are trained to motivate lessons and to make them as interesting as possible. But you should not rely upon your teachers to sugar-coat the materials you study and spoon-feed them into your mouth.

The great wealth of the world's knowledge is poured by society into the schoolroom channels. This heritage of knowledge and culture is at your elbow. Do not attempt to be "smart" and react to it in a bored or casual manner. Do not affect a smug annoyance at being required by your teachers to master a bit of it. Instead, cultivate the attitude of pleasurable anticipation when you settle down with your books; learn to find satisfaction in mastering a generous portion of the world's lore. Cultivate a *feeling tone* (mental state) of enjoyment at your work.

Use mnemonics with discretion.   You certainly depend frequently upon this memory device:

> Thirty days hath September
> April, June, and November;
> All the rest. . . .

And probably you know this one, too:

> I before E,
> Except after C,
> Or when sounded like A,
> As in "neighbor" or "weigh."

These are both examples of mnemonics that everybody employs more or less to help him remember certain things that would be hard to recall otherwise. To a limited degree, mnemonics are helpful and worth while. Occasionally you can make up one of your own, as, for example, one the author employs to remember the rainbow colors in their proper order —red, orange, yellow, green, blue, indigo, violet: "Roy G. Biv." Then, there is the sentence, "Every Good Boy Does Finely," to help one remember the notes on the lines of the music staff: E, G, B, D, F. The word "FACE" aids in recalling the notes between the lines of the staff.

Sometimes, however, mnemonics are misleading, as the pupil found who learned the rhyme:

> In fourteen hundred ninety-two
> Columbus sailed the ocean blue.

When he came to recall the rhyme later on, he got it:

> In fourteen hundred ninety-three
> Columbus sailed the deep blue sea.

And later still:

> In fourteen hundred ninety-four
> Columbus sailed along our shore.

Mnemonics have their place, but when you make one up for yourself, be sure it will not play you false when you want its help. It is ordinarily much better to depend upon logical associations to remember facts than it is to try to remember some artificial rhyme or other kind of "crutch" to help out a shaky memory.

WHY WE FORGET

It is well that we do forget—some things. There is no point in being able to recall the thousand and one details that we are constantly concerned with—as, for example, what you had for lunch nine weeks ago day before yesterday! It was quite interesting and important to you then, but to hold it in memory forever after would be senseless, and your mind would soon become so cluttered up with useless things that there would be no time or space for the important! Along with the unimportant, we want also to forget the unpleasant experiences we have; if all of us stored up and lived over frequently in memory all the harrowing and disagreeable experiences of our lives, we should be extremely abnormal creatures to have around!

It is, then, important to forget—provided always we forget the proper things. Forgetting the things we ought to remember is most unfortunate, and causes, besides, no end of embarrassment and annoyance. Why do we forget the things we seriously need and wish to retain in our minds? There are at least six reasons. Perhaps if we examine each one of them, we shall be helped to remember better in the future. Here they are:

We learn by bits instead of units. If you have material to learn, study it in "hunks," not morsels. Dividing a section up into bits is the infant's way, not the way of the mature learner. Regardless of whether the material is to be learned by the rote or the logical method, the larger the units, the more economical the learning and the better the retention. It is well for anybody engaged in learning, to cultivate the habit of bulking what he reads into sizable mounds and concentrating upon them. This is known as the *whole method of learning*. To memorize a poem line by line, or to study a prose selection sentence by sentence (known as the *part method of learning*), is to destroy the continuity of the material and confuse the mind with a mass of details that should more or less automatically submerge themselves in the wider meanings of the total assignment.

We do not take time to overlearn. Another defect in much of the learning we do is that we stop too soon. Most students, until they are taught better, are satisfied to get some faint glimmer of meaning to what they study; then, by some strangely illogical form of thinking, they presume that the material will clarify itself in their minds and be satisfactorily retained. This is not true. It is important to do more than just to bring the material being studied up to the point where we can express it in vague and faltering language at the moment.

The thing to do is to *overlearn:* that is, to put a little extra time upon the material until we so familiarize ourselves with it that, even after normal forgetting has taken place, we shall still retain the essentials.

Copy the following form on a sheet of paper and make as long a list as possible:

THINGS I HAVE OVERLEARNED

1. My own name	6.
2. The Lord's Prayer	7.
3. Days of the week	8.
4. Months of the year	9.
5.	10. etc.

(This is the sort of thing we repeat so many, many times that we shall never forget!)

Do not stop your study too soon; put a little extra effort into reasonable mastery of it. By the method of recitation, prove to yourself that you really know it before you stop.

We do not distribute our efforts wisely. If you have a poem that will require sixty minutes to memorize, do not put in the entire sixty minutes all at one sitting; put in fifteen minutes today, and fifteen minutes on each of the three succeeding days. If you have a lesson unit that will take two hours to complete, spend a half hour this morning, another half this afternoon, and another hour tomorrow. In other words, distribute your practice over several sittings. Failure to observe this *principle of distributed practice* will result in excessive forgetting. The brain seems to require several "exposures" to a unit of material to be learned; if the time devoted to it is bunched into a single sitting there is bound to be considerable loss.

We do not space reviews properly. As soon as we stop practicing, we begin to forget. Study a foreign language for a year and then discontinue all practice of it for a few months, and you will find that you have forgotten most of it. You have probably had the embarrassing experience many times of turning back toward the end of a term to review lesson units learned—or at least studied—near the beginning, only to find that what you "learned" a few weeks before seems now surprisingly unfamiliar to you. Much of it has been lost through disuse.

Only through observing a famous law of learning—*the law of use*—can you hope to keep materials you have learned fresh in memory. This means that you must constantly review old material if it is to be retained. You should form the practice of going over former units of study rather frequently during the months succeeding study of them, in order to keep them at your finger tips. Later on you will need to review them less frequently. Thus, the principal features of the Elizabethan Age, to which reference was made earlier in this chapter, will require perhaps a monthly review for the first four or five months after you studied them in English history, then perhaps a hasty review every three or four months. Finally reviews no oftener than once in two or three years will suffice. To learn these facts once, and then to let them pass completely out of mind, is to have only the haziest idea of them a year or so later.

We jump from one thing to another. From a psychological viewpoint it is unfortunate that school programs have to be so cut up that you go, let us say, from an English lesson to a Latin, from Latin to mathematics, from mathematics to general science, and from general science to history. By the close of the day you have been "exposed" to so many compartments of knowledge that there is danger lest the entire mass be only a hodgepodge of half-understood material. You pass hourly (or oftener) at the ringing of a bell from one subject to another with little pause. This runs counter to a well-known principle of mental life which requires that the mind shall have an inactive period following an active one, in order that what has been taken in may have time to fix itself firmly in the brain cells.

To achieve the best results from learning, you should have at least a brief period of mental inactivity following application to a unit of work. If it is at all practical, you ought to cultivate the habit of relaxing both mind and body for a few minutes between school periods.

We tolerate conflicting emotions. Why does your tongue cleave to the roof of your mouth when you rise to speak? Why do you forget the answer to a question when a teacher asks it? Why does your mind grow blank when you read over the examination problems?

There is but one answer to these questions: you get panicky! You allow other emotions than confidence and self-assurance to dominate you. You are overcome with fear that you will fail, with concern about the impression you may be making, with apprehension over how your parents will take your impending failure, with perhaps silent rage at the teacher for setting such problems! This is not the way to success in remembering what you have learned. This is the high road to failure! Sweep your mind clear of conflicting and negative emotions when you face the problem of showing what you know, and drive forward with confidence and aggressiveness.

SOME PECULIARITIES OF MEMORY

Perseveration. Has a tune or a line of poetry or a name ever run persistently through your head all day? All of us have this experience sometimes when we are tired, or when we are preoccupied, or when we have been interrupted; it is known as *perseveration*. It is often quite bothersome but can usually be overcome by vigorously turning to some new task.

Crystal-clear images. Another peculiarity of memory, not by any means so common as perseveration, is *eidetic imagery* (pronounced ī-dĕt-ĭk). This is a crystal-clear form of memory image that is as vivid as reality itself. People who have it can recall a face, a scene, an event, a column of figures, or a pattern with perfect fidelity. In the vaudeville and side show, such individuals can often perform prodigious feats of memory, as, for example, adding up mentally six-place columns of figures given orally and on the spur of the minute by anybody in the audience. The figures thus read to them are retained in their minds as clearly as though they were before them on paper, and they can add them and read off the total as readily.

Loss of memory of the past. A somewhat rare abnormality of memory is *amnesia,* or total loss of memory. Occasionally one reads in the papers of somebody who is found wandering about in a strange city, ignorant of who he is and whence he came. Amnesia may be due to brain disease or accident, to shock or hysteria. Some cases of it persist for years; others are restored as soon as the physical or nervous condition of the patient can be repaired. In some cases, notably shell shock in soldiers (see the description of Sassoon's books on page 182), the amnesia is complete; the victim is unable to recall any of the events preceding, during, or following the attack.

HOW PSYCHOLOGISTS WORK

The sphere of memory and forgetting has been for the psychologists a most attractive field of experimentation. Everybody knows, of course, that forgetting occurs, but it has remained for the research men in the field of mental science to determine the rate and amount of forgetting. In general, they have made use of three different methods in studying the problem:

(1) The method of recall
(2) The method of recognition
(3) The relearning method

In using the method of recall the experimenter measures the amount of forgetting by finding the per cent of what has been learned that can be recalled twenty-four hours later, or at some other time in the future. Thus, if on an automobile trip you passed through sixty-three different towns or cities but a week later when you tried to enumerate all of them for your friends you could recall only thirty of them, it is apparent that your rate of forgetting has been very high, and that more than fifty per cent of your impressions have faded away within seven days.

The second method, that of recognition, employs an inter· esting technique. Scattered in among a longer list of items presented to the person whose memory is being tested, are the twenty, or the thirty, or the fifty original items that he has learned; and the subject is asked to identify those which he recognizes. Thus, if you have memorized a list of twenty-five names upon identically mounted photographs and are later presented with fifty, among which are the original twenty-five, your task is to spot the ones you have learned and avoid being confused by the intermixed items. This method is frequently made use of in police courts, when the suspect is placed in a row of persons known to have no connection with the crime, and the plaintiff is called upon to pick out in the group the allegedly guilty individual.

The third method, that of relearning, is sometimes called the saving method. In using it the investigator records the time required by the subject to learn the original data. At some later period—say two weeks--the learner is asked to relearn the data. The lessened amount of time which he requires at the second learning is then taken as a measure of his rate of forgetting. It is the common experience of every student that it requires considerably less time to "brush up" on material that has not been reviewed for a long time than it did to master it in the first place. Thus, if you had studied no Latin since your freshman year, but decided in your senior year to return to the language, you would find that you could freshen your knowledge of it in a very few weeks and soon regain your former proficiency. Teachers and students of "refresher courses" know this principle from personal experience.

Conclusions reached from the use of these three and other methods of studying the problem of forgetting may be summarized in the following general principle:

Forgetting takes place very rapidly in the hours immediately following cessation of practice; subsequently it takes place more and more slowly until a point is reached beyond which one forgets little over a period of many years.

Figure 33 represents the same general principle in graph form.

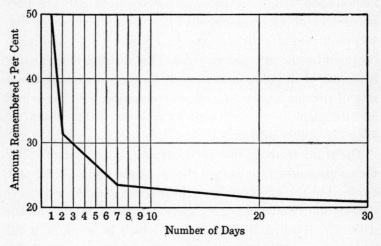

Fig. 33. The curve of forgetting.

Since almost any person taking part in a memory experiment might be familiar with ordinary materials and thus would be at an advantage in the learning as compared with others participating in the experiment, psychologists have found it

helpful to invent a wholly new kind of learning material
which will be equally unfamiliar to every person participating.
This new material consists of *nonsense syllables,* each one of
which comprises a vowel between two consonants, yielding a
three-letter combination without sense. The following list of
nonsense syllables might, for example, be used in a study of
memory:

A LIST OF NONSENSE SYLLABLES

sec	siy
bel	tof
tuv	yaj
nol	viq
vax	siw

Confronted with such a list, every subject is necessarily on
the same footing as every other. The test becomes a sheer test
of memory. Subsequent recall of it becomes a sheer test of
retention or of forgetting. Of course, some learners will be
more clever in their learning of the nonsense list than will
others. Some will make associations of some consecutive sort
with the syllables; some will apply a spur-of-the-minute
mnemonic device; some will introduce rhythm, and so on. But
even so, the good learner of anything is a good learner because he has his own effective and original system.

Try learning the above list for yourself. Note the time required. As soon as you reach the point where you can say the
whole list through without looking at the copy, dismiss the
whole thing from your mind until tomorrow. Then see
whether you can recall the entire list in its original order.

TO HELP YOU LEARN

QUESTIONS TO ASK YOURSELF

1. In what situations during the past week have you used rote memorizing? In what ones have you used logical?

2. Are you in the habit of trying to master sizable units of study materials, or of cutting them up into bits and learning them by the part method? Have you found some types of lessons easier to learn by the part method? Explain.

3. Do you feel that you are inclined to overlearn somewhat, or that you have been guilty of stopping too soon? What advantage do you see in overlearning?

4. What is your practice with regard to (a) distributing your learning time for a given block of material over several sittings and (b) spacing your reviews of material already learned?

5. What experience have you had with the interference of disturbing or conflicting emotions with your learning and recalling?

WORKING WITH PSYCHOLOGY

1. Take the following logical memory test. Read over the quotation below once, very carefully, and then write down as many of the ideas as you can immediately recall. Count up the ideas you have and compare the number with those in the original paragraph. (You will note that each of the forty-five separate ideas is set off by short vertical lines.)

Near the border | of a large | forest | dwelt | in ancient times | a poor | woodcutter | who had two children | —a boy named Hansel | and his sister Gretel. | They had very | little to live upon, | and once when there was a dreadful | season of scarcity | in the land, | the poor woodcutter could not earn | enough to supply | their daily food. | One evening, | after the children were gone to bed, | the parents sat | talking over their sorrow, | and the poor husband sighed | and said to his wife, | who was not the mother of the children | but their stepmother: | "What will become of us? | For I cannot earn enough | to support myself and you, | much less the children. | What shall we do with them? | For they must not starve." | "I know what to do, husband," | she replied. | "Early | tomorrow morning | we will take the children for a walk | across the forest | and leave them | in the thickest part; | they will never find their way home again, | you may depend, | and then | we shall only have to work | for ourselves." |

2. Take the following rote memory test. Learn the Spanish-English vocabulary below to the point where, covering the English words with your hand, you can name them by looking at the Spanish. Keep a record of the time required and compare your rate with that of others. If you have studied Spanish, you should memorize the vocabulary faster than those who have not.

zarza	bramble
retratista	portrait painter
quebrantamiento	violation
desaprovechado	backward
tachuela	tack
relente	dew
necedad	gross stupidity
desalmado	impious
cédula	decree
abacería	grocery store

3. The following are the names of the planets in our solar system in the order of their distance from the sun. (Mercury is nearest of them all to the sun): Mercury, Venus, Earth, Mars, Jupiter, Saturn, Uranus, Neptune, Pluto. Devise some mnemonic of your own to help you remember the planets in their proper order. Test its reliability by seeing whether it will still work twenty-four hours later. Be careful not to think about it in the interim.

4. Try out your memory on the following:

(1) How many windows are there on the front of your house?

(2) How many steps are there in the flight of stairs leading from the first to the second floor of your school?

(3) Draw from memory the design of the wallpaper in your bedroom or living room.

(4) Write the symbol for six as it appears on a watch whose face has the Roman numerals.

(5) Make a sketch from memory of some spire, steeple, tower, or other striking landmark that you pass daily or that you know very well.

Check each product with the original for errors. Report your results in class.

WHAT OTHERS SAY

1. In Biographical Narrative:

Within This Present by Margaret Ayer Barnes. The author chronicles, through the reminiscences of Grandma Sewall, the story of a Chicago family over a period of three generations, culminating, on the eve of the First World War, in the romance, disillusionment, and final reassurance of Sally.

A Goodly Heritage by Mary Ellen Chase. Interesting memories of the author's childhood and youth in a town on the coast of Maine.

Country Kitchen by Della Lute. A description of old-time homes, and especially of old-time cooking and good things to eat.

And Gladly Teach by Bliss Perry. Memoirs of a distinguished literary career in which the author devoted himself to teaching and letters.

Memoirs of a Fox-Hunting Man, Memoirs of an Infantry Officer, and *Sherston's Progress* by Siegfried Sassoon. A trilogy presenting the thinly disguised autobiography of a man who passed through the First World War. He writes poignantly of his experiences as soldier, officer, and shell-shock victim.

2. In Drama:

Smilin' Through by Allan L. Martin. The memory of a tragedy occurring fifty years before embitters the heart of John Carteret and threatens to shatter a modern romance. Only a message from the spirit world finally softens Carteret's heart.

3. In Poetry:

Songs for My Mother by Anna Hempstead Branch. Keen recollections of the hands, the clothes, and the words of the poet's mother.

WHAT'S AHEAD IN CHAPTER 8

Do You Know How to Learn Economically?

Some years ago the world was agog with reports of an unusual horse named Hans. And why not, indeed? For Hans could add, subtract, multiply, and divide, and never make an error! People journeyed far to watch this famous animal perform mathematical tasks that were supposedly only possible to human beings.

The trainer would arrange on the ground in front of Hans a row of placards, on each of which was printed a digit. Then, standing before the horse, he would call out: "Hans, how many are five and four?" Forthwith, Hans would advance and put his hoof beside the placard marked "9."

"Hans," the trainer would continue, "show me how many will be left if I take away three from seven!" Again, Hans would advance to the placard marked "4" and stand beside it.

"Wonderful!" everybody said. "Amazing! Uncanny! A human horse!"

But Hans was not human! He was only an ordinary horse, trained by a patient master, who knew the trick. You will find out in this chapter how all animal trainers achieve their amazing results.

Recalling his first day of school at Salem House, David Copperfield paints a fearsome picture of Mr. Creakle, the master. Said Mr. Creakle to the trembling boys before him: "Now, boys, this is a new half. Take care what you're about, in this new half. Come fresh up to the lessons, I advise you, for I come fresh up to the punishment. I won't flinch. It will be of no use your rubbing yourselves; you won't rub the marks out that I shall give you. Now get to work, every boy!"

After this ordeal was over, as Copperfield recalls, Mr. Creakle came over to where he was sitting and told him that he was famous for biting. Brandishing his cane before David, Creakle cried: "What do you think of *that* for a tooth, hey? Is it a sharp tooth, hey? Is it a double tooth, hey? Has it a deep prong, hey? Does it bite, hey?" And with every question Creakle gave the boy a fleshy cut with the cane until he writhed with pain.

Sandy: Let's play "train of thought"! I'm thinking of General MacArthur.
Andy: All right! General MacArthur makes me think of war.
Sandy: War makes me think of the Philippines.
Andy: The Philippines make me think of islands.
Sandy: Islands make me think of the seven seas.
Andy: The seven seas make me think of seven-league boots.
Sandy: Seven-league boots make me think of Mother Goose.
Andy: Mother Goose makes me think of Jack and Jill.
Sandy: Jack and Jill make me think of "Hey-diddle-diddle."
Andy: "Hey-diddle-diddle" makes me think of cows jumping over the moon.
Sandy: Cows jumping over the moon make me think of milk.
Andy: Milk makes me think of diets.
Sandy: Diets make me think of rations.
Andy: Rations make me think of war.
Sandy: War makes me think of General MacArthur.

Keep this game in mind until you come to the part of the chapter that tells about the Law of Association.

All Learning Is Done Through Association

In all three of these situations, learning either has taken place or is about to take place through association. Hans, the horse, has been able to learn in some peculiar way by connecting his master's language with the appropriate digit. Young Copperfield will be required to learn through associative effort called forth by dread of the consequences of *not* learning. Sandy and Andy have learned through the association of like things or things that have been experienced together.

The reward of learning may be, for Hans, lumps of sugar or appreciative strokings; for Copperfield it will be the dubious negative pleasure of not being "bitten" by Creakle's cane; for Sandy and Andy, it may be the sheer enjoyment of being "quick on the trigger" in carrying through the train of thought until it gets back to the starting point.

In all learning, associations have to be made between a new idea and something we already know; and in all learning some sort of motivation encourages us forward.

✓ ✓ ✓

In this chapter you will become familiar with some very famous rules that operate in all learning, and you will discover how to apply them in your own study. You will find out how animals can be taught to do tricks by an interesting process known as *conditioning,* and how the same principle works in human learning as well. You will discover also whether learning to do one thing, like playing a piano, may make it easier for you to learn something else, like playing a violin or memorizing poetry.

Fig. 34. To win his pilot's license a student flyer must undergo a rigorous course of training, at first with the instructor beside him, later in solo flying. What do you think makes this student so intensely interested in learning to fly?

8. SOME RULES OF LEARNING

Before you start this chapter, recall what laws and principles you know in fields other than that of learning. Use the form below as a guide:

SOME LAWS AND PRINCIPLES I KNOW ABOUT

Who?	Does What?	Because of What Principle?
1. Sanitary engineer	Promotes a clean-up campaign	Germs breed in filth.
2. Weather forecaster	Predicts bad weather	Falling barometer indicates storm approaching.
3.		
4.		
5. etc.		

Try for at least ten illustrations, drawn from as many different fields of human endeavor or experience as possible. It is, of course, because mankind has struggled all through the ages to establish general principles that people today are able to apply them to advantage in managing their own individual lives.

IMPORTANCE OF LAWS AND PRINCIPLES

Every important activity in which human beings engage is governed, in the last analysis, by certain specific laws and principles. The farmer, for example, who is ignorant of the elementary principles of soil analysis, seed selection, and stock breeding can hardly be a successful farmer; the construction engineer who pays no attention to strains and stresses and the other laws of mechanics could never span a river or build a skyscraper; the health officer who ignores the principles of health control could not be expected to preserve and safeguard the physical well-being of his constituents.

The activity of learning is no exception to this general fact. It is regulated by laws and principles which are just as important and just as well understood by psychologists as are those governing activities like farming, engineering, and health control. In the present chapter we shall examine the more significant of these, in order that the student may equip himself to learn more efficiently and economically.

THE LAW OF ASSOCIATION

The fundamental law in all learning. One of the means of developing a good logical memory, as we found in the preceding chapter, is the formation of many associations. So indispensable is this activity that psychologists ever since the days of Aristotle have recognized it as a law: the *Law of Association*. Let us state it: *Of two things previously experienced contiguously* (that is, at the same time or in immediate succession), *the entrance of one into consciousness tends to bring back the other also*. The fundamental thing in all learning is to associate together things that belong together. The fundamental thing in all teaching is to present together those facts, events, and ideas, that belong together, so that they may become correctly associated in the mind of the learner.

Some illustrations of it. Let us be specific. With what do you associate *8 x 9*? With *72,* of course. The year *1775?* With *Paul Revere, Lexington and Concord,* and so forth. The chemical formula H_2O? With *water. The product of the sum and difference of two quantities?* With *the difference of their* *squares.* The *Plains of Abraham?* With *General Montcalm, General Wolfe,* the *Battle of Quebec,* and so on.

Similarly, we associate Pittsburgh with steel; Detroit with automobiles; coffee with Brazil; "The Raven" with Poe; Einstein with mathematical research; Raphael with the "Sistine Madonna"; Roentgen with the X-ray; the Curies with radium; Clara Barton with the Red Cross; Tutankhamen with the Valley of the Kings; Cicero with Catiline; the Louisiana Purchase with Jefferson, Monroe, and Napoleon; the caste system with India.

All these illustrate the operation of the law of association: in each instance two or more events, personages, or ideas were originally learned together—contiguously—and now that one of them is in the mind, it automatically pulls back those with which it was originally joined in learning.

Difference between child and specialist. Basically, the purpose of all drill, of all study of any sort, is to put together in the learner's mind those facts which belong together and which it is desirable for him to remember together. The difference between the grasp which the elementary school child has and the university specialist has of a block of learning material, lies in the number and richness of associations: the school child has relatively few simple ones, whereas the specialist has many complex ones. In both cases, however, the law of association is operative. Similarly, the resourceful writer, the original essayist, the skilled debater, the engaging conversationalist, and the competent man of affairs are all successful in their achievements because they have more ideas and a greater wealth of associations than most people enjoy. Perhaps the best mark of the truly cultured or educated person is the variety and richness of his associations.

Most of us are not, of course, limited to one or two associations with a given idea; rather, we possess scores, even hundreds of ideas tied together in a cluster around any given central theme or idea. It might look, at first thought, as though we would be helpless when a chain of associations began running itself off, and as though we could make no selection among the mass of ideas that must come tumbling into the mind. Actually, it ordinarily happens that only those related ideas that are appropriate to the present need or context are pulled back into the conscious mind, while the hosts of other associates remain at rest. We may distinguish at least five principles that determine which among the hundreds of potential associates shall be pulled back by the present idea into consciousness.

Before considering these principles, go through the following list, one item at a time, and write down the associations which each arouses in your mind—that is, the ideas that are pulled back into consciousness by each name or term given in the list:

STIMULUS WORDS

(1) Banquo
(2) Habeas corpus
(3) War of the Roses
(4) Tierra del Fuego
(5) Polygon
(6) Scarlett O'Hara
(7) Toussaint L'Ouverture
(8) Albatross
(9) Joseph, the son of Jacob
(10) Ohm

Were some of your associations immediate?

Were some of them slow in coming? Can you tell why?

Do some of the stimulus words set off a whole string of ideas? How do you account for so many associations?

Do some of them leave your mind hopelessly suspended, as it were, in mid-air?

The Principle of Frequency

This accounts for the importance of drill. This principle states that *the entrance of one idea into the conscious mind tends to bring back the idea or ideas most commonly experienced with it heretofore.* The combination 7 x 9 suggests 63, not 56; *Abraham Lincoln* suggests the *War Between the States,* not the *Revolutionary War* and the *Articles of Confederation,* because we have so many times put together the former ideas in our study and thinking. The purpose of all schoolroom drill in arithmetic fundamentals, in spelling, in grammar, is to insure that correct associations shall be made over and over again until they have become automatic. If you want to learn such things as these thoroughly, practice them often!

The Principle of Recency

This shows the importance of review. According to this principle, *the entrance of one idea into consciousness tends to bring back with it the idea or ideas that chance to have been most recently experienced with it.* You have many associations with *Lincoln,* but the ones that probably come immediately to mind as you read this line are *Abraham Lincoln* and the *War Between the States,* for the simple reason that you have just experienced these ideas contiguously a few lines back. You might just as well, otherwise, have associated with *Lincoln* either *a city in Nebraska,* or *a county in Maine,* or *a make of automobile,* or *a Cape Cod writer.*

Every student takes advantage of the principle of recency when he reviews his lesson material shortly before an examination. Occasionally a pupil makes the mistake of "cramming," that is, trying to put together in his mind at one sitting so much material that a mental blocking results and he fails to remember most of what he tried to cram. Frequency of association should precede an exam if one is to derive full advantage from the principle of recency.

The Principle of Primacy

The lastingness of first impressions. *The entrance of one idea into consciousness tends,* according to the principle of primacy, *to bring back with it the idea or ideas first or originally experienced with it.* Thus, one's earliest impressions of a person, a community, an article of food, tend to be lasting and are often hard to break down by subsequent contacts. Let a pupil make a poor impression upon his teacher the first few days of a term, or the teacher make a poor impression upon the pupil, and the mischief is done. Let the baby make unpleasant associations with spinach when it is first presented, and it will take persistent effort on the part of the parent to uproot them.

If you like olives, you doubtless liked them from the first; if you dislike them, you probably disliked them the first time you ever tasted them, and whenever you think *olives* you unquestionably associate dislike and perhaps make a wry face. Even though you know several *Olives* and are familiar with *olive oil* and with the *Mount of Olives,* your first association with the word is likely to be the gastronomic one!

The Principle of Vividness or Intensity

The importance of striking experiences. This principle states that *the entrance of one idea into consciousness tends to bring back with it the idea or ideas that have been most vividly connected with it in the past.* Thus, to Mrs. S, *auto-*

mobile always suggests the accident in which she was badly injured and her husband crippled. H, a First World War veteran, associates with *canned meats* all the harrowing experiences of the trenches during the time he was subsisting largely upon "bully beef." To F. J., *Palm Beach* suggests, not *lovely resort* or *Florida vacation,* but *appendix,* because while he was there many years ago he underwent an emergency operation for appendicitis. Vivid experiences that arouse strong feeling, whether we have them in the schoolroom or outside of it, last long in memory. Vivid and interesting learning situations in the schoolrooms therefore make humdrum repetition and drill less necessary.

The Principle of Mood

The importance of our state of mind. *The entrance of one idea into consciousness tends,* according to the principle of mood, *to draw in such ideas as fit into the present mood or attitude of the person.* Children shouting at play under the window may incline the adult in the room above to frown and grumble about "noisy children" or to hasten down and romp with them, depending upon the mental state in which he happens temporarily to be. So, too, a joke may strike one as hilariously funny today and as grossly silly or pointless tomorrow. *School* may suggest *old lessons* and *mean old teacher,* or it may suggest *interesting classes* and *wonderful Miss Blake,* depending similarly upon the attitude of the individual at the moment.

A person may be almost as different in his fundamental personality on two successive days as Dr. Jekyll and Mr. Hyde, all because when he is under the dominance of one mood he associates one series of ideas with everything, whereas while he is under the dominance of another he associates a wholly different series.

Copy the following form on a sheet of paper and enter upon it an original example of each of the five principles of association. Thus, in the sample, Abraham Lincoln might be associated with the *War Between the States* because that is the association that you have made most *frequently* with him in the past.

HOW THE PRINCIPLES OF ASSOCIATION WORK

Stimulus	First Idea Aroused by It	Principle Involved
(Ex. Abraham Lincoln)	(War Between the States)	(Frequency)
1.	1.	1. Frequency
2.	2.	2. Recency
3.	3.	3. Primacy
4.	4.	4. Vividness
5.	5.	5. Mood

(Can you think of more than one example of each principle?)

It should now be apparent, from your study of the preceding paragraphs, that the infinite number of associations which we have with a given idea or situation are apt to follow some sort of determining principle when they come back to mind; they do not ordinarily just rush in "helter-skelter," without rhyme or reason. You will find it very interesting to watch yourself, and the others with whom you converse, to see which of the principles enumerated above determines, in the case of a given stimulus, the order and nature of the immediate ideas associated.

THE LAWS OF USE AND DISUSE

Repeated connections have to be made. Sometimes stated as a single law—the *Law of Exercise*—the laws of use and disuse are related closely to the principle of frequency, discussed under the Law of Association. From the standpoint of the brain and nervous system, all learning results when modifiable connections between a stimulus and a response have been made so repeatedly that they have been strengthened and tend to persist. Use of this nervous connection deepens it and strengthens it; disuse tends to erase it. Other things being equal, the more a connection is used, the stronger it becomes; and conversely, the less it is used, the weaker it becomes.

Thus, the accountant totals up a column of figures quickly and without error; whereas the man who has little or no occasion to use figures finds it a slow and laborious task, and he is extremely likely to get his totals wrong! Likewise, the profane man finds oaths springing to his lips automatically when he is thwarted or angry; the scholar has no difficulty in applying his knowledge to a problem in his field; the sleight-of-hand performer and magician can manipulate small objects so cleverly as to defy detection by the audience.

All of these situations illustrate the operation of the laws of use and disuse in our everyday lives. Rusty or bungling performance ordinarily means that there has not been practice enough, or that the skill in question has been allowed to deteriorate through disuse of the nervous connections.

There must be attention as well as drill.   Mere repetition is usually, however, not enough to attach a response invariably to a stimulus. There must also be attention and purpose. Mechanical or casual repetition conceivably might never result in learning. You have, for example, climbed a given flight of stairs a thousand times and more, but you could not now tell how many steps there are in the flight. You have faced the front of the auditorium in your school perhaps a hundred times, but you could not now describe the details of stage and hangings. Neither could you tell how many light fixtures there are in the ceiling over your head, or the color of your teacher's eyes, or the number of shelves in the bookcase at the side of the room!

Interest and will power are essential. The Law of Exercise requires that the learner shall attend *purposively* to the connection which he desires to make. Mechanically repeating the multiplication tables will never result in mastery of them; lackadaisical and casual listening to a teacher's explanation will never bring the glow of understanding; sleepy or detached reading of a textbook will never fix its contents in the mind of the student. Strong interest, the desire and will to master, and the maintenance of an intellectual curiosity and thirst will mean infinitely more to the student than will the mere slavish repetition of associations. In fact, if the learning experience is kept vivid and dynamic, the number of repetitions needed to fix ideas may be sharply reduced.

THE LAW OF EFFECT

Another significant law of learning is the *Law of Effect*. We may state it in these words: *We tend to repeat those responses that are accompanied or followed by a feeling of satisfaction, and not to repeat those that are accompanied by or result in annoyance.*

How it operates in child training. From the very beginning of a child's life the operation of this law may be observed. It is safe to say that every parent—while he may not be familiar with the wording of the law, or indeed ever have heard of it—understands its importance in the training of his children. A scowl, or an emphatic shake of the head, or a spanking of the baby's hands when his conduct is displeasing, suffices ordinarily to discourage repetition of the undesirable act. Later on, a pained look or a verbal threat or warning will likewise be a strong deterrent to undesirable behavior on the part of the child. On the other hand, a nod or a smile, some simple indulgence, a reward or a favor, will ordinarily encourage the child to repeat the action of the moment.

How the law of effect works in life. Principally through the power of this Law of Effect, most of us learn during the formative years of childhood whatever habits and attitudes of thoughtfulness, obedience, and moral conduct we acquire. Throughout our lives, indeed, the regulative power of social approval and disapproval of our acts continues with undiminished strength.

A habit that satisfies or pleases us or our friends, we tend to continue; one that annoys or bothers, we tend either to uproot or at least to chide ourselves for continuing. Pursuit of a life goal or purpose which we find agreeable and appealing continues to be, if not easy, at least enticing; from goals that offer no beckoning satisfaction we either turn resolutely aside or shut our eyes even as we approach them. Lessons, courses of study, educational experiences, if they are to yield the best results, must be accompanied by a definite feeling of satisfaction and worth-whileness as we pursue them.

Do you get satisfaction from studying? The reason why so much of our educational experience, from the elementary school to the graduate school, is casual and ineffective is that it brings with it little satisfaction, and when a unit of it is over the student feels relieved rather than eager for further study. One undeniable reason, on the other hand, why the extracurricular or extraschool experiences of high school pupils receive a disproportionate share of time and effort is that these activities are in themselves satisfying and interesting, whereas classroom work and study is often the reverse.

To test out your understanding of the workings of this Law of Effect in learning, enter upon a form like the one on page 198 several illustrations of it taken from your personal experience.

HOW THE LAW OF EFFECT WORKS

My Training by My Parents at Home		My School Learning Experience		My Social Experience	
The Act	Workings of the Law of Effect	The Act	Workings of the Law of Effect	The Act	Workings of the Law of Effect
1. Telling an untruth	Parental censure and disapproval (annoying to me)	1. Studying the science of nutrition	Preparing an exhibit of posters designed by the class (satisfying to me)	1. Holding myself aloof from my schoolmates	Experiencing loneliness, envy, jealousy (annoying to me)
2.		2.		2.	
3.		3.		3	
4.		4.		4.	
5. etc.		5. etc.		5. etc.	

(You are a real psychologist if you can do this problem!)

The cause of lukewarmness in students. You should not get the notion, if you are more devoted to the side issues of school, so to speak, than you are to the main issues—classes and studying—that it is necessarily the teacher's fault. About the easiest thing in the world to do is to blame somebody else for one's own deficiencies and shortcomings. You should inquire of yourself rather frankly whether your academic lukewarmness—if you have it!—is not a reflection of your own lack of serious purpose and of the will to make something of yourself, rather than the failure of your teachers to entice your intellectual appetite.

One of the greatest lessons anyone can possibly learn is to find satisfaction in enriching his mind and increasing his mental powers through the mastery of the materials of knowledge. Often a person turns back too late and tries to fill in the gaps in his education and so to find a belated satisfaction years after he has dropped out of school and given it up as of no value or interest.

THE PRINCIPLE OF CONDITIONING

Dead dog! "Bos'n is a clever dog!" remarked his young master proudly. "He'll do lots of tricks."

"What can he do?" queried Mr. Mason.

"He'll play dead!" replied Bill. "Here, Bos'n, dead dog!"

Immediately Bos'n, who had been wagging his tail as though to second all his master was saying to him, lay over on his side and stretched out "lifeless" on the sidewalk.

"Good!" exclaimed Mr. Mason. "What else can Bos'n do?"

"He can sneeze!" informed Bill. "Here, Bos'n, sneeze!"

Forthwith the "dead" dog sprang up and sneezed according to order.

"Wonderful!" admitted Mr. Mason. "How did you ever teach him, Bill?"

"Oh, I just *did,*" replied Bill. "He's a clever pup—Bos'n!"

How all animals are trained. Maybe you, too, have taught a dog, or other animal, to do tricks. If you have, you no doubt used the same technique that Bill must have used with Bos'n. The technique consists in associating together two stimuli— an *adequate* and an *inadequate* one—in such a way that the inadequate stimulus is attached to the response which before was attached only to the adequate one. The *adequate stimulus* is any stimulus which leads naturally or inevitably to a response; the *inadequate stimulus* is one that has no connection with the response. In the case of Bos'n, the adequate stimulus that made him respond by lying down and playing dead was a push by Bill. The inadequate stimulus was the accompanying command: "Dead dog!"

Now there is no connection between a dog's hearing the words "dead dog" and a dog's lying down motionlessly. But by the technique of saying the words "dead dog" *at the same time* that he was pushing him over and holding him quietly on the ground, Bill caused Bos'n to associate the words "dead dog" with lying down. Eventually Bill could eliminate the pushing and holding down of Bos'n: the inadequate vocal stimulus "dead dog" was all that was necessary.

Photo by K. P. Groat for F. P. G.

Fig. 35. By the clever use of the psychological principle of conditioning, wild animals can be trained to be as docile as kittens.

Of course Bos'n didn't understand human language; he merely stretched out motionlessly when Bill gave the command because stretching out and a peculiar verbal combination and tone of voice had been experienced simultaneously by him enough times to make the thing stick. Maybe Bill had to repeat that technique a hundred times or more before Bos'n caught on and was *conditioned*. Maybe, too, Bos'n's memory would fade after a time, and Bill would have to reinforce the association by pushing him down again and repeating the command, thus reviving the *conditioned response.*

Much human learning is also conditioned. Not only is all animal learning done through this process of *conditioning,* but much of our human learning comes about in a similar manner. The baby learns the meaning of "mama," "dada," and so forth through hearing these words pronounced many times and seeing the corresponding personages pointed out simultaneously. By and by the right connection is made in the baby's mind. Similarly, words, commands, warnings, and the like, come to be meaningful to the child because they have been originally connected with adequate stimuli.

So, too, one may be conditioned to like or dislike certain foods through the emotional experiences originally associated with taking them. Fear of anything—animals, certain human beings, the dark, thunder showers—is ordinarily learned by the child through conditioning. The important thing is always that the adequate stimulus and the inadequate one must be presented at the same time or in immediate succession if the latter is to be connected with the natural response to the former.

Conditioning makes association possible. Conditioned learning becomes, from this viewpoint, simply a process in which the Law of Association operates. There is at the outset no inevitable connection between seeing a woman acquaintance and lifting one's hat; between observing a colored object waving and thinking "flag"; between a hot stove and the words "Don't touch!"; between a bottle and one's dinner; between a faucet and a drink of water; between letters on a printed page and meaningful symbols. But after any two stimuli have been associated often enough or vividly enough, one becomes conditioned to the inadequate stimulus, and it becomes thereafter a cue to the original and to all related subsequent experiences.

THE PRINCIPLE OF TRANSFER

Some much debated questions. Does the study of Latin lead to a better understanding of English? Can skill in reasoning out mathematical problems make one more able to think straight politically or economically? Will training of the right hand in penmanship carry over to the left hand and make it easier to learn to write left-handedly? Do muscles trained to react skillfully in handling a tennis racket perform better, by virtue of that training, in baseball or volleyball or basketball? Are fingers that have grown nimble in operating a typewriter for that reason more competent to manipulate a musical instrument? Will memorizing poetry make one better at memorizing prose selections?

These are highly interesting questions. The problem at issue is whether training is *specific* or *general,* whether we learn what we learn and nothing else, or whether the process of learning one thing improves our ability to learn something else. A strong controversy has gone on for many years among educators as to whether learning does or does not *transfer* (carry across) from one situation to another. It used to be believed that the mental "faculties" of reasoning, memorizing, and so forth, were strengthened by exercising them, like a muscle, and that, regardless of the nature of the material with which they grappled, they were bound to improve. Hence all students in the schools of yesterday studied Greek and Latin and mathematics in order to train their mental faculties.

Four scientific conclusions. Recent and extensive experimental investigations of this matter have established the following valid conclusions:

Transfer is limited. The amount and extent of transference are decidedly more limited than the older thinkers believed.

Transfer occurs in similar situations. Transference unquestionably does take place between two subjects or types of activity that are similar in nature or that require a similar technique. Study of one language helps in the study of another; manual skill with the right hand transfers to a degree to the left hand; players who are skilled at basketball are better also at volleyball. There is an identity of material and technique in these related activities which is mutually beneficial. On the other hand, the man who has a keen mathematical mind may be the dupe of any "get-rich-quick" promoter; the student who can memorize a poem in record time may be a hopeless failure when it comes to weighing arguments or working quadratic equations; the specialist in surgery may be the world's poorest orator. There is no essential identity between the pairs of activities mentioned.

Transfer requires thought. Transference does not ordinarily take place automatically, at least to only a very slight degree. It is necessary, if you want your Latin to help you in your English language study, to be on the lookout purposively and consciously for similarities of meaning, construction, syntax, spelling, and the like. The study of a Latin vocabulary, gone at with the idea of finding inherent relationships to English roots, prefixes, and spellings will often be not only most interesting but most illuminating. The student who learns to approach all study with the interesting purpose of relating it to parallel or relevant learning materials will reap a rich reward in the command which he will acquire over the whole field of knowledge.

We learn what we study. While transfer does take place, under the conditions just explained in the second and third conclusions, the student should understand that the principal gains which he derives from any subject of study are limited to that subject. One does not "go east by sailing west," academically speaking. If he studies Latin, he learns Latin, not

English; if he studies mathematics, he learns mathematics, not economics, or banking, or law. The spread from one field to another, while it exists, is not considerable. In general, we learn what we study and not something else.

Character building believed transferable. In a practical sense and in the everyday experiences of life, transfer is believed to play an important role. Parents understand that, when they discipline a child who has been dishonest in handling a small sum of money on an errand for his mother, the disciplinary spread will extend to other honesty-dishonesty situations and make him more honest-in-general. So, too, they presume—and they are probably right—that when they punish him for disobedience in situation x, the training will carry over to situations y and z; or that when they teach him to use good table manners at home and to be thoughtful of his grandparents, they will have started him well upon the road of politeness away from home and thoughtfulness for all aged people.

Teachers, likewise, in emphasizing and insisting upon high ideals of conduct in the schoolroom and on the playground, are convinced that by so doing they are increasing enormously the likelihood that their pupils will carry these ideals with them into home and community life. There is little hope in education otherwise. Unless all the excellent and noble precepts of home, school, and church reach beyond the original setting in which they are taught and influence positively the lives of all of us by making us better citizens and better people, there is little hope for the ultimate salvation of society.

List on a form like the one at the top of page 205 some actual operations of transfer that you have experienced yourself, either in connection with subjects studied at school, or in connection with skills and attitudes developed outside of the classroom:

The Specific Thing Learned	Has Transferred to	With This Result
1. Latin vocabulary	My knowledge of English words	My understanding of the English language has been enriched.
2.		
3.		
4.		
5. etc.		

(How about transfer from music, tennis, Spanish, geometry?)

HOW PSYCHOLOGISTS WORK

Conditioned learning is distinctly a field of research that belongs to the twentieth century. Interest in the subject started with the experiments of a Russian physiologist, Ivan Pavlov by name, in which a dog was used as the subject.

Of course Pavlov knew—anybody would—that when juicy meat is dangled before the nose of a dog, the animal's mouth will run gushingly with saliva. In terms of adequate stimulus, which we have mentioned previously in this chapter, this well-known phenomenon of "watering mouth" may be diagramed thus:

$$S^a \text{(sensing food)} - - - - - - - - - - \rightarrow R \text{ (flow of saliva)}$$

S^a stands for adequate stimulus and R for response to the stimulus. Awareness of the presence of the meat is a perfectly natural stimulus to make the salivary glands discharge anticipatively. Human beings as well as animals experience the same thing whenever they feel hungry and are brought into the presence of savory food!

But Pavlov did not stop with the mere presentation of meat before his eager dog. He did a very peculiar thing: he set up a bell in the laboratory, and every time he held meat before the dog he rang the bell simultaneously. After repeating these two simultaneous stimuli several times, Pavlov made a very significant discovery. When he rang the bell without offering the meat, the dog's saliva gushed forth as plentifully as it had done when meat was proffered! The experimenter was forced to the conclusion not only that an adequate stimulus may produce a response, but that an inadequate or totally unrelated stimulus may, if presented a few times simultaneously with the adequate one, produce the same original response.

Diagraming the learning, or the conditioning, that has taken place in Pavlov's dog, we have the following:

S^a (sensing food) — — — — — — — — — — ⟶ R (flow of saliva)
S^i (sound of bell) ⟍

Here S^i stands for inadequate stimulus, for surely nobody would have supposed that there was any *adequate* associative linking between the ringing of a bell and the gush of saliva in an animal's mouth!

But associative linking there has been, and the dog will now discharge saliva whenever the bell rings! The fact that two stimuli—one of them an adequate and the other an inadequate one—have been associated together suffices to give the latter stimulus the same value as the former one, and we may say that the dog has been conditioned to the bell. The heavy arrow drawn diagonally from S^i to R indicates the linking of this new connection between bell and salivary flow. Our diagram may be simplified now to:

R (flow of saliva)
S^i (sound of bell) ⟋

Since Pavlov's original experiments upon conditioning, both he and many other research students have carried on innumerable studies in this interesting field. None of these has perhaps been of greater challenge than one performed in our own country by Dr. John Watson, at the time a psychologist at Johns Hopkins University.

Watson used for his subject an eleven-months-old boy, Albert by name. Albert is sitting comfortably upon the experimental table, when suddenly a white rat is introduced near him. Curious at once, Albert reaches out his hand toward the rat, but just as he is about to touch the animal the experimenter strikes a resounding blow upon an iron bar behind and out of view of Albert. Now for anybody, of course, a sudden loud noise is the adequate stimulus to arouse fear; Albert reacts as we would have anticipated. He jumps violently and falls forward on the mattress. Diagrammatically, what has happened thus far is this:

S^a(sight of rat) — — — — — — — — — —→R (interest)
S^a(sudden loud noise)— — — — — — — — ➤R (fear)

But after Watson has repeated the noise and the introducing of the rat into Albert's presence for six or seven successive days, he finds that Albert has been strongly conditioned to fear the rat, concerning which at the outset he had not the slightest fear or discomfort.

Diagrammatically, we may indicate what has happened as follows:

S^i (sight of rat)————————————→ R (fear)

Notice that the sight of the rat, which originally was an adequate stimulus only to arouse interest and curiosity, has now become the adequate stimulus to arouse fear in the child. Albert's conditioned fear, moreover, is so persistent and dominant that henceforth he is found to be afraid not only of the rat whenever he sees it, but of other similar furry objects, such as a rabbit, a dog, some cotton wool, a Santa Claus mask, a fur coat. Obviously, the child has learned (that is, been conditioned) to be afraid.

In a later chapter we shall consider the profound importance of conditioning experiences in creating many of the fears that obsess people all their lives.

Meantime, it is the author's purpose here merely to demonstrate the fact that, after all, conditioning is merely the opera-

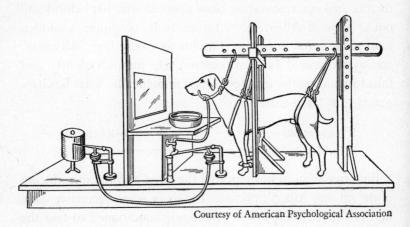

Courtesy of American Psychological Association

Fig. 36. Sketch illustrating Pavlov's experiment with a dog.

tion of the Law of Association. Associate white rat and loud noise together, and you will learn to fear the rat; associate a ringing bell and the odor or sight of food, and your saliva will start flowing at the ringing of the bell. It should, perhaps, be added that a conditioned response, unless it is stamped into the nervous system very deeply by the conditioning experience, will disappear after a time if occasional repetition of the original situation does not occur to reinforce the connection. Thus, Pavlov's dog will not always salivate whenever a bell is rung; but the child Albert will, unless the connection is extinguished in some way, probably always be afraid of rats.

TO HELP YOU LEARN

Some Questions to Answer

1. Can you observe the operation of any of the principles of association in the conversation of a group of people who are together socially for an hour? Explain.

2. Can you mention any skills or abilities in the practice of which you feel yourself to be decidedly rusty at present, though earlier you could use them with facility? What principle of association has been violated?

3. Are you aware of any interference between two types of learning materials on which you are at present engaged? In other words, does the practice of one of them, instead of transferring to the other, actually put you under a handicap when you turn to the second one? For example, one high school student who was studying freshman Latin and freshman German simultaneously wrote "ist" for "est" in the Latin class, and was so confused that she could not straighten out the difficulty.

4. "First impressions are lasting." What experiences can you think of to illustrate the truth of the principle of primacy? Why is it sometimes difficult to decide whether the principle of primacy or the principle of vividness is operating in such cases as you suggest?

5. Have you ever done any cramming? Why is it not a wise practice? How do you reconcile its unwisdom with the wisdom of using the principle of recency in learning?

Working with Psychology

1. Take careful note during the next week of instances in any of your classes in which the instructors are apparently helping the students to transfer their knowledge or skill in one field to some other field. If you are observant in this, you will be gratified to realize that you can actually study out a teacher's design in making his material applicable and usable in fields outside the immediate one. List the instances you detect, and talk them over with the teachers concerned, as well as in this class.

2. Try this game at your next party. Seat the guests in a circle about you and instruct them that when you speak a word, the person at whom you point must respond instantly with the first word that comes to mind. Make up your list of words beforehand, trying to adapt them cleverly to individuals. Thus, give the word "strike" to a baseball player, the word "make-up" to a pretty girl, and so forth. The scene will be more tense and interesting if you assume something of the confident manner of the showman, discoursing volubly upon the power of psychology to pry out innermost thoughts through the laws of association and thrusting your finger directly under the nose of the "victim" as you fling his word at him.

3. Do this experiment. Appoint some member of the class to be the subject, and instruct him that he is to begin, on the signal, to say one hundred disconnected words. Appoint somebody to keep the time, somebody else to act as stenographer and take down the words as they are spoken, and a third assistant to give the "Go!" and the "Stop!" signals. The words given must not be strung together in any connected or serial order, like "one, two, three," and "January, February, March." Rather, they should be disconnected words, like "house, garage, cat, dog, man, go, come." After all the hundred words have been given, go through the list and identify the different chains of associations that linked themselves together in the subject's mind.

4. Review the diagram of Albert's being conditioned to fear a white rat, and construct a similar diagram to show conditioning in an original example. Use the standard form:

$$S^a(\qquad) - - - - - - - - - \rightarrow R(\qquad)$$
$$S^i(\qquad) \twoheadleftarrow - - - - - - - - \rightarrow R(\qquad)$$

With a little practice, you will be amazed to see how many of your responses are conditioned ones, and how readily the process by which they were conditioned may be diagramed.

WHAT OTHERS SAY

1. In Fiction:

The Hoosier Schoolmaster by Edward Eggleston. An American classic. The story of a schoolmaster in the pioneer days of Indiana, who, besides teaching psychologically, falls in love (also psychologically), is persecuted by the settlers, and finally wins through to "happiness forever after."

Tom Brown's School Days by Thomas Hughes. Another classic—an English one. A story of life and learning at Rugby, one of the most famous of the great English public schools.

Fortitude by Hugh Walpole. A strong story of the ultimate triumph over adversity of a man who, because of his brutalized childhood, had fortunately been conditioned to the courageous and noble outlook.

Joan and Peter by George H. Wells. A delicious satire on educational methods that attempt to adapt the learning process to the capacity of the youthful mind.

The Deepening Stream by Dorothy Canfield. A fascinating story depicting the growth and development of Matey as she progresses from one stage to another along the "deepening stream" of her life. The workings of her mind and her associations are exquisitely told.

2. In Drama:

Pygmalion by George Bernard Shaw. An extremely amusing comedy in which a crank on the subject of phonetics not only wagers with a friend that he can transform a flower girl into a smooth-spoken duchess, but actually succeeds so well in his effort that he is able to pass the girl off at court as a veritable woman of nobility.

3. In Poetry:

The Deserted Village by Oliver Goldsmith. Beautiful, nostalgic poem in which the poet's old associations with "Sweet Auburn! loveliest village of the plain" are stirred by the contemplation of the present wretched condition of the village.

WHAT'S AHEAD IN CHAPTER 9

Do We Tire from Work—or from Boredom?

It must be no easy task to unearth and prepare a half-dozen oddities every day in the week for the edification of sixty million people. Yet that is exactly what Robert L. Ripley does. To get the facts for his cartoons, Ripley has traveled into more than 200 different countries, and is obliged to weed through a daily mail pile of upwards of 3,000 letters. He is assisted by a staff of researchers who are said, on one occasion, to have searched through 10,000 books before they came upon a picture of the man whom Ripley was featuring in one of his cartoons—a Mexican President who served for exactly thirty-nine minutes!

A passion to dig out the queer and the unbelievable, and an interest in whatever is unusual or paradoxical have made the name of "Believe-It-or-Not" Ripley almost a by-word in a score of countries in which the 300 newspapers that carry his cartoons circulate.

The chances are ten to one that you don't know either Charles Lutwidge Dodgson, or the book he wrote called *Mathematica Curiosa*. The chances, on the other hand, are ten to one that you *do* know Lewis Carroll, and have read the books he wrote called *Alice's Adventures in Wonderland* and *Through the Looking-Glass and What Alice Found There!*

The surprising fact is that Lewis Carroll wasn't Lewis Carroll at all: he was Charles Dodgson, a staid and sober professor of mathematics in Oxford University! In his workaday life

Dodgson labored hard in his profession. But in his free time, putting on his Lewis Carroll. mask, he went journeying with Alice into Fairyland and created one of the most fascinating tales for children ever written. Who do you suppose will live longer in the memories of men: Charles Dodgson or Lewis Carroll?

Walter Finney—"dead tired," as he expressed it rebelliously to his mother when she met him at the door after school with the request that he run an errand for her at the corner store— voiced strong objection to the idea of doing any more work. What did his mother expect, anyway? This was the usual situation at 4:00 P.M.

At 4:20, after Walter had returned from the store grumblingly, and while he was sitting idly playing with his dog's ears, his attention was drawn to a peculiar yodel, issuing from somewhere down the street. Straightway both boy and dog dashed off in the direction of the yodel, which Walter had recognized as proceeding from the throat of his chum. At 6:20, two good hours later, the boy's father had literally to go across to the vacant lot and confiscate his son's baseball in order to get him home to supper!

Tired? Oh, no, he was not tired; two hours of running and shouting and yelling had left him warm, happy, and *rested,* so it appeared! And all this after he had been "dead tired" from his grueling school experience!

Interesting Work Is Not Tiring at All!

Here are three situations involving work of one sort or another. It is difficult to imagine that "Believe-It-or-Not" Ripley might be bored with his "daily grind"; rather, it is evident that, despite the difficulty he must experience in tracking down his material, he is quite as captivated by his quest for the unusual as are we who read about the oddities he accumulates in his cartoons. Lewis Carroll must have been indefatigable in his dual role of mathematician and fairy-tale writer. It is hard to think of him as bored by either of his occupations! And as for Walter Finney, however "dead tired" the work of the school day may have left him, his fatigue evaporated fast when his chum put in an appearance!

✦ ✦ ✦

In this chapter you will learn what, from the physiological standpoint, true fatigue is, and how its poisons accumulate in our bodies. You will make the discovery also that what popularly passes for fatigue isn't really fatigue at all, but that it is rather a psychological condition based upon boredom. You will learn something, too, about the values of hobbies as a means of making our lives more interesting and saving us from boredom.

Photo by Georgia Engelhard for Black Star

Fig. 37. Mountain climbing is grueling work that tests human endurance to the utmost—and yet fascinating work that grips the imagination and arouses the spirit of conquest. Do you think these climbers, reaching the peak of Mt. Victoria, Canada, are bored or easily fatigued?

9. WORK, FATIGUE, AND INTEREST

Before you begin work upon this chapter, contrast the work habits and attitudes of two different people whom you know well. Use a form like the following to make your entries upon:

HOW TO TELL WHETHER A PERSON'S WORK
INTERESTS OR BORES HIM

Mr. (Mrs. or Miss) X (to whom work is a pleasure)	Mr. (Mrs. or Miss) Y (to whom work is a grind)
1. Goes about work cheerfully and willingly	1. Goes about work sourly and grudgingly
2.	2.
3.	3.
4.	4.
5. etc.	5. etc.

This should make a reliable test that you could apply to anybody. How about applying the items—after you have thought them up—to Johnny Yourself (or Susie Yourself) and determining in the light of them whether you personally are more like X or Y?

WHAT IS WORK?

Two views about work. "The day's work"; "the work of the world"; "my work"; "a day's work for a day's pay"; "the working class"; "working conditions"! These are phrases that we hear used constantly. But what *is* work?

Judging from the mournful complaints of some workers, it is drudgery, almost slavery, with nobody to appreciate one's efforts, and with scanty remuneration into the bargain!

Other workers—and their number is considerable—speak of the satisfaction and joy they derive from their toil, of the essential dignity and nobility of it. Since earliest times philosophers and bards have upheld the virtues of the day's toil, and mankind generally has been always of the opinion that the way of achievement and satisfaction is the way of honest and persistent work.

The consumption of energy. Quite apart from the philosophical and the romantic, as well as the pessimistic pronouncements regarding it, we may define work from the physiological angle as merely the consumption of energy through the use of muscle and nerve. This energy has been derived by the body from the food and oxygen which have been taken into it and transformed into power. Purely from the viewpoint of the organism, the child shouting at play is *working* because he is expending energy in the process; so are the swimmer, the golfer, the reader of a "thriller."

Energy is unquestionably being consumed in doing those things which we ordinarily think of as restful or recreational, just as truly as it is in running a lathe, or building a house, or studying a lesson. People often come back after a vacation period more tired than they were when they went away because in their play they have been expending more energy than they had been in their workaday lives. On the other hand, people may perform their daily tasks for years and years and never know what it means to feel tired.

Prepare a form like the one at the top of page 218 and enter upon it all the kinds of work you do that you find interesting and enjoyable, and all the kinds which you find uninteresting or actually distasteful.

Apparently then, work may or may not lead to fatigue, and play may or may not lead to fatigue. Fatigue seems to be only partially related to the expenditure of energy.

MY DAY'S WORK

These Things Are Play to Me	These Things Are Work to Me
1. Studying ——————— (Subject)	1. Studying ——————— (Subject)
2.	2.
3.	3.
4.	4.
5. etc.	5. etc.

(Include all kinds of tasks that you customarily do in the course of the day at school, at home, and elsewhere.)

WHAT IS FATIGUE?

How a tired muscle feels. Such being the case, we need to inquire a little more carefully into the nature and meaning of fatigue. Let us start out by recalling the feeling which accompanies a tired muscle. Suppose you have been writing rapidly for an hour or longer. The muscles in your wrist and forearm and shoulder are cramped and aching, and it becomes increasingly harder for you to continue to move your pen across the paper. Very likely when the condition has become extremely uncomfortable, you will stop writing for a moment to put your fingers and wrist and arm through a miniature calisthenic exercise; you open and close your hand forcibly several times, rotating your wrist and perhaps massaging the muscles with your other hand; you may extend your arm downward passively for a few seconds; or you may raise both arms behind your neck and yawn and stretch vigorously before going back to your writing.

When you do resume, much of the stiffness and discomfort of the moment before will have gone, and you can continue to write for a considerable period without further annoyance. During the entire process your *left* arm and hand remained comfortable and unprotesting, and only the *working* muscles in your right arm ached.

Fatigue toxins, or wastes. Everybody knows that when coal is burning in a stove it is not only throwing off heat but is also producing wastes—ashes and clinkers—that must be removed if the fire is to continue to glow and burn freely. Precisely in the same way, when a muscle works it burns up the food and oxygen in it; at the same time wastes accumulate around it in the form of chemical substances that must be

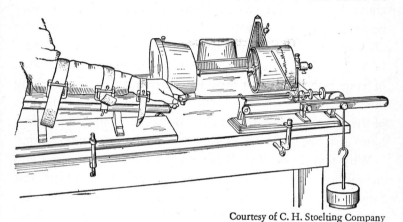

Courtesy of C. H. Stoelting Company

Fig. 38. Sketch of an ergograph, an apparatus for measuring and recording the onset of fatigue in a working muscle. The subject's arm is held in position at a comfortable angle by being strapped lightly along a slanting board. The middle finger is inserted in a loop attached to a weight which is suspended over a pulley. At each beat of the metronome (the top of which can be seen at the right) the subject bends his finger, thus drawing up the weight. A revolving drum is so placed that a pen, automatically moving to and fro as the weight is raised and lowered, records in a wavy line each contraction of the finger. In this way a record is provided of the rate at which fatigue is produced in the working muscle. During the first few contractions the pen writes boldly and the lines are high; but as the finger becomes more and more paralyzed by the accumulation of fatigue poisons around the muscles that operate it, the lines grow lower and lower, until at length the subject is totally unable to raise the weight. The wavy line then becomes straight.

removed or the muscle cannot keep on burning fuel. These wastes are often spoken of as *fatigue toxins,* that is, poisons which cause fatigue.

While you were writing rapidly, these toxins were being deposited around the working muscles and nerves somewhat faster than the blood could ferry them away. The blood was doing its best, and had you been working more slowly, it could have kept the channels clear of wastes. As it was, they became clogged, and you had to pause for a few seconds to allow the blood to cleanse them away so that more fuel could burn and yield its energy. If you compared the temperature of your two hands you would have found that the working one was much warmer than the resting one, a good indication of the fact that blood was circulating faster through the former hand as it brought in more fuel and ferried away more toxins.

Why toxins pile up. Wherever, in the body, muscles and nerves are working, food energy is being consumed and fatigue toxins are being thrown off into the blood stream. Up to a certain limit this building up and breaking down process remains balanced, and nature can ferry in the fuel and ferry out the toxins, thus enabling the organism to keep up its work for many hours. When the tempo of the activity is stepped up above the limit (as in the example of rapid writing) or when it is prolonged beyond the capacity of the body to maintain the balance mentioned, fatigue develops. It follows from this, of course, that the more vigorous the work performed, the more swift the onset of fatigue.

WHY MENTAL WORK CAUSES FATIGUE

Mental work uses up energy, too. What about *mental* work? Is it only the laborer, the physically, or muscularly, active person, who gets tired? Every school child knows better than that. Brain workers fatigue just the same as muscle

workers do; and students, teachers, professional men, accountants, bookkeepers, and the like, have just as much right to be
weary after a day's work as do teamsters, truckmen, builders,
ditch diggers, and athletes.

In the first place, even mental work involves the continuous
use of muscles; the brain worker must maintain his body in
an upright or sitting posture for hours at a time; he must use
the fine eye muscles in more or less constant reading or writ-

Photos by H. Armstrong Roberts and Black Star

*Fig. 39. Both this brain worker and this muscle worker are using
up energy. Which way of working is easier for you?*

ing; he must use hand, arm, and shoulder muscles to operate
adding machine or typewriter, to do handwriting or figuring.
These muscles consume energy and throw off toxins exactly
as do any other muscles in the body. In the second place, we
know that when nerve fibers conduct currents, as they have to
do in mental as well as in physical work, they also use up

energy and undergo chemical changes which lower their efficiency and yield fatigue toxins.

After all, then, there is no essential difference between physical work and mental work. The muscle worker has to use his brain and nervous system to regulate and direct his work; the brain worker has to use his muscles to take in the materials and to execute his ideas. About the only way we can distinguish between these two forms of activity is that in mental work the seat of fatigue is likely to be in the nerves and in the finer and smaller muscles, whereas in physical work the seat of fatigue is commonly in the larger, grosser muscles.

IMPORTANCE OF SLEEP AND REST

"Tired nature's sweet restorer!" When fatigue toxins—whether of muscular or nervous origin—accumulate in the blood in considerable quantity, the body feels tired and needs rest. About every sixteen hours or so they accumulate to the point where only rest through sleep can restore the efficiency of the organism. During sleep the consumption of energy is reduced to the very minimum; the cells are bathed with fresh energy through the intake of oxygen; the last traces of yesterday's toxins are removed along with the outgoing carbon dioxide; the muscles and other tissues that were damaged during the day are repaired.

Occasional rest periods are beneficial. But the body needs rest also between the times of nightly sleep. At intervals during the working hours we need to pause for a few moments to relax and "let down." Schools have recess periods and intermissions for this purpose. Industrial experts have found that when brief rest periods are introduced, during which the machines are shut down, the employees turn out more work, suffer fewer accidents, maintain a better mental attitude, and come through to the end of the day less fatigued than industrial workers used to be in the days when there was no respite from morning till night.

Housewives and workers in the home often take advantage of a few spare minutes in which they can sit down or lie down and rest. It is a good habit for any of us to form—taking time out for a "breathing space" once in a while during the active period of the day's tasks. By so doing we shall finish in much better form and feel distinctly less fatigued when night comes.

BOREDOM AND PSEUDO FATIGUE

The "fatigue" that quickly disappears. It is easy to fool ourselves about the degree of genuine fatigue we feel. Thus, the small boy who protested against going on an errand for his mother, on the ground that he was "all tired out" from a hard day in school, appeared anything but all tired out when a few minutes later his chum appeared in the offing and the two engaged in lively play for two full hours before the call to supper came! Similarly, the "fagged out" stenographer who arrives home from the office "half dead" finds it possible to dance for several hours in the evening, and the "tired" business man can trudge for miles over a golf course, while his equally "all in" wife can revive from her onerous household duties sufficiently to play bridge during half the afternoon and attend the theater with her husband in the evening!

Get tired of being bored! It looks as though the whole story was not always being told when we sympathize with ourselves or solicit sympathy from our friends because of an alleged condition of worn-outness! And the whole story is distinctly *not* being told. As a matter of fact, much that passes among us all for fatigue is not fatigue at all but *boredom*. It is not so often that we consume great amounts of energy during the day's work as it is that we are "bored to tears" by that same day's work!

In the case of the student who claims to be "dead tired" well before the end of the school day, the real fact is almost always that he is bored by the monotonous routine of school, by the sameness of the teacher's methods, by the unappealingness of the materials of knowledge, by the enforced physical inactivity that accompanies the traditional schoolroom experience, by the never-interrupted sequence of classes and study hours and lesson preparations, and perhaps by his own limited capacity and outlook. What he feels is not fatigue in any genuine sense, but a kind of pseudo fatigue which looks like the real thing and which is so commonly experienced as to be considered genuine by the rank and file of us.

Complete the following list:

THINGS THAT BORE ME

1. A dull conversation
2.
3.
4.
5. etc.

(It's easy to spot these things because they make you yawn and feel restless, "bore you to tears," give you a kind of pseudo fatigue.)

Almost nobody escapes boredom. The office worker, like the student, mistakes for real weariness the ennui and boredom that are attached to monotonous motions, unchanging surroundings, the unstimulating routine of adding figures, or typing, or taking down dictation, and the generally prosaic nature of the daily tasks. The factory or mill worker is "weary" not so much from the expenditure of energy as from the lack of stimulation, of interest, of variety in movement. The housewife tires of the ever-recurring round of meal planning, dishwashing, bedmaking, laundering, and housecleaning, with which her life is filled. In brief, whoever the worker and whatever the work, monotony almost always tends to increase the subjective feelings of fatigue without providing a justifiable objective basis for them.

If only there could be provided for everybody an interesting task and stimulating surroundings in which to do it, the daily "fatigue" that assails most of the workers of the world would be sharply reduced, and what remained of it would be un-questionably genuine.

AN INTELLIGENT ATTITUDE TOWARD WORK

This discussion of boredom suggests the importance of a sensible mental attitude toward the work we have to do. We have already referred to this matter in Chapter 5. Here we need only to add the plea that every young person facing a vocation of any sort whatever shall understand that his own day-by-day attitude toward it will determine pretty largely whether it is to be monotonous and boring to him or whether it will be stimulating and challenging.

The world of work is no vale of tears!   If you move through your daily tasks as through a vale of sorrow and hardship, you will lead an unhappy and perhaps even rebellious life. If, on the other hand, you see in the work you do not only an honest and honorable contribution to society but—more im-portant still—a medium through which you may express your originality and demonstrate your respect for honest work, even though it may have to be performed under drab circumstances and amid monotonous surroundings, your life will be im-measurably more satisfying and worth while.

By contrast with the man who goes grumblingly and un-willingly to the day's toil and performs it skimpingly and sullenly, the one who brings to his day's work optimism, interested curiosity, and the purpose of full and unreserved self-investment, is the happy and successful individual.

INTEREST AS A MOTIVE

A release from monotony. If every worker in every line of endeavor derived interest from the performance of his tasks, society would rarely be faced with strikes, lockouts, and industrial unrest. Even delinquency and crime, which so often take root in discontent and monotony, would be decreased unbelievably. Furthermore, the indifference and unwillingness that exist so widely among people in their routine workaday activities would be replaced with pleasurableness and enthusiasm, and the work of the world, as well as the workers, would benefit by a most healthy and stimulating upswing.

Immediate and derived interest. Interest in a task ordinarily springs from the personal enjoyment which one obtains from its performance. Something in the intrinsic nature of the job itself appeals to the doer, and he finds himself experiencing pleasurableness at his work. If the task stimulates him from the start, his interest may be said to be *immediate;* if early performance leaves him indifferent, but continued attention to it day after day and week after week leads him to experience an increased fascination with it, his interest may be said to be *derived.*

While some work is of such a nature as to challenge from the start, it must be expected that most work in which people engage requires an initial period of performance during which one has to learn to appreciate its importance and to enjoy doing it. Interest, in other words, grows upon the performer with the passing of time.

Enter upon a form like the following several illustrations of immediate interests and of derived interests that you yourself take pleasure in pursuing:

SOME OF MY INTERESTS

Immediate Interests (I've Always Had Them)	Derived Interests (I've Learned to Be Interested in Them)
1. Adventure stories	1. Collecting Washingtoniana
2.	2.
3.	3.
4.	4.
5. etc.	5. etc.

(Maybe the examples suggested do not apply in your case. Think out your own illustrations of both sorts of interests.)

How interest boosts our performance. Once the attitude of interest has been established, it becomes a strong motivating force in any line of work, driving us forward with new zest and bringing us new satisfactions. It is the incentive for many inventions that men set themselves to accomplish as side lines of their particular vocations; it is behind the efforts of the explorer to find new territory or new conditions of life; it goads on the artist, the architect, the craftsman, the writer, the actor, the specialist in any field. In fact, it is hard to see how one could achieve much success or satisfaction in any vocation or any line of endeavor if he lacked the stimulating incentive which interest in his task provides. "Get interested!" would be an excellent slogan for anybody in his vocational life.

Many careful experiments have been carried out by industrial plants, business houses, and even schools, to find out to what extent performance improves as interest in the work increases. Thus, in one instance, change from the daily set wage to the piece-work or bonus plan in a certain factory doubled production and aroused workers to a new interest in their work. In another instance, removing a group of delinquent boys from the humdrum atmosphere of the typical reform school and placing them in an educational environment where they could choose what they wished to do, so stimulated them that they gained a whole year in educational status in four months' time.

HOBBIES AND OUTSIDE INTERESTS

Interest in one's vocation is unquestionably, as we have seen, of prime importance. Still, as the old adage has it, "all work and no play makes Jack a dull boy." Most people are possessed of very much more potential energy than that used up in gaining their livelihood. The vocational day leaves large areas of their brains untouched and leaves them eager for the release of their unused powers. After the work of the vocational day is over, the avocational day should begin. Then is the time for all of us to busy ourselves with the special individual interests or hobbies that we happen to have.

Through our everyday contacts, vocational or otherwise, we should come upon at least one thing that arouses our curiosity and intrigues us to follow where it may lead. Such an interest may arise out of the special kind of work we do for a living— as, for example, the interest a postmaster developed in collecting rare stamps; or again, it may have no basis in our workaday life but may be touched off by some experience or contact wholly outside—as, for example, the interest which a housewife developed in cultivating an herb garden in her back yard because she happened to read a book about such a garden. Sometimes our interests, in whatever way they are derived, become so strong that they color and motivate much of our thinking and activity. Anybody who has a strong interest or hobby becomes almost a new individual as he cultivates and develops his taste.

THE COLLECTING INTEREST IS A GOOD ONE

One of the most fascinating of all hobbies is the collecting interest. There is no end nor limit to what collectors may devote themselves to. Stamps and old coins probably head the list in popularity, but the range of collectible objects is unlimited. Some collectors take the historical slant, as with Washingtoniana, period furniture, and glass; others indulge a literary bent and collect old books, first editions, or manuscripts; still others enjoy artistic objects and collect paintings, daguerreotypes, or vases.

Most collectors follow a particular lead because they chance to come into possession of something curious or unusual and are stimulated thereby to find other collectible objects that are similar, until before they know it they have become enthusiastic fans at collecting.

Thus, a high school boy who came into possession of the signature of a popular big-league player, sought and found means of inducing others of his favorite idols among ball players to send him their autographs. A lady who discovered in an attic some old bottles became so interested in them that she used them for the nucleus of what has since become a large and valuable collection. A thirteen-year-old girl in poor health, urged by the family to be out of doors a great deal, became so interested in butterflies and moths that she began a collection which yielded her, within three or four years, several thousand specimens from every quarter of the globe and a scientific interest that will be always with her.

INTERESTS AND MORE INTERESTS!

Collecting is, of course, but one of many avocational interests which may be indulged by any of us. A business man devoted years of study to the life and work of Jan Vermeer, a noted Dutch artist of the seventeenth century, and has become probably the best living student of Vermeer. A printer devoted most of his spare time for seven years to producing a miniature copy of the quatrains of Omar Khayyám, which is so tiny that the pages can be read only with a magnifying glass and the entire book can be tucked into the setting of an ordinary signet ring.

A housewife, discovering that she could whittle, has spent much of her time for years carving wooden animals which net her good prices at a local arts-and-crafts shop. A woman having some leisure and a good reading voice spends several hours each week reading to the inmates of a city home for the blind. A teacher with imagination and a good sense of rhythm writes poems that are published regularly in standard magazines.

A professional man spends much time hooking rugs of intricate pattern and has produced scores of them during his off hours. A high school girl, a good debater and a good organizer, has brought about the formation of a debating society in her school and led it several times to victory over competing schools. An office worker, fascinated by genealogy, haunts historical societies and libraries, tracing down family lines for her friends.

A storekeeper enjoys building ship models and devotes most of his evenings to his hobby. A newspaper man with a good voice has organized in his city a light opera club which produces two or more Gilbert and Sullivan operas each season. A barber, interested in the evolution of the tonsorial art through the ages, has spent much time and money in obtaining possession of historical implements and panels depicting the progress of barbering through three thousand years.

INTERESTS EVERYWHERE: FIND THEM!

The opportunities for finding and pursuing avocational interests in the ordinary environment in which we live are innumerable. Leisure hours filled with activities like these are hours profitably spent: membership in literary clubs, play-reading clubs, orchestras, choral societies, music appreciation groups, amateur theatrical groups, fraternal organizations, photographic clans, outdoor sports clubs; interest in the theater, in motion pictures, in nature study, in church work, in social service, in making scrapbooks, in wood turning, in modeling, in sketching, in block printing, in reading, in writing, in local history, in athletics; enrollment in self-improvement courses; interest in handicrafts and the decorative arts, in microscopy and scientific research; enjoyment of hunting, fishing, mountain climbing, riding, motoring, boating, yachting, scouting, mechanics, amateur radio, dancing, camping and musical training.

These are just a few of the myriads of possible interests and hobbies which are available in any environment and which people find highly agreeable. Participation in one or more of these, or in any other avocational activity which happens to allure us, is the finest way in which we may find new channels of expression, new viewpoints and ideas, new friends, new opportunities to develop our originality and resourcefulness.

List your own hobbies in the left-hand column and those of people you know in the right-hand column of a form prepared like this one:

SOME HOBBIES AND INTERESTS

My Hobbies	Hobbies of Other People I Know
1.	1.
2.	2.
3.	3.
4.	4.
5. etc.	5. etc.

(Maybe you have in mind some additional hobby or interest in which you think you would find enjoyment sometime. If so, include it in your list, marking it with an asterisk [*].)

THE USE OF LEISURE TIME

A problem of the machine age. It does not make much difference what one does in his free hours, provided only that he does something that appeals to him and affords him a healthful and constructive means of self-expression. The advent of the machine age has served to reduce sharply the number of workaday hours in business and industry and has in consequence left millions of people with large quantities of free time on their hands.

Our forefathers, in the simpler economic environment in which they lived, were compelled to toil early and late to win their livelihood. The working day in many lines of endeavor began at sunrise and continued until sunset. The modern worker, with his day already reduced in many occupations to eight hours and even less, is faced with several hours of waking life before bedtime. Sociologists are rightly concerned over the nature of the activities pursued during this new-found leisure which people now enjoy.

If the hours following the day's work are unfilled by anything constructive or self-improving, we shall be likely either to spend them in destructive and harmful ways or else to fritter them away in idleness and in lounging aimlessly about. Idleness, at best, begets smugness, stupor, pseudo fatigue and a colossal indifference to everything, including our daily work.

It's a wonderful age to live in! With plenty of spare time on our hands and unlimited possibilities for enjoyable avocational pursuits, we of the modern age ought to have infinitely richer and more satisfying lives than any other people in history have ever had. In past ages only the wealthy leisure class could indulge their fancies; in the present age nearly everybody has the leisure once enjoyed only by kings and nobles.

It will be interesting to take a glance at your own leisure time—the time at your disposal after your school and home duties of the day are completed, or when you are not engaged in any of them. Use the following form as a model for working out your daily calendar of leisure time:

HOW I SPEND MY TIME

Time Spent in School	Time Spent in Doing Home-work	Time Spent in Helping at Home	Time Spent in Earning Money	Time Spent in Bed	Time Spent in Other Duties	LEISURE TIME ON MY HANDS
Monday						
Tuesday						
Wednesday						
Thursday						
Friday						
Saturday						
Sunday						
TOTALS						(This is the important item!)

Learn to enjoy life!   People who have attractive personalities are nearly always those who have learned how to live satisfyingly through the pursuit of many interests and ambitions. They are not dumb creatures with impoverished souls and narrow outlooks; instead, they are keenly alive to the vast resources of enjoyment and enduring satisfaction, and they are wise enough to tap these resources at many points. If you would be numbered among those fortunate and happy folks who enjoy being alive and are in turn a never-failing source of enjoyment and inspiration to their friends, get interested in something worth while and see what a difference it will make in your outlook upon the world and in the world's attitude toward you!

HOW PSYCHOLOGISTS WORK

Experimentation in fatigue, as it relates itself to physical and mental efficiency, has yielded some very interesting conclusions. One investigator, a young woman graduate student, set herself the task of multiplying four-place numbers by four-place numbers for twelve hours without a break. She started in at eleven in the morning and continued her task until eleven at night. At the close of the experiment, she was still going forward with her multiplying, but she was taking almost double as much time per problem as she required earlier. Only the strongest kind of motivation, of course, could have held her to such a consuming task; even her strong scientific desire to find out whether, if a person drove herself hard enough, she could keep working efficiently, could not stave off the effects of accumulating fatigue.

Another investigator, a man, repeating the multiplication experiment, started in at eleven o'clock at night after a heavy day's work. For the first hour, he felt little subjective fatigue, but by the third hour he was making constant errors, and by the fourth he was so completely exhausted that he gave up and had to be helped to bed. His conclusion was that there finally comes a limit in mental work, when the mind simply refuses to function, and that that limit comes suddenly.

Experiments have been made also in physical work to determine the nature of fatigue curves. In industrial plants it has been found by careful research that the rate of work improves at first as the worker warms to his task and gets under full momentum. The peak of production has been found to come for most workers at about eleven o'clock in the forenoon, with a falling off during the last hour before lunch. Following

lunch the curve of production sags again and then swings up
to the afternoon peak by about three o'clock, falling off again
toward the close of the day.

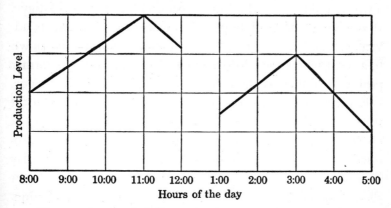

Fig. 40. Graph of daily production in an industrial plant.

A study of accidents in industrial plants and factories indicates the significant fact that when fatigue is highest among
the workers the number of accidents rises. Accidents occur
commonly also during times of the day in which momentum
either has not been worked up or else has died down. There
seems to be even a weekly rhythm, more or less identical in
pattern with the daily one in the factory. Monday is the day
of the smallest output and the most accidents; Thursday is
the peak day, when production is at its best and accidents are
diminished; and Saturday shows a diminution of output and a
rise in accidents.

The introduction of brief rest periods during production
hours has been demonstrated by several investigators to be of
advantage, both in bringing the worker through to the end of
the day in better form, and in increasing his volume of output.
Uninterrupted wheeling of bricks and mortar will, for example, result in a falling off in efficiency before many hours

have passed. Increasingly fewer barrow loads will be wheeled per hour, and the workman will show needless strain. Introduce a brief rest period of not more than five minutes once in a while, and he will wheel more loads with diminished fatigue. If the length of the idle period is extended, however, its advantage will be lost, because the momentum will die down to a point where the effort required to build it up to its former peak will counteract the good effects of recovery from fatigue.

Experiments carried on in industrial plants in England at the time of the First World War by the British commission in charge of labor relations showed rather conclusively that production is actively increased when the twelve-hour work day is reduced to an eight-hour one. Even under the stress of war the patriotic motive appealed to in the workers failed to stimulate them to as high an output in twelve hours as they were able to produce in eight. Knowledge that the work day is short is a powerful motive in encouraging the worker to keep his level of production reasonably high.

Similarly, these same experiments in England proved a six-day week to be better than a seven-day one from the standpoint both of factory output and of worker morale.

TO HELP YOU LEARN

Some Questions to Answer

1. How can anybody distinguish between work and play? May work be play? May play be work? May either be relatively non-fatiguing? Explain each answer.

2. Can you tell in your own words exactly what it is that causes muscles and nerves to be genuinely tired after exercise?

3. What happens during sleep that causes the body and the brain to feel refreshed and free from fatigue afterwards? Have you ever awaked in the morning feeling unrefreshed? What explanation can you offer?

4. Do you know of any hobby or interest that so fascinated someone that it changed the whole course of his vocational life? Explain.

5. What great men of history or well-known characters in literature can you name who were driven forward by tremendous interest in their work?

WORKING WITH PSYCHOLOGY

1. Make a survey of the principal leisure-time activities for which your community offers opportunity. Include, in addition to theaters, dance halls, and other commercial amusement places, such agencies as boys' and girls' clubs, men's clubs, women's clubs, athletic fields, public parks, community centers, libraries, and the like. If possible confer with the director or another official of one of the organizations on your list and try to form a reliable picture of the leisure-time services which it renders to the community: the number of people who benefit weekly from it, its sources of income, its per capita cost, its personnel, and so on.

2. Do the following experiment. Using the diagram, Figure 38, as a guide, construct a simple ergograph for studying the accumulation of fatigue poisons in your hand and forearm. A simple way to do this would be to tie a two-pound weight on one end of a string three feet long and make a loop on the other end. Pass your middle finger through the loop and lay your forearm along the side of a table top, allowing the weight to hang freely. Then, keeping your eyes on the second hand of a watch, draw up the weight every two seconds, allowing it to drop back immediately. Count the number of times you can pull the weight up before fatigue paralyzes your hand and arm. Pay careful attention to the feeling of fatigue as it progresses in your working muscles.

3. Make a visit to some near-by establishment where several workers are employed—for example, a factory, a store, a telephone exchange—and find out in what way or ways the management is trying to promote good attitudes and increase production. Some ways would be making the workroom attractive, keeping the

machines in A-1 condition, providing comfortable rest rooms, introducing occasional rest periods during the working hours. Does it seem to you that the management understands how important it is to keep work from appearing to be a form of drudgery in which the employees are exploited for the sake of what they can turn out?

4. In the days before the industrial revolution, mass production was unknown; each master workman produced at his own bench, unit by unit. Apprentices served under him until they became skilled enough to open their own independent shops. There were shoemakers' guilds, weavers' guilds, cabinetmakers' guilds, coopers' guilds, and so forth. Think out the advantages and the disadvantages of the guild system and of the modern factory system of mass production, keeping in mind the effects of both upon worker and product, and prepare an oral defense of one or the other system. If there is disagreement among the students, here will be an interesting opportunity for the class to have a debate on the subject: "Resolved, that the guild system was superior to the factory system."

WHAT OTHERS SAY

1. In Autobiography:

An American Doctor's Odyssey by Victor Heiser. An absorbing account of the labors of a physician engaged in a great international campaign to wipe out the most malignant diseases of man. Dr. Heiser's profound interest in his task illumines every page.

I Married Adventure by Osa Johnson. To leave a comfortable home in Kansas, marry a man whose consuming passion was to photograph cannibals and wild animals, and go adventuring with him into the most dangerous corners of the world—this was the life of Osa Leighty. On the evening before his tragic death, her husband remarked: "Even the hard part has been fun!" That's the true spirit of work!

2. In Fiction:

The Life and Strange Surprising Adventures of Robinson Crusoe by Daniel Defoe. A classic tale of the shipwreck, escape to a desert island, and subsequent adventures of the hero. Crusoe's methodical and unflagging industry in conquering his harsh environment is portrayed.

The Adventures of Tom Sawyer by Mark Twain. A romantic saga of the Mississippi, full of fun and mischief. Occasionally bored with life, often working like a beaver to carry through his plans, Tom is a perfect example of a good bad boy. An American classic you ought to read. And while you're about it, read also Mark Twain's *Huckleberry Finn*.

Big Doc's Girl by Mary Medearis. Set in the back country of Arkansas, this tale of a cultured family, devoted to the task of bringing happiness and delight to unschooled but generous people, is movingly sincere.

3. In Drama:

Dear Brutus by James M. Barrie. After living unsatisfying lives that have been largely wasted, would not any nine people feel a new zest and enthusiasm if they could be given a chance to live their lives over again? It actually happens in this play, but only one of the nine profits by the opportunity.

4. In Poetry:

The Village Blacksmith by Henry W. Longfellow. Vivid picture of a toiling smith who

> Each morning sees some task begun;
> Each evening sees its close.

An unmatched glorification of honest work, with good cheer in the doing of it and gratitude for the chance to wet his brow with "honest sweat."

Do Your Emotions Help You or Hinder You?

One day when she was about thirteen years of age, a French peasant girl, Joan of Arc, believed that she heard the voice of an angel speaking thus to her: "I come from God to help thee to live a good and holy life. Be good, Jeannette, and God will aid thee!"

From then on for the next four years, Joan continued to hear the voices of angels addressing her and urging her to be faithful to God and to country.

Meantime, the wars in which Europe was engaged brought an English army against France, and the city of Orleans was laid siege to. Convinced by the voices that heaven had decreed that she should lead the French defenders, and impassioned with a patriotic fervor that swept all opposition from her pathway, Joan received the blessing of King Charles VII and set forth to raise the siege of Orleans. Clad in a suit of mail and bearing aloft a white banner, she rode her charger at the head of the French columns, and actually succeeded in turning back the attacking hosts.

Even the treachery of the Burgundian soldiers who captured her and sold her to the English, her subsequent trial as a sorceress and heretic, and her final condemnation and burning at the stake failed utterly to dull the fierce glow of her devotion to God and country. Four and three-quarters centuries later, in recognition of her fidelity and faith, Joan of Arc was beatified by Pope Pius X.

In ancient times it was customary in China to compel any person suspected of a crime to undergo the "ordeal of rice." Chun Moy, for example, has been accused of having stolen Sun Tong's rice. The magistrate assembles the populace and the trial gets under way.

Into Chun's mouth is thrust a small handful of dry, uncooked rice, and he is commanded to chew it. After he has turned the rice around and around in his mouth for some time, working his jaws actively the while, Chun is directed by the magistrate to spit out the rice upon a sacred fig leaf which has been placed in front of him. In great fear and trembling, Chun does as he is bidden, and the magistrate examines the mass. If he finds that it is wet, indicating that Chun Moy's saliva has been flowing properly, he declares Chun to be innocent of the crime and acquits him of the charge. But woe be to Chun Moy if his rice is dry! Fear has dammed up his saliva: his own mouth has condemned him as the guilty man!

Can you see any fallacy in the "ordeal of rice"?

Alice Strong and Patty Wentworth are both seniors in the Jefferson High School. Patty is a popular girl, well liked by everybody in her class—everybody, that is, except Alice! The trouble is that Alice, who has never seemed to make any close friends among her classmates, is extremely jealous of Patty, whose popularity has increased rather than diminished during the past three years of high school. She has done well in sports, has captained the girls' soccer team, has always had plenty of masculine attention at school parties, and has stood pretty well in her studies.

Alice, resentful and envious of Patty, has held herself aloof from most school activities, especially those in which Patty is prominent, and has become more or less of a recluse. Nobody notices her very much, and she has never had any attention from boys. Piqued by Patty's success, Alice has not hesitated in times past to make disparaging remarks about her, to minimize her successes, and to ignore her studiedly in everything she does.

Jealousy, that green-eyed monster!

Emotions Are Powerful Human Drives

Something of the range and power of human emotion may be felt in these three examples. Religious fervor, love of country, zealous pursuit of what is noble and unselfish inspire men and women to invest their lives in great causes; fear, apprehension, terror make their tongues literally cleave to their mouths; jealousy, envy, resentment distort their views of their neighbors and make them sour and sometimes hateful in their attitudes toward them.

It appears that our emotions are powerful determiners of our actions and conduct.

✦ ✦ ✦

In this chapter you will investigate some of the principal emotions that drive men. You will learn why we have rage, fear, sympathy, love, and all the rest; why our emotions are of such constructive value if rightly used. You will learn also some right and some wrong ways to express emotion.

Photos by Keystone View Company and by Roy Pinney for Monkmeyer

Fig. 41. How would you interpret the emotions of these six men? What common emotions are missing?

10. OUR FEELINGS AND EMOTIONS

Before you begin work on this chapter, take time to record on a form prepared like the following as many situations as you can think of in which you commonly experience (1) pleasurable feelings and (2) feelings of annoyance.

MY GAMUT OR RANGE OF FEELING

In These Situations I Usually Experience Pleasurableness	In These Situations I Usually Experience Annoyance
1. Reading an interesting story	1. Hunting for something that I've misplaced
2.	2.
3.	3.
4.	4.
5. etc.	5. etc.

Since life is filled every day with the pleasant and the unpleasant, you will have little difficulty in doing this exercise. On some days everything goes smoothly; on other days things go badly. This intermingling of the gratifying and the annoying is what makes life. We can hardly expect our day-by-day experience to bring us only the pleasant and agreeable.

THE PLEASANT-UNPLEASANT GAMUT OF LIFE

Our feelings are like a pendulum. The pendulum of life seems to swing back and forth between experiences that are pleasant and experiences that are unpleasant. True, a given feeling tone of pleasurableness may stay constant for a considerable period, unlike the incessantly changing pendulum of the clock; and a given feeling tone of unpleasantness may likewise linger for minutes, or even hours. Sooner or later, however, for most people pleasurable feelings diminish and tend to be replaced by the opposite, and vice versa. This is life, and however earnestly we may strive to keep the pleasurable within our grasp, it is inevitable that the unpleasant will ultimately have its inning.

Feeling is a difficult term to describe, for we have no sense organs specifically to report feelings to us, as we do to report sensations.

The physical side of our feelings. Yet we are agreeably conscious of pleasant feeling tones and disagreeably conscious of unpleasant ones. In general, it appears that when our organism is carrying on smoothly and adequately, we tend to experience feelings of pleasurableness; when it is functioning inadequately, we experience the reverse. Thus, from the purely physical angle, when we are eating a toothsome meal, or when the meal is digesting smoothly, or when we are warm and sleepy and the conditions are right for going to sleep, or when we are relaxed and resting comfortably, or again when all the internal processes are going on harmoniously and smoothly, we experience a vague feeling of pleasantness and well-being.

On the other hand, let food be lacking or digestion be disturbed; let the body be chilled; let our nerves be profoundly wrought up; let opportunity for sleep be lacking; or let there be anywhere within our inner organism pain or malfunctioning, then we experience either a vague or a pronounced feeling of ill-being and annoyance. There is some basis for the common belief that the man with a good digestion is an optimist, whereas the man with a poor digestion is a pessimist.

OUR HIGHER FEELINGS FOLLOW THE SAME GAMUT

Blocked ideas and smooth-flowing ones. On higher levels than the physical, too, agreeable feeling is associated with smooth internal functioning and disagreeable feeling with impeded or disturbed organic processes. If, for example, you are in a group in which you find it difficult to hold up your end of the conversation or to express yourself satisfactorily, the unpleasant feelings you experience are undoubtedly associated with a blocked nervous system or speech apparatus, or perhaps with circulatory disturbances that give you a flushed face and an uncomfortable feeling of warmth. Let your ideas flow freely, however, and let the conversation be of such a nature or in such surroundings that you are stimulated to throw yourself agreeably into the situation, then your obvious feeling of pleasurableness reflects an unhampered nervous discharge, ready speech muscles, and an exhilarating consciousness of internal harmony and strength.

Some kind of feeling is always present. Similarly, you may feel pleasurableness when among friends, when on the threshold of a new and exciting experience, when reading a good story, when doing your lessons easily. You may, on the contrary, feel annoyance or disagreeableness when only strangers are about, when you are tired or bored by the sameness of experience, when you are reading an uninteresting but required book, when your lessons "come hard." No matter what the situation or the setting, subtle and usually vague sensations from the internal organism go along with either a pleasurable or an unpleasurable feeling tone. In general, free, unhampered, and smooth inner functioning favors the former feeling, while impeded or jerky functioning favors the latter.

There are relatively few life experiences that are so neutral as to fail to arouse feeling of one sort or the other. At any given moment we are likely to be either comfortable or uncomfortable, pleased or displeased, gratified or annoyed. To the extent that we can keep the pendulum of feeling on the agreeable end of the gamut, we shall be happy and content. To the degree that conditions, either within or without, push the pendulum over to the opposite end of the gamut, we shall feel frustrated and uncomfortable.

HOW DO EMOTIONS DIFFER FROM FEELINGS?

Emotions are born of feeling. At the extremes either of pleasantness or of unpleasantness, feeling merges into emotion. Whenever an experience becomes so intense or overpowering as to stir up the entire physical organism internally, we experience emotion, such as fright, rage, hate, and ecstasy. When we are under stress of powerful emotions such as these, the face may blanch or flush, the muscles may grow taut, the pupils of the eye may dilate or narrow down to a pin point, the hair may literally stand on end, the organs of speech may erupt, or the posture may assume a pattern of defiance or of flight.

It is usually not very difficult for an observer to identify the particular emotion which a person is experiencing at any given moment by outward signs such as these. Even though we become surprisingly adept in covering up many of our feelings and milder emotions, we are usually quite at the mercy of the more intense ones and find it next to impossible to conceal them from those around us.

INTERNAL ACCOMPANIMENTS OF EMOTION

Do we act first or feel first? An emotion is always accompanied by a definitely agitated or stirred up state of the internal organs. Some students of emotion have insisted that it is this internal agitation that leads up to the brain and sets off an emotion; others have felt that our conscious awareness that we are angry or afraid spreads downward from the brain and arouses the visceral, or internal, organs to abnormal activity. Those who, following the earlier psychologists like William James and Carl Lange, subscribe to the first point of view say that we feel fear because we run away, that the involuntary act of running away sets off the emotion. Those who, like W. B. Cannon, put the thing the other way around are of the opinion that the organic agitation we feel during emotion follows rather than precedes the mental state, that we run away because we feel afraid.

Emotion stirs the body profoundly. Whichever may be ultimately shown to be the correct viewpoint, nobody discounts the fact that in times of emotion there is a profound upheaval of internal processes and functions deep within our bodies. The apprehensive man loses his appetite and cannot eat; or if he eats, his food does not digest but lies "like a lump" in his stomach. The angry man experiences a pounding heart, and an abnormal volume of blood is shot into his muscles to help him to defend himself. In both cases nature withdraws blood from the digestive organs, where it is not immediately needed, and concentrates it in strong volume in muscles that may require it for purposes of self-defense, of offense, or of actual flight to safety.

Swift bodily changes occur. Brilliant experimental work has shown also that during highly emotional states there is a rise in blood pressure, an improvement in muscle tone throughout the entire body, a release of sugar from the liver into the blood, an increase in the number of red corpuscles, a reduction of conscious fatigue, and, if the body is wounded, a more rapid coagulation of blood than normally occurs.

All these radical changes obviously prepare the body of the emotionally aroused individual to meet the emergency of fright or of anger more adequately. A rise in blood pressure increases the power of the organism to use its resources; an improvement in muscle tone makes the body more alert and ready; a release of sugar into the blood stream furnishes immediate energy for the muscles to use; an increase in red corpuscles brings more oxygen from the outside so that the energy from the food can be more promptly used; a reduction of fatigue makes it possible for the individual to struggle on without exhaustion until safety or satisfaction is achieved.

OUR SIMILARITY TO ANIMALS

It is easy to see how animals living in the jungle and confronted constantly by dangers that must be met or fled from are benefited by these internal bodily changes. It is not so easy to understand why it is that human beings, especially civilized human beings, who rarely need to exert themselves either in physical combat or in taking to their heels, should have this same internal equipment for emergency action that the animals have. About the only explanation appears to be that, though we no longer live the primitive forest life that our ancestors once lived, we still possess the internal body mechanisms and impulses that they had.

Civilization has removed the need for violent internal agitation to conquer physical emergencies, but the capacity is still undiminished. Society may frown alike upon a physical attack upon an enemy and upon a cowardly running away from danger: the impulse to attack and the impulse to take to our heels is still present, along with all the internal physiological aids that are set off automatically whenever we feel anger or fear, or any other strong emotion. We shall discuss a bit later in this chapter the importance of learning to regulate our emotional life so that the body may not suffer damage from the internal agitation that accompanies strong feeling.

THE TWO STRONGEST HUMAN EMOTIONS

Anger is a universal emotion. We have all experienced anger! From the earliest weeks of our lives we have sought to get our own way and to impose our will upon others. Whenever any person or any thing impedes us, or restrains us, or belittles us, or is otherwise felt to be interfering with our plans, he or it is apt to feel our wrath.

The baby kicks and screams if he is held too tightly, or if his dinner is not forthcoming when he wants it. Grown older, the child flies into a passion when his belongings are taken from him, when he loses in a game, when his prestige is challenged. The high school pupil resents slights, suspicions of his motives, sarcastic remarks, unfair treatment, being babied. The man of affairs is angered by unfair business competition, by misrepresentation of goods, by deceit and trickery, by lack of appreciation from his superiors, by defiance in his home.

List for yourself some of the common things that "make you boil," "get your goat," cause you to lose your temper. Use the form below.

THINGS THAT MAKE ME ANGRY

1. Seeing anybody strike a child
2.
3.
4.
5. etc.

(Worth-while people usually rebel—openly or silently—against many things. Are you worth while, in this sense? Your list will show.)

The good and the bad in anger.   There is literally no end to the conditions that arouse our anger. From annoyance at a persistent fly that buzzes about our head to bitter hatred of the base deeds of war lords and tyrants, we react characteristically. This powerful emotion leads to crime, or to needful reform; to work for peace, or to work for war; to the instigation of wrong, or to the righting of wrong. It motivates great areas of our human conduct, inspiring us on the one hand to champion,

against their aggressors, the weak, the poor, the underprivi-
leged, and on the other hand to plot vengeance, destroy
property, incite rebellion. As the righteous wrath of the reformer, anger has led to most of the great and enduring social
achievements of the race. As the blind hate of the antisocial
individual, it has led to devastation and carnage. Like Galahad
of old, men still despise the evil in the world, and even if
they do not ride forth, like him, to overthrow it and establish
justice in its place, they throw the weight of their influence on
the side of social betterment.

As we come to resent injustice and vice and their ugly role
in the drama of life upon the earth, we are likely to join forces
with other like-minded crusaders and to battle against whatever we believe to be retarding human progress and happiness.
Those who champion the weak, the poor, the underdog; those
who strive to rid society of its slums, its child labor, its crime,
its selfishness, its ignorance and disease—these people are activated fundamentally by indignation. Anger or wrath thus
becomes a powerful ally to the forces of good in the world.

Fear is a powerful deterrent.   Perhaps when you were very
young, somebody frightened you with threats of the "ragman's
bag," the "dark closet," the "bogeyman," the "policeman," the
"doctor-man," or with some other dimly understood power
that was calculated to make you behave properly when nothing
else could. Poor punishments in themselves, these appeals to
fear often lay the basis in children for much nervousness and
apprehensiveness.

Pity the poor child!   As if this sort of mishandling by adults
were not enough, the child finds as he grows older all sorts
of mounting fears across his pathway. He is warned not to
tell lies and not to be naughty; he is cautioned against catch-
ing cold, being friendly toward strange dogs, making too
much noise at his play, breaking dishes and windows; he

either receives, or lives in imminent expectation of receiving, scoldings and sarcasm from parents and teachers; he is reminded pointedly by his elders that all his deeds and even his thoughts are being noted by the recording angel; he suffers now and again the blame for occurrences which he did not engineer; he is scolded for being impolite, heedless, bold; for being shy, timid, reserved; for being sleepy when he ought to be wide-awake, or wide-awake when he ought to be sleepy; for forgetting errands, indulging in horseplay, upsetting the family tranquillity.

Considering all these disconcerting experiences, it is small wonder that many of us grow up the victims of all sorts of fears and dreads.

An example of conditioned fear.   A common source of fears that often persist for life is *emotional conditioning*. In a previous chapter we referred to conditioning as a principle of learning. The case of Betty Pomeroy is a striking example of how fear of a thunderstorm was firmly established in a child by conditioning.

A loud crash of thunder! A blinding flash of lightning! A shriek from the tense lips of a nervous aunt! That was all; but it was enough to condition a seven-year-old girl to a lifetime's fear of electrical storms. It all happened one summer day when the aunt was visiting in the little girl's home. The family was gathered about the dining table, at lunch. Little Betty was the first to finish her meal, and, attracted by the growing dusk, she slid back her chair and ran to the window to look out at the sky. There was a casual remark or two at the table to the effect that a shower seemed to be coming up, but nobody appeared to be particularly concerned about it: that is, nobody but the aunt, who kept turning her head in the direction of the window behind her and shuddering nervously at the sight of the lowering sky.

"Oh, don't I hate thunderstorms!" she exclaimed.

The child's mother, possibly sensing the danger of conditioning Betty, glanced hastily in the girl's direction to see if she had heard. It appeared she had not, for she drew a chair up to the window and climbed up on it. Her nose pressed against the pane, she was watching in fascination the gathering clouds and the first dashes of rain.

Then, suddenly, nature's artillery was touched off and the storm broke.

The nervous aunt screamed in dismay.

"Get away, Betty!" she cried, half cowering behind her raised hands. "Don't stay in that window! You'll be struck!"

The child whimpered with fear and scrambled hastily down from the chair into the outstretched arms of her mother, who did her best to distract Betty. But Betty could only bury her face on her mother's shoulder and sob fitfully. A second crash of thunder and a second shriek from the aunt did not help the situation any. Neither did a third, and a fourth. The mother rose shortly and led Betty from the dining room. The child peered furtively at her aunt through her tears, as she went out, only to behold the spectacle of a very frightened woman with her hands pressed over her ears and her eyes tightly closed. Betty was conditioned by this very dramatic incident to a fear of thunderstorms.

Recall some of the things of which you have been at some time or other afraid, listing them on a form like the one at the top of page 254.

CHRONIC WORRIERS

Sources of worry. As a natural result of threats and punishments received in childhood, of warnings and scoldings repeatedly administered, and of conditioned fears learned from others, many of us grow up victims of all sorts of dreads, fears, and anxieties. By the time adulthood is reached we are apt to be afraid of many objects or conditions that should not arouse

FEARS I HAVE HAD

Object or Situation	Age at Which I Was Afraid of It	Probable Reason for My Fear	My Present Attitude
1. Cats	4 to 6 years	Once a cat jumped on my bed and startled me.	I like cats a lot.
2.			
3.			
4.			
5. etc.			

(Most people have some conditioned fears, or have had them at some previous time. If you have not, you are very fortunate.)

fear at all. People who are particularly sensitive or imaginative are likely to suffer the most from these needless worries.

In the adult world of affairs such individuals tend to become chronic worriers about one thing or another. They worry over their jobs, over the status of their business, over the kind of impression they make on their associates. Their minds conjure up the certainty that they are sick or are going to be shortly, that their friends are untrustworthy, that their children are going to die. They are apprehensive about a thousand things that the rational individual dismisses utterly from his mind.

What worry does to us. At the extreme, of course, these people shade off into the neurotic and the unstable; at best, they waste their energies over minor forebodings and anxieties and tend to build their lives rather about fear than about confidence and serenity. The unfortunate long-time effects of such chronic states as these upon the health and efficiency of the individual, involving as they do profound internal physical disturbances, can only be estimated. A temporary state of fear stirs up the physiological organism badly enough; but when the emotional state is prolonged into a chronic condition of apprehensiveness and anxiety, the subtle effects upon the whole organism are obviously multiplied.

OTHER IMPORTANT HUMAN EMOTIONS

Love "makes the world go round." Anger and fear are unquestionably the strongest of all our emotions. They are also the earliest ones to be exhibited by the infant, and for that reason also they may be presumed to be the most significant. If the only emotional states we ever exhibited were those of rage and fright, however, our lives would be lived necessarily on a rather primitive level. We expect savages to be motivated in large part by these two great drives; we expect something quite different of civilized human beings. Love and sympathy, for example, represent powerful driving forces in our lives. The former is associated with filial devotion, parental sacrifice, matrimonial stability, the communion of friends, and, on a higher level, reverence for the Deity.

If love does not actually "make the world go round," it certainly does exert a profound influence over us and over our affairs. Sympathy, born of understanding and a warm imagination, is associated with all actions that aim to help the sick, the bereaved, the unfortunate, the impoverished, and the wronged. Sympathy sometimes arises from anger or resentment; sometimes it springs from the ability of a person to imagine himself in somebody else's place.

The world would be immeasurably poorer had it not been for the many men and women of history who have been activated by warm human sympathies and by love for their fellow men in the establishment of reforms, movements, and institutions intended to benefit the race.

On a form similar to the one at the top of page 256, see how many benefactors of mankind, both men and women, you can identify.

CONTRIBUTIONS OF LOVE AND SYMPATHY TO CIVILIZATION

Name of Individual	Contribution to Society
1. Clara Barton	1. The Red Cross
2.	2.
3.	3.
4.	4.
5. etc.	5.

(History is quite as much a record of unselfish and generous deeds as of wars and intrigues.)

A few emotions from a much longer list. Other important emotions include the following: disgust, shame, tenderness, coyness, awe, reverence, joy, grief, jealousy, pride, greed, hatred, ecstasy, remorse, excitement, envy, worry, zeal. In all of these, and in many others to which we are periodically subject, the underlying condition is a stirred-up organism, as we have seen.

Thus, in our experience of disgust, for example, we are aware of a highly unpleasant tension in the chest and abdominal organs and a strong impulse to react explosively. In the emotional state of pride, we feel an internal expansiveness, a surging of blood through the upper body and the face and perhaps a tingling spine. Sometimes the organic accompaniments of an emotion are agreeable; sometimes they are disagreeable. In any event, an emotion always arouses feeling—pleasurable or otherwise.

EMOTIONS PROVIDE COLOR, INTEREST, DRIVE

It would be a drab world without emotion! Fancy what sort of creature one would be if he had no emotions! And fancy what sort of world it would be if nobody in it ever experienced any emotion! Life would proceed on a vegetative level, if indeed we continued to exist at all. There would be nothing to elevate and nothing to debase, nothing to love and nothing to hate, nothing to defend and nothing to destroy. One of the principal values of emotion is the tingeing of life with color and the supplying to it of interest and motivation. At its best, emotion makes life exciting, surrounds it with adventure and charm, drives it to achieve, to conquer, to win recognition. Emotion creates and enables us to enjoy beauty, art, literature, music, drama. Emotion fashions our dreams, inspires our visions, whets our appetites.

Emotion both creates and destroys. At its worst, of course, emotion leads to crime, to exploitation, to plottings and intrigues; it fires men with hatred, with lust and cruelty, with the thirst for blood and vengeance. Just as, on the positive and constructive side, emotion uplifts, so, on the negative and destructive side, it debases and destroys. At the one extreme, driven on by his sympathies and his ideals, is a St. Francis of Assisi; at the other extreme, goaded on by his lusts, appears an Attila or a Nero. Both history and literature are filled with the struggle between these two poles of emotion.

On a form like the one following, list striking instances from literature, in which the characters were swayed by strong emotion, and indicate in each case the action which grew out of the emotion:

EMOTIONS IN LITERATURE

Character	Literary Work	Emotion Illustrated	What It Drove the Character to Do
1. Jean Valjean	*Les Miserables*	Sympathy	Steal bread for children
2.			
3.			
4.			
5. etc.			

(Here is a good test of how well you remember some of the books you have read!)

Emotions are contagious.   We tend to take on the emotions of those with whom we associate. This is true in the more limited sense—as, for example, when we experience anger or sympathy because a friend is doing so—and also in the wider sense—as, for example, when almost with one accord a whole nation and a whole people may be aroused to think alike and to act in unison in times of national or social crisis. Fundamentally, perhaps, it is an underlying passion for security that drives men together emotionally at such moments as these.

Opinions or acts contrary to the ideals and principles of the hour, which are represented in the attitudes and behavior of the group, tend to isolate the nonconformist and to destroy his feeling of security and of belonging to the group. Only the most brazen freethinker is content to antagonize the group and jeopardize his security in it by persistence in his radicalism. Thus, in times of war, millions of people may unite under the common banner of self-defense or of conquest, and the emotional drive of the hour can be relied upon to sweep the entire populace into a fervor either of patriotic zeal or of mass defiance and hatred of the enemy.

MISUSE OF EMOTION

Children use tantrums to gain their ends.   It is understandable that any human attribute having the power that emotion has will sometimes be wrongly used to gain ends or to achieve satisfactions that are unworthy and undesirable. The temper tantrum, commonly used by children to get their own way, and sometimes displayed by adults for the same purpose, represents a by-no-means unusual misuse of emotion.

You have seen, no doubt, many a child, having been denied the privilege or favor he coveted, fly into a passion of rage or rebellion in order to frighten the parent or nurse into acquiescence to his desires. If such a trick works once, and the adult gives in, it will be trotted out again and again; before long the child may find himself in possession of a weapon so powerful that it gets him all the boons he covets! We all know of a few parents who are thus "led around by the nose," helpless to regain control of their own two-year-olds! Let a parent be of the panicky or apprehensive sort, and lacking in a little backbone, and let the young son and heir throw himself into a bristling heap on the floor, screaming and kicking and turning purple in the face, and the chances are more than good that the former will yield and the latter will triumph.

Adults have tantrums, too!   There are altogether too many grown-up people in the world who also resort to childish tantrums to get their own way. They may not actually fall screaming to the floor, but by "getting sore," refusing to speak, "flying off the handle," sulking, weeping, indulging in self-pity, or trotting out some similar mechanism, they club their relatives, their friends, or their associates over the head and compel them to grant special considerations, favors, or privileges.

This is an obvious misuse of emotion, but it is one that we all have to be on our guard against, lest we ourselves be guilty of employing it! It is temptingly easy to act in these cowardly ways, even though one has presumably "put away childish things."

Taking it out on the door!   *Substitution,* or emotional transfer, is another unfortunate but common example of the misuse of emotion. Instead of limiting anger or fear to the situation arousing it, one may allow himself to vent his wrath upon some wholly innocent agent. The man who, for example, returns home at the end of the day incensed at his boss and proceeds to "take it out" on his wife or children is a case in point. He may be surly or positively mean all the evening. Similarly, in times of anger one may bang the door, dash a dish to the floor, or kick the cat. Nothing is wrong with door, dish, or cat: the trouble is all with the man himself, who is allowing his wrath to spread from its original cause and to encompass these lowly and unoffending objects.

The clever propagandist! Appeal through propaganda is still another example of the way in which our emotional make-up may be capitalized to our own disadvantage and to the aid and comfort of the propagandist. So much of this sort of thing goes on that it is difficult to know where the line should be drawn between justifiable propaganda and unjustifiable. It is legitimate to appeal to our sympathies when a community drive for local charities is under way, or to our resentment and wrath when subversive influences are found to be at work against our institutions, or to our fears and apprehensiveness when the enemy knocks at our gates. It is certainly not legitimate when a pressure group seeks to arouse popular support for projected reform or legislation in which selfish interests rather than the general public good are obviously at stake.

Professional propagandists understand how universally the rank and file of people may be counted upon to respond emotionally toward whatever is advertised as being the latest in style, or the most improved, or the best on the market; to purchase allegedly superlative or indispensable commodities; to swing into obedient line behind party whips and political agents to the support of legislative blocks and pressure groups. Sooner or later too many of us "climb on the band wagon" and add our shouts and hurrahs to those of the original handful who were first victimized by the propagandist. We shall return at much greater length to this theme in a later chapter.

CONTROL OF EMOTION

Give your mind a chance! Perhaps the acid test of anyone's character is the degree to which he rules his life by intelligence rather than by emotion. On every hand we observe individuals who live on a frothy, emotional level, having little stability in their make-up and affording society little of the solid common sense upon which its security must ultimately depend. The world needs people who can withstand the wiles and artifices of the rabble-rouser, the gloom dispenser, and the irresponsible painter of Utopia. It requires people who can resist the mob spirit; people who can think for themselves and not be stampeded by the "half-baked" ideas that issue from innumerable quarters all around us; people in short who can keep their emotions where they belong and give their intellects a chance to save the day.

Indicate below some flattering instances in which yourself conquered negative emotions:

CONTROLLING MY OWN EMOTIONS

Emotion-Arousing Situation	Emotion I Felt	What I Felt Like Doing About It	What I Actually Did About It
1. A person gossiped untruthfully to me about my friend.	Resentment	Making an angry retort at the gossiper.	Called attention calmly to one of my friend's good points.
2.			
3.			
4.			
5. etc.			

("He that is slow to anger is better than the mighty; and he that ruleth his spirit than he that taketh a city.")

The conquest of anger. In the home and on the playground the child needs to discipline himself in the control of anger. It is easy for any young person to get into the unfortunate habit of grumbling, sulking, scolding, falling into a passion, abusing his mates, holding resentments and jealousies.

He needs to school himself continually in the fine art of controlling himself and to learn early that, while anger has its place in the world, that place is not on the playground or in the bosom of the family, where everybody needs to be always on good terms with everybody else. He must appreciate that other people besides himself have rights and privileges, and that he who always carries "a chip on his shoulder" soon becomes insufferable and unacceptable to his mates and his friends, if not indeed to his own family. If he can learn to reserve the expressions of his anger to situations where somebody is being made to suffer unduly, or where there is deceitfulness, dishonesty, or trickery, he will be mastering an excellent lesson in self-control.

Conquering our timidities. Fears and timidities, too, have to be kept under control if we are to get the most out of life. To give way to them to any extent is only to weaken our aggressiveness and destroy our confidence. That person who is too timid to put himself forward when the surroundings warrant it, or to covet and demand the honest respect of others on all occasions, or to insist upon his principles, ideals, and opinions—always provided of course that they are sincere— or to wrestle valiantly with the problems of everyday living, is certain to be the person who gets little satisfaction out of his own life and brings little satisfaction to others. Fears and timidities should be limited to situations or possibilities fraught with real physical or moral danger to the peace of mind of the individual or the welfare of the group.

The world needs intelligently bold people who are not afraid to invest themselves and their influence on the side of aggressive citizenship and intelligent social advance. Fears and timidities need to be replaced with courage and faith if our nation and the world as a whole are to achieve the goals of peace and democracy.

HOW PSYCHOLOGISTS WORK

Psychologists have commonly made use of three different methods·of studying emotions: the method of observation, the method of introspection, and the method of laboratory experimentation.

The first two methods mentioned are somewhat unsatisfactory in that they are altogether too subjective. How can the observer be sure, for example, that in observing the manifestations of an emotion in his subject, he is getting at the real inner emotional condition of the individual? There is too great a chance that the individual under observation may be falsifying, or covering up, or otherwise controlling his present feelings. Similarly, the psychologist who attempts to study his own emotions at a given instant by introspection may, by the very act of looking within his own mind, change the nature of the emotional state he seeks to examine!

The third method, that of experimentation in the laboratory, has come in recent decades to supplement encouragingly the older methods of studying emotions. It will be interesting to summarize briefly some of the findings that the laboratory technique in the investigation of emotions has established.

The following internal changes have been demonstrated to occur during aroused emotional states:

(1) Digestion slows down in the stomach and intestines and may actually stop. X-ray photographs indicate these changes.

(2) The pulse rate is speeded up. The *sphymograph* records the changes.

(3) The blood pressure rises, as indicated by the *sphygmomanometer*.

(4) The rate of breathing is modified, inspiration being deeper. The *pneumograph* studies these changes.

(5) The *adrenal glands* (ductless glands next to the kidneys)

secrete more of their powerful *hormones* (substances which increase bodily activity) into the blood, as blood analysis plainly indicates.

(6) The *sweat glands* discharge more perspiration upon the surface of the skin, thus making the skin more susceptible to the passage of mild electrical currents through it. The *galvanometer* measures this variation in the sweat glands.

Proceeding from the knowledge that deep organic changes take place in any individual who is in the grip of strong emotion, laboratory men have originated a most interesting and complex device known as the *polygraph,* or, in popular terminology, the "lie detector." Figure 42 shows one type of polygraph.

A polygraph is really a device which combines many separate pieces of laboratory apparatus and synchronizes them upon the same individual. Several of the kinds of apparatus mentioned above—the sphymograph, the sphygmomanometer, the pneumograph, the galvanometer—are hooked up together and connected with mechanical pencils that trace graphically every recordable change occurring internally in the subject.

Ordinarily, when the polygraph is to be used upon a suspect, the experimenter prepares beforehand a list of stimulus words that contain both neutral and "loaded" words. The latter are interspersed among the former at varying intervals.

The suspect sits as comfortably as possible (considering all the instruments that are attached to his arms, chest, and so forth!) and responds to each word with the word that comes first into his mind. The supposition is that if he thinks of a word that would give him away, he will cover it up with a fake word. All the time, of course, the polygraph is writing on a slowly revolving drum an indelible record of the behavior of the suspect's heart, lungs, and skin structures. If he hesitates, or takes an unusually long time to find a fake word, or repeats, at every "loaded" word, a stereotyped word that ob-

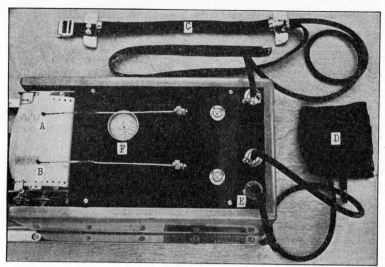

Fig. 42. Blood pressure, pulse, and respiration recording units of the polygraph, or lie detector. A: Respiration pen. B: Blood pressure-pulse pen. (A synchronous electric motor which drives the strip chart is located beneath the chart bearing the respiration and blood pressure-pulse recordings A and B.) C: Respiration or pneumograph tube, which, with the aid of a strap, fits around the subject's chest. D: Blood pressure-pulse cuff, of the same type as that used by physicians in determining a patient's blood pressure. During a test it is fastened around the subject's arm. E: Air pressure coupling and tube for inflation of blood pressure-pulse cuff. (The air pressure supply for this purpose may be obtained from a hand operated bulb; or, as in the case of this particular instrument, from an electrically operated air compressor controllable by means of valves situated on a panel of the table supporting the instrument.) F: Pressure dial (sphygmomanometer) for measuring the air pressure in the blood pressure-pulse cuff.

viously has no connection with the stimulus one, or if he otherwise deceives, the internal fear which he feels at the ordeal will be intensified, and the instruments will detect it.

If, then, after the curves have been proceeding normally for several seconds, one of the "loaded" words suddenly causes the subject to "act up" abnormally, it may be concluded that the fear emotion has actually been tapped, and that in spite of his best efforts to disguise any knowledge he may have of the crime, the victim is condemning himself relentlessly through the stirred-up condition existing throughout his physical organism.

It has been claimed in police work that the polygraph has failed to discover the liar in fewer than one tenth of one per cent of the cases investigated.

Figures 43 and 44 are sketches showing polygraph records of changes in circulatory and respiratory functions previous to, during, and immediately after the presentation of a "loaded" stimulus word.

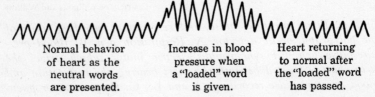

Normal behavior of heart as the neutral words are presented.

Increase in blood pressure when a "loaded" word is given.

Heart returning to normal after the "loaded" word has passed.

Fig. 43. Polygraph record of suspect's pulse and blood pressure.

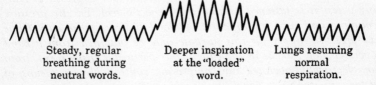

Steady, regular breathing during neutral words.

Deeper inspiration at the "loaded" word.

Lungs resuming normal respiration.

Fig. 44. Polygraph record of suspect's respiration.

TO HELP YOU LEARN

SOME QUESTIONS TO ANSWER

1. In what ways is the animal's body mechanism so well adapted to life in the jungle that when an emergency arises it can meet the situation appropriately?

2. Has the fear emotion any constructive value? Or would we be better off if we had no fears and timidities?

3. Would not our human society be better off, too, if people never got angry and never flew into a rage?

4. Do you personally feel that you do little worrying and have few apprehensions? Or are you limited in your possible achievements by such negative motivation as timidity and fear?

5. Is there such a thing as being overintellectual and under-emotional in conducting our lives? In other words. are not people more human if they give some rein to their emotions? Explain.

WORKING WITH PSYCHOLOGY

1. Do the following introspecting: The next time you find yourself in an especially pleasant (or unpleasant) mood, try to observe whether your physical body is contributing anything to the feeling tone of the moment. Note whether you are receiving any sensations from internal organs, or from muscles or skin, which might lead you to understand that feeling is tied up in some definite way with body functioning.

2. When people's emotions are strongly aroused—especially those of anger, fear, jealousy, hatred, and greed—they will go to almost any extremes in conduct. Check through some metropolitan daily paper for news items in which crimes are reported, and try to decide which emotions influenced the criminals. Use a form like the one at the top of page 268.

3. Gather ten magazine advertisements that are calculated to appeal to potential customers through arousing such emotions as shame, envy, anger, fear, love, or pride. Do you find advertising appeal directed toward any emotions besides these? See also whether

CRIMES REPORTED IN THE PRESS

Crime Committed	Probable Emotions Responsible
1.	
2.	
3.	
4.	
5. etc.	

you can find any advertisements that are clearly and frankly intellectual in their appeal. If you do, compare their persuasive power with that of the emotionally loaded ones.

4. Determine what negative emotion (fear, jealousy, anger, and so forth) is retarding or interfering with your best personal development, and start at once a campaign to bring it under control. If it is a tendency to quick temper, school yourself to stifle the hasty remark, to change the subject of conversation, to go for a brisk walk, or in some other way to control your impulses. If it is fear of asserting yourself in class or in a social group, compel yourself little by little to participate actively in various social situations. It will be helpful to you if you keep a line-a-day sort of diary of your successes and failures.

What Others Say

1. In Fiction:

For Whom the Bell Tolls by Ernest Hemingway. A novel of the Spanish Revolution, depicting the horrors of the struggle so vividly that some readers find themselves unable to read it in its entirety.

The Yearling by Marjorie K. Rawlings. A portrayal of the keen love of a boy for a fawn, and the overpowering emotions he experienced when his pet was killed. An excellent picture, not only of boyish affection but of the rough tenderness of an understanding Southern father.

All Passion Spent by Victoria Sackville-West. After an eventful life in which she had always been gentle and submissive, Lady Shane amazed her children by escaping to a little Hampstead cottage and living her declining years in detachment and content. A beautifully written fantasy showing the serenity of feelings possible in one whose "passions are all spent."

Darkness and Dawn by Aleksiei N. Tolstoi. A picture of the chaos and stress in Russia between 1914 and 1919, during the Revolution. A chronicle of violence, brawls, bloodshed, and utter disregard of death.

Out of the Night by Jan Valtin. Revolutionists—torture chambers —fanatics pledged to terrorism—death and destruction—these represent the grimmest portrayals of events leading up to and culminating in the Second World War. Every human emotion is stirred to the depth in the reading.

2. In Drama:

The Barretts of Wimpole Street by Rudolph Besier. One of the best examples of strong emotions in modern drama. Fear, anger, resentment, love, sympathy are all revealed as the fascinating story of Elizabeth Barrett and Robert Browning is enacted.

3. In Poetry:

Renascence by Edna St. Vincent Millay. The portrayal of a college girl's deep feelings about life and of the surging emotions that well up in her soul as she contemplates it.

Can You Think Straight?

When, in 1590, the young Galileo Galilei, an Italian philosopher, took in his hands two weights—one of them a heavy one and the other a light one—and climbed up the narrow stairway of the Leaning Tower of Pisa, it is safe to say that professors and students alike were agape with interest. For here was a youthful mathematician who dared to deny the centuries-old contention of Aristotle to the effect that heavy bodies fall more rapidly through space than do lighter ones. He was actually brazen enough to try out the problem for himself, and prove once and for all whether he was right, or Aristotle.

In this famous experiment Galileo proved the old Greek philosopher wrong. Incidentally, too, he got himself a lot of unfavorable criticism from the wise men of the day, who had swallowed Aristotle, "hook, line, and sinker"! By clearing away much of the old intellectual rubbish of antiquity, the young Italian set the stage for a new day in mechanics. Galileo could think, and think straight.

George Washington Carver, more than anybody else, put the humble peanut on the map of the South. A Negro, born of slave parents in Missouri, stolen as an infant by night raiders, ransomed for a racehorse valued at three hundred dollars, he eventually worked his way through school and college and became one of the outstanding members of his race.

He was not only a brilliant agricultural chemist at Tuskegee Institute, but was prominently associated with the Bureau of Plant Industry of the United States Department of Agriculture. His contributions won him many honors, including the Spingarn Medal for the most distinguished contribution of a Negro to science.

When Southern farmers needed a crop to replace cotton in rotation, Carver persuaded them to grow peanuts. Faced with the problem of how to develop the new product commercially, he began work in his laboratory, and he found more than three hundred uses for peanuts. From them, and from sweet potatoes and pecans, he found ways of producing milk, condiments, axle grease, plastics, ink, flour, insulating board, coffee, starch, preserved ginger, and scores of other commodities. Because of his ingenious research, the peanut industry today ranks second only to the cotton industry in the South, more than one and one-half million acres being under cultivation.

Warren Tully's face flushed angrily.

"There!" he exclaimed. "I might have known it! Bad luck was bound to come to me today!"

"Why, what is it, Warren?" called his sister, Florence, who was studying in the adjoining room.

"Bother take it all!" scolded Warren. "I'd got my drawing for Mr. Hatch all finished, and then when I was labeling it, a big drop of ink had to go and splash on it! I knew something would happen to me before the day was over!"

"How'd you know that?" queried Florence, coming to the door and regarding the splash on her brother's paper.

"Oh, Verner's old black cat had to go and run out across the walk just ahead of me this morning, when I was on my way to school!" complained Warren. "I said then I'd have bad luck today! It never fails!"

"And you a senior!" remarked Florence, going for a blotter and eraser. "I'll help you clean it off."

"What's being a senior got to do with it?"

"A senior in high school ought to think straighter than that!" replied Florence. "Blaming Verner's cat because your pen leaked!"

"It's bad luck when a black cat runs across your path!" Warren reiterated doggedly. "Took me two hours to make this sketch, anyway!"

Thinking—Good and Not So Good!

Here are some interesting specimens of thinking. Galileo, by a simple—but in his day, daring—experiment sets aside the traditional belief and establishes a new principle of mechanics. George Washington Carver, starting out with a strong feeling of need, arrives at new ideas that revolutionize the role played by the humble peanut. Warren Tully, appalled by the spectacle of a black cat dashing in front of him, reasons that bad luck will stalk his steps all day, and when he carelessly spills ink on his paper attributes the disaster to the malign influence of a feline!

Florence Tully, you note, thinks a little more sensibly than does Warren!

✓ ✓ ✓

In this chapter you will learn that in order to be able to think and reason we have to have ideas gained from experience. You will find out about mental images, through which some of these ideas are retained, and about verbal symbols, through which others are preserved. Your attention will be called to a few rules that need to be kept in mind by anybody who aspires to think clearly and logically.

Fig. 45. "The Thinker" by Auguste Rodin. This famous statue symbolizes the power of the human mind when it is turned upon the solution of some problem which confronts mankind.

11. THINKING

Before you start out, see how many problems of pressing importance you can think of that are confronting people in our country today—problems that are or are not being attacked intelligently. Use a form like the one below for recording them:

SOME PRESSING NATIONAL PROBLEMS OF TODAY

1.
2.
3.
4.
5. etc.

There are numberless problems before us all the time. How conscious are you of them? Only as students in our high schools and colleges—who are to be tomorrow's leaders and thinkers—become mentally alert to the importance of these pressing, unsolved riddles that clamor for solution, may we ever hope eventually to thread our way through them.

LIMITED POPULAR MEANING OF THINKING

To think means more than to recall. When most people use the term "to think," they mean one of two things. In the first case, they have in mind the same thing as "to remember," or "to recall." Thus, one often says, "I can't think what his name is," meaning, "I can't recall it." Or John's teacher asks, "What is the capital of Virginia?" and John replies, "I think it is Richmond." Or again, Mr. Brown inquires what time the letter came, and Mrs. Brown answers, "I think it was about two o'clock."

Obviously what each of these three persons does when he "thinks" is to bring back to mind something he has experienced before. Thinking in this sense is limited to looking backward into the happenings of the past, with a view to recalling them when and if they are wanted.

Thinking is more than reverie. A second common meaning of the term "to think" is merely to allow ideas to run more or less freely and passively through the mind.

"What are you thinking about so hard, Bill?" queries Tom, noticing his friend gazing vacantly out the window.

"Oh, nothing much," Bill replies, blinking, and coming back to earth. "I was just thinking what I'd do with a million dollars if I had 'em!"

Similarly, old Mr. Telford sits placidly by the fire and thinks of old times, while his granddaughter permits her thoughts to wander away from tomorrow's history lesson which she is preparing, and is soon lost in a "brown study," or in "building air castles," or in otherwise paying attention to loosely-knit ideas that flow interestingly through her mind.

Obviously, what Bill and old Mr. Telford and young Miss Telford are all doing while they are "thinking" is to enjoy the more or less passive flow of ideas, either drawn from the past or imaginatively painted across the future.

WHAT THINKING REALLY IS

Recall and reverie are not enough. The world would never advance far if thinking were limited to these two kinds of mental activity. To be able to recall what one has previously learned—for example, in economics, in history, in English— may be of the greatest practical and immediate value to any of us, and we should not discount its importance. And to spend

otherwise dull moments in reverie and in playing with un-
reality may also be decidedly good for us sometimes. But the
mere recall of a past experience or the mere flight into the
dream world of fancy does little or nothing to help one settle
a problem, or to lead him to new conclusions, or to pave the
way to a new discovery. After one has thought of the thing
he is trying to remember, and after he has come back to earth
from a fanciful flight of imagination, both he and the world
are as poor as before.

Take the case of Columbus. Christopher Columbus, everyone will admit, did more than merely recall what he had been
taught, and more than merely indulge in a pipe dream. He
had been taught, we must suppose, that the earth was flat;
that the mariner who navigated his bark too far in a straight
line would soon sail it over the edge of the world and plunge
it downward into a bottomless precipice of fire; that India,
with its treasures, lay to the east, and that to reach it one
must sail eastward. He had dreamed, we must suppose also,
of fame, of fortune, of thrilling adventure in the eastern lands
and on the great sea, just as thousands of other youth had
done before him and have done since.

Exciting questions, these! Still, Columbus did not stop
with his recalled lessons and his idle fancies. These were only
starting points for him. He had been taught that the earth
was flat. He began to wonder why its shadow in an eclipse
was always curved; why a ship's topmasts always rose into view
from behind the horizon before its hull became visible; and,
if his thinking was sound, why he could not reach India by
sailing westward.

These were rather exciting questions, and they made Columbus eager to find the answers. "To go east by sailing west"
emerged in his thinking as something far more than a play of
fancy. It came to be the strong, consuming purpose of his life;

and he talked it, argued it, and pleaded for the means of setting forth on a voyage to investigate. The unexpected outcome of the trip he finally was able to make in no way detracts from the genius of a man who refused to let other people do his thinking for him, and who refused also to be content with mere fancies and dreams.

Recall other well-known historical instances of independent thinking, recording them on a form like this:

STRAIGHT THINKERS OF YESTERDAY

Person	The Belief He Exploded	The Truth He Established
1. Copernicus	The earth is the center of the universe.	The sun is the center of our universe.
2.		
3.		
4.		
5. etc.		

(Scientific progress depends upon the search after truth. Many notable people of the past have participated in the quest.)

Our best thinking seeks for solutions. Thinking, in its truest sense, is always concerned with reaching some sort of rational solution to a problem that has presented itself to the mind. Now in such a world as the one in which we live it is perfectly apparent that there is no end to the number of problems that press for solution. They originate from many sources of our experience. Following are a few such sources:

The need to meet a practical life situation.
Reflecting about something one has learned.
Doubting what the books or newspapers say.
Comparing this bit of evidence with that bit.
A vexing feeling of uncertainty about something.
Curiosity about something.
Trying to explain something previously held unexplainable.

However it arises, or from whatever source it comes, a problem is easily recognized, when it does come, as a perplexing question or situation which needs to have new light thrown upon it.

HOW THE MIND IS SET FOR THINKING

Mental resources emerge automatically. One of the most amazing things about our minds is that when a problem arises for solution, somehow those very ideas that are most likely to help us in solving the difficulty come tumbling into the arena of our minds. The psychologists say that when the mind faces a problem, all its resources tend to be *set* (placed in readiness) to help solve it.

Thus, if you are trying to think through an original in plane geometry, your mind is set for mathematics, and not for general science or literature; and if you are searching for an explanation of why wool is preferred to cotton for clothing in the desert, your mind becomes set automatically for ideas relating to cotton, wool, heat, perspiration, and desert life, and not for ideas concerning food assimilation, or radio frequencies, or the magnetic compass. In other words, the very act of thinking about a particular problem automatically sets the mind to yield up whatever ideas it contains that seem to touch on the problem.

Selection is needed. Of course, not all the ideas that present themselves will necessarily help in solving the problem. Some of them can be discarded at first sight; some of them presently; some of them only after careful study. Good thinking means that one is intelligent in what ideas he discards and in what ones he accepts as helpful.

Enter on a form similar to the table at the top of page 279 some of the problems which you are attacking in your various classes.

1. Why are some cities adopting a commission form of local government?
2.
3.
4.
5. etc.

(Include problems from all subjects: literature, natural science, social studies, and so on.)

THINKING SHOULD LEAD TO ACTION

The goal of all thinking. When at length what seems to be a valid conclusion has been reached, or the problem has been solved, the real thinker has another responsibility that cannot be ignored. He must act accordingly!

Suppose I am confronted by one or another of the following problems:

What is the best investment for me to make?
Who is the better candidate for councilman?
What are the responsibilities of a citizen in going to the polls?
For what vocation am I best suited?
Is public ownership of utilities desirable?

It is idle for me to be concerned about these and scores of other problems requiring thought unless I intend, after having reached a conclusion, to adjust myself and my activities accordingly.

If my reasoned and thoughtful study convinces me that XYZ is the best investment for me to make, then I shall proceed to invest in XYZ. If I am persuaded that Candidate K will make a better councilman than Candidate L, then I shall throw the weight of my influence toward Candidate K's support. If thoughtful self-analysis suggests that I may become a good lawyer, or policeman, or factory hand, then I shall proceed to make myself into the best lawyer, policeman, or factory hand possible. If I am convinced from the arguments that the government ought to own and operate the utilities, then I shall be an advocate of government ownership and operation of the public utilities.

But don't get the cart before the horse! The first essential in all these situations is that I come to my conclusions only after rigid and careful *thinking*. The order is essential: first, *thinking;* then, *doing*. It is unfortunate if one makes the mistake of omitting to think and proceeds thoughtlessly into scatterbrained *doing*. There are altogether too many people in the world who leap first and look afterward—if they are still alive and *able* to look!

List on the following form several historical incidents in which poor thinking was done by a person or a group:

SOME HISTORICAL EXAMPLES OF POOR THINKING

The Error	The Date	The Place	What It Led to
1. Belief in witches	1690's	Salem	Hanging innocent people
2.			
3.			
4.			
5. etc.			

(The pages of history are frequently marred by these instances of man's ignorance and folly.)

TO THINK ONE MUST HAVE IDEAS

Without ideas one is helpless. All of these things suggest that only a person who has ideas can do much thinking. Infants and idiots can hardly be expected either to have many problems to solve or to be able to solve them intelligently.

Fancy how far Thomas A. Edison would ever have gone forward in the invention of the incandescent lamp unless he had had wide experience with electricity and its properties! Or how far his friend, Alexander Graham Bell, would have advanced in the invention of the telephone had he not spent years and years collecting ideas about sound vibrations and diaphragms and transmitters and a score of other related matters!

You could not yourself even sit down and write a page theme for your English class unless you had at least a few ideas about something fluttering about in your mind somewhere! And how could you help your side win a debate about "the desirability of discussing controversial subjects in the social science course" if you did not know at least what controversial subjects are? You could not take part in a class discussion about trade unions, our chief exports, our solar system, exploration in the Antarctic, the life of Charlemagne, or Scott's best novels, unless you had garnered some ideas about these topics.

Whence do we get our ideas?   In the last analysis, there is only one source of ideas: the everyday experiences of living. These experiences include the following specific sources and many more:

Parents
Teachers
Friends and acquaintances
Books, newspapers, magazines
Broadcasts
Moving pictures
Conversations
Lectures, sermons, discussions, debates
Contacts with natural objects, such as birds, flowers, and stars
Games and sports we engage in or watch.

We gain still more ideas by working over in our minds all this mass of everyday experience, by thinking about it, classifying it, and adding to it.

The number and variety of ideas that students of today have are unquestionably far beyond those available to their elders when they were young, because nowadays people are exposed to so many new sources of information that did not exist a generation ago. If ideas were all that was needed to guarantee clear thinking, surely the modern age might well be labeled the Age of Reflection.

TWO KINDS OF IDEAS

Images of all sorts. The simplest ideas we have are the *images* left in our minds from our experiences. These include:

(1) *Visual* (or sight) images, such as houses on your street, faces of friends.

(2) *Auditory* (or hearing) images, such as a friend's voice, a ringing bell, screeching brakes.

(3) *Olfactory* (or smell) images, such as onions, ether, perfume.

(4) *Gustatory* (or taste) images, such as olives, turnips, candy.

(5) *Tactile* (or touch) images, such as the feel of velvet, of sandpaper, of new shoes.

Verbal symbols. Much more complicated ideas than these exist in our minds as language symbols, or words. These symbols are ordinarily not so vivid as the mental images we have just listed. But even though less vivid, they are of the greatest help to us in our thinking.

Suppose you are asked to decide what would be a suitable definition for "patriotism." Possibly you might get a fleeting visual image of the flag waving, or you might have an auditory image of the national anthem being sung or played. These images would be quite understandable to you, but their presence in your mind would hardly represent a definition of the term "patriotism"!

Rather, your definition would be chiefly a verbal thing; that is to say, you would feel yourself actually thinking in terms of words. This verbal thinking is often so vivid that you can almost feel the speech muscles in your throat forming the words that flash through your mind. For this reason, thinking is often called *inner speech* by the psychologists. Probably when you try to think of a definition of "patriotism" you find something like the following words running like silent whispers up from the speech muscles in your throat and over your tongue and lips: "'Patriotism'? Why, 'patriotism' is being true to my country; it's—well, it's just believing in America."

Inner speech. Now you will notice that you probably didn't have any real images at all while you were making your definition. You were simply thinking in words or language symbols; that is to say, you were carrying on inner speech. If you did have any images—like visions of waving flags or of marching men or of bands playing—these were of little help to you in formulating your definition. You were simply thinking in words. Real thinking does not depend upon images, but upon language symbols.

Of course infants and younger children can't do much verbal thinking, for their knowledge of words has not been developed enough. Young children have to depend upon images for what elementary thinking they can do. Animals, too, are unable to think in any human sense because of their lack of speech.

IMPORTANCE OF THINKING IN SYMBOLS

Verbal symbols indispensable to thought. The importance of being able to think without bothering with images can hardly be overestimated. If man could use only ideas that had

Photo by Brown Brothers

Fig. 46. Beethoven at work on a new composition. Creative thinking in the field of music depends not so much on verbal symbols as on musical symbols and auditory images. Is this real thinking?

been aroused by definite and particular images, he could never think in abstract terms at all. How could he, for example, reason about politics, or about the problems connected with law, with public health, with foreign policies, with education, with public welfare, with social security, and with scores of other questions that confront him at every turn? Thinking of this sort is of a distinctly higher order than thinking about this house, or that automobile, or your necktie!

Try it for yourself, and see! Do a little thinking right now about the causes of crime in the United States, or about the efforts of organized labor to improve working conditions in America, or about the importance of public education in a democracy. Isn't it immediately apparent that the only way to reason about important matters of this kind is to compel one-self to apply inner speech, or language, to them?

A sobering responsibility. The habit of verbal thinking is an important one to cultivate. Not all of us can hope to become great thinkers, like Edison, or Marconi, or Einstein, but we can all learn to think clearly and logically. After all, the welfare of our nation does not depend upon a few great thinkers nearly so much as it does on the presence of intelligent thinkers in great numbers in the population. Those who —like yourself—have had at least a high school education must be the citizens of tomorrow who will do most of the thinking for our democracy. There will be millions who have never had the opportunity of secondary education, whose thinking will always be weak and ineffective.

FIVE RULES FOR A GOOD THINKER

How can one become a clear thinker? There are just five things he can do, and they are all that anybody can do. Here they are:

Observe widely and intelligently. In this way you get a rich background of experience. You should try to get information about just as many worth-while things as you can, so that your mind will have plenty of facts at its disposal to think with. Wealth of experience, range of information—these must be the first goals of anyone who wants to become a clear and logical thinker.

Cultivate an active, reflective mind. It is not enough merely to have a good fund of information, necessary as that is. The person who would really think needs to work over this information and put it to use. Facts are of no value to anyone until he can make them a part of his "stock in trade." The habit of making active use of the knowledge and information you have is a wise one to try to form. Facts thus fitted together by an active mind have ways of leading to new facts and new ideas. Only those facts that remain in the mind unsorted and disconnected have no value.

Master as large a vocabulary as you can. Most of our thinking, as we have seen, is carried on in inner speech. This fact suggests the importance of cultivating a good command of language. The ready and capable thinker is likely to have a large vocabulary. Through the splendid command of language symbols that he has, he is able to use inner speech considerably better than is the individual whose speech symbols are few and clumsy.

Converse much with others. Intelligent conversation helps immensely in thinking. By means of it we tap new sources of ideas in our friends, and at the same time learn to express our own ideas clearly and logically. Conversation stimulates thinking about all sorts of interesting and important problems; it encourages us to collect more facts and wider experience upon which to draw. Conversation is a fine art, one that is almost essential to good thinking.

Form the habit of doing your own thinking. In a world where there are newspapers, radio commentators, and propagandists of every sort on every hand, it is easy to let these agencies do your thinking for you. We need such informational agents as these to provide us with facts and with a knowledge of the events that are going on in the world. But we need to do our own *interpreting* of this ever-accumulating mass of information, misinformation, and propaganda. The thoughtful citizen is not stampeded by any sort of pressure-group activity; rather, he turns the force of his own thinking upon everything that comes to his attention. In the light of this thinking, he reaches his own conclusions and forms his own opinions. Our democracy needs such thinkers, and needs them badly.

We shall return to this discussion in the next chapter.

On a form like the following, list some instances of real thinking which you yourself have done within the past twenty-four hours:

SOME PROOFS THAT I CAN SOLVE A PROBLEM

What Aroused Me to Think	What I Did About It	The Result
1. I saw a new kind of bird in the park.	I searched through my bird book to identify it.	I learned to recognize the Myrtle Warbler.
2.		
3.		
4.		
5. etc.		

(The mentally alert person meets dozens of problematic situations every day and seeks for clues to interpret them.)

HOW PSYCHOLOGISTS WORK

> *Major Premise:* All men are mortal.
> *Minor Premise:* Socrates is a man.
> *Conclusion:* Socrates is mortal.

Upon this framework practically all of the earliest and much of the more modern reasoning of men has been constructed. The pattern is called a *syllogism,* and its conscious use dates back to one of the first great philosophers, Aristotle. It comprises three parts: (1) the major premise, which is some universally recognized truth; (2) the minor premise, which is some particular phenomenon that has been observed; and (3) the conclusion, which is the logical deduction from the two preceding premises. In the syllogism given above, since all men are without exception mortal, it follows plainly that Socrates, being a man, must also be mortal.

Syllogistic thinking, or *deductive reasoning,* is commonly used in many of our everyday observations, conclusions, and opinions. Provided the major premise is *invariably* true, and provided the minor premise is properly related to it, this kind of reasoning is valid and reliable. Thus:

> All iron is heavy.
> This is a piece of iron.
> It is heavy.

Nothing could be more logical than this. Of course, one does not necessarily go through these three distinct stages in his everyday use of syllogistic reasoning. When, for example, you stoop to pick up a bar of iron, you brace yourself and put forth more energy than you do when you stoop to pick up a sofa pillow three times as large! Something like this probably goes through your mind: "This is going to be heavy: it's iron."

Similarly, we complain, "It's going to rain today," when the morning sky is cloudy and the air feels damp. We do not bother to state the entire pattern:

> Whenever it is cloudy in the morning and the air feels damp, it rains before night.
> It is cloudy this morning and the air feels damp.
> It will rain before night.

One of the common flaws in deductive reasoning is illustrated in the last syllogism. *Sometimes,* when the conditions are as stated in the major premise, it *doesn't* rain, but clears before night! It is of prime importance in all deduction that the major premise shall be universally valid, with no exceptions. Do you detect the flaw in this syllogism?

> All cows have horns.
> Brindle is a cow.
> Brindle has horns.

Or in this one?

> All foreigners are untrustworthy.
> Z is a foreigner.
> Z is untrustworthy.

Yet how many faulty deductions we make because of our prejudices, or our misinformation, or our willingness to accept as a universal truth a major premise that is wobbly!

Here is an example of false reasoning because the minor premise is not properly related to the major premise:

> The first word in a sentence always begins with a capital.
> The word "House" in this sentence begins with a capital.
> "House" is the first word in the sentence!

Try this one:

> Men are stronger than women.
> Antelopes are stronger than women.
> (Men are stronger than antelopes?)
> (Antelopes are stronger than men?)
> (Neither conclusion is true?)

In the opposite kind of reasoning, called *inductive reasoning,* the thinker starts off with a single particular observation. Later on, he makes other individual observations of the same nature or in the same category as the original one. Finally, after he has made a large number, he reaches a degree of confidence in which he feels justified in drawing a general conclusion, or in making the "inductive leap." Here are some specimens of inductive thinking:

> This fire is hot.
> That fire is hot.
> Those fires are all hot.
> The fire in this stove is hot.
> The fire on that grate is hot.
> *All fire is hot.*

> This apple has a core.
> That apple has a core.
> Those apples have cores.
> The apples in that basket have cores.
> The apples I ate yesterday had cores.
> *All apples have cores.*

The inductive way of reasoning is the way of all scientific research. Painfully, slowly, analytically, the searcher after knowledge in any scientific field gathers his specimens, his particular facts, and after making many comparisons and contrasts he at length feels safe in making the inductive leap. Charles Darwin collected his data over a period of many years before he would allow himself to state his inductive principle of natural selection or the survival of the fittest. His purpose in being so thorough was to make sure that there was not a single exception in his observation of particulars.

Everybody uses the inductive method a great deal in building up his concepts and ideas. The child learns that all fire is hot by a few vivid experiences of it; that honesty is the best policy by individual examples of its wisdom, or of the unwisdom of its opposite. The high school student learns that the good-natured person is the likable one through observing the relationships of particular individuals; that one part of carbon and two parts of oxygen unite to form carbon dioxide through actual individual demonstration of the principle. The man of affairs reasons that ABC stock is a good investment because many people recommend it to him, because it has weathered all the depressions so far, because it has always paid good dividends.

The weakness in many of our inductions lies in our proneness to jump at conclusions without sufficient individual observations to warrant the leap. To conclude that because Tom B. and Henry Q. are both redheads with quick tempers, *all* red-headed people are quick-tempered is absurd, but very human. To reason that the good person is always poor, from the particular cases of John C. and William B., both of whom are good and poor, is equally ridiculous, and equally human! The fact of the matter is that we are so ridden by our prejudices, so convinced of the validity of our "hunches," and so influenced by our superstitions and misinformation and biases, that we find it difficult to refrain from snap judgments and hasty conclusions in almost every area of our experience.

Many an adult is little more logical in his thinking life than is the four-year-old who asked to go out in the rain so that he might grow fast, or the five-year-old who dug up the kernels of corn his father had planted earlier in the day to see if they were growing, or the six-year-old who pictured Aunt Hattie when he first saw her as being dreadfully old because her eyes were gray! Consulting a palmist to know one's future; refraining from starting a new enterprise on Friday because Friday is a day of bad luck; concluding that "doctors don't know anything" because they did not cure Uncle Bob—these are inductive leaps that are quite as ridiculous as any of the most infantile conclusions reached by five-year-olds.

TO HELP YOU LEARN

Some Questions to Answer

1. In the light of your study of this chapter, can you better appreciate the truth of the old adage: "Look before you leap"? Explain.

2. Why is it more important for people to be able to think straight in a democracy than in an autocracy or dictatorship? Can you understand why it is so essential for the high school student to become a good thinker?

3. Can you see actual growth in your own English vocabulary since you came to high school? What is responsible? Can you think of practical ways in which you can consciously improve it still more? Explain.

4. Do you find it easy to carry on a conversation with others? Or do you find it hard to express your thoughts? How can you develop greater ease and confidence in conversation?

5. As you size yourself up as a thinker, what seems to be your strongest point? Your weakest? In what ways will your study of this chapter help you to think better in future?

Working with Psychology

1. Do this introspective problem: Determine upon some question of the day to think about for five minutes (for example, public ownership of utilities). As you think over arguments pro and con, try to observe the inner speech going on in your speech muscles. Note especially whether you cannot almost feel your tongue and lips forming the words, as your ideas proceed, and whether there is not actually a slight tension in your throat in the region of your vocal cords (Adam's apple).

2. Find in literature—either classic or contemporary, prose or poetry—good examples of the use of vivid imagery employed by writers in their descriptions of places, people, events, and experiences. Can you not, for example, hear plainly in your imagination the events in the following:

> While the plowman, near at hand,
> Whistles o'er the furrowed land,
> And the milkmaid singeth blithe
> And the mower whets his scythe.

Much of the beauty and richness in language depend upon the appeal which it makes to our various kinds of images.

3. Look through current issues of magazines having wide circulation (for example, *The Saturday Evening Post, Time, Newsweek, The Reader's Digest*) and find out what are the leading problems of the day about which writers and thinkers are concerned. Supplement your study by finding what editorial writers are concerned about in their columns and what radio speakers and news analysts are discussing. From these sources you will be able to construct a good picture of the present-day human problems about which people are thinking. You will also find that not all whose voices are heard are in agreement.

4. Do the following bit of research. Using dictionaries, encyclopedias, and other reference books, find out how many words there are in the English language. Find out, too, how many of these words are actually used by the ordinary individual in his daily talking and writing and reading. It will prove very illuminating if, after you have learned how many words there are that might be used, and how many of them most people actually employ, you can find out how many words *you* know well enough to use. Ask your teacher to give you a standard vocabulary test that will demonstrate in half an hour's time the size of your total vocabulary.

What Others Say

1. In Essay:

How to Think Straight by Robert H. Thouless. A highly readable analysis of correct thinking and many examples of incorrect or crooked thinking.

2. In Fiction:

Private Worlds by Phyllis Bottome. A story of the inability of the staff members of a psychopathic hospital who, though clever enough in treating the emotional and mental disturbances of their patients, fail to apply their knowledge to themselves and are at a loss to diagnose their own emotional maladjustments.

Babbitt by Sinclair Lewis. Through the satirical delineation of the character of a middle-class business man, the author portrays the crudeness and the confused thinking of a shallow individual who feels himself very important and clever.

The Heritage of Hatcher Ide by Booth Tarkington. The account of a boy who thought he knew it all, and who could talk his way to almost anything. Interesting analysis of a bossy adolescent, possessed of a swelled head.

As a Man Thinks by Augustus Thomas. A serious and inspiring study of modern life and character which penetrates deeply into society. Through his insight and wise tolerance, Dr. Seelig assists in solving the problem of an unhappy family.

3. In Drama:

The Little Foxes by Lillian Hellman. A rather startling portrayal of the effects of twisted thinking and scheming upon the lives of the Hubbard family, some of whom "eat the earth" while others "stand around and watch them do it."

4. In Poetry:

If by Rudyard Kipling. The poet writes in appreciation of anybody who can let his head rule him and not be stampeded by his emotions into extravagances of conduct and attitude.

Are You Easily Taken in by Propaganda?

A certain bank in California, wishing to show up the ridiculousness of all get-rich-quick schemes, placed in one of its show windows a placard urging people to invest in the California Ranching Company. The company was starting two ranches, one of them a cat ranch and the other a rat ranch. The former was to operate with 100,000 cats, each of which could be counted on to produce twelve kittens per year. The cat skins would sell for thirty cents each, and a force of 100 men could skin 5,000 a day, yielding the investors a net profit of $10,000 daily. Meantime, the rat ranch next door was starting with 1,000,000 rats which, breeding twelve times faster than the cats, could be counted on to feed the cats adequately. The rats, in turn, were to be fed the carcasses of the cats after they had been skinned.

In spite of the fact that beside the placard was a large sign stating that this was a wildcat scheme, but no more wild than many other similar attempts to gouge money from gullible people, the bank was so swamped with inquiries in person and by mail that it was compelled to take down the advertisement!

Ponce de León was a wealthy man, but his wealth could not keep him from growing old! Famed as explorer and soldier, as voyager with Columbus on his second expedition to the New World in 1493, as conqueror and governor of Porto Rico—he yet could not stay those telltale years that were stealing up behind him. Like many a man or woman, he was ready to follow any will-o'-the-wisp that would promise to keep him young! Tales of a wonderful Fountain of Youth somewhere to the north on a legendary island of the Bahama group, called Bimini, had long fascinated him. Now, past fifty, he set off in search of the magic fountain from whose elixir he might drink and receive back his lost youth.

Poor Ponce de León! After years of seeking, disappointed and far older than when he had set out, he still had found no such magical waters. Instead, an arrow from the taut bow of a dusky Indian had wounded him mortally, and he died in agony in the Florida jungles.

"I hate it!" exclaimed Janet Crowder, looking up suddenly from the magazine she had been looking through.

"Hate what, Janet?" asked Betty Treslow, her chum.

"Being so gawky and self-conscious!" cried Janet. "I haven't any more natural grace than a cow!"

"What set you off on that tangent, anyhow, Janet?"

"Oh, I don't know," Janet replied. "I want to be charming —have personality—like—like—like the girl in this ad!"

"What's the ad?" Betty queried.

"Just listen to this!" cried Janet, pointing at the glamour girl in the advertisement and reading:

You don't have to be what your mirror says!

You can walk as rhythmically—be as un-self-conscious—be as poised as this girl!

You can sit down, stand up, turn around, walk *charmingly!*

You can learn to wear your clothes as becomingly as the most lovely actress!

You can learn to apply your cosmetics with all the artistry of the most accomplished beautician!

You can have a personality that is winsome and dominating!

You can have the world at your feet!

"Goodness, Janet!" exclaimed Betty. "What do you have to do?"

"Just send and get this self-improvement booklet!" explained Janet enthusiastically. "It's free! Now won't I make that flashy Joan Pindar envy me!"

"What's the address?" demanded Betty. "I'm going to send and get one of those booklets, too!"

Riches, Youth, Charm—Universal Wishes!

Wish-thinking! The "promoters" of the cat and rat ranches knew perfectly well that they could rely upon the universal desire for easy wealth to float their enterprise. Ponce de León knew that if he could find the Fount of Bimini he would remain forever young himself and become the race's greatest benefactor through the conquest of age and death! The promoters of the self-improvement course that so captivated Janet Crowder and Betty Treslow knew that they could count upon the keen desire of womankind for charm and personality, to induce hundreds to swallow their bait.

Riches! Youth! Charm! Powerful wishes, these!

⟡ ⟡ ⟡

In this chapter you will learn about the amazing role which wish-thinking and the will to believe play in our lives. You will understand why we tend so often to throw logic and common sense out of the window; why we try to pass ourselves off as more worth while than we are; why parents seldom think ill of their children; why we become smugly satisfied with ourselves; why we are taken in by fakers who promise us whatever we want; why we become easy prey to propagandists of every conceivable type and variety.

*Fig. 47. A medieval astrologer. For ages men have sought to fore-
tell their destinies from the stars. Astrologers are frequently patron-
ized today by those who wish-think.*

12. WISH-THINKING AND PROPAGANDA

Before you start your study of the chapter, it will be helpful for you to pause to recall from history some striking instances in which people were deluded by wish-thinking. Record your examples on a form prepared like the one below:

SOME SPECIMENS OF WISH-THINKING IN HISTORY

1. "Making the world safe for democracy." (1917-1919)
2.
3.
4.
5. etc.

Go to ancient and medieval as well as to modern history for your examples. The records of the past are filled with the driftwood of exploded ideas which were the embodiment of somebody's wish-thinking.

THINKING THAT ISN'T THINKING AT ALL

Wish-thinking. "If wishes were horses," the old maxim has it, "beggars could ride!" Stated more appropriately for the present age: "If wishes were automobiles, every beggar could have his own car!" The implication is, of course, that a person who lacks certain things he would like to have, commonly spends a lot of time and energy wishing that he had them.

Most of us do more or less of this sort of thing in moments when we are particularly discouraged with our achievements or dissatisfied with our possessions. It is a pardonably human trait, strongest perhaps in childhood and youth, but one that we probably never entirely outgrow.

Unfortunately, though, many a person does not stop with an occasional wishing that things were different. His fanciful dreams prove so alluring that they soon come to filter into his thinking. Before he knows it, if he isn't careful, he half believes that what he wishes is really true, or is going to come true shortly. A willing victim of this wish-thinking, he comes to look with bias upon every situation and condition that confronts him. Instead of weighing the evidence pro and con, he ignores or dismisses all the features of it that do not dovetail into his own peculiar hopes and wishes for himself, for his friends, and for the world in general.

WISH-THINKING IN THE AREA OF ACHIEVEMENT

Get-rich-quick schemes. There are many areas of experience in which this kind of thinking—which cannot properly be called thinking at all, of course—is commonly found to be operating. Take, for example, the area of achievement. A clever but unscrupulous promotor comes along with some get-rich-quick scheme and represents that here is a sound and safe investment by means of which in just a few weeks' time you can double or triple your money—or perhaps even multiply it by a hundred, or a thousand!

You are immediately allured. You wish for wealth—have always wished for it—and here is wealth at last in the guise of golden opportunity knocking at your door. Logic, common sense, probability are all thrown out the window. Your powers of thinking never even have a chance to protect you. So strong and so overpowering is your wish to get easy wealth, that you, like hundreds of other victims with the same ambition, are drawn into the web and fleeced of your hard-earned dollars.

Wish-thinking blinds its victims. Wish-thinking one's way to accomplishment leads a person to put confidence in all sorts of dubious means of achieving his goals. Closing his mind to the logical and reasonable analysis of the means and schemes that offer, he allows his wishes to overrule his better judgment. The hope which "springs eternal in the human breast" aids tremendously by goading the person on to keep his faith in what he wish-thinks, even after all sensible support for it has been overthrown. Thus, a man who has been duped in some wildcat, get-rich-quick scheme may continue for a long time afterwards not only believing in the returns the venture will ultimately bring him, but even throwing in more good money in the vain hope of retrieving his vanishing fortunes.

On a form prepared like the one below, enumerate as many as possible of the characteristics of some person you know who is an inveterate wish-thinker:

CHARACTERISTICS OF A WISH-THINKER I KNOW

1. He is certain he is going to be rich some day by playing the races.
2.
3.
4.
5. etc.

(Remember that in wish-thinking all the evidence seems to point to the contrary conclusion, or at least does not warrant the complacent faith of the wisher!)

WISH-THINKING IN THE AREA OF SELF-ESTEEM

Undesirables in our midst. In the area of the leadership of others, of domination, of impressiveness, too, much wish-thinking goes on. Many people, eager for prominence among their fellows, for fame, for preferment, cultivate the pretense that they are of far greater social or civic worth than they really are. Through wish-thinking they shortly reach the point at which they really consider themselves worthy of the admiration and perhaps even the veneration of their friends and associates. Thus, in their own minds, they become what they would like to be. Since they believe themselves to be far more inspiring or interesting to others than the facts indicate, they are in grave danger of becoming insufferable boasters and social ignoramuses.

Most of us probably could think of at least one person we know who has wish-thought himself into an unenviable conceitedness and surrounded himself with a halo of virtuousness, or of long-suffering humility, that is most disagreeable to everybody but himself.

WISH-THINKING IN THE AREA OF FAMILY LIFE

Why parents idealize their children. In the area of family life, too, much wish-thinking goes on. This is probably most strikingly true in the wish-thinking of parents about their children. Since their offspring are flesh of their flesh and bone of their bone, it is quite understandable why mothers and fathers believe so staunchly in their children. The faith and hope they have in them is proverbial, and this is as it should be. Where else save to their parents could boys and girls look for belief and trust during the long years from infancy up through the teens?

If parents, looking through the eyes of love, fail to see the imperfections that others can see in their offspring, it is only because they idealize them and are apt to behold them through rose-colored spectacles. It is good for the parents and good for the children that the former do so much wish-thinking about the latter. Not having had too many opportunities and advantages when they were young themselves, some parents covet these jealously for their children and believe implicitly in their capacity to achieve.

Children do not always measure up. Sometimes, though, the child lacks the mental capacity to do or to become what his parents dream for him, or else he proves himself unworthy and brings sorrow and shame upon them. In the former case, the fault is likely to rest with the parents, who have failed to understand the intellectual limitations of their child and who may perhaps have forced a college education on a lad who lacks the capacity for college work. In the latter case, the fault is likely to be in large measure the child's for departing so far from the parental standard.

To the glory of mothers!   It has been only a few years since an incredulous mother, confronted with indisputable evidence that her son had committed a dastardly murder, shook her head wonderingly and made the simple remark: "I know he didn't do it; he isn't that kind of boy." Poor, blind wish-thinker to the end! She could see in her fine, upstanding son only the virtues she had wished for him. To their eternal glory be it said that most mothers are like that!

THE WILL TO BELIEVE

A common failing.   Wish-thinking depends upon what William James, a great American psychologist of yesterday, called the "will to believe." Most people are surprisingly gullible, particularly about those things they *want* to believe and those things they do *not* want to believe. It is the easiest thing in the world to dismiss evidence that is damaging to our own preconceived ideas and beliefs, or to find confirmatory "evidence" that can be constructed as favoring or substantiating them.

If John Doe be a Democrat, he discerns no good in Republicanism, and he becomes adept in so sifting the evidence that he is able to trace everything constructive and good in our body politic to the Democrats and everything vicious to the Republicans. If he be a Republican, he can do the opposite with equal confidence and assurance.

Similarly, an individual may find virtue only in *his* church, *his* family, *his* community, *his* system of ideas, and *his* slant on life. For the other fellow's religion, or family, or community, or ideology, or slant on life, he has nothing but criticism or scorn. From one person's viewpoint the "good old days" were the best when "a man was a man" and right was right; from another person's point of view, the old times were all wrong, and only ultramodern or "advanced" standards and ideals are good.

The poor man can easily believe the worst about rich men; the rich man can as easily despise the poor man. To one who is city-born and bred, ruralites are dull, uninteresting, crude; to one who is country-born and bred, urbanites are "stuck-up," overbearing, fast. If a person be young, the older generation is stodgy and reactionary; if he be middle-aged, youth may seem to him indifferent, irreligious, and shockingly indiscreet.

Our vision becomes narrow. And so it goes on! The will to believe makes us, if we do not take care, blind to our own faults and overkeen to detect shortcomings in the other fellow; it makes us smugly satisfied with our own special attainments and outlooks and at the same time highly critical of those of other people. We choose to think that persons, places, and things not immediately connected with ourselves or not in line with our interests are of small worth. We grow contented with things as they are and resist change, growth, progress. We wish-think ourselves into becoming narrow-minded and smug.

On a form like that on the next page list several instances in which your own judgment has been distorted recently by an insidious "will to believe."

EASY MARKS FOR THE PROPAGANDIST

The clever soothsayer. Wish-thinking and the will to believe tend to make people uncritical of clever schemes designed

1. I "reasoned" that I would get ahead faster if I left school and began to earn money.

2.

3.

4.

5. etc.

(The will to believe motivates much of our ill-thought-out conduct and opinion.)

to win their support or their dollars. Wish-thinkers, that is, willing believers, consequently are easy victims for the snares of propagandists of all sorts and varieties.

One of the very large areas of human experience in which the propagandist finds fertile soil for his schemes is that concerned with foretelling the future. Ever since the earliest Assyrian astrologers looked up to the stars and claimed to be able to read in them the inevitable happenings of tomorrow, mankind has been spellbound by the possibilities of foretelling the events of the morrow, especially as they touch the individual searcher.

"A fool and his money are soon parted!" Throughout all the ages since then, soothsayers, diviners, astrologers, palmists, and necromancers have vied with one another in making dupes of men and women who have found it easy and enthralling to believe the mutterings of the oracle, or the arresting visions of the crystal gazer, or the inscrutable wisdom of the mystic and the palmist and the astrologer. Passionately desiring reassurance for the future, many a credulous mortal has deposited his money and his faith on the altars of the seer and the mystic. The will to believe provides him with half the conviction he needs to accept the augury; the clever impressiveness and dark mysteriousness of the practitioner provide nim with the other half.

Make a form like the one below and list as many kinds of people as you can think of:

THESE PEOPLE CAPITALIZE ON THE WILL TO BELIEVE

Who They Are	Why They Succeed
1. Operators of slot machines	People believe they may get much for little.
2.	
3.	
4.	
5. etc.	
(You'll have a long list if you will think sharply.)	

A case in point. As I write, there is upon my desk a printed flier which is one of hundreds that have been recently circulated through the community. "Let this man help you solve your problems" is the inviting message at the top of the face side of the flier. This is followed up in bold-face type half an inch high by the modest title: "Famous Psychic and Adviser and Expert Astrologer." After the name and address the reader learns that "consultation and reading have been reduced to $1.00 if you present this card." On the reverse side he is assured, again in bold type, that "Psychic and Astrological Advice Means Rehabilitation of Reasonable Hopes and Ambitions, and will be of great value when you are in doubt or worried about anything or anybody."

Additional alluring "facts" emblazoned on the flier include the following: "This expert psychic and astrologer suggests what you are able to accomplish, your talents and possibilities." "Astrology gives you definite information on every subject: business, marriage, talents, habits, hopes, wishes, or difficulties! Remarkable knowledge of your affairs and astonishing readings." "Definite information on any subject any human being may be interested in." "A brilliant, truthful, and com-

pelling reading of yourself and those whom you are interested in."

Who is not curious about the future?   It is fair to suppose
that this "psychic" is finding it extremely profitable thus to
capitalize upon the average individual's keen personal interest
in what the future may hold in store. The will to believe may
be safely counted upon to guide many an eager consultant to
his rooms. His art and his stock in trade may consist principally in clever advertising and the knowledge that a new
sucker is born every minute.

To this same order belong the astrologers' columns in the
newspapers, the elaborate charts of the palmists and phrenologists, and the cards, crystals, and tea leaves of the fortuneteller. Yet neither in the stars, nor in the lines of the palm, nor
in the inscrutable interior of a crystal do the fates reveal themselves to the psychics.

Of like nature also are the spirit manifestations of mediums
who not only claim to be in touch with the spirit world but
who also claim to be able to photograph the spirits of de-
parted loved ones still hovering over those bereaved. So yearn-
ingly would many be assured that all is well with those who
have preceded them in death that they put implicit and wondering trust in those "spiritual" individuals who are able to
pierce the veil and report their findings.

"Cures" for human ills.   Not only do wish-thinkers desire
to be reassured regarding otherworldly matters; they want also
to stave off as long as possible the encroachments of old age,
illness, and death. In consequence of this universal desire to
continue in good health and to postpone the inevitable hour
when infirmity or death will intervene, wish-thinkers are eager
to grasp at any and all health-preserving and health-restoring
programs, medicines, and cure-alls with which clever advertisers can capture their fancies.

Magazines, billboards, placards, radio programs, and pamphlets vie with one another to flash into the ready eyes and din into the willing ears of wish-thinkers the indispensableness of this, that, and the other alleviator of human suffering and woe. Superlatives are employed most extravagantly in the claims for these products made by their promoters. From

Photo by Culver Service

Fig. 48. In frontier days medicine peddlers drove their rigs over the countryside selling to gullible people their cure-alls for baldness, for consumption, or for what-ails-you. Are people less gullible about patent remedies in these enlightened times?

dentifrices and mouth washes to fat reducers and cancer "cures," these preparations cover the entire range of human ills and deficiencies.

Most of them worthless or even harmful! And millions of people, driven forward by the strong will to believe the claims of the manufacturers, seek every year to preserve their health, or to regain it, by investing in worthless or positively harmful products. For years the American Medical Association, in conjunction with the United States Pure Food and Drug Administration, with the Federal Trade Commission, and with state and municipal boards of health, has been analyzing these "remedies" and disseminating information about them to the general public. Included in the list of panaceas and "treatments" that the Association has exposed have been cancer "cures," consumption "cures," cough "cures," epilepsy "treatments," rupture "cures," diabetes "cures," kidney "treatments," obesity "cures," and "cures" for deafness.

The truth about these and innumerable other specific drugs, nostrums, and "remedies" has been proclaimed throughout the country in books, in pamphlets, and in professional articles carried in the popular and the scientific medical journals. The appalling extent of the traffic in these "cures" testifies in no uncertain terms to the eagerness with which ill or apprehensive people will turn to them as well as to the false faith which they continue to repose in them. The will to believe in an advertised patent "remedy" is overpowering, and the sufferer wastes precious weeks and perhaps months fooling with such "cures" as these when he ought to be receiving genuine curative treatment at the hands of reputable physicians before it is too late.

Skin-deep beauty! A prominent area of wish-thinking is that concerned with physical charm and beauty. What woman —young or old—does not wish for these priceless boons? Manufacturers of cosmetics and beauty preparations find ready feminine markets for their products, for which the most alluring claims are made. The sale of creams, ointments, and paints for the skin, of dyes and washes and beautifiers for the hair, of depilatories and deodorants, has grown to a major industry in our country. Some of these preparations are decidedly harmful to the skin, and a few have had fatal results. Yet the strong urge for physical charm drives millions of women yearly to purchase them in the fond belief that by their use they may either enhance their beauty or stay the encroaching signs of age.

"Pep-producers."   Related to the wish for charm and physical beauty is the desire to keep fatigue away in order that one may do more work or indulge in more prolonged activities. This urge has been strong enough to tempt certain foolish people who ought to know better to drug themselves with a very powerful "pep-producer" known as *benzedrine sulfate*. The immediate effect of this substance is to increase the heart action, raise the blood pressure, heighten the keenness of the senses, eliminate fatigue, and produce temporarily a gratifying consciousness of elation and power. The reaction is, however, sharp and sure. The victim is shortly rewarded with sleeplessness, headache, and a feeling of excessive fatigue; a deathly pallor spreads over his features, total collapse is not infrequent, and subsequent nervous disorders are common.

The following excerpt from an article by Dr. Iago Galdston in *Hygeia* (October 1940) is illuminating in this connection:

Patented "pep-producers" bombard us on all sides, claiming to bolster us with exuberant vitality or to enable us to meet fatigue. . . . Among the panaceas offered to the public for that "tired feeling" is one which has as its active ingredient a sweetish substance . . . identical with the . . . acid of gelatin. A leaflet supplied with each package of this pep-inducer modestly contained claims that it fills the customer with "a desire and ability to undertake tasks that before were irksome and difficult. The tired, sagged expression of the face changes. The patient gains strength, and life for him is altogether different from what it was before." (!) Such tablets will do about as much good as a spoonful of corn syrup.

Thus it goes for a score of preparations that are being advertised and bought as pick-me-ups. Either they are superfluous and useless, or they do pick you up, only to let you down with a terrible crash. . . . *It is significant that none of the fatigue laboratories of the world has ever recommended or manufactured a patented pick-me-up.*

The principal addicts of this benzedrine intoxication are reported to be overworked professional men, executives, clerks, secretaries, and students; they make the mistake of believing that they can burn the candle at both ends and escape the consequences. What a fine thing it would be, indeed, if we never got tired and worn out! But fatigue is unavoidable, and there is no way to wish-think otherwise. "Pep pills" passed around at social parties may revive weary revelers for an hour, but the inevitable "hang-over" is a highly dangerous condition of exhaustion and physical depletion.

List on the following form some of the commonest specimens of wish-thinking that people exhibit:

COMMON FORMS OF WISH-THINKING

1. One can disregard the laws of health and continue to keep well.
2.
3.
4.
5. etc.

(You find on every hand people who are wish-thinking their way through life!)

THE POWER OF PROPAGANDA

Popularizing the cigarette. The tremendous power that propaganda wields in shaping public opinion may be illustrated in innumerable ways, but perhaps in no connection more strikingly than in the popularization of cigarette smoking. In 1915 somewhat less than eighteen billion cigarettes were produced in the United States. In 1940—twenty-five years later—ten times that number were produced. The curve of consumption followed a similar pattern, of course, and this notwithstanding the counter influence which the schools attempted to exert by teaching "the ill effects of tobacco." Wide advertising and the carrying on of favorable propaganda were of course the principal factors that accounted for the steady rise in the production and consumption of cigarettes.

Propaganda works both ways. Propaganda may be relied upon to win popular interest in and support for anything, good or bad. Propaganda elects men to office, or defeats them; it enacts legislation, or kills it; it impassions men to war or to peace; it popularizes and dictates our food and drink, our amusements and our relaxations, our likes and dislikes; it induces men to gamble or to turn thumbs down on gambling, to drink or to abstain, to accept or to reject, to think or not to think.

Seekers after fame. Propaganda, moreover, fires mediocre people with the conviction that they can be leaders of men, or write romances and songs and verse, or be winsome and radiant and compelling in their personalities, or achieve wealth and fame and an enviable place among their fellows, or transform sievelike memories into phenomenally retentive memories. All that is necessary is for the would-be notable to "try our system" of personality culture, or of memory training, or of creative writing, or what not. Here, as in all wish-thinking, the tantalizing and all-pervading will to believe impels the seeker after fame to throw himself into the eager arms of the clever promoter. The latter gets the former's dollars and the former gets the latter's inconsequential and usually worthless or downright vicious formula for success and achievement.

The promoter of such a scheme seldom gets prosecuted or even privately criticized because the victim either continues to believe in the "system" to the end or he is too ashamed of his own gullibility to admit that he has been duped.

NATIONAL AND INTERNATIONAL PROPAGANDA

Winning wars without bullets. Propaganda at perhaps its cleverest is to be witnessed in the studied and highly effective efforts of dictator nations at war to win blind support for the policies of their leaders. So indispensable do modern dictators feel propaganda within their realm to be that they coolly and unapologetically elevate some powerful figure to be minister of propaganda and charge him with the function of whipping into line every last man, woman, and child in the country and of blotting out every person, place, or thing that attempts to hold out against the avalanche.

By controlling the press and the radio, by maintaining a universal system of espionage, by the power of oratory, and by the appeal to fear, dictators find it possible to coerce their nationals—outwardly, at least—into conformity with the aims of the government.

Insidious work abroad. They go further than this. Aware of the effects of long-time propaganda, they early send their henchmen into other countries, both near and far, and charge them with the responsibility of arousing and maintaining attitudes favorable to totalitarian methods. This type of propaganda may take either the form of disseminating biased information, or the more insidious form of endeavoring to undermine the theories of government locally subscribed to and creating through fifth-column activities discontent with the *status quo* and a desire for co-operation or alliance with the totalitarian state. By these means dictators hope not only to hold in line their own nationals at home but also to arouse favor and support abroad.

HOW PSYCHOLOGISTS WORK

Investigators distinguish many subtle propaganda devices by which some individuals or groups seek to influence the opinions of other individuals or groups.

The Institute for Propaganda Analysis, in New York City, has identified seven different techniques made use of by pressure groups in influencing public opinion. Here they are:

(1) The technique of *Name Calling*. Through being associated in the public mind with undesirable or blameworthy persons or practices, some epithets have come to be so strongly tinged with emotion that they are flung by the propagandist at individuals, organizations, or philosophies as a means of discrediting them in the eyes of the public. Examples of such emotionally toned names are "Communist," "fifth columnist," "Puritan," "chiseler," "obstructionist," "demagogue," "dictator." To apply any of these terms to a person is to arouse attitudes of disgust or resentment in large numbers of people who are not clever enough to see through the trick.

(2) The technique of *Glittering Generalities*. The reputation of any movement can be surprisingly damaged or bolstered by the propagandists' use of vague but popularly appealing terms in referring to it. Some examples of damaging terms are "fraud," "paternalism," "slavery," "in cahoots with." Words calculated to bolster a cause and facilitate its development include "the American standard," "equality," "freedom," "democracy." The latter are designed to make, the former to break, a movement. Everybody understands, of course, that these latter terms may be used accurately to tell the truth about a genuinely good cause, as well as to bolster a dubious one. It is principally because such terms as these have real validity that the propagandists press them into service.

(3) The *Transfer Device* technique. A promising means of

creating popular approval and support for a cause or a product is to assert that it has the confidence of admittedly reputable groups or institutions. The advertised or propagandized commodity or movement is thus cleverly aided by its alleged association with the good and the creditable, and the esteem enjoyed by the latter is thus transferred to the former. Such transfer devices include the assertions that the propagandized agent "has the full support of the city government," or "is recognized by the leading physicians," or "is subscribed to by businessmen throughout the country." People tend to be readily influenced by the assurance that a thing is approved by reputable groups having prestige in the community.

(4) The technique of the *Testimonial*. About the first questions the ordinary individual asks about a new proposition or a new gadget or commodity are: "Who else has one?" "What do other people think of it?" If the promoter or the salesman can have up his sleeve a sheaf of testimonials from "satisfied users," he has a powerful reply for such questions. And if the testimonials he flaunts bear the signatures of some individuals of prominence—a movie star, an aviatrix, a person of wealth or social position—they will have all the more drawing power, and the scheme will be the more likely to work.

(5) The technique of the *Plain Folks Device*. This is an especially clever method for the propagandist to employ since, by claiming to be "one of the plain people," an aspirant to office can always count upon striking a responsive cord in the breasts of his constituents, most of whom are plain people, also. However aristocratic he may be at heart or in deed, and however out of tune he may be with the lives of the common people, if he can put on the "plain folks" act in his public appearances and utterances, he will fool nearly everybody. To admit that one is a "plain dirt-farmer," or that he "came up through the mill," or that he "started out with nothing," or that

he "always feels at home among his people," is nearly always to win votes. And if, in addition to these verbal assurances, he can also call a few key people in his audience by their first names and can take time out to kiss a few dozen babies whose fond mothers hold them up in front of him, he will clinch still more firmly his hold upon the people.

(6) The *Card Stacking* technique. This is a particularly vicious technique, for it depends upon outright misrepresentation of facts for its appeal. By broadcasting half-truths or actual lies, a propagandist can stack the cards against almost anybody or anything. By choosing his "facts" judiciously and placing emphasis upon the wrong aspect, he can do the same thing. The "whispering campaigns" that flourish in many an election are good specimens of the card stacking procedure; through such insidious propaganda the opposition may easily ruin the prospects of the opposing candidate and thus enhance their own.

(7) The *Band Wagon* technique. Users of this device make their appeal by advising everybody to "go along with the crowd," by asserting that "everybody is doing it" and that now is the time to "get in line." Psychologically speaking, nobody wants to be alone in the sense that he is not one of the crowd; hence, to appeal to the natural desire to "stand in," to be "on the band wagon" is a clever way to motivate a man's allegiance to a cause. "Uncle Sam says," "America calls," "used by millions," "eight out of every ten people prefer it"—these are examples of the band wagon technique. "Five million people can't be wrong," "follow the crowd to Blank's basement," and "a nation's breakfast food" are others.

TO HELP YOU LEARN

SOME QUESTIONS TO ANSWER

1. What is the difference between indulging in fancy and wish-thinking? Between wish-thinking and thinking?

2. Can you identify any characters in literature who exemplify wish-thinking? Explain.

3. Do you think all gamblers are wish-thinkers? Why, or why not? How do you explain Monte Carlo?

4. Have you ever consulted a palmist or fortuneteller of any variety? If not, do you know somebody who has done so? Can you account for any true facts or predictions that were given?

5. Why should anybody need a "pep-producer"? What more intelligent way to keep full of vim and energy for the day's work and the day's play would you be inclined to recommend?

WORKING WITH PSYCHOLOGY

1. Search carefully through the advertising sections of some home magazines which you happen to have available and find as many different appeals as possible made by advertisers to the gullibilities of readers. Note particularly the cleverness with which the ads are directed toward the awakening of or the catering to ambitions whose realization by the rank and file of people is improbable.

2. Cut from local or metropolitan newspapers several columns conducted by astrologers, clairvoyants, "psychics," and so forth. Check through the clippings and note the clever appeal which they make to thoughtless or gullible people looking for the fulfillment of their ambitions for easy wealth, beauty, popularity, success, happiness.

3. Appoint some member of the class to write to the American Medical Association, Bureau of Investigation, 535 North Dearborn Street, Chicago, Illinois, requesting literature on useless or harmful drugs and nostrums they have investigated. After the material has been received, analyze it from the standpoint of the appeal to wish-

thinking, and the will to believe which the "remedies" are designed
to make.

4. Identify several specimens of propaganda from the international
scene, dealing, for example, with such matters as coloring the news
for home consumption; minimizing the extent of military reverses
and exaggerating the importance of military successes; misrepre-
senting social, political, or governmental crises; belittling the resources and strength of hostile or competing nations; and the like.
Valuable sources for this project include, in addition to newspapers
and periodicals, publications of the Foreign Policy Association, of
the government, and of propaganda bureaus.

WHAT OTHERS SAY

1. In Fiction:

The Magnificent Obsession by Lloyd C. Douglas. A highly
idealistic example of wish-thinking, in which the theory is developed
that good deeds, when done altruistically and in secrecy, always
redound to the benefit of the doer.

The Closed Garden by Julian Green. A young French girl of
eighteen, seeking refuge from the cruelty and isolation of which
she is the unhappy victim, retires into a dream world of wish-thinking in which she is madly in love with a stranger who lives next
door. The story shows how wish-thinking, when unbridled, may
lead to complete mental breakdown.

The Emperor of Portugallia by Selma Lagerlöf. The story of a
man who pathetically wish-thinks his absent daughter into a great
lady of royal rank, and himself—a humble peasant—into an
emperor.

2. In Drama:

Peter Pan by J. M. Barrie. A delightful play in which Peter Pan,
a young boy, in his wish to escape from growing up, runs away to
Never-Never-Land. There he meets Wendy, Michael, and John,
and the four of them have many exciting adventures with Tinker
Bell, Tiger Lily, and the terrible Captain Hook.

The American Way by George S. Kaufman and Moss Hart. A
propaganda play designed to stimulate tolerance and sane patriot-

ism. It ruthlessly arraigns the American way of handling social, economic, and political problems.

If I Were King by Justin H. McCarthy. A fascinating melodrama in which are unraveled the fortunes of a dissipated rhymester who, deploring the manner in which France is governed, wishes that he might be king so that he could set matters right. Louis XI, over-hearing the wish, makes him Constable of France for one week.

3. In Poetry:

Justice Denied in Massachusetts by Edna St. Vincent Millay. A strong propaganda poem inspired by the famous Sacco-Vanzetti Case. The author is pessimistic about the future unless men acquire a nicer sense of justice.

Do Our Ancestors Make Our Lives, or We?

What would you have said if, while making a survey of jails, you had chanced upon six different people in the same prison, all of them related and all awaiting trial for different crimes? That was exactly what Robert Dugdale, of the New York Prison Commission, found in one county institution. Four of the six were men; the other two were women. Two of the men were charged with murderous assault; another, with receiving stolen goods; and the fourth, with burglary. One of the women was charged with vagrancy; the other was being held as a witness against her own father.

Of course, being a scientific-minded person, Mr. Dugdale was immediately made curious by this unusual array of criminals in the same family. The subsequent study which he made of the Jukes Family was one of the first and most interesting of the investigations that have been made in the field of heredity *versus* environment. Laboriously, painstakingly, he traced the lineage of these six criminals back over more than a century, cataloguing more than 700 persons of an approximate 1200 in the complete line. Here are the records some of them left behind: 180 were paupers; 250 were arrested and tried for crime; 140 were convicted as criminals; 60 were habitual thieves; 7 were murderers; 50 were notoriously immoral; 300 died in infancy.

There's a family record for you! A record of "unending crime, pauperism, disease, viciousness, and immorality."

The famous Bach family of musicians included fifty-seven persons of such prominence as to merit inclusion in standard biographical dictionaries of musicians. Sebastian Bach's father was a distinguished organist; his first cousin, J. Christopher, was one of the most noted musicians of the age in which he lived; his son, Guillaume Frederick—"Bach of Halle"—was a man of great power and learning; Emmanuel, another son, called "Bach of Berlin," was the founder of pianoforte music; another son, Christopher, called "Bach of England," was a famous composer. And so the story runs! Talent and musical genius appeared phenomenally in this amazing line.

Quite a different record from that left by the descendants of worthless, drunken, shiftless Max Jukes!

Heredity? Yes, undoubtedly. But do you suppose a child born in the Jukes environment had anything like the chance of one born in the Bach environment? Are not the opportunities offered by one's surroundings related to achievement?

Gordon Stanley wasn't really Gordon Stanley at all. Mr. and Mrs. Stanley, who adopted him when he was five years old, could find out but little about the boy's family, except that his father had deserted when Gordon was two years old and that his mother had died about a year later. Gordon could dimly recall his mother, but of course could remember nothing about his father. He brooded a lot about his family, and by the time he got to high school he had pretty well convinced himself that his paternal heredity, at least, was bad and that there wasn't much chance for him ever to amount to anything.

Then one day in class, Mr. Barry, the science teacher, in talking about heredity, made two remarks that electrified Gordon Stanley. One of them was: "Of course, heredity isn't everything. Look at Abraham Lincoln; his father didn't amount to much, but that didn't stop his son." The other one was: "A famous old Roman once said, 'It is of no consequence of what parents a man is born, so that he himself be a man of merit.' We build our own lives; our parents don't. It's up to each one of us what we shall make them."

Gordon Stanley walked home on air that afternoon, his ears ringing with these two statements of Mr. Barry's. He was beginning already to feel new courage and self-confidence.

"I never thought of it that way before!" he said to himself.

Heredity and Environment Both Important

Here are interesting situations. The Jukes family provided its descendants with a poor heredity and a poor environment. The Bach family provided its children with good parentage and a good environment. Gordon Stanley's real parents provided an uncertain heritage; his foster parents, a good environment; his school, good advice and training. It should be apparent that Gordon had a far better chance to amount to something than he would have had if his name had been Gordon Jukes! It should be apparent also that there was a possibility that he might turn out to be as noted a person as if his name had been Gordon Bach!

✓ ✓ ✓

In this chapter you will find out something about the mechanism of heredity, something about racial and family similarities and differences, and something about the difficulties scientists encounter in their efforts to fathom the mysteries of human inheritance. You will learn that environment is of perhaps equal importance with heredity in determining what each of us shall become. You will discover that there is much loose thinking about heredity and will meet some common-sense attitudes about it that should help to counteract these popular misconceptions.

Fig. 49. Must a person be descended from a brilliant line in order to achieve renown? The life of Louis Pasteur, one of the world's greatest scientists, answers this question. His ancestors were peasants. His father was a tanner with little education, but he provided Louis with a good home and a good education. While both his environment and his own tirelessness helped make Pasteur famous, no one can deny that he was born a potential genius, in spite of his ordinary inheritance.

13. WHAT WE DO AND DON'T INHERIT

Before you begin studying about heredity, prepare a form like this one and enter upon it some of the more obvious traits of your own parents, and whether or not you can distinguish in yourself some of them:

FAMILY TRAITS

In My Father (Paternal Side)	Am I like Him in This Trait?	In My Mother (Maternal Side)	Am I like Her in This Trait?
1. Brown eyes	Yes	Blue eyes	No
2.			
3.			
4.			
5. etc.			

Sometimes the similarity to one or another parent is very clear; sometimes a child differs markedly from both parents in some trait.

IS HEREDITY OR ENVIRONMENT MORE IMPORTANT?

Two inevitable forces. Heredity and environment are both powerful forces in our lives. None of us can escape the influences of both factors; we inherit what we inherit, and we are surrounded by what surrounds us! Both are highly important, and both are inevitable. About the first—heredity—we can do nothing whatever; about the latter—environment—we can often do much. It would be far more profitable to abandon the popular controversy one meets on every hand regarding which is the more powerful factor, and to use all our mental energies in trying to make the most of the opportunities for developing our inherited capacities in the environment in which we find ourselves.

THE GENES

The word *gene* is an important one that everybody should remember. It comes from the same Latin root as the word *genesis,* which means *beginning.* Biologists use the term *genes* to apply to the factors in the *germ plasm* (contents of the germ cell) that determine in the beginning what our inherited qualities are to be. It is believed that there are many thousands of genes in the parental germ cell. These carry our inherited traits and characteristics, physical as well as mental. Each parent contributes to the new cell one set of genes; the two sets combine to form the particular traits of the new individual, such as eye color, length of nose, or shape of fingernail.

Why you might have been different. Now since there are many thousands of genes in the germ cell of each parent, and since the genes are quite diverse, it follows that when these innumerable and varied genes unite to form the new individual, there are infinite possibilities in the resulting traits. *Geneticists* (scientists who study heredity) estimate that the possible number of different combinations from a single mating amounts to trillions! The wonder of it all is, not that people are so unlike each other, but rather that they are not infinitely more unlike!

With the multitude of possible combinations among biparental genes, it is little short of amazing that any two people in the world can look or act in the remotest degree alike! Yet in thousands of years of human history on the earth, so relatively limited have these potential variations been that men have differed surprisingly little from one generation to another, or from one age to another.

WE ARE ALL ALIKE—YET ALL DIFFERENT

Common traits in us all. If you were to study a thousand normal adult white males, you would find they would all resemble one another in numberless ways. Structurally, for example, they would be of relatively similar height and weight. True, some might be only five feet tall, or even a little less, while some might be more than six feet tall; some might weigh barely a hundred twenty-five pounds, while others might weigh more than two hundred fifty. None, however, would be three feet tall, nor eight feet; nor would any weigh seventy-five pounds or three hundred pounds. They would all have two eyes, two ears, two hands, and two feet; their skins would all be white and their eyes colored; they would have hairy scalps and hairless palms, jointed fingers and toes, movable necks and backs and immovable noses, thirty-two teeth (now or formerly!), twenty-four ribs, twenty nails; they would all have mouths and tongues and vocal cords capable of making sounds.

From the activity point of view, these thousand men would all have minds and be able to use them in varying degrees; they would all either jump or be startled on hearing a sudden noise; they would fight if attacked, recoil if afraid, laugh if amused. All of them would experience, on occasion, emotions like anger, hatred, jealousy, grief, and fear. All of them would prefer comfort to discomfort, pleasure to pain, joy to sorrow. All of them would covet self-expression, mastery, and self-determination. In all of these fundamental characteristics, our thousand subjects would resemble each other very closely. In their physical make-up and in their various instinctive drives, they could not differ much, because nature does not often permit marked variations from the normal in these respects.

RESEMBLANCE IN THE SAME FAMILY

No two people are exactly alike. The traits that we have been enumerating in the two preceding paragraphs are principally traits which the thousand men would have by virtue of the fact that they all belonged to the human race and to the white race; they are, in other words, largely racial characteristics. If, now, we could take each one of these thousand men in turn and study him against his own particular family background—including his grandparents, parents, brothers and sisters, aunts, uncles, and cousins—we should find a surprising amount of difference between him and some of his relatives, and a striking resemblance between him and others of them.

What studies in human heredity show. Let us be more specific; and we can be, because geneticists have conducted many careful investigations of family resemblance, and mathematicians have shown them an easy way to express these relationships in understandable terms.

Let us suppose that Mr. Black—one of the thousand men—has an identical twin, that is, a brother born at the same time as he and so closely resembling him that the two can barely be told apart. Investigation reveals the fact that identical twins are more alike than any other people in the world, excepting other identical twins, of course! If we let perfect resemblance be expressed by 1.00, then the chances are that Mr. Black and his twin will resemble one another to a degree expressed by the decimal .90.

If instead of being one of a pair of identical twins, Mr. Black had been one of a pair of fraternal, or ordinary, twins, the degree of his resemblance to his brother would be reduced to something like .50. Likewise, the correlation between Mr. Black and his non-twin brothers or sisters would be about .50. Using the same mathematical notation, Mr. Black's resemblance to his parents may be expressed by the decimal .40, and his resemblance to his grandparents by .15. Any first cousins he may have will rate at about .25.

Clearly, there must be something to heredity, for if we compare Mr. Black's resemblance to the other nine hundred ninety-nine men in the group, the chances are that the decimal will be reduced to zero. Not only this, but it is apparent from the correlations mentioned in the preceding paragraph that the more closely people are related, the more likely they are to resemble one another in their traits. Conversely, the further back one goes, the less he tends to resemble his forebears. Children resemble their grandparents little (.15); they resemble their parents more (.40); they resemble their brothers and sisters still more (.50, or more). Cousins, descended on one side from the same line, of course, are half as much alike as brothers and sisters (.25).

TRAITS CAN'T BE PREDICTED ACCURATELY

Even though we know the traits of two parents fairly well, it will be impossible to predict with much reliability how their children will fit into the family pattern. To some degree only (.40) can we foretell what the probable resemblance to the parents will be; this is, however, too low a figure to justify any very confident prediction of the total characteristics of the offspring. We can speak only in terms of probability.

The law of chance in heredity. There is another reason why it is never safe to try to predict the traits of an individual from what we know about his parents. This, too, is a reason which the mathematicians have provided us. Because of the law of chance, the children in any family will cluster about the bi-parental average; some of them will diverge considerably; more will diverge but little. There is no way of foretelling, assuming there are to be several children, which of them will be nearest to the parental average and which will be farthest from it; and if there is but one child, nobody can predict where he will fall on the curve of chance: it may be that he will be almost a duplicate of the parental average; it may be he will diverge strikingly from it.

Geniuses and idiots. One child in a million births may so depart from parental average as to be a potential world genius; another may be the lowest type of idiot. It is impossible to forecast when and in what particular family a Michelangelo, or a Lincoln, or a Pasteur, or a Paderewski will make his appearance. Neither is it possible to forecast the birth of a child who is doomed to remain a helpless idiot all his life. All we know is that these striking departures from parental patterns occasionally occur, that less striking departures are everyday occurrences, and that rather slight departures are commonest of all.

Every race and every country has produced great men and women who have left indelible imprints upon those who came after them. On a form like the one below, list the ten persons whom you consider the greatest in all history.

MY TEN GREATEST WORLD GENIUSES OF ALL TIME

Personage	Century	Race	Contribution
1. Jesus	First	Jewish (Semitic)	Spiritual interpretation of life
2.			
3.			
4.			
5. etc.			

(Don't forget the great men you studied in ancient history.)

DIFFERENT RACES ARE SURPRISINGLY ALIKE

How about "superior races"? We who belong to the white race are tempted to believe naïvely that the white is a superior race; if we were Japanese, we should be just as prejudiced in favor of the yellow race. What are the facts?

A number of careful samplings have been made of the intelligence of various races and racial groups, both in the United States and in their native habitats. More and more research men incline to the position that, when due allowance has been made for differences obviously due to better opportunity and to a more stimulating environment, the original differences among the races of the earth approach the vanishing point.

True, it can be shown—and has been—that Negroes and Indians, when tested for intelligence, rate distinctly lower than whites. As we shall see in a later paragraph, this difference is easily explainable in terms of the general poverty of environmental and educational opportunities available to the former. It appears that there is no "superior race" of people. The fact that Anglo-Saxons and Nordics, whether in Europe or in the United States, rate higher on the tests and appear to have achieved more in the history of modern civilization is explainable in terms of an easier environment, better educational facilities, and the stimulating influence of surrounding culture and opportunity.

The myth of racial superiority. Variations within any given racial group are found to be much more significant than differences between racial groups. There are exceptionally stupid individuals in every race and group. What a person can achieve seems to depend far more upon his own make-up and the opportunities he enjoys than it does upon any mythical racial trait which he inherits from his ancestors. Give a Negro a few generations of educated forebears, with the present cultural and educational stimulation which this entails, and you will have a superior Negro. Give a white man a few generations of ne'er-do-well and illiterate forebears, with the present cultural and educational stagnation which this entails, and you will have an inferior white man.

It is high time we stopped talking and boasting about "superior races" and began to talk about improving the environments of men everywhere. Superiority is not greatly, if at all, a racial characteristic; it is rather a combination of good heredity and stimulating environment.

PROOF OF MARKED ENVIRONMENTAL INFLUENCE

Studies of canalboat children. There is plenty of evidence to indicate that environment greatly influences what people achieve with their minds and their capacities. One study that shows this clearly was made of the intelligence of the children of canalboaters in England. The parents of these children were illiterate, and the children themselves were exposed to no culture and received practically no formal education or schooling. The investigator made the startling discovery that, whereas four-year-old and five-year-old canalboat children rated within the normal range of intelligence, the older ones were found to be thirty points below the younger in intelligence. The inevitable conclusion is that an unchallenging and unstimulating environment actually reduces the amount of measurable intelligence with which a child originally started out in life.

Studies of Gypsy children. The same investigator found a similar decline of intelligence with age among Gypsy children, who live likewise characteristically in an environment lacking in opportunities for formal schooling and for intellectual stimulation.

Children in industrial areas. A query into the intelligence of children in a large industrial area in the United States revealed the fact that, whereas the six-year-olds tested at about normal, children older than six tested progressively lower at each age up to and including thirteen. The thirteen-year-olds were a good fifteen points lower than the six-year-olds. The suggested conclusion is that an impoverished environment, inadequate schooling, and frequent moving about from one part of the area to another, as the parents followed the shifting

Fig. 50. A children's modeling class at Hull House, the social settlement founded by Jane Addams and located in Chicago's slums.

demands for their labor, operated to lower the intelligence level of these boys and girls.

Children in orphan asylums. Another investigation yielded the discovery that continued living in an orphanage had a stunting effect upon the children. Many who rated well upon entering the institution showed a drop of several points at the end of a few years of residence. On the other hand, those whose intelligence was low at admission were found to have gained somewhat by continued residence. The inference here is, of course, that the environment provided by an orphanage is too poor to stimulate the brighter children to develop

Do you think these children will have a better chance to become intelligent citizens than those who have to play on the streets?

normally as they should, but is enough better than what those of lesser intelligence had earlier known to provide some small degree of stimulation.

Another study demonstrated the fact that eight years spent in a good foster home resulted in a gain of more than ten points in intelligence, while still another showed a similar ten-point gain among malnourished children after they had undergone treatment for some time in a first-rate children's hospital.

These and many other investigations that might be cited testify to the influence which environment unquestionably has upon intelligence; a fortunate and stimulating one promotes intelligence, while a meager and unstimulating one depresses it to a measurable degree.

The above discussion should not be interpreted as suggesting that in an unstimulating environment a child of original superior intelligence might be actually reduced to idiocy; nor that a child of poor intellectual endowment might, if he were placed in a superior environment, grow up to be a gifted individual. There must unquestionably be good endowment in the first place if an individual is to achieve much, later on; the best environment cannot make up for lack of brains to start with. With good endowment, an individual can often conquer his environment; without it, he is likely to be conquered by it.

In the form below, list a large number of environmental influences that make it easy for young people to turn out poorly when they grow up:

THESE THINGS IN THE ENVIRONMENT ARE BAD

1. Gambling dens
2.
3.
4.
5. etc.

(Sociologists and psychologists recognize scores of unfortunate environmental forces.)

LOOSE THINKING ABOUT HEREDITY

The fallacy that heredity is everything. A number of well-known studies have been made in years past of both famous and infamous families, among them the Edwards Family, the Kallikak Family, and the Jukes Family. The Kallikaks and the Jukes were, in the one case, feeble-minded, and in the other, worthless and criminal lines. Because of the fact that over a period of more than a hundred years these two infamous lines produced hundreds of feeble-minded, ne'er-do-well and criminal descendants, it has been commonly assumed that heredity must have been all-important.

Actually, the environment provided by the Kallikak and Jukes parents in each generation studied was a wretched one, and the stupidity or ill-repute of their descendants was certainly quite as much due to the surroundings in which they grew up as to the germ plasm from which they sprang. It is the loosest kind of thinking which neglects one line of evidence and magnifies another.

The Jonathan Edwards line has also been studied, and similar disregard of the environmental factor has been committed. Here was a line of men and women famous throughout the history of New England for its notable and superior citizens, many of them occupying high office and high responsibility in their communities. To argue, as many have done, that it was the superiority of the Edwards stock that was responsible for the long and distinguished line of people issuing from it, is to ignore completely the obvious fact that because of its superiority this line was able to provide culturally superior surroundings for its offspring to grow up in. Here is another example of incomplete thinking.

Nobody would argue for a moment that heredity was of no importance in producing either a Kallikak or an Edwards; the item that is overlooked is the inevitable contribution which their homes and surroundings and opportunities (or lack of opportunities) for education and culture made toward their development.

"It runs in the family!" How often we hear it remarked of an individual who possesses this or that affliction, physical or mental: "It's to be expected! That runs in his family!" Among the inherited deficiencies that have been thus attributed to the family germ plasm are the following: tuberculosis, cancer, insanity, feeble-mindedness, epilepsy, deafness, and color-blindness.

As a matter of fact, with the exception of feeble-mindedness, there is no proof that these things are inherited, and even feeble-mindedness is frequently found in families in which there is no history of the defect. Tuberculosis and cancer certainly are not inherited, although it is believed that a child may inherit a weakened constitution from a tuberculous parent. Even so, if he is properly protected from infection in his early life, there is no more reason why he should ever contract the disease than somebody else who has inherited no tendency toward it. Likewise, epilepsy may be associated with an unstable nervous system, but there is no definite proof that it is inherited. Proper control of the environment would prevent its occurrence even in those individuals who might have inherited a constitutional weakness of nerve structures.

The facts of the matter. About all we can safely say regarding the alleged "running in families" of such defects as these is that there is no valid evidence that they do, but that those individuals in whose family lines these conditions have appeared seem to develop them more easily than those whose lines are free of them. In other words, regardless of inherited tendencies and constitutional weaknesses, almost anyone's life can be so ordered that he will escape these afflictions.

If you have weak lungs, keep away from people ill with tuberculosis and learn to live hygienically. If you feel that you have inherited an unstable nervous system, learn to live serenely and confidently and to avoid extremes of conduct. If you have an ancestor who died of cancer, have a periodic check-up by a physician to forestall any development of cancer in your own body. These precautions, you will observe, are just as sensible for those who have no hereditary bugbears or apprehensions as they are for those who have. Hygienic living is the only sane rule for all.

See what additional popular superstitions about heredity you can think of, using the following form for recording them:

"IT RUNS IN THE FAMILY!"

The Popular Belief	The Fact of the Matter
1. "With that heredity, this boy couldn't do anything else but grow up to be a crook."	His heredity probably hasn't anything to do with it. He *learned* to be a crook.
2.	
3.	
4.	
5. etc.	

(It's easy to blame heredity, when most of the trouble that people get into can be traced to bad environment and training.)

The fallacy of inevitable insanity. "There is insanity in my family; therefore I shall go insane!" Here is a bit of false reasoning so common as to merit a special paragraph or two in refutation. Granted that an examination of a thousand psychopathic family lines and of a thousand sane or normal lines would reveal more individuals who are definitely insane in the former, the thing is by no means *inevitable*. Insanity neither afflicts everybody in the former nor avoids everybody in the latter. As a matter of fact, even though there is mental disease or weakness in your own near ancestry or among your relatives, you may take comfort in the reflection that there are few families who do not have peculiar people, sane or insane, in them.

A rash conclusion. To conclude that, because there is nervous or mental disease in your family, it is bound to come to *you* sooner or later is entirely unwarranted. Insanity is a state due either to actual physical disease that attacks the nervous system, or else to a failure on the part of the individual to adjust his emotions and his values to the world of reality in which he finds himself. Long continued overwork, excessive fatigue, and poisoning from alcohol or syphilis rank high among the causes of mental disease. So also do such things as chronic worrying, overstimulation, and physical and emotional excess.

Conditions such as these may be experienced by any person who does not live wisely, whether there is insanity in his line, or whether there is not. The only difference is that one who comes from the former type of stock should exercise greater wisdom in ordering his life, so that a none-too-stable nervous system may be strengthened and fortified by his daily experiences rather than distressed and disrupted by them. In other words, he must try somewhat harder to obey the simple rules of health and to keep his mental outlook serene and satisfying. If he cares to do these things, he will be likely to continue through life to be as sane and well adjusted as anyone else.

The fallacy of inherited badness. This is another kind of false reasoning that bothers many people. The implication is that any "bad streak" in a parent is a heritable streak and will necessarily be passed down to the child. There is not a shred of evidence to support such a fatalistic notion. The bad in R's father does not exist in the germ plasm which he received from his father, and which he has passed on to his son. Badness is an acquired trait, and acquired traits cannot ordinarily be inherited. R's father *learned* badness, and the only way R, in turn, can be bad is likewise to learn badness, either from his father or from somebody else.

Of course, R may always have had the parental example of badness before him and hence may find it easy to imitate it; on the other hand, he may find the parental example distasteful and so find it easy to renounce it.

One should beware the unjustifiable fear that he has inherited an immoral or a criminal nature from some unconforming ancestor: he has *not!* At the worst, he may have been brought up in an unfortunate environment, or he may have been assured by critical neighbors that he could come to no good end because of what he had "inherited."

All this is, of course, unfortunate. Almost anybody possessed of the will and the determination to rise above a poor environment can succeed, and thus give the lie to ignorant and skeptical onlookers. The bad in this world is not something handed down by one generation to another; it is acquired anew by each one as it comes along. Neither, unfortunately perhaps, is the good in it handed down; it, too, must be acquired anew by each succeeding generation.

COMMON-SENSE ATTITUDES TOWARD HEREDITY

Heredity important but not all-important.   No one would wilfully choose to be descended from a family line of crooks, morons, or psychopaths. The hereditary genes are unquestionably important—very important—in determining the traits and the achievement level of the individual. However, the significance of such nonhereditary influences as our homes, our friends, our play, our work, our education, our reading and writing and thinking, in moulding our characters and determining our achievements, must never be overlooked.

The genes that you and I have received from the ancestral plasm can provide only the foundations, the broad general patterns, upon which we build our lives. The nature of the superstructure, its proportions, its symmetry, its stability, will depend principally upon our own workmanship as builders. As the poet has it:

> *We* [not our ancestors] build the ladder
> By which we rise [or ought to]
> From the lowly earth
> To the vaulted skies.

Human heredity is a baffling matter. The knowledge about heredity which scientists have amassed and put to work in the growing of better fruits and vegetables and flowers and in the raising of better animals is rather extensive. It is a far cry, however, from better roses and better horses and cows to better human beings. Experimentation in human heredity is extremely difficult, partly because it is impossible to get pure original strains with which to experiment, partly because it would require too many years before results in successive generations could be analyzed, and partly because the relationships involved in such a study are too intimate and delicate to be brought under controlled experimental conditions.

Much notable work has been done by scientists to improve the quality of animals and plants through careful breeding, careful seed selection, and so forth. On a form like the one at the top of page 341 see how many examples of such improved varieties and stocks you can record. Where would you look for information on this subject?

For a long time to come we shall have to recognize the fact that the laws underlying human heredity are too elusive to be understood, and that any reliable and scientific knowledge we may have about them must continue to be necessarily meager. Whatever claims, therefore, one may come upon, professing to define or predict or control human traits through the manipulation of alleged "laws of heredity," may be sharply discounted.

WHAT SCIENTIFIC SEED SELECTION AND ANIMAL BREEDING CAN
ACCOMPLISH

Name of Scientist Concerned	Scientific Field	Stock or Breed Improved	Results of Work Done
1. Luther Burbank	Horticulture	Berries	Ten new varieties
2.			
3.			
4.			
5. etc.			

(Investigate roses, gladioli, pompons, race horses, hogs, wheat, plums, and so forth.)

Heredity should not be a scapegoat! A certain middle-aged drunkard, when upbraided by an acquaintance for being little more than a sot, excused himself for his lapses by attributing them to his paternal great-great-grandfather. "I've been told," he explained, "that he never knew a sober minute! I inherited the taste from him." In this way, you see, the drunkard was able to excuse himself for his shortcomings by projecting them upon a long-dead ancestor who, incidentally, was not around to defend himself! How much more sporting—and altogether true—it would have been if he had hung his head and said: "I know! I'm just too weak-willed to take hold of myself and reform!"

There are many people in the world who are willing to make heredity a sort of scapegoat at whose door they may lay every unlovely trait they possess. They seize upon some fancied hereditary weakness or shortcoming as the explanation of their own follies and foibles, and adopt a fatalistic, ever-say-die attitude toward them. Don't be deceived by this submissiveness to a genetic "destiny" that has no basis in reality. Rather, common sense suggests that, if a person is aware of ancestral tendencies that he wishes might be otherwise, he should himself put forth all the greater effort to win out in spite of the hereditary handicap.

Don't be dazzled by good heredity! On the other hand, if one is fortunate enough to have sprung from a flatteringly prominent line of people, he should not, because of that circumstance, be dazzled by his own luster! It is disgusting to hear a person brag about his ancestry, or to see him regard it as a prerogative to rank or position or privilege, or to see him sit back serenely because of it and expect the world to provide him with its best without effort on his part. From him that hath much, much shall be expected. Not only is it an easier task for an individual of good hereditary background to amount to something, but the obligation of such a person to society, as well as society's rightful expectation from him, cannot but be infinitely greater than is the case with the poorly endowed individual.

HOW PSYCHOLOGISTS WORK

"Wooden legs do not run in families, but wooden heads do!" This is an often-quoted statement of fact. It refers to the well-known scientific principle that acquired traits, like mutilations from accidents, for example, are not passed down to the next generation, but that traits in which there is abnormality of the genes, like feeble-mindedness, or webbed toes, are likely to recur in subsequent generations.

One of the most important developments in psychological science in the past quarter of a century has been the invention of ways to measure an individual's intelligence, in order to determine whether he is gifted, dull, or average in his mental endowment. It goes without saying, of course, that one's intelligence is inherited from his forebears, and that while an unfortunate environment may prevent it from developing normally, or a favorable environment may promote its maximum development, environment cannot *create* intelligence. Only the genes can give us our basal intelligence.

One of the most exact and widely used tests of intelligence is the test known as the Stanford-Binet Test, developed by Dr. Terman, at Stanford University. In its present revised form, this test can be given to children as young as two years of age. It can also, of course, be given to anybody else, up to and including the genius.

The Stanford-Binet Test consists of a series of thinking-situations or action-situations for each age-year from two upwards. Sample situations taken from the test are listed below. Owing to the fact that a very careful technique has to be observed by the examiner, both in administering the test and in the subsequent interpretation of it, only experienced psychologists who have been properly trained to do so are competent to apply the Stanford-Binet Test to an individual. Only one person can be examined at a time, and the test sometimes requires more than an hour to administer. The testee is ordinarily alone with the tester, so that the distracting influences of other people in the immediate vicinity may be avoided.

Tests for the various age levels include problems or situations involving comprehension, word-naming, drawing designs, memory for digits, giving differences and likenesses, and defining words. The following problems are taken from the two-and-a-half-year level:

(1) Tell the use of the following miniature objects attached to a card: cup, shoe, penny, knife, automobile, flatiron.

(2) Identify parts of the body, using a picture of a doll: hair, mouth, ears, hands.

(3) Name familiar objects in miniature: chair, automobile, box, key, fork.

(4) Recognize familiar objects in a picture: shoe, clock, bed, chair, scissors, house, table.

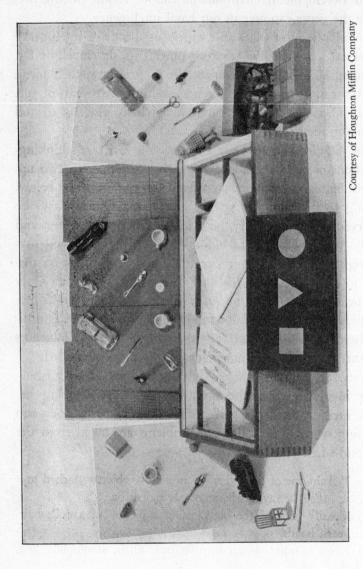

Fig. 51. Stanford-Binet materials used in testing intelligence.

(5) Repeat two digits after the examiner.

(6) Replace three insets in a simple form board: circle, square, triangle.

The complete setup of the Stanford-Binet tests is shown in the following table:

Age	Number of Tests, or Problems	Value of Each in Months of Mental Age
2	6	1
2½	6	1
3	6	1
3½	6	1
4	6	1
4½	6	1
5	6	1
6 to 14	6 for each year	2
Average adult	8	2
Superior adult I	6	4
Superior adult II	6	5
Superior adult III	6	6

If the testee can pass all the tests at his level, he is given twelve months of mental-age credit for the year and is allowed, of course, full credit for all the years preceding. Furthermore, if he can pass some tests at levels beyond his calendar age, he is credited with the equivalent number of additional months of mental age.

The *I. Q.,* or *Intelligence Quotient,* of a person is computed by dividing the total number of months of mental age earned in the test by the number of months of chronological, or actual, age. The resulting quotient is his I. Q.

In the following sample the procedure in reckoning mental age (M. A.) and in computing I. Q. is shown; the child tested has a chronological age (C. A.) of 4 years and 2 months, that is, of 50 months.

Credit assumed for first three years   36 months of M. A.

Year		tests passed		
3½	5 tests passed		5 " " "
" 4	3 " "		3 " " "
" 4½	2 " "		2 " " "
" 5	2 " "		2 " " "
" 6	1 " "		2 " " "

Total 50 "   "   "

M. A. = 50

$$I. Q. = \frac{M. A.}{C. A.} = \frac{50}{50} = 1, \text{ or } 100.$$

Dr. Terman's interpretation of the value of I. Q.'s is indicated in the table which follows:

I. Q.	Interpretation
Above 140	Near genius, or genius
120-140	Very superior
110-120	Superior
90-110	Normal, or average
80-90	Dull
70-80	Borderline
Below 70	Feeble-minded

Since the Stanford-Binet Test, like other individual examinations of intelligence, can be given to but one person at a time, and then only by properly trained examiners, the need was felt for some kind of group test of intelligence that could be given simultaneously to a large number of testees, such as the pupils in a particular grade or school, draftees for military service, applicants for admission to colleges or technical schools, and candidates for scholarships.

This need has been met by the construction of a large number of group tests of intelligence, with some of which you may be familiar through having taken one or another of them during your school career. Tests of this sort may be administered simultaneously to as many persons as can be seated at desks or tables in the largest auditorium or hall. The examiner merely reads the standardized directions from his instruction manual. The checking and scoring are done mechanically or with stencils or answer sheets, so that the tester's opinion or attitude has no influence whatever upon the results achieved by the testees.

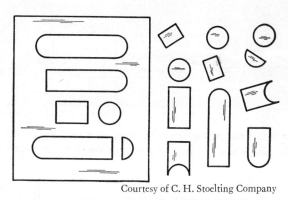

Courtesy of C. H. Stoelting Company

Fig. 52. Form board used as a performance test. The pieces at the right are to be fitted into the form at the left.

Group tests of intelligence are paper-and-pencil tests, for the most part: the examinee is required to mark as true or false certain statements in the examination booklet, or to indicate his choice among several alternatives, or to match ideas that belong together, and so forth. While these group tests are far less exact than the individual tests of intelligence, they do have the enormous advantages of being adaptable to large numbers of people, of requiring no preliminary training on the part of the tester, and of lending themselves easily to the task of selecting in half an hour's time those pupils in a school, for example, who are quickest and brightest, or those conscripts who should

Courtesy of C. H. Stoelting Company

Fig. 53. One of the picture puzzles used as a performance test looks like this when the parts have been correctly assembled.

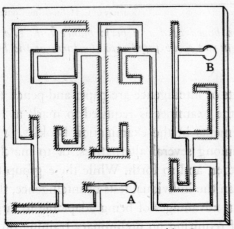

Courtesy of C. H. Stoelting Company

Fig. 54. Maze used as a performance test. The object is to make a pencil line as quickly as possible from A, the starting point, to B, the finishing point.

make good officer-training material, or those job applicants who are possessed of the keenest minds. For these reasons, group intelligence tests have tremendous practical value. They are in far wider use today than are the less flexible individual types of test.

For use with examinees who are illiterate, or who for any reason are unable to comprehend the instructions on a group test, performance tests, or nonverbal tests are available. These test the individual's ability to use his hands in manipulating objects like a form board, a picture puzzle, or a maze. Figures 52, 53, and 54 illustrate devices commonly used in performance tests. Most examiners find it best to employ both verbal and nonverbal tests, thus tapping both the academic and the nonacademic, or nonverbal, forms of intelligence in the testee.

TO HELP YOU LEARN

SOME QUESTIONS TO ANSWER

1. What is your present understanding of the term "genes"? How is it that the genes are ultimately responsible for the differences among people?

2. How may we account for the birth of a genius in an ordinary family?

3. How can you account for the dominance of the white race, and accept at the same time the findings of investigators to the effect that races differ little, if any, in intellectual capacities?

4. If there is a mental disease, epilepsy, or a history of "badness" in a particular family line, what should be the attitude of any young member of the line toward his heritage?

5. Does it seem to you, after studying this chapter, that every normal individual holds the key to his own destiny? Why, or why not?

WORKING WITH PSYCHOLOGY

1. You have learned in this chapter that everybody is somewhat different from everybody else, even though in basic traits we are all more or less alike. Make a survey of your own class to find out interesting ways in which its members differ from one another. Pay particular attention to such things as different scholastic interests, musical abilities, skills, ambitions, likes and dislikes. Use your own originality in determining how best to record your findings and conclusions. Try your hand at predicting, from the evidence you amass, fields of achievement in which each member of the class would be most likely to succeed.

2. Begin an investigation of your own family genealogy that will lead eventually to the constructing of your family tree back as many generations as you can trace it. Confer with your two parents for any data they may have, and with your grandparents, if possible, to learn the names and traits of *their* parents and grandparents— your great-grandparents and your great-great-grandparents. If possible, carry the study back at least four generations beyond yourself. Prepare some sort of form for keeping your records. One patterned after the following might be helpful for recording the names of your ancestors, but you will want to record their traits, too.

MY FAMILY TREE

Myself	Born	My Parents	Born	My Grand-parents	Born	My Great-Grand-parents	Born
Peter	1930	Father: John Mother: Sara	1900 1903	Paternal: Rufus Edna Maternal: George Mary	1865 etc.	Paternal: Jodiah Ruth Thomas Patience Maternal: William Abigail Austin Frances	1827 etc.

3. The most surprising thing about one's ancestors is that there are so many of them! Ordinarily we think of our parents and our grandparents, and do not bother to think back beyond the latter.

Assuming that your first ancestors to come to America reached this country 300 years ago, and estimating three generations to the century, find out how many of them there have been in a direct line down to yourself. Next, count up all the other living relatives you know of at the present time and assuming that each of your direct-line ancestors had an equivalent number of relatives in his generation, figure out the number of thousands of people there have been altogether in your family in 300 years.

4. Abraham Lincoln once remarked that God must have loved the common people because he made so many of them. It is true that most people are common, in the sense that they are average. We have referred in this chapter to the law of chance. This law may be best represented on a curve, called the curve of chance, or the *curve of normal distribution*. Here it is:

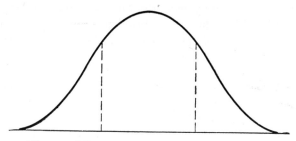

Fig. 55. The curve of normal distribution.

We can represent any trait in the human family upon this curve. You will note that the greatest number of people possessing the trait fall in the middle of the curve; that is to say, they possess the trait in the average or typical amount. Thus, 55% of people have average intelligence; 22½% have less than average and another 22½% more than average intelligence. There are as many stupid as brilliant people in the world; there are more moderately stupid people than very stupid, more moderately superior people than superior. Similarly, there are more people just middle average than there are either low average or high average. Lincoln was right!

Now that you understand the significance of the curve of normal distribution, relate to it other traits, like height, weight, honesty, goodness, patriotism, and figure out all the implications involved.

What Others Say

1. In Social Research:

Mental and Moral Heredity in Royalty by F. A. Woods. A study of the reigning houses of prewar Europe. The author traces the effects of marriages between related people of royal blood, including more than 600 individuals. He makes out a strong case for heredity as opposed to environment.

2. In Fiction:

Growth of the Soil by Knut Hamsun. A Nobel prize winner, this tale shows how the Norwegian hills and mountain wilds shape the lives of a simple peasant and his wife. It demonstrates the powerful influence of environment upon man.

The Three Black Pennys by Joseph Hergesheimer. A three-generation book, dealing with the careers of the various Pennys, in whose family line there is an hereditary trait of moodiness and impatience at restraint. The scene is laid in the iron region of Pennsylvania.

Rogue Herries by Hugh Walpole. The first of four books dealing with the English Herries family and showing the influence of a coarse heredity and an eighteenth-century environment upon a dreamer-rogue.

Sanctuary by Edith N. Wharton. A story which deals with the efforts of a woman of fine character to save her son from the consequences of the hereditary taint which he has inherited from his unstable father.

3. In Drama:

The Royal Family by George S. Kaufman and Edna Ferber. A fascinating play dealing with the Cavendish family, one of the most notable families of actors on the American stage. It reveals a case of the "cluster" of acting ability in several members of the same family.

4. In Poetry:

Chicago by Carl Sandburg. One of the most interesting attempts to portray in modern poetry the brutality and the laughter of a great industrial city. The poem contains striking descriptions of how environment fashions people.

Do You Attack or Run Away from Obstacles?

Robert Bruce of Scotland was discouraged and downhearted. He was Scotland's king, and the Scots had flocked loyally to his banners. But the advancing hosts of Edward proved too much for Bruce's army. Defeated in battle, he was compelled to flee. For a time he hid himself in the Grampian Hills; later on he concealed himself on a small island at the north of Ireland. Six times he had attacked the enemy; six times he had failed. And now, lying in a lonely hut on a heap of straw, he was debating with himself whether it might not be better to give up and leave Scotland to herself.

Just at that moment, Bruce's eye was caught by the spectacle of a spider trying to swing itself from one rafter to another. One, two, three, four, five, six times it failed.

"So have I!" muttered Bruce. "If it tries again, and succeeds, I too will try again!"

The spider gathered all its energy and flung itself again! This time it bridged the chasm successfully and proceeded to attach the filament of its web to the beam.

Robert Bruce, too, tried the seventh time—and succeeded!

Mr. Wilkins Micawber, a notable character of Dickens in *David Copperfield,* was not one to face his problems aggressively. Poor, indebted to everybody, and surrounded by a large family of wretchedly dressed children and a loyal but shabbily clothed wife, he was wont to discourse at length upon his ill luck.

"I have no scruple in saying, in the presence of my friends here," he affirmed to Copperfield on one occasion, "that I am a man who for some years has contended against the pressure of pecuniary difficulties. . . . There have been times when they have been too many for me, and I have given in, and said to Mrs. Micawber in the words of Cato: 'Plato, thou reasonest well. It's all up now. I can show fight no more.' But at no time in my life have I enjoyed a greater degree of satisfaction than in pouring my griefs (if I may describe difficulties chiefly arising out of warrants of attorney and promissory notes at two and four months, by that word) into the bosom of my friend Copperfield."

Mary Brown had always admired nurses. Throughout her high school course, she looked forward with anticipation to the day when she could begin training. The fact that a local hospital operated a successful nurses' training school made it a simple matter for the girl to set out upon the trail of her objective. When the time finally came, Mary, with a great deal of enthusiasm, donned her uniform and embarked upon what she was sure was to be a most agreeable profession.

The realities of day-by-day training, however, soon became very distasteful to her. In her emotional anticipation of becoming a full-fledged nurse, she had been carried away with grandiose ideas of "wearing a uniform," of "nursing the sick and dying," of "alleviating human suffering," and the like, and had failed to make allowance for the decidedly steep and rugged path all nurses have to climb before they achieve their goal. In consequence, Mary was neither mentally nor emotionally prepared to scrub floors and clean wards and dispose of wastes, and to do the thousand and one other humdrum but essential duties that fall to the lot of the young student-in-training.

The upshot of it all was that Mary abandoned her objective after about four weeks of training, thus turning her back in defeat upon a goal that she had fondly visioned for years. Some time later she entered a business school and set out on a career of stenography.

Overcoming Obstacles Takes Real Effort

In these three situations are seen various ways of meeting obstacles. Robert Bruce, discouraged and defeated, marshals his resources for a seventh time and attacks! Wilkins Micawber does not know the meaning of the word *attack!* Instead of fighting, he exhausts his energies pouring his troubles into the ears of Copperfield. Mary Brown makes an initial attack, but at the first sign of trouble she loses heart and falls back. The world is filled with people like Micawber and Mary Brown, some of them too easygoing or indolent by nature to care to drive ahead; some of them showing an initial eagerness to achieve, but too easily discouraged when the hurdles begin to rise before them.

✦ ✦ ✦

In this chapter you will learn a good deal about the mental conflict that arises in the individual who has been thwarted in reaching his goals. You will see that sometimes retreat is the most sensible thing when obstacles are insurmountable; but that *mere* retreat without compensating attack in fresh directions is disastrous to character. You will learn about various insidious ways in which people excuse themselves for their failures.

Fig. 56. Glenn Cunningham overcame the obstacle of being so badly burned that doctors had no hope of his ever walking again. Have you read the inspiring story of how, in spite of his handicap, he became one of the world's champion runners?

14. MEETING OBSTACLES

Before you go further in exploring this matter of meeting obstacles, complete the following record of some of your own outstanding successes and failures in the past year:

SOME OF MY OWN EXPERIENCES WITH OBSTACLES

I Attacked These:	I Fell Back Before These:
1. Getting a new job for Saturdays. (I applied at five different places. I wanted a job very badly and was willing to try my hardest to locate one.)	1. Practicing my music an hour every day. (I really want to learn to play better, but I just can't make myself settle down to practice oftener than once or twice a week.)
2.	2.
3.	3.
4.	4.
5. etc.	5. etc.

The successes you list at the left make up a part of the credit side of your account with you; the failures you list at the right comprise, on the other hand, a part of the debit side of your account with you. Let's hope you will have a favorable balance on the credit side!

THE ROLE OF CONFLICT

Our basic wants. In an earlier chapter we listed a considerable number of wants which are found universally among humankind. Prominent among these items were the following: companionship, security, domination, change, mental activity, and self-perpetuation. These human wants, as we saw, are so powerful in every one of us as to constitute the principal goals or objectives of our lives. Intimately connected with our instinctive urge for self-expression, these powerful wants loom ever across our pathway, challenging us to the very depths of our being.

Defeats are inevitable. How gratifying it would be if we could always be successful in attaining our objectives and satisfying our wants! And if we could have the assurance that all that is needed to reach our goals is to "peg away" at them persistently until we ultimately achieve them! Unfortunately, few of us ever have the pleasure of satisfying all our wants and attaining all our life objectives. By reason of faulty methods of attack, or of inadequate equipment for the battle, or of vagueness or elusiveness of our aims, many of us, while succeeding in reaching some of our goals, are doomed to disappointment in the case of others.

Thwartings are inevitable for us all on occasion, and when thwartings of the stronger human urges are experienced, emotion is usually aroused and we tend to fight on blindly and vainly to reach the objective denied us. Often we rebel bitterly at fate or circumstance, and our whole personality becomes a battleground of strong inner conflict.

Hamlet's conflict. Everybody is familiar with the famous soliloquy of Hamlet, which is one of the most striking illustrations of mental conflict to be found anywhere in English literature:

> To be, or not to be: that is the question!
> Whether 'tis nobler in the mind to suffer
> The slings and arrows of outrageous fortune,
> Or to take arms against a sea of troubles,
> And by opposing, end them?

Thwartings are everywhere. One does not have to go to the characters of literature to find illustrations of disappointment and of the resulting mental conflict. We rub elbows every day with real flesh-and-blood people who have been rebuffed in their ambitions and who, in consequence, are miserable unless and until they can find some way of adjusting their lives to the new conditions which have been imposed upon them by an unkind fate.

Some frustrated people brood over their disappointment— like Hamlet—often for the rest of their lives; others reconcile themselves to the inevitable and turn to some other substitute goal for their happiness and contentment. Happiness, of course, we must all have—somehow or other. Even the thwarted individual, who remains miserable and complaining and self-pitying for years and years after the disappointing experience, unquestionably gets more or less satisfaction out of his miserableness. Many people not only enjoy poor health: they also enjoy being miserable!

Prepare a form like the one below and record upon it some striking instances of frustration that you know about, indicating in each case the adjustment made by the individual concerned. It may be that some of your examples will have less favorable endings than the one suggested.

SOME THWARTED AMBITIONS

Who?	What Was the Original Objective?	What Defeat Occurred?	How Was the Conflict Eliminated?
1. Mrs. Bolling	To keep her child and watch him grow up	The child was killed in an accident.	Mrs. Bolling got interested in orphan children.
2.			
3.			
4.			
5. etc.			

(Not all thwarted ambitions are adjusted as bravely as Mrs. Bolling adjusted hers.)

BILL MASON'S TRAGEDY

The case of Bill Mason affords a good illustration of thwarting and conflict. Bill was making good on the high school team. An all-round athlete, he was an unusually fine football player. Early in his career he had proved himself to be an invaluable member of the squad. In interscholastic contests his magnificent playing was unquestionably a factor in the victories scored by his school. He was hailed by everybody as a young football prodigy.

And then, in the summer of his junior year, with a most promising athletic future before him, Bill was struck down by the dreaded infantile paralysis. Not only was he compelled to lose a half year of school, but the disease left him with crippled legs that would in all probability never again carry him down the field with the pigskin clutched tightly under his arm.

Remorseful and bitter—for what thwarting can be more complete than to see one's fondest dreams of achievement dashed to pieces? —Bill became cynical and despairing. When he could drag himself back to school, months later, he honestly felt that life held for him nothing more. Morose and rebellious, he spent the remainder of his school days as in a treadmill, without spirit or ambition.

Bill's disappointment over his lost objective was keen, and the conflict that seethed in his breast, between what he had dreamed of becoming and what he was now compelled by stern reality to be, was turbulent. Thwarting at its worst may not only change an entire outlook on life but may also completely transform the personality.

CONFLICT IS UNIVERSAL AMONG US

Even children have conflict. There are all kinds and degrees of thwartings and failures to achieve objectives that we have set for ourselves, or that have been set for us by somebody else. Conflict begins in childhood. When the child wishes to play, he is required to rest or work; when he wants to enjoy freedom, he must pore over books; when he desires to "hog" his toys or his sweets, he is counseled to share them with others; when he is tempted to tell a falsehood to protect himself from punishment or censure, he is ever mindful of the parental warning to tell the truth.

Besides all these sources of conflict there are in childhood all manner of worries and apprehensions about disgraces and belittlements suffered at the hands of other children, as well as about school work, school standing, teachers' scoldings, parents' scoldings, and so forth. Life, for the ordinary child, is a series of thwartings and of perplexing problems that clamor for solution.

Youth has its conflicts. At the high school level young people find plenty to nurture their conflicts. Ambitions and achievements do not coincide; right and wrong vie continually for the uppermost position; the voice of conscience and the exciting appeal of "the world, the flesh, and the devil" cannot be reconciled. Besides, much inner annoyance and turmoil may be occasioned by the realization that nature has been unkind in afflicting one with a turned-up nose, or with freckles, or with stringy hair, or with a blemished skin, or with a sallow complexion. All of such liabilities make it appear the harder for the sensitive youth to be accepted by his mates, who (as it seems to him) have none of the defects or shortcomings that he has been cursed with.

Add to these difficulties the awareness that one's intellectual endowment is poor, that he compares poorly with other pupils, or that he is lacking in social graces and polish, and you have reason enough for the inner rebellion that is often so strong in the adolescent.

Conflict in the adult world. Thwartings and conflict in the adult individual are likewise found on every hand. As a man finds the objectives at which he aimed in his youth retreating ever before him like some tantalizing mirage, he experiences chagrin, disillusionment, and sometimes despair. Consider, for example, the impact of the following conflicts upon one individual:

Awareness that he is losing out, or that competitors are outstripping and ruining him;

Being compelled to compromise with his ideals;

Consciousness that his way of life "is fallen into the sere, the yellow leaf";

Rebellion at being obliged to keep his nose to the grindstone perennially;

Regret at missing much of the essential happiness of life;

Being confronted with family problems that are baffling or disturbing;

Awareness of tension and friction between his own and other personalities;

Being assailed by doubts and uncertainties in wide areas of experience;

Knowledge that his future security and that of his family are not assured.

All these and other disturbing thoughts would tend to keep anybody in a condition of suspense and apprehension during most of his waking life, and might even make much of his dream life troubled.

It thus appears that there is thwarting at every age level of life—in childhood, in youth, and in adulthood. No age can escape the failures and bafflements and the nonachievement of objectives that characterize our human experience. Nobody, regardless of age or station, can expect to escape a considerable amount of disappointment and discouragement. These mental and emotional reactions represent the basis for conflict in us all.

Still, while these states are inevitable, it is a fact also that *surrender* to defeat and dejection is not inevitable.

SOLVING THE CONFLICT BY A FRESH ATTACK

"Don't give up the ship!" It is surprisingly easy for any of us, if we find some obstacle in the pathway to our goals or objectives, to give up the attack after the first unsuccessful skirmish and withdraw from the encounter. This is a very foolish thing to do, unless and until we are soberly convinced that success is impossible.

How commonly do we come in contact with people who consider themselves failures, yet who have never really tried to be successes! In their first enthusiastic attempt to achieve a goal, buoyed up by an emotional conviction that the objective was to be an easy one, they lost the skirmish. Either they had not intelligently appraised the nature of the task, or they had failed to attack it wisely, or they misjudged their attacking strength, or for some other reason they suffered initial defeat in their maneuvering!

Weakhearted, or too easily discouraged, or made too keenly conscious of their lacks, they lost not only the battle but the campaign as well. Thenceforth they were content to abandon all attempts to reach their objective.

Robert Bruce again! The way to overcome obstacles is to *attack* them. Rebuffs and thwartings should not deter a person, unless of course the goal sought is an obviously unachievable one for the particular individual. Assuming the achievability of a goal, one cannot afford to be turned aside by the first difficulties he encounters. Sometimes by a different method of approach, sometimes by a marshaling of forces, sometimes merely by a more determined and sustained attack, a person finds it possible to win through to his goal. "If at first you don't succeed," advises the old adage, "try, try again!" This is a much more sensible procedure than to adopt a policy of defeatism.

Is the goal an achievable one? On the other hand, we must admit that some goals which some individuals set themselves are, for one reason or another, impossible of achievement. For one to continue to bang his head against a stone wall, in the vain endeavor to break through it, is the part of folly rather than of wisdom.

The first thing for any of us to do when setting up an objective is to make a frank and realistic survey of our likelihood of success in achieving it; then, being convinced that it lies within our power, we should drive steadfastly and with full determination forward. It is far better, from the standpoint of our mental health and serenity, to turn aside from an unachievable goal than it is to permit our personalities to become discouraged or embittered by cumulative failures in striving to reach it.

SOLVING THE CONFLICT BY SUBSTITUTION

Finding new satisfactions. But we must do something more than merely turn aside from the unachievable goal. To do no more would be to admit total defeat, besides leaving a gap in our life program. The sensible individual will, when compelled to relinquish a goal, seek to substitute for it some other that will yield compensatory satisfaction. In so doing, he is able to turn his momentum and his energies upon the new objective and to escape that feeling of defeat and frustration which he might otherwise experience. Chagrin, self-censure and conflict over the thwarted goal may thus be escaped, and in their place a new consciousness of achievement and success may be substituted.

Most people find themselves compelled now and again to turn aside from original goals and to set out on the highroad that leads to new ones. Self-confidence and satisfaction may be achieved just as surely through these substituted objectives as through the original ones. In fact, greater happiness is often attained than would otherwise have been possible.

Make the substitution wholehearted. There are two dangers that a person must be on guard against when he substitutes one objective for another. The first danger is that he will continue to lament his earlier failure, and will carry over to the new effort an emotional tie-up with the old which leads him to rebel at his lot, or to be envious of those who are succeeding where he failed, or otherwise to undertake the new task halfheartedly. This will not do at all: there must be no lingering animosities or jealousies or attitudes of rebellion. Once a substitute goal has been set up, one should accept it as a full equivalent for the thwarted objective.

If, for example, a mediocre student who aims at college but finds it impossible to get satisfactory grades in high school transfers to a vocational school, he must carry over no envy and regret but apply himself wholeheartedly to the new plan for his vocational life. If a plain young woman, thwarted in her desire to be beautiful, sets herself the substitute task of developing a winsome personality and charm of manner, she must nourish no jealousies of more attractive young women but must concentrate her energies on achieving satisfaction in the new role she has undertaken. To harbor wistful or bitter thoughts about "what might have been" is to defeat the highest purpose of life, which is to find contentment and happiness in one's total experience.

Don't overdo your substitution! The other danger in substituted goals lies in the tendency to *overcompensate.* While there are many forms of overcompensation, a common one is for the individual to go to extremes of conduct in the mistaken supposition that in extremes he will find the approbation of others and the personal pride and thrill which he has always coveted but been denied. Anxious as everybody is to be approved, to be well thought of, to attract the favorable notice of others, it is easy for the individual who finds it impossible to win these goals by routine methods to adopt some bizarre or out-of-the-ordinary means of gaining them.

Thus, a person may compel others to take notice of him by affecting a striking or peculiar or immodest mode of dress, or by doing spectacular or breath-taking stunts, or by expressing radical opinions, or by indulging in "advanced" forms of conduct, or by shocking other people into at least momentary notice of him. Through such extremes of conduct or opinion, people frequently win, in place of the good repute and respect they covet, only a questionable notoriety which is far less enduring and less satisfying than genuine approbation.

Enter on a form like the one below a number of examples of thwarted ambitions, with the substitute goals set up and the resulting effects upon the individuals involved:

SOME SUBSTITUTED OBJECTIVES: WISE AND UNWISE

The Original Goal	Nature of the Thwarting	The Substitute Goal	Result upon the Individual	Was the Adjustment Wise or Unwise?
1. A young fellow I know wanted to go to college.	He was needed at home to help support a large family.	He went to night school and evening classes.	He felt he was doing right and was happy.	Wise
2.				
3.				
4.				
5. etc.				

(Thwartings don't matter: it's what we *do* about them that counts!)

TWO UNHEALTHY SOLUTIONS TO CONFLICTS

Running away. We have seen that the only sensible and healthy ways to meet defeat and settle the conflict arising from it are either to make a fresh attack or else to adopt a new objective. Unfortunately, many people do neither of these things. Thwarted in their efforts and haunted by their failures to win through, they turn about and flee from the skirmish, in the vain belief that if they can retreat far enough from the arena of action they will find mental peace and happiness.

Among those who thus haul down their colors and withdraw from the fray may be included people like the hobo, who has "taken to the road"; the hermit or recluse, who shuts himself away from human contacts; and certain of the mentally diseased, who find in their delusions not only withdrawal from the rational give-and-take of life but a type of satisfaction which, though to us shadowy, is to them substantial and real.

Each one of these types is running away from life, from responsibility, from sustained effort and struggle. True, not every hobo is in deliberate flight, any more than every hermit or insane individual is. Fate and circumstance unquestionably force many of the maladjusted people about us into their peculiar types of withdrawal. The fact remains, however, that great numbers of the thwarted and the unsuccessful might have found far happier and saner adjustments for themselves if they had had the perseverance to reattack or the wisdom to substitute new objectives for unattainable ones.

Protecting our ego. It is not very flattering for an individual who has failed to win his goal to admit that it is his own fault. Above everything else, we like to believe in ourselves; we are anxious to protect our ego, to maintain our self-respect and our faith in ourselves. To acknowledge defeat is to injure or destroy these powerful personal motives. In consequence, when thwarted, instead of placing the responsibility at our own door we seek about for some plausible explanation that may account for our defeat and at the same time leave us convinced that we ourselves are blameless.

This unfortunate tendency in the thwarted individual is decidedly bad for his mental health, for to excuse himself for his shortcomings and place responsibility for them upon some other person or condition or thing is to destroy aggressiveness and self-confidence.

KINDS OF POOR ADJUSTMENT TO FAILURE

Sour grapes. You know the old fable perfectly well. The grapes hung too high for the fox, and when he had failed to reach them by jumping up at them, he sauntered away with the mental soliloquy: "They are sour, anyway: I don't want them!" A lot of people are like Mr. Fox. Rebuffed or thwarted in the attainment of their desires, they turn aside and comfort themselves with the reflection that the objective was not worth the effort of achieving it. This neat little way of adjusting themselves to defeat consoles them, leaves no awareness of personal inadequacy, and saves from regrets and self-criticism.

You know quite well, no doubt, the attitude adopted by the plain girl toward good-looking girls—that they are "beautiful but dumb"! You know, too, the contention made by the unsuccessful applicant for a job—that the job would have been too confining, anyway; or that made by the poor man—that riches are "the root of all evil"; or that made by the unpopular person—that popularity must be purchased by silly or extravagant conduct, and in such he will have no part!

The grapes aren't really sour! The fact of the matter is, of course, that none of these adherents of the *sour-grapes philosophy*—not even excepting the fox himself—really means that the thwarted objective is undesirable. Any of them would give anything if he could win through—the plain girl achieving good looks, the job applicant landing his job, and the unpopular person gaining popularity and acclaim. The sour-grapes attitude is merely a salve to disappointment; one consoles himself by arguing that it is silly to reach for what is after all worthless or vicious; and at the same time he maintains his own self-respect unimpaired by contending that he has not failed but rather has *succeeded* in avoiding what would no doubt have been undesirable!

Look out for boomerangs! The sour-grapes adjustment is a boomerang to the personality for another reason. If Mr. Fox had observed, after his own failure to seize the grapes, that another fox was successful, he would thenceforth have been jealous of and perhaps have developed a decided dislike for his competitor. Likewise the plain girl is apt to be jealous or envious of the good-looking girl, and may be heard to say unkind things about her; the unsuccessful applicant for a job may harbor bitterness against society, or against the man who got the job, or against all men who have jobs; the unpopular person resents the popular one and will have nothing to do with him.

The effect of such hostile and unsocial attitudes as these upon the character and personality of the individual who harbors them is certain to be unfortunate. Thus does defeat, when it leads to the sour-grapes adjustment, not only deprive the individual of the successful accomplishment of his purposes, but also sour him and make him into a decidedly unattractive and shut-in personality who peers critically out of his narrow window and glowers at the passers-by.

Projection: blaming somebody else. You have, no doubt, at some time or other observed the spectacle of a pompous-looking gentleman stumbling as he walked along a perfectly smooth sidewalk, and going through startling motions calculated to restore his balance. Ten chances to one, as soon as he was again properly upon his feet, the gentleman glared at the unoffending sidewalk as though it and not he himself had been at fault!

The same principle of wishing to protect one's personality from self-censure obtains here as in all other thwarting experiences. It is unflattering for a man who stumbles to call himself a stupid or absent-minded fool who didn't watch his step; it is far more flattering to transfer to the sidewalk the responsibility for his graceless exhibition. This blaming of our failures upon something or somebody else is sometimes referred to as *projection,* since in all such situations we tend to project the blame for our shortcomings upon some cause other than ourselves.

Are you ever guilty? Projection occurs surprisingly often in many of us. Just glance through the following illustrations of projection:

The ball player who strikes out blames his bat, or the pitcher, or perhaps the umpire!

The student who gets a poor grade on an examination blames the teacher for asking a question he couldn't answer!

The bungling carpenter blames his tools for his bungling!

The automobilist involved in an accident blames the other driver, or the pedestrian!

The illegible writer blames the scratchy pen he is using!

The disappointed cook blames the recipe, or the oven, or perhaps the flour, for the flat, soggy cake!

The drunkard blames a long-dead ancestor, from whom he claims to have inherited the thirst!

The defeated political candidate blames the unfair campaign of his opponent, or the stupidity of the voters, for his defeat!

And so it goes! None of these thwarted individuals is eager to seek for possible fault that might lie within himself: it is so much easier and more flattering to blame the other fellow. The blaming alibi is a great deceiver, of course, and while many of us may see through ourselves if we look sharply, the fact remains that many people escape all self-censure by the handy device of projection.

Rationalizing.   There is a vast difference between *rational-*

izing and reasoning. The latter means, as we know, thinking straight and logically toward some conclusion; the former means one-sided reasoning, with the cards all stacked beforehand, so that the rationalizer is bound to be right in the final outcome. Almost anybody with average intelligence can think up "good" reasons to explain his conduct or his actions.

For example, the man with an income too meager to warrant the purchase of an automobile can rationalize his purchase of one by arguing that he is getting too old to walk so much, or that he wastes too much time on buses and trolley cars, or that his wife is beginning to look peaked and needs to be taken on long, restful motor rides in the country, or that it is not right for his children to have to walk so far to and from school! The decision is reached at the very beginning; there are no counter arguments!

His true motive, of course, is to secure the approval of his neighbors, to be regarded as "getting along well," and to experience the compensating flattery and thrill of being a man behind a wheel. His poverty, the fact that his wife hasn't had a new coat in ten years, or that his children are out at the heels, or that his house is sadly in need of repairs—these arguments on the other side are completely ignored in his blind distortion of facts.

Daydreaming. Defeated in our goals, we may still experience a fancied success in *daydreaming*. The unlettered or toilworn man or woman may experience vicariously the thrills of wealth, fame, power, and position by following, wide-eyed, the glamorous adventures of some movie star on the silver screen. For two or more hours one may completely lose his identity and be totally submerged in the affairs portrayed by the actor.

Among children, especially, this form of adjustment is common. By reading Cinderella stories, magic carpet adventures,

Aladdin's lamp tales, and fairy godmother stories, children who are deprived of things they would dearly love to have find joy and momentary forgetfulness of their own misfortunes and failures through the tinseled charm of daydreaming.

Behold! the conquering hero comes!   One form of day dreaming takes the pattern of the *conquering hero*. In this fantasy, the boy who, for example, has failed or been thwarted in any of his purposes, daydreams himself into a hero who rides victoriously through the streets with the applause and hurrahs of thousands roaring in his ears! Returning in imagined triumph to the scenes of his belittlement or ridicule, he dazzles the eyes of his former detractors by the splendor of his bearing and the brilliance of his retinue; with head held high and a flush of pride on his cheek, he rides majestically through the crowd scarcely deigning to notice the acclaim and the veneration everywhere accorded him.

A daydream like this is a joyous one, of course, but the awakening may be rude when the dreamer comes back to earth with a thud, only to find his old failures and rebuffs still there waiting for him.

Tom Sawyer envisioned his own funeral!   At the other extreme of the conquering hero is the *suffering hero*. You recall how Tom Sawyer, falling into fancy one evening shortly after he had left his home, beheld in his mind's eyes the spectacle of his own lifeless body lying in state before the eyes of his fellow townsmen—and especially before those of his aunt, who had heaped what he felt were unjust indignities upon him. Everybody was doing homage before his bier. As he dreamed on, Tom could see the tears and hear the laments of his old friends and neighbors—and his *aunt*—who now with one accord were prostrate with grief for having been so unkind to him! Only now when he lay dead before them did they appreciate that here indeed had been a real and genuine hero!

There is a somber sort of joy in a dream of this sort, too, but the awakening, again, is likely to be a rude one when the dreamer comes back to earth to find that nobody *is* lamenting him, and that he is the same old failure, or outcast, or recluse that he was before!

On a form like this one, list a number of instances of sour grapes, projection, rationalizing, or daydreaming that you can detect in your own behavior in recent weeks:

HOW I REACTED TO RECENT THWARTINGS

What Happened	How I Was Affected by What Occurred	Name of This Adjustment
1. My side was defeated in a debate.	I maintained stoutly that the judges were biased.	Projection
2.		
3.		
4.		
5. etc.		

(Few people avoid adjustments like these to thwarted efforts. If they can "see through" themselves, it isn't so bad!)

THE HEALTHY PERSONALITY FACES REALITY

It pays to unmask. The adjustments to failure that we have been discussing are decidedly poor ones to make. Granted, of course, that all of us tend on occasion to indulge in sour grapes, in blaming others, in rationalizing, and in fantasy, it is of the first importance that we recognize the fact when we are so indulging, and cut ourselves short when we find we are doing it persistently.

There is no point in trying to make ourselves believe that we are happier, or better off, when we fail; or that our failures are due to no fault or weakness of our own; or yet that only those arguments that advance our own personal advantage or interest have validity. Neither is it the part of wisdom to be content with substituting fancied triumphs for real ones.

Blaming oneself. The healthy, normal person faces things as they are. He does not attribute his defects and shortcomings to the unfair or evil plottings of other individuals; on the contrary, he recognizes his own weaknesses and places at his own doorway the responsibility for his thwartings and failures. He understands, further, that each individual is called upon to work consistently toward his goals, and that when he finds them unachievable, the blame—if blame there be—is not ordinarily to be sought beyond himself.

HOW PSYCHOLOGISTS WORK

Figure 57 represents diagrammatically the obstacle situation:

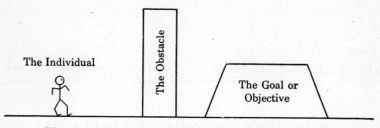

Fig. 57. Diagram of a person meeting an obstacle.

In the path leading to his objective, the individual comes upon an obstacle of some sort. He is either temporarily or permanently thwarted in reaching his goal. As we have indicated in the preceding pages of this chapter, the thwarted individual may attack, or he may turn aside. If he turns aside, he may strike out toward a substitute goal, and experience a substitute satisfaction either with or without regrets over what he has lost; or he may build up some kind of defense or escape mechanism and work out an internal adjustment that requires no attack and that at the same time excuses him for his failure.

We have referred to the sour-grapes adjustment, the projection adjustment, the rationalizing adjustment, and the daydreaming adjustment.

The purpose of these undesirable forms of escape is to reduce conflict. The individual who is frustrated in reaching his goal accounts satisfactorily for his defeat by recourse to these mechanisms; otherwise, he would have to be honest and admit his own weaknesses, and that would mean a continuing self-criticism and internal conflict. That is why these adjustments are called *escape mechanisms.*

Psychologists distinguish several other forms of escape mechanisms besides the four discussed above. The following are to be noted particularly. Remember that every one of them is seized upon by the thwarted person as a way out, and hence it becomes habitual with him as a way of explaining his failure and adjusting himself to it without self-criticism.

(1) *The Mechanism of Identification.* In this form of escape, the individual experiences success vicariously by identifying himself with somebody who has succeeded in achieving the goal he has failed to achieve himself. A lazy, unambitious youth may lose his own individuality, at least for the time being, by identifying himself with the personality of some strong character in a romance he is reading. Similarly, the small boy, none too powerful of brain or muscle in his own right, easily transfers his personality into that of his idolized father, who represents to him the embodiment of power and success. Under the spell of this identification, he may strut about, swagger, boast of what he can do, warn his obstreperous chum that "My daddy can lick your daddy!" and in general stride a conqueror among his mates.

(2) *The Mechanism of Sympathism.* Sometimes called the *martyr complex,* this mechanism inspires the individual to take recourse from his difficulties in the gratifying escape of sym-

pathy and pity offered by his friends and relatives. If his work is too hard for him, he may refrain from doing it, knowing that he will have plenty of indulgent sympathy from people who ought to know better. Thus, in the satisfactions he receives from his indulgent friends he experiences no glimmer of regret or consciousness of failure.

(3) *The Mechanism of Regression.* A thwarted individual sometimes escapes the admission of his failure to himself and the consequent uncomfortable feeling of conflict by turning back the hands of time and reverting to earlier or childish kinds of response. Having failed in his work, or in the achievement of his objective, a person may become petulant, seek endearment, make infantile excuses, tell white lies, pity himself, or otherwise react as a child rather than as an adult. In such behavior, he experiences again the soothing feeling and sense of importance that he enjoyed when, at the age of five, somebody made a face at him and his mother soothed and comforted him.

(4) *The Mechanism of Malingering.* In this mechanism, the individual who is not willing to put forth the effort to reach his goal feigns some sort of illness or incapacitation which renders it obviously unreasonable for him to be expected to try any more. This is a neat little escape trick—and trick it is, for unlike some other escape mechanisms, it is consciously and with malice aforethought adopted by the individual. Fake illness and indisposition are too commonly encountered by us all to require further discussion here.

(5) *The Mechanism of Repression.* A certain modern school of *psychoanalysts* (physicians who try to help people adjust their conflicts) known as *Freudians* (so called because they follow the viewpoints of the late Sigmund Freud, a Viennese psychologist) hold that our unachievable goals and ambitions, as well as the unpleasant experiences that would

otherwise harass us plaguingly, are forced out of our conscious and into our unconscious minds and are there forgotten (or would be forgotten if they did not seethe and clamor to get back again into the conscious mind). If a person does something that he is ashamed of, and so compromises his ideals, he is helped to avoid the logical feeling of chagrin and conflict by thus quietly forgetting all about the affair!

(6) *The Mechanism of Worry and Anxiety.* While worry and anxiety are classified as escape mechanisms, they are actually nonadjustive, for they do not release us from conflict. Sometimes the thing worried about is not related to the unattained goal, but represents an emotional reaction to something

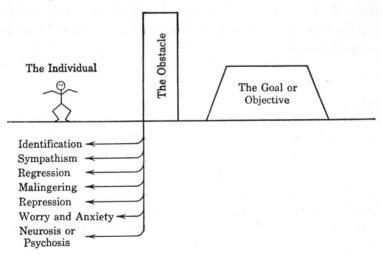

Fig. 58. Diagram of a thwarted person turning aside into some form of escape from the obstacle.

quite remote. There are many people who have failed in one specific area of life who develop vague anxieties and fears touching other areas.

(7) *The Mechanisms of Neurosis and Psychosis.* Some people who have failed to achieve their ideals or goals take

refuge from their sense of futility and defeat by developing personality disorders, either of a mild or of a major sort. The milder upsets are called *neuroses,* and include those peculiarities of conduct that are less extreme than those found in people who are definitely insane, who have actual *psychoses.* By escape, in the one instance, into nervousness, restlessness, insomnia, strange interests, or odd mannerisms, the individual avoids conflict over his awareness of failure; by escape, in the other instance, into insanity, he undergoes so complete a transformation of his mental life as to remove all trace of the frustrations he experienced in achieving his goal or goals.

Figure 58, on page 377, shows diagrammatically what takes place if the thwarted individual in Figure 57, after meeting the obstacle in his pathway, turns aside into some form of escape behavior.

TO HELP YOU LEARN

Some Questions to Answer

1. Why is conflict inevitable whenever we find ourselves thwarted in achieving a goal or objective which we have set ourselves?

2. What are some of the various things that make people give up after the first unsuccessful skirmish and withdraw from the encounter?

3. What was lacking in Mary Brown to lead her to abandon so easily the pursuit of a career that she had looked forward to for several years? Are there few or many people like Mary?

4. Why is it that folks find it so hard to admit to themselves that they are failing in reaching their objectives?

5. What safeguards to personality must a person adopt who has substituted a new goal for one that he has found unattainable? Explain why these safeguards are necessary.

Working with Psychology

1. Consider this short, short case study: Mrs. White's two-year-old Donald one morning was winding a ball of twine in and out between the legs of the table in the kitchen as his mother worked near by. Mrs. Conrad, a neighbor, stopped in to invite Mrs. White and Donald to take an automobile drive uptown with her. Mrs. White hastily pulled Donald's coat on, and in a few minutes all three of them entered the car and drove off. Within ten minutes Mrs. Conrad's car was in a traffic accident and Donald White was killed. For more than fifteen months afterward, Mrs. White refused to allow anybody to remove the twisted string from the table legs, and she spent hours every day weeping over the gnarled twine. She was in grave danger of insanity from grief. If you were a consulting psychologist to whom Mr. White came for advice, what would your recommendation be?

2. Collect from your reading and conversation as many instances as possible of the use of sour grapes, of projection, of rationalization, and of fantasy made by persons whose desires or ambitions have been frustrated. It is nothing short of amazing how commonly we take refuge in this type of excuse to explain away our failures and shortcomings.

3. History is filled with the records both of those who struggled valiantly to achieve their goals and of those who gave up the fight after an initial attack or two and went down to defeat. In modern affairs these same two sorts of people can be identified—the attackers and the quitters. You find them in every community, and on every street. Keeping their identity concealed, describe orally the characteristics of one of each of those two sorts of individuals in such a way that the contrast between them will be quite apparent to your class. Notice that you will not have to go only among the lowly to find frustration and running away, nor only among the rich and fortunate to find courageous struggling against odds. Both of these attitudes cut across all strata of society.

4. Youth in every generation meets frustration. Young people have so many ambitions, so many goals, so many beckoning purposes, that it is inevitable that defeat and discouragement shall come in considerable amount. Spend a part of your next class period talking over some of the most obvious frustrations and failures

suffered by the young people of the present generation. Do not be satisfied merely to enumerate grievances; pay particular attention to ways and means of improving and enlarging the opportunities that are available to modern youth.

What Others Say

1. In Fiction:

No Hero—This by Warwick Deeping. The diary of Stephen Brent, who enlisted in the army, fought gnawing fear, and finally conquered it. The reactions of a sensitive man to army life.

Les Miserables by Victor Hugo. The magnificent story of a man who was victimized by society all his life, and who, while struggling manfully to express his innate nobility, was yet doomed to slavery and shame.

Black Daniel by Honoré Willsie Morrow. The dramatic story of Daniel Webster's decision to assume an all but unbearable burden, when it would have been simple and easy to walk in a serene path with no burden.

2. In Biography:

The Americanization of Edward Bok by Edward Bok. The dramatic memoirs of an immigrant who, by dint of strong ambition and hard work, became a great editor and a great American philanthropist. An inspiring story for anybody to read who appreciates the spirit that conquers obstacles.

The World at My Finger Tips by Karsten Ohnstad. A vividly dramatic account of the experiences of a boy who became blind, and of his struggles in learning to perceive through his finger tips.

3. In Drama:

Golden Boy by Clifford Odets. The tale of a moody lad who, though handicapped by his appearance, yet longs for success. Overcompensating for his failures, he becomes increasingly brutal and meets an inevitable death in trying to forget.

4. In Poetry:

The Vagabonds by John Townsend Trowbridge. An old beggar and his dog pass along the street. The old man has been broken by his own weaknesses and failures. Only his dog is faithful.

WHAT'S AHEAD IN CHAPTER 15

Have You Decided upon Your Life Work?

Keats, the noted English poet (1795-1821) started life very humbly. Son of a stablekeeper in London, he was orphaned before he had grown up. His guardian, wishing to start the boy off in some sort of work, apprenticed him to a surgeon in Edmonton. For five years he served as the surgeon's helper, and for two additional years as an assistant in a hospital.

Then, one day, he read *The Faerie Queene,* by Edmund Spenser, and from that moment his life was changed. Haunted by the enchanting melody of the poem, he knew that only in poetry could he find himself. He forsook his work at the hospital and devoted himself to writing the verse which today is adjudged by critics to be unsurpassed in English literature for pure melody and lyric beauty.

If John Keats had not been struck down by tuberculosis, much more poetry as beautiful as *Endymion* and *The Eve of Saint Agnes* might have been created by this great master. As it was, he died when only twenty-six years of age. His entire literary career was limited to the last three years of his life, but he produced verse of such a high order of merit that it won for him the enviable title, "The Poet's Poet."

George Arliss is recognized as one of the greatest actors of his time. The story of how he happened to enter acting as a profession has been interestingly told in his autobiography, *Up the Years from Bloomsbury.* One Christmas time, when he was only a boy, a party for the children was prepared, with three actors participating. The actors were older boys, one of whom had written the play which they were to produce. It was called "Mrs. Bottlewasher's Apartment." At the very last minute one of the three was unable to appear, and the suggestion was made that young Arliss take the part. George went into a hasty coaching which lasted half an hour!

The production was "an enormous and overwhelming success," and young George Arliss was profoundly convinced that only acting as a profession could satisfy his soul. Throughout a long and brilliant career he never flagged in his ardent devotion to the stage as a profession.

"How pleasant your grounds always are!" remarked more than one visitor on the Selvern piazza, looking down across the well-kept and tastefully arranged gardens of the hostess.

"All thanks to Eleanor!" Mrs. Selvern would reply. "She has a flair for that sort of thing. She's going to be a landscape gardener, you know, some day! She always arranges our flower beds herself and decides what to plant in them and where to locate them."

And it is true. Now in her final year at high school, Eleanor is looking forward enthusiastically to landscape gardening as a vocation. Some of her friends try to dissuade her, insisting that landscaping is a man's job rather than a woman's. But Eleanor only smiles indulgently at such an idea and continues reading her horticulture and floriculture magazines and books, studying catalogs of herbs and shrubs, and planning and caring for the Selvern grounds. She almost literally haunts the nearby nursery and hothouse belonging to her uncle and spends every spare hour among the shrubs and trees. Sometimes she helps her uncle draw landscaping plans for some property owner or land development concern, and actually supervises the men when they set a hedge or arrange a quadrangle.

"The young miss knows her onions!" the workers often remark admiringly as they follow out her suggestions.

Enthusiasm for Your Job Is Important

In these three anecdotes, you are impressed with the enthusiasm which young people properly feel when they finally discover a kind of life work in which they know they will experience satisfaction through the years. John Keats was ready to give up the start he had received in medicine during seven years to begin all over again in something he was convinced he would like far better. George Arliss grew up from boyhood with the ideal of being an actor ever before him, and he became great in his chosen profession. Eleanor Selvern, while it is too early yet to predict the final outcome, is so devoted to landscaping and floriculture that there is no question in anybody's mind about her present enthusiasm for it nor about her future achievement in this vocational field.

Three similar people—Poet Keats, Actor Arliss, Landscaper Selvern!

✓ ✓ ✓

In the present chapter you will learn how many thousands of possible occupations are open to the youth of the twentieth century. You will discover that, notwithstanding the wide range of vocational possibilities, the nearly two million young people who leave school each year to seek their fortunes in the work of the world have almost no background of information or of self-analysis for choosing a life work. You will learn that 95% of all college students wish to work in four occupations! You will be helped to evaluate vocations in terms of your own aptitudes for them and will be supplied with some suggestions about preparing now for future occupational success.

Fig. 59. Aviation is a field that is rapidly expanding to include more and more different jobs. In 1935 there were sixteen ground workers for every plane in the air, while in 1940 there were forty ground workers for every plane. What effect has the war had on aviation as a vocation?

15. YOUR VOCATION

Before you read the chapter, it will be helpful for your class to prepare a vocational chart indicating the preferences of each person in it for a life work. The following form may be used, or a more elaborate one may be constructed:

VOCATIONS WHICH INTEREST MEMBERS OF OUR CLASS

Student's Initials	Sex	Vocation Most Appealing at the Present Time	Reason for This Interest
1. J. E. P.	Girl	Nursing	Admiration for someone who is a nurse.
2. L. H. C.	Boy	Truck farming	Likes gardening.
3.			
4.			
5. etc.			

After the chart is completed, find the totals for all the occupations mentioned and arrange the choices in order of their popularity. It will be interesting also to devote a little class time to an oral defense of several choices by the pupils who made them.

THE PERENNIAL QUESTION

What shall I be? "What are you going to be when you grow up?" From almost the earliest days of childhood you have been asked this question over and over again by your relatives and friends, and more recently, no doubt, by your teachers and counselors.

For the most part you have probably not taken the matter of occupational choice very seriously up to the present, for you have been too immersed in going to school to have very much time to think seriously about vocations. Besides, you have realized that you still have some months or years of schooling ahead and have come to feel that there will be plenty of time to choose your vocation by and by.

How our ideas about vocations change.   No doubt you have had several different ambitions during the years that have passed. Perhaps at one time, attracted by the buttons and uniform of a police officer, you planned to be a policeman. Maybe you were impressed with the adventure of railroading and dreamed at some time of being an engineer, with "your hand upon the throttle and your eye upon the track." Or it may have been aviation, or big business, or medicine, or seafaring, or farming, that captivated you for a season, one ambition fading into another as you were brought into successive contacts with the varying occupations of men.

If you are a girl, you perhaps have decided at different times to be a nurse, or a teacher, or an actress, or a stenographer, or an air stewardess, or a dressmaker, one ideal again merging into another as your experience broadened to encompass more and more of the vocational opportunities open to women.

Rarely, perhaps, does anybody cling for a lifetime to his original choice and follow the vocational path upon which he set his foot at the beginning; although it occasionally happens that an individual knows from the very first what he wants to become and hews his way consistently and persistently in an invariable direction. Such single-mindedness is becoming less and less common in these days of economic upheaval.

How many different vocational ambitions have you had in the past dozen years or so? Use a form like the one on the next page for recording them.

THINGS I HAVE THOUGHT I WANTED TO BE

At About the Age of:	I Thought I Wanted to Be:	Because:
5	A policeman	I was fascinated by the uniform w o r n by my brother, who was on the force.
8 etc.	A locomotive engineer	One day my uncle let me get into the cab of his engine.

(Some of us would have to live several lives if we were to engage in every occupation that at some time or other had intrigued us!)

RANGE OF OCCUPATIONS OPEN TO AMERICANS

Only a few vocations two centuries ago. One of the most amazing things that has taken place in our country during the past century and a half has been the unbelievable increase in the number of vocations by which people earn their livelihood. In colonial America, previous to and including the period of the Revolutionary War, there were scarcely more than a dozen occupations in which one *could* engage. Outside of the ministry, teaching, farming, fishing, cobbling, and small trading, little offered itself in the way of occupational opportunity. In such a period of simple culture there was neither need nor opportunity for much else. Each home was largely self-supporting and self-sustaining and provided, chiefly through the efforts of its own members, the necessary food, clothing, and shelter, and such luxuries as existed.

Immeasurably more vocations today. Contrast with this limited range of vocational opportunity available to the young person of that period, the occupational possibilities of the middle of the twentieth century. The United States census lists more than 20,000 separate kinds of occupations in our country! Thanks to the machine and the resulting expansion of manufacturing, agriculture, mining, distribution, transportation, communication, and so forth, the modern young person facing the problem of selecting a career has a choice that would have made his colonial ancestor dizzy at the mere contemplation! Think of it: *twenty thousand possible kinds of work* that one may choose to do!

CHIEF CLASSIFICATIONS OF THE WORLD'S WORK

The nine major vocational groupings. This tremendous range of occupations is not, of course, so confusing as it might seem at first thought. Actually the entire 20,000 types of employment may be classified into the following nine groups:

(1) Agriculture, forestry, and animal husbandry
(2) Extraction of minerals
(3) Manufacturing and mechanical industries
(4) Transportation
(5) Trade
(6) Public service
(7) Professional service
(8) Domestic and personal service
(9) Clerical occupations

A simpler classification. The Yale University Department of Personnel has presented an interesting analysis of human occupations in three groupings: (1) work that deals primarily with people; (2) work that deals primarily with ideas; (3) work that deals primarily with things. These three are further subdivided as follows:

(1) Work dealing primarily with people
    (a) Directly
        Professions
        Medicine
        Ministry

Law
Teaching
Personnel Work
Industry
Social service
Business
Management
Selling
(b) Indirectly
Advertising
Journalism
Educational administration
Public relations, investigations, etc.
Social investigation

(2) Work dealing primarily with ideas
Invention
Research
Pure science
Artistic and creative professions

(3) Work dealing primarily with things
(a) Working with the thing itself
Engineering and construction
Technical and production side of manufacturing
Agriculture, forestry
Transportation
(b) Working with symbols of things
Accounting and statistics
Drafting, designing
Credit work
Investment and insurance
(c) Work dealing with commercial exchange and distribution
Newspaper and advertising
Retail store
Department store
Chain store

Mail order house
Purchasing
Trading companies, domestic and foreign

This is, of course, a very much abbreviated and simplified list, but it is sufficient to indicate something of the range of specific kinds of occupations open to the young people of America. Somewhere in it, or in the thousands of subtitles that would have to be included if the list were complete, you and I and everybody else in the land, will ultimately find his or her place in the world of work. The important thing—supremely important, too—is that all of us shall find a niche in which we may not only pass our vocational lives but pass them satisfyingly and agreeably.

THE ANNUAL ROLL OF YOUTHFUL JOB SEEKERS

A new army every year. Approximately 1,750,000 young Americans leave our schools each year to take their places in the occupational world, or at least to look for available places for themselves. Only the smallest fraction of these hundreds of thousands of youthful seekers have clear ideas of what they want to become. The vast majority of them have neither any understanding of their capabilities and of their probability of success in a given line of work, nor in most instances any reasonable conviction of what line of work they would prefer to attempt. It is safe to say that most of them have never given any prolonged and serious thought to their occupational futures.

"Their need," says the American Youth Commission of the American Council on Education, "is occupational adjustment, and when that need is adequately met a major national problem will be solved." At the outset, "most of them have only daydreams and wishful thinking."

Vocational bottlenecks! Unaware, on the one hand, of the thousands of possible lines of work which they may enter, and inclining rather generally to look with favor upon four or five leading occupations that seem to them most flattering because of a traditional superiority which they seem to enjoy over other vocations, the young searchers tend to flock into types of work that are already overcrowded! Studies have indicated that as high as 95% of college students wish to enter four occupations! It has been estimated by competent authority that nine out of ten children now in school will enter eighty-seven occupations only! This leaves only 10% of them for the other 19,913 kinds of jobs that must be filled! This unfortunate pressure upon a few occupations is bound to result in students' disappointment and delay in finding their place in the world's work.

GET AS MUCH EDUCATION AS YOU CAN

A mistake too often made. How many of the older generation lament the fact that they left school too soon in order to go to work! Some of them were compelled by hard circumstance to begin to earn just as early as they possibly could; others of them—probably the majority—had the mistaken idea that schooling was superfluous and that the thing of first importance was to get a job and earn some money. Of course, it is pleasant to feel that one is earning, that he has money of his own coming in all the time, and that he is on the way to achieving financial independence and self-determination. Unquestionably this is one of the great goals and the great motivators of life.

It is unfortunate that so many young people, dazzled by the lure of a job and an income, drop out of school prematurely and in so doing compel themselves to enter the great army of workers unprepared and unfortified by the boon of a good basic education. Except for the lucky few, the great mass of such youthful deserters of our schools will soon find themselves either in blind-alley jobs or else enrolling in evening schools, vocational schools, correspondence schools, and the like, to add to their meager educational background in the confident hope that at length they will be in a position to better themselves vocationally.

The need of a high school education. There is no better guarantee that a young person will succeed occupationally than that he start out on his career with a good general education. It makes little difference what line of work he follows: the better educational background he has, the greater the likelihood that he will establish himself agreeably in his vocation. A high school education, while less essential a generation and more ago, is today practically indispensable for success in the workaday world.

Should you decide later that you wish to enter one of the professions, you will find none of them open to you unless you have a high school diploma to start with. Should you choose business, or trade, or any of the other occupations, you will find advancement in them dependent to a large degree upon whether or not you completed the secondary school. Those who fall by the educational wayside, who drop out of school for one reason or another, are, barring exceptions, of course, not likely to win advancement and promotion in their jobs to the same degree as their wiser or more fortunate fellows who stayed in school. True, they may get an earlier start, but they will be ultimately outstripped by the better educated group.

QUESTIONS TO ASK ABOUT ANY OCCUPATION

Will this job bring me satisfaction? It is the part of folly to enter blindly any vocation or job. The intelligent young person will want to stop to ask himself whether the work he is thinking of undertaking is the kind of work that will yield him a reasonable degree of satisfaction. After the novelty of it has worn off, will it still continue through the years to appeal, or will one grow tired of it after a time and so become another individual in the large group of workers who are vocationally morose and unadjusted? If a job is satisfying only because it represents a source of livelihood, it is a poor vocation in which to spend a lifetime.

Not by bread alone! A person's job should be much more than his bread and butter; it should be for him always a source of genuine interest and satisfaction. In day-by-day pursuit of it, he should find his feelings pleasantly stirred, his ambition aroused, his mental or physical powers fully engaged. If one cannot put his soul into his work, as have all the immortals who have achieved fame in their callings, he should at least throw the best of his energies into it and make it always a vital part of his total life experience.

Unless you can anticipate a reasonable guarantee that the line of work you enter will thus challenge you and your capacities, you would better either adjust your expectations and your character so that it will, or else seek for some other occupation that will meet this requirement. The shops and factories and offices and business establishments of the world have in them altogether too many workers who derive scant satisfaction from their jobs and who bring to them each day little more than bitter tolerance and self-pity. Probably in more cases than not the fault lies, not with the job, but with the adjustment of the worker to it.

Will there be a chance for advancement? While some jobs, by their very nature, are blind-alley jobs, or one-story jobs, which lead to nothing better, either horizontally or vertically, it is unquestionably true that most occupations in which people engage are not of that sort. Extremely few types of work are so cut and dried as not to offer abundant opportunity for growth or advancement to those who have the ability and the character to climb.

Industrial managers and directors of production in innumerable varieties of manufacturing establishments are constantly on the lookout for those among their employees who have ideas, or who indicate ability or promise somewhat above the rank and file. For such young workers, there is seldom any limit to the possibilities of advancement. At the bench of the apprentice, or in the ranks, any young fellow of ability is likely to be singled out promptly and slated for promotion. When our system of mass production becomes perfected, it will undoubtedly provide as many new jobs each year as there are people leaving school and seeking for them, and it will single out those workers who are promising and push them along, thus leaving room each year for the new group of beginners.

There is no justification for the commonly voiced opinion that mass production makes machines out of workers, and that there is no individuality demanded of them, no future before them, no interest or enthusiasm expected of them. On the contrary, industry as it is organized in the twentieth century is so dependent upon improved and quicker ways of doing things that it is more on the alert than ever for those in its ranks who have ideas and ingenuity. The trouble is not so much with the heartlessness of industry as it is with the mediocrity and indifference of those whom it absorbs. Few, indeed, are the types of work that leave a person stranded and hopelessly bogged down.

Is there room for me in this vocation? It is unfortunate, as we pointed out earlier in this chapter, that so many young people limit their vocational preferences to so few jobs. It has been estimated that the public schools are preparing 90% of their students for 10% of the jobs. It goes without saying that the 10% of the jobs toward which these students are steered are the so-called "white-collar jobs." For young people with strong inclinations toward the professions, or toward some sort of office or clerical or managerial position, the advice and encouragement the schools offer are sound and proper.

On the other hand, for the great numbers of youth who are looking forward to manual occupations, there needs to be a

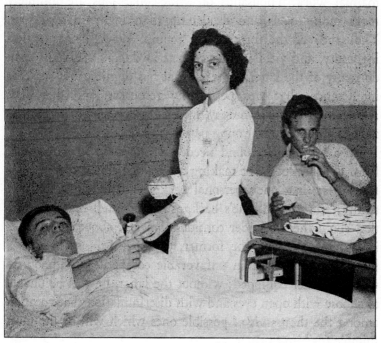

Photo by Ralph Pierson for Monkmeyer

Fig. 60. Is the field of nursing an overcrowded one? What qualifications must a girl have to become a good nurse?

new emphasis placed upon the attractiveness of the mechanical trades. Here is the field where absorption is greatest, and where there is always room at the top.

In choosing your job, after analyzing your interests and

preferences, do not forget to consider the possibility that the vocation of your choice may be already absurdly overcrowded. The question of demand and supply is a significant one when it comes to selecting a life occupation.

Most work requires manual skill. Do not cultivate a foolish prejudice against work that calls for the use of your hands as well as your head. Two thirds of the work of the world is manual work. Thousands of white-collar jobs are infinitely more monotonous and deadening than many manual jobs. Thousands of the former, too, require less skill, arouse less ingenuity, and yield smaller returns in dollars and cents than do many of the latter. Any job that has dignity, that requires intelligence, that taps personality resources, and that pays reasonable returns in money, in self-respect, and in security is a worthy one for any young person to select.

Have I the background needed for success? Background, from the standpoint of making a wise vocational choice, is of two sorts: first, one's personal background of education and ability; and second, one's background of intelligent information about the job under consideration and about occupations in general. Without the former, the youthful seeker after a job will find himself in unfavorable competition with others who are better equipped; without the latter, he will be unable to choose with open eyes and with discrimination that vocation among the thousands of possible ones which will be the most suitable for him to enter.

My own personal background. The question of personal background resolves itself into two rather complex queries: first, have I enough general intelligence and education for this job; second, have I the special aptitudes needed to make good in it? Some kinds of work, by their very nature, necessitate specialized aptitudes or knacks if one is to succeed in them. Others require no such particular knack but instead demand a good average level of intelligence and a reasonable minimum of schooling. For the latter, you need only your own honest self-appraisal. For the former—those jobs which demand a special aptitude for a given kind of work—you may find it wise to seek the advice of some well-informed vocational counselor.

What jobs can you think of that appear to require some kind of special knack or aptitude on the part of those who are to be successful in them? List as many as you can on a form like this one:

JOBS THAT REQUIRE A SPECIAL KNACK

Occupation	Do I Have the Knack for It?	Who in My Class Has This Knack?
1. Automobile repairman	No	Fred L.
2. Tradesman	Yes	Bill C.
3.		
4.		
5. etc.		
(Don't leave out the girls!)		

Some day, without question, all high schools and colleges will have vocational counselors; at the present time, however, that is unfortunately not the case. Consequently you may be in some doubt regarding your fitness for such specific vocations as drawing, music, law, salesmanship, and so forth, and should try to secure the advice of a competent psychologist or counselor before you make your decision.

Psychological testing for aptitudes. It may well be that you have heard about the work done by the Human Engineering Laboratory, at Stevens Institute of Technology, Hoboken, New Jersey. From his original study of applicants for employment in the General Electric Company plant, Mr. Johnson O'Connor, founder of the Laboratory, became convinced that psy-

chological testing would help to indicate the future success
or failure of young persons as they faced their life work.
In the quarter of a century since the Human Engineering
Laboratory was established, it has tested tens of thousands of
people, many of them of high school or college age. Hundreds
of tests have been developed for the purpose.

In order to reach a greater number of people than could be
served at the Institute alone, temporary testing laboratories
have been set up in a score or more of secondary schools. In
these centers vocational testing is made available at cost, the
Laboratory being a nonprofit enterprise. The number of persons tested by the Human Engineering Laboratory has doubled
each year.

In addition to the actual testing done at the Laboratory and
in the branch centers, the organization publishes brochures
giving young persons who wish for it guidance in their vocational quest. The brochures cover the following fields:

(1) Executives
(2) Executives in manufacturing and public service companies
(3) Lawyers
(4) Physicians and surgeons
(5) Engineering executives
(6) Lawyers; women in law
(7) Men and women in advertising, merchandising, and general
sales work.

Gathering information about occupations. The second
kind of background essential to success is your information
about occupations. It is the height of folly to select a vocation
at random from the list and proceed to enter it without first
having collected a good bit of information about it.

There are many sources from which this information may
be culled. Your school library and your public library can

furnish you with bibliographies on vocational information, and can even loan you some books dealing with occupations. Magazines and journals frequently carry articles on this subject. Trips or visits to business houses, government agencies, factories, and farms will yield rich information about actual working conditions and opportunities. Talks with people who hold different kinds of jobs will also be helpful. Vacation opportunities to work in various types of employment will bring you into actual first-hand contact with the workaday world and aid you in your evaluation of different jobs.

Armed with all the information you can gather from these and other sources and with a fair and impartial recognition of your personal assets and liabilities, you should find the ultimate selection of a vocation somewhat simplified.

HOW CAN A STUDENT PREPARE FOR SUCCESS?

Develop a good presence.   Other things being equal, of two applicants for a position, the candidate who can make the better personal impression upon the employer will be the one to get the job. Schooling and training are important things, of course, but the importance of personality, of poise, of good manners, cannot be lost sight of when you are interviewed by an employer. While nobody can adequately evaluate personality and character during an interview, there is no question but that many of the elements that make up good character and personality do show up when you find yourself face to face with a prospective employer. Your sincerity, your politeness, your fundamental culture, your confidence in yourself can hardly be concealed. These are traits that play large roles in personality and character.

These are traits, too, that may and ought to be cultivated zealously during your school years. There may not be much opportunity in your school for vocational exploration or guidance; but there is no reason why you cannot develop these intimately personal traits that are so essential both in obtaining a job and in holding it afterwards. Initial employment and subsequent advancement are in no small degree dependent upon you yourself and your own character.

Develop industry and perseverance. No matter what sort of job you get, it will require hard work and aggressiveness if you are to make good in it. These are mental attitudes that cannot wait for the actual coming of vocational age and appointment; they must be under cultivation every day in your school career. If you are developing slipshod habits, if you tend to be indolent or ambitionless, if you are a shirker or a delayer or a quitter, you can hardly expect that your negative traits will be miraculously transposed into their opposites when you start looking for a job. Work habits and attitudes cultivated during school life ordinarily cling to a person after he leaves school. Almost anybody who knows you well today could predict pretty accurately whether or not you will be likely to make good in the workaday world tomorrow.

Learn how to talk. Can you talk with another person without stuttering, or fumbling with your hat, or flushing and paling alternately, or using inelegant forms of speech, or "murdering" the English language? Can you control your thought and couch it readily in acceptable words, well pronounced and enunciated? Has your voice variety and range, so that listening to it is not monotonous and uninteresting?

One of the most important aims of high schools and colleges is to equip the student with a good practical command of the English language, both spoken and written. Through study of language and grammar, through practice in oral and written composition, through the give-and-take of classroom and assembly and extracurricular activity, and through the opportunities provided by social functions, your teachers are striving not only to make you socially at ease when in the presence of others but also to make you a good talker and writer and a pleasant conversationalist. These are assets that you will find to be invaluable steppingstones to success in the occupational world, where facility in the use of language is so commonly indispensable.

Be practical about occupations. Altogether too many of our future workers have decidedly impractical ideas and visionary ambitions concerning the jobs they are soon to secure. The desire to be an actor or a movie star, for example, is a decidedly barren idea to play with from the standpoint of probable attainment. Many young women who are obsessed with the idea of going to Hollywood would do much better to dismiss such an empty notion from their minds and start searching about for some likely vocation nearer home. Failure and disappointment strew the pathway of most of those who pursue absurd ambitions of achieving fame and fortune behind the footlights or upon the screen.

We do not expect very young children to be too stable in their vocational preferences. But we do expect most young people to be more constant in their vocational interests and to narrow them down to practical and achievable jobs. Too-early selection of a vocation is not, of course, desirable. By the time you leave high school, however, you ought to be in possession of some very definite ideas on the matter. Throughout the closing years of high school you should at least keep yourself alert to occupational opportunities in the great world beyond the school.

Learn tolerance and appreciation. One of the most unfortunate things about our industrial age is the fact that there is none too much sympathy between types and levels of workers. The strife arising between labor groups and between labor and capital springs in considerable measure from misunderstanding and misinformation. It is tragically easy for an individual who works in some nook or cranny of the world's occupations to speculate feelingly as to how much better off somebody else is who occupies some other nook or cranny, or to resent his own failure to rise, or to grow envious of his boss or of his employer, or to deplore the conditions amid which he toils. Strikes and walkouts and all the other evils that arise from such situations would be shortly done away with if each employer and employee could understand the other fellow's problems and point of view.

Collar color is unimportant! If you choose either the teaching or the theological profession, you should realize from the outset that your returns in dollars and cents will probably never equal the returns you might have enjoyed had you gone into business. If you choose business, you should realize that in so doing you are sacrificing much of the quiet reflection and culture and moral and social leadership that commonly falls to the lot of the professional man. If you choose a white-collar job, do not forget that the black-collar and the blue-collar and the uncollared jobs are likewise essential. If you find yourself holding an uncollared job, cultivate respect for the holder of the white-collar job and the problems which he faces. In short, learn to be tolerant and appreciative of all workers, of whatever types and levels.

The work of our country depends for its performance upon the perseverance and faithfulness and contentment of tens of millions of men and women distributed among 20,000 different varieties of jobs, of which few are any more indispensable than any others.

What factors or conditions can you think of that tend to make for jealousies and intolerance between workers in different fields or at different levels within the same field? Record your ideas on a form like the one on page 403.

1. They are envious of those who get higher wages.
2. They underestimate the importance of other people's work.
3.
4.
5. etc.

(There are many factors that belong here. This is an excellent opportunity for you to do some real research.)

HOW PSYCHOLOGISTS WORK

A question with which psychologists have been for some time concerned is that dealing with the relationship between intelligence and successful performance in the various occupations. It is obvious, of course, that some vocations and professions require, by their very nature, a higher intelligence than is demanded by certain others, if those who enter them are to make good.

In 1917 and 1918, at the time of the First World War, many hundreds of thousands of men in their twenties and early thirties were tested by the army psychologists to determine their varying degrees of intelligence so that the most promising of them might be placed in special training classes and advanced rapidly to officers' positions. The scores obtained by the draftees were later classified in terms of the occupations of the men examined.

The table on the next page gives the average scores of those draftees who were engaged in the twenty selected occupations. Slight changes have been made in a few instances as a result of more recent information obtained from non-army groups.

Inasmuch as the scores obtained by draftees may be assumed to be representative of those of the population as a whole, we are doubtless reasonably safe in supposing that our occupa-

INTELLIGENCE SCORES IN TWENTY OCCUPATIONS

Average Score	Occupation
161	Engineer
152	Clergyman
137	Accountant
127	Physician
122	Public school teacher
114	Draftsman
111	Y. M. C. A. Secretary
110	Dentist
109	Minor executive
103	Stenographer, typist
101	Bookkeeper
99	Nurse
96	Clerk
85	Telegraph, radio operator
83	Railway conductor
78	Shipping clerk
69	Policeman, detective
65	Automobile mechanic
65	Carpenter
59	House painter

tional groups rate approximately as indicated in this table, with engineers, clergymen, accountants, physicians, and teachers heading the list. The scores recorded in the table, it should be noted, are not I. Q. scores.

Another important question that confronts society perennially concerns the vocational content of the high school curriculum. In recent decades we have seen an increasing emphasis in the secondary schools upon vocational guidance, vocational testing and counseling, and vocational preparation. In a technical, mechanical age, it is apparent that the schools are obligated to prepare their students to live in the world of work as much as in the world of ideas. In consequence, we find that the conventional academic subjects are sharing their place with those more definitely vocational.

It is now rather generally agreed among secondary school administrators that every young person should, when he leaves high school, understand how to manage a machine and have a good comprehension of some one broad field of work. Rather than narrowly specializing, the student should become familiar with processes that are common to a number of occupations and industries. Shop training is essential, but it is recommended that instead of spending six semesters in any one

Photo by Brown Brothers

Fig. 61. Michael Faraday as an apprentice. In the old days a youth got his vocational training by serving his apprenticeship under a master workman. Would that be a good system for today?

shop, the student would better spend one semester (and never more than two) in a machine shop, a metal shop, an automobile shop, a woodworking shop, and a foundry. In this way the prospective worker avoids narrow specialization and is more likely to "find himself" vocationally.

A striking illustration of the penetration of vocational consciousness into the high schools is to be seen in the movement to introduce aeronautics into the secondary school curriculum. To prepare youth for the air age, which, most people agree, has already begun, aeronautical education is considered extremely desirable.

At a conference held in New York State on the subject of Education for the Air Age, the section on secondary education adopted the following provisions as a general policy to guide high school aeronautics courses:

(1) Strengthening and extension of aeronautical shop instruction wherever possible;

(2) Teaching of all courses with the implication of the air age in mind;

(3) Formation of aviation clubs, with flight or glider training programs;

(4) Specific courses in pre-flight aeronautics open to both sexes and carrying regular academic credit.

The group recommended that pre-flight aeronautics should include the study of aerodynamics, navigation, meteorology, civil air regulations, general service of aircraft, communications, airplane structures, power plants, and propellers. The completion of two years' study of mathematics and one year of physics in high school is required of those who take pre-flight aeronautics.

Thus does the secondary school curriculum reflect promptly the present and future needs of people who live in the air age.

TO HELP YOU LEARN

SOME QUESTIONS TO ANSWER

1. Whether or not you have made any vocational choice, in which of the nine classifications of the world's work given on page 388 do you find your vocational preference falling?

2. If it is true, as is sometimes contended, that 65% of all the jobs in the United States require no training other than three days or less on the job itself, of what advantage could it possibly be for students to study vocations and vocational choices, as you have been doing in Chapter XV?

3. Do you know, or have you heard about, any worker who is "a square peg in a round hole"? How might this misfitting of worker to job have been avoided? Do you think most, if not all, of such vocational misfits are found in the strictly manual jobs? In the white-collar jobs? If not, how are they distributed?

4. Do you thoroughly believe that vocational advancement depends chiefly upon the worth of the candidate? Or do you feel that only those get ahead who have "pull" or "friends at court"?

5. Can you think of any white-collar job that is more monotonous than many manual jobs? Explain.

WORKING WITH PSYCHOLOGY

1. Reckon, in terms of dollars and cents alone, the relative value of four years spent in high school as compared with the same four years that might have been spent instead in working and earning. Take the long-range view of over twenty-five years, from the age of fourteen to the age of forty. Be as fair as possible in estimating your annual earnings in either situation. Where could you obtain information on this subject? A form like the one at the top of page 408 may be suggestive.

2. Arrange a class trip to some easily accessible business concern, factory, or industrial establishment for the purpose of finding out about the type of work done, the number and classification of workers, wages paid, conditions under which the work is carried

DOES A HIGH SCHOOL EDUCATION PAY?

Without a High School Education		With a High School Education	
At Age	I Could Probably Earn	At Age	I Could Probably Earn
14⎫ 15⎬ the 4 high 16⎭ school years 17	$ $ $ $	14⎫ 15⎬ the 4 high 16⎭ school years 17	$ $ $ $
18 to 40 (at $ per year)	$	18 to 25 (8 years before promotion at $)	$
		26 to 35 (10 years after first promotion at $)	$
		36 to 40 (5 years after second promotion at $)	$

on, preliminary training required of employees, vacations, pensions, hours of the working day, and so forth. Plan before making the trip the essential information you desire, so that the official whom you question may not waste his time. Make as thorough a tour of inspection and maintain as lengthy an interview as time and conditions warrant. Spend some time in class afterwards comparing notes and drawing conclusions. It will be extremely valuable if during the year your class can make several such trips. A courteous letter requesting permission to visit the concern will ordinarily meet with sympathetic approval on the part of the directors.

An alternative plan would be, of course, to invite some representative of a business enterprise to come to your class to speak and to answer queries about his type of work.

3. Make a vocational survey of your community, listing all the types of jobs in which men and women are engaged for a livelihood. If you live in a large city, you will need to limit your survey to your own neighborhood, or perhaps your own precinct. In a smaller community, you will be able to make a reasonably complete analysis of jobs in which people are engaged. After your study is completed, list in some kind of orderly classification, similar, for example, to the one on pages 388-390, the principal vocations discovered.

4. Quite as important to occupational success as intelligence or special aptitude are certain traits of character and personality in the worker. On a rating scale similar to the one on the next page,

rate yourself on certain of these qualities that loom large in the successful performance of any job:

TRAIT: *Perseverance*

Shilly-shally	Halfhearted	Plodding	Fairly Aggressive	Indomitable

TRAIT: *Sincerity*

Two-faced	Likely to be Insincere	Usually Straightforward	Frank, Undissembling	Completely Guileless

Try your own hand at constructing a scale for the following traits: self-confidence, politeness, co-operativeness. Rate yourself similarly upon each.

WHAT OTHERS SAY

1. In Fiction:

The Song of the Lark by Willa Cather. A story of the struggles of a girl reared in the Colorado deserts and of her eventual triumph as a grand opera singer. The book shows the dominant force of genius compelling a person to work out her vocational destiny.

The Honorable Peter Stirling by Paul L. Ford. The classic story of a young Harvard graduate who enters municipal politics as a vocation. In the midst of intrigue and corruption, he maintains his principles.

Work of Art by Sinclair Lewis. A tale of the dogged and persistent climb of a young Connecticut hotel employee who dreamed of owning and operating the Perfect Inn. An excellent portrayal of the problems confronting those who would succeed in this vocation.

2. In Biography:

One Foot in Heaven by Hartzell Spence. In this absorbing story of his father's life as a clergyman, starting off with straight-laced ideas and ending with a lovable liberalism, the author presents the trials and tribulations of a practical-minded parson.

Barnum by M. R. Werner. An absorbing biography of one of the greatest showmen America has produced. As interesting as any western adventure tale is this story of a Yankee genius who devoted his life to the vocation of amusing people.

3. In Drama:

Stage Door by Edna Ferber and George S. Kaufman. How Terry Randall, through thick and thin, fights her way up in the theater to a place as a promising young actress. Here's a good play for your class to put on.

4. In Poetry:

The Dauber by John Masefield. The evolution of character in a young man who followed the sea as a vocation is strikingly portrayed in this appealing poem. Finally, the Dauber won everybody's heart.

WHAT'S AHEAD IN CHAPTER 16

What Do We Mean by the Good Life?

"T. R.," as Theodore Roosevelt was popularly known, was the acknowledged leader of the progressive element in the Republican Party. Physically weak and in poor health, he journeyed as a young man in the twenties from his native New York to the vast plains of North Dakota. There, as a ranchman, he not only developed health and robustness but achieved physical hardihood to a degree that made it possible for him to devote himself strenuously to public life for the next quarter of a century and more.

"T. R." organized the Roughriders and fought conspicuously in Cuba on behalf of the forces of freedom. As governor of New York State, he began a long career of "trust busting," reform in state administration, and extension of the civil service. He won national fame as president of the New York City Police Board through his reorganization of the department in the interests of honesty and efficiency.

As twenty-sixth president of the United States, he continued his drive against trusts and organizations in restraint of trade, stood out strongly for American rights in the international arena, got the Panama Canal built, negotiated the Treaty of Portsmouth that terminated the Russo-Japanese War, established the Census Bureau and the Department of Commerce, vastly increased the army and navy, and accomplished other notable deeds.

"T. R.'s" honesty, sincerity, and fine character won for him a host of friends in all parties.

"When I grow up I will have a large house, but it will not be built among the other large houses, but right in the midst of horrid little houses like these!" So exclaimed Jane Addams, a frail little Illinois girl when she went one day with her father into the poorer district of the city where they lived.

True to her promise, when she was grown up Miss Addams opened the famous Hull House in a foreign quarter of Chicago. To it the poor and the needy and the sick and the stranger were admitted and ministered unto. A day nursery for the children, classes and clubs for the older people, a friendly graciousness to puzzled and friendless immigrants of thirty-six different nationalities—these original offerings of Hull House soon grew into the complex activities of the most famous of all American social settlements. Today Hull House, after half a century of conspicuous service, is respected and revered alike by those unfortunates whom it has befriended and Americanized and by social workers and sociologists throughout the world.

Jane Addams has been widely recognized as one of our foremost citizens. Great honor has been given her on many occasions, at one of which she received the Nobel Peace Prize.

Ettie Chin was a little Chinese girl. Her father ran a small retail store in a large American city. It was a strong wish in the Chin family that both Ettie and her brothers should go to high school, and after that to college. And they all did!

A girl with a strong character and a keen desire to help her people, Ettie resolved early that she would go back to her ancestral homeland some day and help the Chinese to improve themselves. To China she went, upon graduation from college, and in China she has remained ever since. Ettie found her opportunity in Ginling College, in Nanking, at which she became a teacher. About four years after her arrival at Ginling,

Ettie and her associates on the faculty realized that the Japanese would soon overrun Nanking and their beloved college.

Then began one of the most amazing and inspiring journeys ever undertaken! Collecting together the college books and apparatus and furnishings, Ettie and the rest transported Ginling College on their backs and in such rude conveyances as they could find to a safe haven far in the interior of China. Students and faculty alike wended their slow, painful way a thousand miles into Szechuan Province, where today Ginling College is training hundreds of Chinese youth for the great new day which sometime will dawn for China!

Good People Are Not Necessarily Great

Theodore Roosevelt, Jane Addams, and Ettie Chin are three of an innumerable company of people, living and dead, who by the fineness of their characters and the nobility and integrity of their spirits have inestimably benefited mankind through their lives and influence. Fortunately, such individuals are not limited to the great and the near-great. In the humblest of surroundings, such as those of little Ettie, character is nurtured, and the ideal of service is instilled.

↑ ↑ ↑

In this chapter you will learn what is meant by the good act and the good life. You will learn about the conflicting motives and the conflicting examples presented in the lives and conduct of people in the economic world and in the social and political world, and will understand how difficult it is for the young person to chart his course clearly and safely among these contradictory influences. You will discover an interesting relationship between our emotions and our conduct, and will become familiar with the six fundamentals of character.

Fig. 62. Ignace Jan Paderewski has been acclaimed the most brilliant pianist since Liszt. A man of sterling character, beloved by his countrymen, he was made premier of Poland in 1919.

16. CHARACTER

Before commencing to study about character, it will be helpful for you to contrast some notable examples of good character and of poor character, both in historical personages and in your own contemporaries. Use this form for the purpose:

TWO KINDS OF CHARACTER

Exponents of the Good Life, Good Character, Good Citizenship	Exemplified in	Exponents of the Selfish Life, Poor Character, Poor Citizenship	Exemplified in
1. Socrates	Acts of morality and self-discipline	1. Caligula	Acts of cruelty and tyranny
2.		2.	
3.		3.	
4.		4.	
5. etc.		5. etc.	

The world is filled, in each succeeding generation, with good people, bad people, and indifferent people. The indifferent rarely leave any permanent imprint upon mankind. Only the outstandingly good and the outstandingly bad affect their fellows strikingly.

WHAT IS CHARACTER?

Don't confuse character with reputation! A well-known test of intelligence asks the question of the individual being tested: "What is the difference between character and reputation?" Research indicates that the average individual sixteen years of age knows the difference: that one's reputation is the opinion others have of him, whereas one's character is his real and inherent goodness or badness.

A person of poor character may have an excellent reputation, provided he conceals his true nature from his neighbors and takes care to do his evil under cover. Some knaves are clever enough to hide their true characters for a lifetime, or the greater part of a lifetime, and their real natures begin to show up only after they have done most of their evil in the world. Other knaves may be known and recognized as knaves all their lives, their character and their reputation coinciding rather closely.

The stability of character.   Character—whether good or bad —is tolerably stable and consistent in any individual. It expresses itself in the *customary* way by which a person responds to the world in which he lives and to the surroundings in which he finds himself. He possesses certain attitudes and points of view that are permanent, and his habits are consistent and for the most part unvarying. He may be counted upon to react in his characteristic way at all times and in all circumstances. His interests do not change every morning, nor his desires every night. His emotions, attitudes, and ideals are integral parts of *him*. His moral and ethical code is *his* moral and ethical code, and it remains relatively stable and consistent from day to day and from year to year. His friends and relatives and associates know how to take him, and what sort of reactions to expect of him.

Even though a man may be a vacillating, weak-willed individual who never stands up for anything, he is still consistent, and nobody ever expects him to be aggressive and strong-willed. These characteristics are *his* characteristics, just as much as decisiveness and initiative may be characteristics of somebody else, and in both cases they are associated constantly with the respective individuals.

GOOD CHARACTER LEADS TO GOOD ACTS

A definition worth remembering. We expect people of good character to do good deeds, and we are not surprised when people of bad character do bad ones. The good act is associated with the good life, the bad act with the bad life. What is the good act? There is perhaps no better definition of it than the following: "The good act aims at as many and as worthy satisfactions for as many people as possible over as long a time as possible."

Worthy satisfactions. In this definition there appear to be three implications regarding character. In the first place, the emotional returns which we derive from our conduct are to be in the nature of *worthy* satisfactions, not unworthy ones. The goals of the individual possessed of good character are goals that do honor to him; they are not mean, or sordid, or low. They are goals which he possesses in common with all people who are activated by ethical principles and desirable standards of conduct.

Conduct beneficial to others. In the second place, an individual of good character tries to keep in mind the welfare and the satisfactions of other people besides himself in whatever he does. He is unwilling to benefit himself at the expense of other people. If the satisfaction he seeks is of such a nature that it might cause embarrassment or pain to somebody else, the person of fine character denies himself the satisfaction which he might otherwise enjoy. By his deeds, he seeks always to assure the greatest possible pleasure and satisfaction to as many other people as he can. The conduct of the man of good character is beneficial to his immediate family and friends; his conduct is also calculated to be of benefit to those quite removed from his immediate circle. In his good thoughts, his good intentions, and his good acts, he tries to embrace the whole race of men. He is a good citizen alike of the community, the nation, and the world.

The long view. In the third place, the individual of good character is not content to seek a momentary satisfaction that is gone shortly; rather, he takes the long view, and so orders his life and conduct that his influence may be lastingly good. Satisfactions of the moment, he knows, are better not experienced at all if in the long run they are going to make him impatient, or reduce his capacity to enjoy life tomorrow, or cause him to see things in the wrong perspective, or make him callous and indifferent to the happiness and comfort of others. "For as many people as possible, over as long a time as possible!" These are important phrases in the definition of the kind of act that characterizes the good life.

On the form below list a number of kindly deeds done by the people you know or have heard about:

THE GOOD ACT IN EVERYDAY EXPERIENCE

1. Mrs. Williams sat up all night with a neighbor's sick child so that the tired mother might have a good night's sleep.
2. Mr. Soper arranged a party for some poor children at Christmas time.
3.
4.
5. etc.

(When we stop to think about it, it is pleasant to realize how many kind acts are done in the world.)

SOME CONFLICTING INFLUENCES

The power of home example. What are the sources of a person's character? Surely, character is not innate—born in us! By no means, indeed! An individual shapes his own character through his contacts and experiences. In his childhood home the foundations of his character were laid by the habits and attitudes and ideals which fastened themselves upon him before ever he left its doors for the outer world. The precepts that were taught him, the training that was given him, the standards that were held up before him—these were the foundational stuff out of which his character was fashioned.

What parent does not covet for his child the good life and the good deed? What parent does not strive to inculcate into his child good standards of obedience, of honesty, of kindness, of thoughtfulness? If we all turned out to be the kind of people that our parents hoped we would become and tried to help us become, nearly all of us would have the finest of characters.

Examples of a different color!   The examples of the childhood home are apt to be lofty. But when one passes beyond its doors into the outer world, he finds, alongside of the good, another and quite different kind of example and influence. At first these other forms of conduct and ideals do not thrust themselves very strongly upon the young fledgling from the parental nest. The moral momentum which his home has provided him, and continues to provide him, is sufficient for a time to carry him safely past the opposing examples and forces that men of base or poor character set loose in the world about him. The reality of these other ideals and values, however, cannot long be disregarded, for they exist side by side with the good and the enduring.

From the day on which the child first passes through the parental doorway, if indeed he has not already sensed it before, he is confronted with a whole range of conflicting ideals and practices in the world of men. Let us pass in brief review some of the more obvious and powerful of these diametrically opposed principles of life and conduct.

Conflicting motives in the economic world.   In the business world the observant young person soon becomes aware that, while justice and fair dealing activate many of those who are in control, many others are activated by such selfish motives as seeking enrichment at the expense of their fellows, conniving to gain or to retain control over the production or distribution of commodities, winking at or actually setting aside the law and tending to become laws unto themselves.

Selfishness and greed, in other words, are observed to be strong motives that preside over the activities of men on every hand, often outglaring the generosity and sympathy that one may find also in the world if he looks for it. Injustice, oppression, unfair methods, and disregard for the rights and feelings of others are observed continually by us all, and unless we are careful to look for their opposites, we are extremely likely to conclude that justice, honorableness, and co-operativeness do not exist at all.

These opposed points of view are not confined, of course, to captains of industry and leaders in the business world. One sees the same types of character among the hirelings of industry and in the rank and file of those who do the actual labor of the world. There are those who slight their jobs and those who throw their whole beings into their jobs; there are those who are lazy and untrustworthy and those who are ambitious and absolutely reliable, regardless of whether or not the boss is watching them. It is usually not very difficult for anybody who employs a workman, whether in a shop, or about his home, to form a reasonably accurate notion of his honesty, or his industriousness, or his reliability, and to do so rather promptly after he starts work.

The skimper, the chiseler, the loafer—these are all found in the ranks of those who work, and the rewards they receive are not infrequently quite as great as those enjoyed by the other class of workers who are possessed of good standards and good character.

More conflicting motives. In the social and political world, too, the young person surveying the modern scene finds the same opposed philosophies of conduct and performance that exist in the business and economic world. There are socially acceptable forms of conduct and socially unacceptable forms. There are the law-abiding people and the law-breaking people; the moral and the immoral; the selfish and the unselfish; the provident and the improvident; the high-minded and the low-minded; the pleasure-mad and the well-balanced; the hypocritical and the sincere; the community-minded and the self-centered; the good citizens and the bad.

These opposite types of people make up the adult world upon which the young person looks out when he first ventures away from the parental roof and seeks to get his bearings in a world that is bewilderingly confused and complex in this twentieth century of ours. It would be easy, and the outcome would be inevitable, if only the good example and the fine influence were met on all sides by those who embark upon the great adventure of living in a modern world. Unfortunately, however, the opposite examples and influences are there to be reckoned with, and none can dispute their power to attract the youthful adventurers.

Using the form on page 422, list examples of these "diametrically opposed principles of life and conduct" that you yourself encounter in the world about you.

HOW OUR EMOTIONS AFFECT OUR CHARACTER

Something needed besides intelligence. We took the position in an earlier chapter (see Chapter 10) that the acid test of character is the degree to which a person regulates his life by his intelligence rather than by his emotions. While this is unquestionably true, it must not be supposed that our emotions play little or no part in the building and maintenance of

SOME SPECIMENS OF CONFLICTING INFLUENCES IN SOCIETY

Helpful and Encouraging Influences	Harmful and Discouraging Influences
1. The "golden rule" philosophy	The "every man for himself" philosophy
2.	
3.	
4.	
5. etc.	

(The rate of social progress is perennially retarded by the struggle that must go on between these two forces in the world.)

character. A man's intelligence can tell him what is right and what is wrong in conduct, but unless the warmth and the power of his emotions fill him with a respect and admiration for the good, his character will not ring altogether true. A coldly intellectual analysis of life and its affairs will never drive an individual to crusade for the right, never make him a strong advocate of the good life, and never enable him by the winsomeness of his own personality to attract others to a life of service.

Emotional sincerity is important.　Character is not, in other words, merely a reasoned acceptance of a moral or ethical code. It is something vastly more than an intellectaul assenting to one set of rules for conduct and dissenting from another set of rules. Intelligent acceptance and rejection of rules of conduct there may and should be; but along with the mental act there should be also an emotional sincerity and conviction that give color and direction and driving power to the way of life adopted.

What draws us to our friends?　We are drawn to our friends for the most part, not by their mental or intellectual caliber, but by the attractiveness of their personalities. We admire them, seek them out, and enjoy their companionship because of the feelings of pleasurableness and responsiveness which their spirits arouse in us.

One's character is, to a very large degree, his emotional or feeling life. If he feels keenly, he will be likely to act aggressively and positively, and to win others to his side. If his emotions play only a minor role, he will act mechanically, without spirit, dash, or contagion, and we shall be repelled. True, his emotions may mislead him, and may perhaps victimize us and others; that is not, however, the fault of the emotions: it is only because they are misdirected or out of bounds. And in any case, whether his conduct be good or bad, it is in considerable part an expression of his characteristic emotional slant.

The emotions impel one person to be a reformer, a pioneer for the right, a campaigner for justice, fair dealing, and human welfare; they inflame another to crime, treachery, oppression, evil-doing. It is unthinkable that either saint or sinner could be devoid of strong feelings and powerful emotions.

POSITIVISM *VERSUS* NEGATIVISM IN CHARACTER

Some people never get enthusiastic! Deliver us from spineless, negative people who have no strong ambitions to work out, no enticing goals to pursue, no fascinating hobbies to ride, no keen interests and curiosities to satisfy! Unfortunately, we all know plenty of individuals who never get enthusiastic about anything, indeed whose characters are consistently negative and indifferent to their external surroundings, and almost to their internal drives, too. They move mechanically through the daily round, never eager, never hopeful, never on tiptoe to press further beyond the innumerable portals that open before us all. They take everything—home, country, personalities, experience, God—apathetically and unemotionally. They warm up to nothing and nobody. They pass their days "as a tale that is told."

Community deadwood. Saint John made a telling criticism of all such indifferent people when he exclaimed: "I would thou wert cold or hot." Lukewarm people are likely to be as insipid and unaggressive as the term "lukewarm" indicates. They are never heard from in the civic sense, any more than they are in the vocational or the social or the personal sense. They have no concern for the welfare and the progress and the strengthening of our moral attitudes, or our institutions, or our common way of life. They represent the deadwood in our lodges, our churches, our clubs and organizations. Never strongly "sold" on any institution, they sit comfortably and serenely back and withhold their support and their backing. All movements calculated to improve the community have to reckon without them. Although profiting continually from the existence and the program of this, that, or the other organization or institution with which they may or may not be identified, they contribute little or nothing of themselves to perpetuating it in the community.

About the best thing that can be said about the "luke-warms" is that they are no more aggressive in crime and anti-social movements than they are in beneficial, worthy enterprises. They are neither social liabilities nor social assets, although their very negativism tends to make them more properly classified under the former category than under the latter.

EVOLUTION OF THE HIGHEST FORM OF CONDUCT

Why children are likely to be unsocial. We are not surprised when the conduct of a baby is disagreeable and annoying. We take it for granted that the small child will be thoughtless, or selfish, or disobedient, or saucy, or cruel, or otherwise lacking in what we assume to be the fundamentals of good character as judged from an adult standpoint. The reason for the unsocial conduct of the child is an obvious one: he has not yet had sufficient experience to enable him to understand the full significance of his behavior and to choose the more desirable conduct.

Early childhood must be, perforce, a more or less servile condition in which the new individual is compelled by his parents to do as they believe best for him to do. Under such circumstances, he may be expected to throw off occasionally the restraining parental hands and precepts and demonstrate lustily his own personality and individuality. In a sense, all children are slaves to the conventions and the habits and the general behavior demanded of them by their elders. Conduct, at this childhood level, is necessarily therefore the expression of the thinking and the willing of the adults in the background of the scene, not of the child in the foreground.

From slave to free agent. But when the child becomes an adult, he puts away childish things! From the unstimulating role of being almost a slave to other people, he has gradually become a free-willed individual who must make his own choices and decisions. The parents are no longer at his elbow to counsel and caution and direct. The child of yesterday has become today's adult, for the most part subservient to no authority except himself.

This final emergence from parental restraint makes possible the highest form of human conduct—that dictated by free will. When one has arrived at the stage in his evolution where he has become his own authority, he may well glory in the fact that he is now personally accountable for his conduct and for his observance of the laws—written and unwritten. He has achieved the peak of human experience in the sense that he is now guide of his own life and behavior. For better or for worse, he has passed beyond the reach of the restraining hands of his elders and become almost entirely self-determining.

From passive to active morality. The standards which such an individual sets up for himself and the choices which he makes are to be henceforth his *own* standards and choices. In contrast to an earlier condition of passive morality, in which he did right—or at least refrained from doing the wrong—because others imposed good conduct upon him, he now makes his own decisions for the good life or the bad, for the high path or the low. Actively now, he must forge out his own character and by the same token be prepared to take the consequences in his own person. The motives that drive him become of first significance. In general, the high school years are the years in which the essential ideals of life are determined and in which, therefore, final character is shaped.

Think over the change that has taken place in your own character from an earlier condition of passive morality to the present one of active morality. List on this form some specimens of your behavior at both stages:

MY OWN PROGRESS FROM PASSIVE TO ACTIVE MORALITY

Early Stage (Passive Morality)	Later Stage (Active Morality)
1. I told the truth to avoid being punished for lying.	1. I tell the truth because I have a real sense of personal honor.
2.	2.
3.	3.
4.	4.
5. etc.	5. etc.

(Thus does one become a free moral agent, responsible for his own decisions and his own acts.)

SIX IDEALS OF CONDUCT AND THEIR PRACTICE

We may distinguish among the myriads of ideals that characterize the good life at least six that are basic for us all. Let us list and examine briefly these six fundamentals of character.

Honesty and reliability. We may say without reservation that the dishonest person is a potentially vicious individual for whom very few have any respect. If a person cannot consistently tell the truth, even when it may take courage; if he cannot be entrusted with another's money; if he cannot be relied upon to keep his word, to stick to the job, to do faithfully the things expected of him—then we are inclined to be somewhat skeptical regarding his total character—and we have a right to be. Honesty is so fundamental that, lacking it, a man forfeits his right to be respected and trusted by his fellows.

Different morals in different situations! Yet honesty has been found to be, unfortunately, a relative term. There is no *general,* all-inclusive factor of honesty in any individual, so far as studies have indicated. The degree of a person's honesty has been found to depend upon the particular situation with which he is confronted. The same individual will be honest with this person, or in this situation, but decidedly dishonest with that person or in that situation. It all depends upon what is at stake, or what personalities are involved.

It is a bit disconcerting to find, as certain investigators have demonstrated, that even though children have been brought up to be honest by their parents and have attended Sunday School regularly, they still have different codes for different situations. The same child who will be scrupulously honest in a classroom is not unlikely to cheat in an athletic contest; and the same child who would not think of stealing money may not hesitate to copy the answers to test questions from an answer sheet if he is sure he will not be detected. In other words, there seems to be a school code, a home code, a Sunday School code, and a club code, rather than a uniform code that covers all situations.

It is somewhat more difficult to investigate honesty and reliability among adults and near-adults. The probabilities are, however, that we, too, are extremely likely to follow different codes at different times and with different personalities. At least, we may do so until we learn from wide experience the importance of being upright and trustworthy all the time and under all circumstances. Those of us who fail to learn this great lesson will find it difficult to inspire much confidence in our friends and associates. We ought not to be surprised if they lose faith in us and look somewhat askance upon our general character.

Co-operation and loyalty. From the very first months of your school life you have been taught the necessity for co-operation and loyalty—co-operation with the school authorities, the club leaders, the civil authorities; loyalty to the home, to the school group, to the church, to the employer. No family, no community, no nation, no principle or ideal can ever succeed without the faithful support of earnest individuals.

In our homes, every member of the family must work with every other member if that harmony which makes a happy home is to exist. The disloyal member of a family group, who will not co-operate in the common tasks, makes any home uncomfortable and unhappy.

In our schools, similarly, teachers and pupils are engaged upon a common adventure into the wonderland of learning and experience, and unless everybody plays the game with everybody else, the goals cannot be achieved. School loyalty and co-operativeness imply a faithfulness and even an eagerness to carry the banners forward in every area of school life, whether it be the mastery of lessons, or the maintenance of the social atmosphere, or the support of the faculty, or getting behind the team and rooting for it on the athletic field. Let the group spirit in any school be poor, let there be uninterested or disloyal people within its walls, and the good repute of that school in the community is likely to be destroyed.

In the great world beyond the school, this same demand for loyalty and co-operativeness is everywhere insistent. The citizen who believes in and supports his community and his government; the worker who identifies himself unstintedly with his job and is loyal to it and to those who provide it; the

Photo by S. W. Patrick for F. P. G.

Fig. 63. Are you a rooter or a slacker? Is your school spirit as praise-worthy in the classroom as on the athletic field?

friend who is faithful to those who honor him with their friendliness—these are examples of persons who possess the essential traits of loyalty and co-operation.

On the other hand, those citizens who are only halfhearted in their commitment; those workers who plot and connive against their employers; those false friends who remain true only in fair weather—these are examples of people who make exceedingly poor members of the social group. In whatever walk of life one may be, and regardless of the personalities with whom one comes in contact, the character traits of loyalty and co-operativeness are of first importance.

Courage. Courage, as a trait of human character, means something far more than mere physical bravery. That form of courage which inspires a person to stand up for what is morally right as he sees it is of a sort quite as noble as that form which fortifies a soldier to face the enemy on the field of battle.

The present age seems to be one in which we all find it easy to follow the crowd, to "do as the Romans do," rather than as the Romans *ought* to do. If the crowd could be counted on to be always in the right, this tendency would not be so bad; but unfortunately the crowd is often in the wrong. To hold out against the conduct and ideals of the crowd and to follow our own code requires real courage, and courage of a high order. It is so easy to lower ourselves if our friends have lowered themselves; to cheat if our friends cheat; to turn our backs upon the higher virtues of life if our friends have forsaken them.

Holding to principle, when that principle is contrary to the example and conduct of others, is one of the most unmistakable earmarks of real character. Those who would follow the good life learn sooner or later the lesson that one cannot compromise with principle, with ethical and moral codes. These things stand eternally valid and are eternally a challenge to all of us.

Appreciations. Still another prominent earmark of character is the degree to which an individual feels gratitude for the good things of life that come his way—appreciation of the simple and obvious blessings he enjoys.

It is easy, in a complex age of material things, to wander far afield from the simpler and more substantial joys of life and to seek for the elaborate and the spectacular. When you have reached the point where you can be grateful for the sunlight and for the storm cloud; for the light and for the shadow; for health and vigor; for hunger and for food; for parents and home and love; for play time and for work time; for simple gifts that have love behind them; for homely services rendered and for the opportunity to repay them in kind; for protection offered by home and country; for the opportunities of school and church and club—then and only then may you properly feel that you are carving out for yourself a character that will endure as long as the sun.

If the unusual and the spectacular blessings come to you some day, well and good: you will be better able to enjoy even them if you have first learned to be grateful for the simple and ordinary.

Sense of justice. How fair-minded are you? How openminded? Do you like to see everybody have a "square deal"? Do you feel a degree of resentment when somebody has been wronged or when an injustice has been done? Do you feel ready and glad to lend the weight of your influence to the support of legitimate movements calculated to do good? Do you aim to be counted upon the side of law and order, of justice and equality, of the right because it is right? If you can answer all these queries in the affirmative, you may feel reasonably certain that, so far as character depends upon the possession of a strong sense of justice, you have a good character.

We must distinguish, of course, between those who possess a merely verbal or philosophical sense of justice and those who are actively desirous of helping the good and the right to come to pass in the world. The former assent readily enough to the theory of the "square deal," but their deeds are not directed consciously and earnestly toward the bringing about of their ideals; the latter represent the doers, the bringers-to-pass. We must distinguish, also, between the serious-minded, sane workers for righteousness, and the wordy, impassioned howlers for human rights who lend little save oratory toward the achievement of the social millennium. A proper sense of justice and fair-mindedness expresses itself in quiet, sincere, and consistent deeds, not in bellowing words and empty protestations.

Self-control and sportsmanship. Self-control, in one sense the very keystone of character, means far more than overcoming temptations, essential as that unquestionably is. In its broadest meaning, self-control involves keeping serene and in good humor when everything goes wrong; continuing to try when failure looms across our pathway; being a modest winner and a sportsmanlike loser; admitting it when we are wrong and graciously accepting the correction; being kind and thoughtful when others are saying or doing or implying the unkind thing; resisting distractions when other people are chasing hither and yon after every will-o'-the-wisp; sacrificing our own personal stake for the good of the team or the group.

Viewed from this angle, self-control and good sportsmanship are seen to be perhaps the most essential and fundamental of all the traits that go to make up our character.

Find in the daily papers and in your contacts with people around you several outstanding instances of each of the six ideals of conduct developed in this chapter. List them as indicated in the table on page 433.

HOW PSYCHOLOGISTS WORK

Psychologists have devised a great many different tests and scales for measuring or estimating a person's character. We may distinguish three types of such tests:

(1) *The rating scale.* Measures of this sort are pencil-and-paper measures. A typical rating scale comprises a considerable

PRACTICING THE SIX IDEALS OF CONDUCT

Honesty and Reliability	Co-operation and Loyalty	Courage	Apprecia-tions	Sense of Justice	Self-Control and Sports-manship
1. A man returned some money he found. 2. 3. 4. 5. etc.	Some employees gave a testimonial dinner for the president of their company.	A political candidate denounced graft in his city.	A grateful patient endowed a bed at the hospital.	A social worker championed the cause of the unemployed.	A driver kept calm after an automobile accident.

(These are good rules to live by!)

number of questions about the individual being rated, the rating being done by another person who presumably knows him well enough to judge his character traits. A series of questions like the following are presented:

> Is he prompt in keeping engagements?
> Does he know how to direct his own work?
> Does he have a sense of responsibility?
> Can he be trusted to do what is honest and fair?
> Is he courteous?

Instead of embodying a list of standard questions, a rating scale may be constructed as a horizontal line, with positions along it at which a given individual is to be placed with regard to the trait named. Here is an example of such a rating scale:

ROBERT ALLTON

Extremely Trustworthy	100% 75% 50% 25% 0%	Entirely Untrustworthy

Invariably Polite	100% 75% 50% 25% 0%	Invariably Impolite

Always Punctual	100% 75% 50% 25% 0%	Always Behind Time

(2) *The self-rating scale.* In this type of scale the person may be given a standard series of questions and asked to judge himself with reference to each trait touched upon by a given query. Note the following typical questions on a self-rating scale:

Do you believe lying is ever justified?	Yes	No
Do you lose your temper easily?	Yes	No
Do you enjoy having friends?	Yes	No
Do you like other people?	Yes	No
Are you frequently irritable?	Yes	No

A variation of this "yes-no" variety of self-rating scale is the "How I feel" form, intended to disguise the fact that a person is rating himself. A specimen situation in such a scale would be the following:

When Other Folks Praise Me

(a) How I feel:

dislike	rather not	don't care	like some	like a lot

(b) How most boys feel:

dislike	rather not	don't care	like some	like a lot

(c) How I think I ought to feel:

dislike	rather not	don't care	like some	like a lot

(3) *Objective tests of character.* Tests of the third variety actually sample the behavior of the tested individual in situations in which his actions are being observed without his suspecting it. There are many of these objective-type tests. In one of them, two different tests, known to be of equal difficulty,

are given to a class. The first is so proctored that there is no possibility of anybody's cheating; the second provides ample opportunity for cheating. Any considerable improvement in scores obtained in the second over the first is indicative of the probability that there has been cheating.

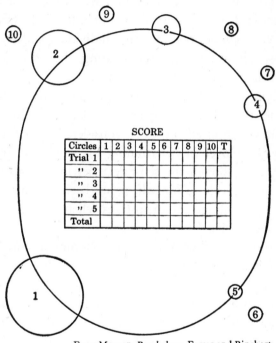

Circles	1	2	3	4	5	6	7	8	9	10	T
Trial 1											
" 2											
" 3											
" 4											
" 5											
Total											

SCORE

From Morgan, *Psychology,* Farrar and Rinehart

Fig. 64. Objective test of honesty.

Figure 64 illustrates another objective test of honesty. The testee is confronted with the task of inserting numbers, in order, in the circles indicated. He must keep his eyes closed while working. Five trials are allowed him. Since it is obviously impossible for anybody to enter numbers in such exact positions without vision, it follows that any person who is able to do so has peeked, and therefore is dishonest in the test.

Human character is such a complex thing and is so difficult to evaluate, that obviously tests such as those described above are not entirely adequate to diagnose it. In the use of the rating scale, the rater may easily overestimate or underestimate the amount of any given trait present in the ratee, either because he does not know him well enough or because he is prejudiced in his favor or against him. Only when several competent judges rate the same individual and pool their judgments can anything approximating the true character evaluation of the person be determined.

In applying a self-rating scale, a person tends to rank his traits higher than they actually are, especially if he knows that his estimates of himself are to be considered by a teacher or prospective employer in determining his worth or eligibility. Moreover, even though the self-rater tries to be conscientious in applying the scale to himself, it has been found that most people are poor judges of themselves when it comes to analyzing specific traits.

Most psychologists who are experimenting in the field of trait analysis and character rating incline to the opinion that a given test of honesty, for example, may measure well enough the person's honesty *in the situation tested* (as in taking an examination), but it affords no reliable basis for predicting how honest he will be in another specific situation (such as returning the correct change).

In other words, honesty, like all other character traits, is not a general term but rather a specific condition in situation X, situation Y, or situation Z. The same person may be 95% honest in X, 50% in Y, and 5% in Z! The needs, opportunities, and surroundings of the moment are more potent in shaping the moral reactions of a person than is any generalized, abstract "honesty" that might be presumed to preside over his conduct as a whole.

TO HELP YOU LEARN

SOME QUESTIONS TO ANSWER

1. What is your present definition of character? How has it been modified by your study of Chapter 16?

2. "If we all turned out to be the kind of people that our parents hoped we would become and tried to help us become, nearly all of us would have the finest of characters." What is your reaction to this statement in the light of parents and children as you know them?

3. Suppose that only the good existed in the world. What would be the effect upon character building? Which character should be the finer—the one that struggles against the bad and achieves the good, or the one that never comes in contact with the bad and hence always remains good?

4. Why is it that emotions are so important to character? How would you justify the statement that "it is unthinkable that either saint or sinner could be devoid of strong feelings and powerful emotions"?

5. Do you know any lukewarm people? How dominant a role do they play in the life that goes on about them?

WORKING WITH PSYCHOLOGY

1. The author clearly means by *courage* far more than mere physical bravery. Adhering to principle, holding out against the crowd, acting nobly, even self-sacrificingly—these are implicit in true courage. Search your memory for notable characters in literature who possessed courage of this grander type. Make a list of such characters, following a scheme similar to the one at the beginning of this chapter, entitled "Two Kinds of Character."

2. Let the class agree upon some contemporary figure prominent in world affairs—preferably a citizen of some country other than our own. Each member of the class, working independently, is to rate the individual on each of the traits indicated on the scale below. A score of 100 means that the person possesses the trait to an out-

standing degree; a score of 0 denotes that he is utterly devoid of the
trait (that is, has just the opposite trait).

THE INDIVIDUAL: M————————

Completely Fair- Minded	100%	75%	50%	25%	0%	Entirely Preju- diced
Enjoys Fullest Confidence of His Fellows	100%	75%	50%	25%	0%	People Have No Confidence in Him at All
Has Extraordi- nary Powers to Get His Ideas Accepted	100%	75%	50%	25%	0%	His Ideas Are Completely Re- jected by Others
Works Hard, Is Conscientious	100%	75%	50%	25%	0%	Is Extraordi- narily Lazy

Other traits may be added to the scale, at the discretion of the
class, after the individual to be rated has been decided upon.
Average all the ratings in each category; note the range of judgments and try to account for any striking differences you find.

3. Appoint one member of the class to write to the C. H. Stoelting
Company, Chicago, Illinois, for a list of the personality and adjustment scales which they publish. When the list comes, select one
of them (the Heidbreder Personality Traits Rating Scale or the
House Mental Hygiene Inventory would be excellent for the
purpose) and order a quantity sufficient to administer to everybody
in the class. Your teacher will send the order and find means of
paying the cost. Study the results of the test in your class and work
out a set of conclusions.

4. Make a catalogue of the principal agencies in your community
that are engaged, to some degree at least, in building or promoting
character. Some of the agencies, like the churches, may be engaged
primarily in this task; others, like the fraternal organizations, may
exert this influence only incidentally. If you approach this project
thoughtfully and discriminatingly, you will be able to identify a
surprising number of agencies—public, semipublic and private—
that further the good life.

What Others Say

1. In Biography:

Portrait of an American by Robert P. Tristram Coffin. An idealized biography of the poet's father as seen through the eyes of the son, who sees only the best qualities of his sire.

2. In Fiction:

Jane Eyre by Charlotte Brontë. A famous autobiographical novel of a girl of very strong character and original ideas who revolts against the social conventions and narrownesses of the day and strives for self-realization.

Eyeless in Gaza by Aldous L. Huxley. An absorbing story of the transformation of character in a man who passes from cynicism, disillusionment, and an utter sense of futility to personal idealism, inner peace, and compassion.

The Last Puritan by George Santayana. An analysis of the old New England character through its principal exponent, Oliver Alden, who is convinced that he ought to renounce Puritanism, yet who finds it impossible to do so. This is a brilliant and absorbing work.

3. In Drama:

Valley Forge by Maxwell Anderson. A play which throws a new and strong light on Washington, who, during the black days of 1778-9, showed the splendor of his spirit in his struggles against treachery and pettiness.

Craig's Wife by George Kelly. This Pulitzer prize play (1926) presents an admirable character study of a woman of tremendous power but complete selfishness, who drives out of her home her husband, her husband's friends, and her own relatives.

4. In Poetry:

General William Booth Enters into Heaven by Vachel Lindsay. Moving description of Booth's arrival in heaven, followed by the varied multitude of men and women redeemed through the Salvation Army.

Have You Learned to Live Harmoniously?

Alfred, King of England—Alfred the Great—did not shut himself up in his castle and live in royal solitude apart from his people. Rather, he lived very close to them.

He roughed it with his soldiers and slept with them on the ground. He ate at the table of many a swineherd and toiled in the field with the peasants. He had boundless faith in common humanity. He introduced trial by jury into England and laid the foundations of English common law, upon which our own system of law is so largely based. At the Ox Ford he organized a school where England's sons might receive learning—a school known throughout the world today as Oxford University. He taught and exemplified in his own life those virtues of loyalty and sympathy toward others that made him truly Alfred the *Great*.

He was more than a great king: he was a monarch who threw off his royal trappings in order the better to understand his people and lead them to a higher and nobler plane of existence.

Henry David Thoreau, one of America's greatest naturalists, was just twenty-eight years old when he built his famous hut near Walden Pond, at Concord, Massachusetts. Born in Boston and educated at Harvard, he taught school for five years, but abandoned teaching for a kind of life that would bring him into close contact with nature and with himself. Grudgingly working at surveying, carpentry, and simple handicrafts, sufficiently to provide food and clothing, he devoted the greater part of his days to the study and contemplation of nature.

For two years he lived the life of a hermit at Walden recording his experiences and his reflections in a book called *Walden, and Life in the Woods,* a volume that has been ever since then a classic source book for nature lovers. During the last fifteen years of his life (he died when he was forty-five), he continued his work as a naturalist, spending much of his time in the forests and fields of his native Massachusetts and of near-by Maine.

Thoreau liked people, but he dearly loved to be alone with the birds and the flowers of his beloved New England.

Ted Miller was decidedly "in bad" with Coach Maloney.

"What do you think football is, anyway, Ted," demanded the coach—"a sideshow in a circus, with you the principal exhibit?"

Ted's face was red, and he fumbled with his locker key.

"You're a good player, Ted," the coach went on unrelentingly, "but the trouble with you is, you've just got to make those crazy plays to the gallery that disgust everybody and lose us the game! Now, this afternoon we might have made that last touchdown just as well as not if you could have followed the signal and passed the pigskin to Joe! You ought to have seen that they had you blocked and you couldn't possibly break through! But, no! You just had to try to be a one-man squad and streak down the line for the touchdown *yourself!* A good football player—just like a player in any other team game—has to learn to take directions. You've never learned that little lesson, and it doesn't look as if you ever would! That's the third game this season you've lost for Jefferson High! It's about enough!"

Ted was too shamefaced even to look at Coach Maloney. "I—I'll—try—to do better!" he stammered. "I—I guess I understand."

Some Are Leaders, Some Followers

King Alfred was a great leader because he found pleasure in mingling with all kinds of people. Henry Thoreau found the solitude of woods and fields more satisfying than the company of his fellows. He was content to follow where nature led. Ted Miller found pleasure in being in the limelight, and in drawing people's attention to himself. He was unable to follow the leader and to be, on occasion at least, inconspicuous.

✔ ✔ ✔

In this chapter you will learn a good deal about leaders and followers, about taking directions from the man higher up, about adjusting harmoniously to others at work or at play around you. On the other hand, you will be helped to realize that, in a restless age like the present, one must also learn to find resources within himself which will enable him to escape once in a while from the "madding crowd" and to be contented just to be alone.

Fig. 65. Can you live with yourself happily and peacefully? Or are you at perpetual odds with yourself?

17. LIVING HARMONIOUSLY

Before you start your study of the chapter, take time to think out what it is in a person that makes him a social individual, interested in people and responsive to their influence and presence. Use this form for recording your ideas:

TRAITS THAT HELP IN GETTING ALONG WITH OTHERS

1. Possessing a genuine interest in others.
2.
3.
4.
5. etc.

It will help you in considering this matter if you will call to mind some of the people you know whom you regard as the best "mixers," the most gracious, the best liked, the most unselfish.

LIVING WITH OTHERS

Our changing world. This is a social world, not a solitary one. Every new machine invented, every advancement made by science, every achievement of the institutions that make up civilization, draws people nearer together, makes them more socially conscious, reduces the size of the world, and makes human beings closer neighbors. Unfortunate is the person who, in the midst of all this reduction of frontiers and this drawing together of peoples, must still hold himself apart as a solitary individualist.

The world was a somewhat different place in our grandfathers' time. Means of communication were few and slow;

transportation was difficult and often dangerous; machines were still simple; cities were smaller; people lived further apart, both geographically and socially.

In contrast with this world of yesterday—which has passed forever away—the present world is highly socialized and integrated. We can no longer get on in it as recluses and individualists. Happiness and good adjustment to it require that we shall know how to live with our business or vocational neighbors, with our social neighbors, with our political neighbors. The unsocial individual, living in a world that is geared to run smoothly only when the human beings comprising it can work harmoniously with one another, is by all means a misfit, and he must find it extremely difficult to achieve any reassuring satisfactions as he watches life go by him.

The importance of group living. Social-mindedness is indispensable to good adjustment. To live acceptably among other people is to win true happiness and contentment. The power and strength of the group cannot be underestimated. Life is a co-operative enterprise; when it is lived at its best it requires the full and unreserved participation of every individual. Only when one has learned to cast his lot hopefully with others, to adapt himself to the personalities that surround him, to enjoy the give and take of social intercourse in all the areas of his experience, can he be regarded as being well adjusted to his surroundings. The social isolationist, the wallflower, the hermit—these people are all maladjusted, and almost all of them, even though they may appear self-satisfied and self-sufficient, really tend to be miserable and cynical.

Agreeing—yet disagreeing. Social-mindedness and good adjustment to the group do not mean, of course, that the individual must be a slave to the group and must submerge his personality and his ego in the group personality and the group ego. Nothing could be farther from the fact. One can be group-conscious and group-minded, and at the same time be an individual personality. He can disagree with the group, criticize it, seek to reform it, and yet maintain his social adjustment.

Photo by J. C. Allen and Son

Fig. 66. Can you get along harmoniously with people entirely different from yourself? These young people know how to work together without getting on each other's nerves.

It is highly important for all of us to preserve our originality, to safeguard our sense of values, to uphold our ideas of right and wrong, even in the face of counter group influence and ideals. Our personal sense of the fitness of things may be decidedly at variance with that of the crowd, and yet we may continue to be social-minded. Our moral standards may depart radically from those of the other people making up the group, and yet we may continue to be group-conscious and group-minded.

Poor reformers. Very often the group morals may differ entirely from yours or mine; yet we cannot afford to antagonize the group by flaunting our attitudes, martyrlike, before it and withdrawing from its "contaminating" influence. If the standards of a group are ever to be raised to those of the best individuals comprising it, the transformation must come about through the friendly, consistent practicing of the higher patterns of conduct *within the social setting,* not outside of it. Haughty recluses and "holier-than-thou" people rarely make good reformers. Stay in the group! Maintain your ideals firmly but unobtrusively! By and by your quiet, constructive example and your wholesome influence will win supporters to your banner.

Prepare a list of those contemporary forces, movements, and scientific advances that are drawing the peoples of the world inevitably closer together. Use this form for recording your ideas:

THESE THINGS ARE MAKING OUR WORLD SMALLER

1. Clipper planes
2.
3.
4.
5. etc.

(What has happened to the circumference of the earth since Magellan, sailed laboriously around it in 1520?)

LEADERSHIP AND FOLLOWERSHIP

It takes all sorts to make a world. This would be a queer world if it was made up exclusively of leaders, and had nobody to be followers! It would be an equally strange place if it contained no leaders and everybody was a follower! Leaders must have followers; followers must have leaders. It takes both sorts --and all sorts of both--to make a world.

Followers are needed. Followers are extremely important people. Not all of us can be leaders in the business world, captains of industry, managers of campaigns, planners and executors of new enterprises and conservers and guardians of old, pioneers and pace-setters in literature, science, art, or politics. Progress is quite likely to be as dependent upon the more humble people as it is upon the more exalted. The business magnate may map out his production schedule or his sales program, but a long line of workers must create the goods, and transport them, and sell and deliver them. The military genius may plan the details of a campaign, but its success must depend upon the faithful obedience and support of perhaps tens of thousands of soldiers.

> Theirs not to make reply,
> Theirs not to reason why,
> Theirs but to do and die.

The naval commander may signal the fleet to attack, but the outcome of the encounter with the enemy will depend upon the courage and obedience of the humblest mechanics in the engine rooms; and, if victory results, the credit must be attributed to the faithfulness of the latter as well as to the genius of the former.

It is a great mistake for anybody to suppose that "hewers of wood and drawers of water" are of only minor importance. There is no reason why the toiler at his daily tasks, the plain man in overalls, the grimy and besooted worker returning homeward at the day's end with his dinner pail, the operator of a loom or a lathe or a band saw, should feel inferior. So long as the work one does is honest work, essential to somebody, it should be regarded as worthy, and those who perform it should feel themselves indispensable to society. The dignity of work, of whatever kind, is undeniable.

Leaders are also needed. Leaders are important people, too. Society must have those who are able to make its blue-prints and engineer its progress. If in the natural course of events it should devolve upon you to be one of that very important company of leaders who must think and plan for others, it is to be hoped that you will not only be properly equipped for such responsibilities as may come to you but will also be able to maintain a saving humility and sympathy, without which no one ever becomes a great leader.

Appreciation essential to leadership. Of those who control the comforts and even the lives and destinies of men, much is required in addition to mere proficiency and fitness for the task; a warm human concern, and an appreciation of the contributions to progress and happiness made by those who furnish the brawn and muscle, should rank as of first importance. One cannot be a good leader without being an understanding and appreciative director of men. If you desire the respect and loyalty of your underlings, you must see to it that you respect and are loyal to them. The attitude of giving one's best to his followers, not of requiring that they make all the sacrifice, is essential to effective leadership.

Capacity is essential, too. The fundamental requisite in the leader must always be, of course, ability. It is unfortunate when little men aspire to be big men, when those who lack the endowment or equipment for leadership succeed by fair means or foul in achieving places of responsibility among their fellows. Any enterprise suffers under such irresponsible and inadequate management. The social group, too, suffers when its leaders are found wanting. Unless you are sure you possess the fundamental *capacity* to assume control of men, or of enterprises, do not presume to do so. First, make sure you have the ability; second, strive to cultivate the human traits necessary to get on with those whom you are to lead; and third, forge ahead. There is no limit to the possibilities of achievement and of contributions to the race which leaders thus endowed and equipped may bring to pass.

ADJUSTMENT TO SUPERIORS AND CO-WORKERS

In a culture such as ours, in which people carry on their occupational tasks in working groups or shifts under the direction of overseers and supervisors, it is of great importance that everybody shall know how to get on harmoniously with everybody else in the firm or occupational setup. As workers, we are all called upon with varying degrees of frequency to take orders from somebody higher up. Unless the employee can accept this situation as a part of the ordinary routine, he is not going to be a very desirable member of the enterprise. It behooves everybody who aspires to be an acceptable, not to say a desirable, employee, to cultivate a cheerful willingness to accept the requirements of his superiors and to maintain the steady purpose of carrying them out to the letter.

Telltale faces. It behooves everyone, too, to learn how to be cheerful at his work, considerate of and friendly toward his co-workers, co-operative with the buying or trading public, and loyal to the organization of which he is a part.

If you will but note the uninspired motions, the lackadaisical manners, and the dissatisfied or annoyed facial expressions of numberless clerks, salesgirls, waitresses, waiters, office workers, and other employed people with whom you come into incidental contact now and again, you will be struck by the telltale language you can discern. Eloquent character sketches are written indelibly on their faces.

No wonder personnel managers and employers are always on the lookout for cheerful, pleasant faces at the application desk, and are glad to reward generously those of their employees who, under stress of the day's work, can maintain their good nature, their patience, and their loyalty to the organization.

Watch your attitude! A long face, a surly manner, a resentful bearing, a martyrlike resignation—these are fatal in the employee. The salesperson, for example, who slams about, who makes you feel that he or she is doing you an extraordinary favor by attending to your wants, who is critical and even jealous of other salespeople in the establishment, who takes directions from a superior with all but open hostility—such an employee is destined, at best, to remain behind a counter all his or her life, and, at worst, to be invited in the not-very-distant future to give way to some more co-operative and tractable individual who is waiting to step into the job. And justly so!

List, as suggested below, some of the common ways in which people who work for others indicate an obvious lack of co-operation with and loyalty toward their employers:

CHARACTERISTICS OF THE UN-CO-OPERATIVE EMPLOYEE

1. He resents any suggestions made by his employer for improving the quality of the work done.
2.
3.
4.
5. etc.

(Look around you in stores, shops, offices, and homes!)

Can you take direction? Living agreeably with others involves the willingness to accept a certain amount of direction from the "boss," of suggestion for improved performance or for increasing output. Certain opinionated "know-it-alls" find it irksome, if not quite impossible, to accept such surveillance. Supervision is reacted to as interference or meddling. It is sometimes ludicrous—or would be if it were not so tragic—to see the ill nature with which some people resent any suggestion or recommendation from their superiors. In a highly specialized and industrialized civilization such as ours, it is inevitable that there must be supervision at every level of vocational activity. Foremen, superintendents, overseers, department heads, production managers—all of these and many others in supervisory capacities are charged with getting the maximum of returns from all workers under their control. Suggestion, direction, and even dictation become matter-of-course in their plants.

For those who can co-operate and can profit from the supervisory oversight, promotion is always a possibility as openings become available. On the other hand, those who rebel at suggestions from their superiors are extremely likely to be overlooked when promotions are made from the ranks. Living harmoniously with others involves co-operation to the limit with everybody, and not least of all with the "boss."

BEING A GOOD LISTENER

A fine art, but a neglected one. Frequently throughout this book we have insisted that various human relationships bear all the earmarks of fine arts if they are properly carried on. Being a good listener belongs distinctly in the category of a fine art. We hear much about being a good conversationalist; in fact, we may read alluring advertisements in the popular magazines of "systems" or "courses" that will guarantee their patrons the ability to be easy and attractive conversationalists and so to experience the joy of being popular, sought after, the "life of the party." Advertised systems of instruction in the art of *listening,* however, are never encountered. Here is a real art that greatly needs to be cultivated.

Preoccupation kills good listening. Without for a moment discounting the importance of being an interesting and ready conversationalist, the writer would insist that to be an interested and ready listener is of equal importance. Why are not more people good listeners? What is going on in their minds while you are speaking to them?

The answer to these queries is not difficult to give. To be a good listener, a person must for the time being forget his own importance and grant the other fellow credit for having ideas worth attending to. Poor listeners are not able to do these things well. They may be overconscious of their own relative superiority; they may be preoccupied with their own thoughts, or achievements, or deeds, or plans; they may assign to the person with whom they are thrown for the moment a status of inferiority; they may be bored by his conceit or his stupidity; they may be just plain self-centered and uninterested in anything and anybody outside of themselves and their own personal affairs. These and other preoccupations fill the minds of poor listeners and make the task of conversing with them a most uncomfortable and annoying one.

Three rules worth noting. What, then, is one to do if he would cultivate the attitudes and traits of the good listener? First, let him look for something of interest in the other fellow. Everybody has *something* in his personality that is worth searching for.

In the second place, let him school himself to *listen*. This is not always easy; for some people it is downright impossible, or nearly so. It is, however, a habit that can be cultivated if a serious determination is present.

In the third place, let the good listener develop in himself a readiness in drawing out the other person and encouraging him, by simple, well-worded questions, to talk about himself and his hopes and ambitions. It is so absurdly easy for most of us to be impressed with our own personal interests and values that we find it hard to tap the mental resources of another person and to find pleasure in listening to *him* while *he* talks. An important attribute of the good listener is the ability to make this mental contact with the ideas of another individual.

BEING A FRIEND

Many essays and many books have been written on the subject of friendship. Mythology, history, and literature recount the tales of many classic and beautiful friendships, such as those of David and Jonathan, of Damon and Pythias.

What friendships mean to us. Everybody knows what friendship means, at least ideally. A friend is interested in what you are interested in; a friend takes pride in your achievements; a friend weeps with you when you weep and rejoices with you when you rejoice; a friend warms to your spiritual touch as a violin vibrates to the hand of the master; a friend can be relied upon, is the same yesterday and today and tomorrow, has faith in you, trusts and understands you. There is no fairer word in the language than *friend*. Friendships are of incalculable blessing to us all.

Why some people have no friends. But there are some individuals who have no friends, and who do not seem to feel a strong need for friends. They tend to be avoided, or at least they do not arouse warm sentiments in others. There is something in their personality that repels, something in their manner or bearing that warns people who would be friendly.

Basically, such people are too selfish and self-centered to win friends. They have an exaggerated sense of their own importance, or else they are absorbed in their own personal affairs, or perhaps they have lost all touch with the gentler human attributes, like sympathy, simplicity, and genuineness. Immersed in selfish or thoughtless ends, they may at first lack the time and subsequently the inclination to enjoy the pleasures of friendliness. There is many an Old Scrooge in the

world who, at least until a miracle or near-miracle happens, becomes increasingly self-centered and self-sufficient until at
length he is shunned, if not actually despised, by everybody
who knows him.

Some key questions. How about you? Can you forget
yourself sufficiently to let your friends shine out once in a
while? Can you experience joy when your friend is gay,
sympathy when he is sorrowing, pride when he is receiving
praise? Can you feel the thrill of companionship, the spon-
taneity of the understanding heart? If you answer these questions affirmatively, then you know what friendliness means. If
you are a stranger to these mental states, then be advised to
set about cultivating them with diligence.

Youth is the golden age for forming friendships that will
last through the years. Have a few intimate friends, but avoid
exclusiveness. Strive to be friendly with everybody in general,
and with a select few in particular. Avoid laying yourself open
to the criticism that you belong to an "inner circle" and are
not cordial to all.

LIVING WITH YOURSELF

A change of scene nobody can have! You are your most
constant companion! Have you ever stopped to think of it?
You must live with yourself twenty-four hours each day, seven
days each week. If you get tired of your own companionship,
there is no way by which you can "walk out" on yourself, or
go for a change of scene, or otherwise escape from your own
society. However much time you spend in the company of
other people, you cannot avoid spending a good deal of time
by yourself. And however enjoyable you may find the companionship of others, you ought to learn to be happy when
you are by yourself. If your friends bore you, or aggravate you,
you can go off and leave them; but no matter how harshly

you may grate on your own nerves, or how out of sorts you may get with yourself, there is no escape. Since this is the case, it would seem to be the part of wisdom for each of us to try hard to make himself into the sort of individual that he can live with comfortably and without friction.

A restless age. Unfortunately, we live at present in an age which is restless and topsy-turvy. Everything and everybody seems to be "on the go." Most of us are so caught up in this mad whirl of life that we are uncomfortable unless we are driving ahead at full speed. In our work, in our amusements, and in most of our social activities we are operating in high gear. The very rush and roar of existence deafens us to the quiet inner life that all of us ought to be cultivating along with the more strenuous outer one.

List on such a form as the one below some of the social influences and economic conditions about us that make the present age a restless, tumultuous one:

WHY PEOPLE ARE RESTLESS IN THE PRESENT AGE

1. It is an age of machines, and machines drive men fast.
2.
3.
4.
5. etc.

(It may help you to make a longer list if you will stop to analyze the differences between living today and living fifty years ago.)

"Live alone and like it" (sometimes)! Quiet places are coming to be few and far between. Quiet moments and hours have been reduced almost to the vanishing point in an age which barely takes time out for sleep. We are so strung up by modern intense living that we are in danger of forgetting how to let down and relax. We are finding it more and more difficult to withdraw ourselves from the crowd, the social group, the give-and-take of living with others, and to spend time by ourselves.

This slavery to the stimulating—and often overstimulating— presence of other people is highly dangerous. When a person becomes so dependent upon the artificial excitation provided by his companions that he is helpless and miserable when left five minutes in his own company, he is in serious danger of

Photo by Dick Hanley for F. P. G.

Fig. 67. An agreeable way to spend an afternoon alone.

losing his individuality and his sense of self-direction. This is a condition that all of us must fight strenuously to keep it from dominating us.

The world desperately needs a new birth of the ability in

mortals to shut out the call of the exciting and the glamorous and the intoxicating, and to attend to the inner affairs of the spirit. To be able, on occasion at least, to live alone and like it —or at least not be driven to desperation by it—is something toward which everybody ought to strive.

Can you settle down quietly and comfortably, when nobody else is with you, and think out some of your personal problems that need solution? Can you find pleasure and companionship with books? Can you gather your thoughts together and map out a course of action, or plan a line of attack? Can you shut out for the time being the insistent and often bewildering call of people, even of chums and intimate friends, and find your bearings and plot your course?

If you cannot do these things, it is unfortunate, and you ought to take vigorous steps to learn how to do them; if you already possess the ability, by all means hold fast to it and exercise it a little every day! The only way in which we can ever learn to live with ourselves is actually *to compel ourselves to live with ourselves;* that is the only possible way in which we shall ever find the motivation and the driving force to make ourselves into the sort of people we should like to associate with!

A UNIVERSAL GOAL

There is just one main goal that people strive after—consciously or unconsciously—in this world: the goal of *happiness*. Nobody wants to be miserable; everybody wants to be happy. Of course, what will make one person happy may make somebody else decidedly the opposite, but the fact remains that happiness, however individually achieved, is the common objective of us all. Many times it happens that what we thought was going to bring us satisfaction brings instead annoyance or misery. Still, the *objective* was happiness, not misery or grief.

No matter how young or how old we are, nor to what social group or station we may belong, nor what occupation we may follow, nor in what part of the world we live, the same thing is true: we covet happiness and shun unhappiness. We do our daily tasks, plan our lives, and order all our affairs in such ways as appear to us likely to yield the greatest present happiness as well as the greatest possible likelihood of future satisfaction.

It is easy for the happy person to live with himself; it is distressingly hard for the unhappy person to live with himself. The happy individual finds pleasure alike when he is associating intimately with others and when he is limited to his own company. The unhappy individual, on the other hand, is likely to flee continually from himself and his miseries and seek to stifle them by mingling with other people. The fine art of achieving happiness, of attaining a satisfactory adjustment to life, is a fine art indeed, and fortunate is he who understands it and is able to accomplish it.

Let us see what are some of the most likely sources of happiness and of skillful adjustment to life.

WAYS OF ACHIEVING HAPPINESS

Keeping faith in yourself.   If you lack faith in yourself, you can hardly hope that other people will put much confidence in you. We pass in this world for about what we are worth, and other people are apt to put nearly the same estimate upon us that we put upon ourselves. All of us need to have faith and confidence in ourselves, partly in order that we may have the courage to do the things we wish to do, partly in order that we may enjoy the respect and confidence of others about us.

Self-confidence and faith in ourselves fortify us to strive to reach our goals, and inspire us to do the right thing, the hard thing. These qualities seem to create courage and ambition and to supply us with the necessary energy and push to move forward along a projected pathway of achievement. Lacking them, we can hardly expect to get very far on the road to any objective.

> There is a tide in the affairs of men,
> Which, taken at the flood, leads on to fortune.

True enough, but the person who is lacking in self-confidence will certainly not have the boldness to launch himself on this flood tide of opportunity and hence cannot hope to be swept on its bosom to success. Self-distrustful and diffident people are rarely able to brace themselves for herculean efforts. The timid, the wavering, the weak-willed—these people languish under the banners of defeatism instead of advancing beneath the pennants of victory.

The rugged determination and heroism of the youth who bore "a banner with the strange device" meets no responsiveness in the souls of defeatists. Their slogan is not "Excelsior!" but rather "Ever say die!" Only those who have a reasonable self-confidence are truly serene and adequately adjusted.

Cultivating humility. We said above that faith in oneself is extremely important as an element of happiness and contentment. So, indeed, it is; but there is a vast difference between the sensibly self-confident person and the conceited, top-heavy individual. Often the latter is at heart quite lacking in self-confidence, and he trumps up a kind of arrogant self-sufficiency that belies his true nature. In any case, whatever the reason back of it, conceit is an unlovely trait in anybody. For the person who "can't be told anything," or who "knows it all," or who is vain and arrogant, few of us have much use.

No truly great personality is ever vain, or ever lays claim to being a superior individual. Always open to new viewpoints, always ready to learn from any and all who have worth-while ideas, always meek and humble in the face of the Great Mystery that holds the secrets of life and progress, these great souls would be the last people in the world to strut across the stage of human experience and vaunt their achievements or their genius before the eyes of their fellows.

Humility is a virtue well worth cultivating by us all. If we have gifts or abilities superior to those possessed by our fellows, it is unbecoming and discourteous to draw other people's attention to them; if we are inferior, or if our achievements are disappointing, it is dishonest and cowardly to attempt to dress ourselves up in misleading attire in the hope of "throwing dust in our neighbors' eyes." Besides, our true personalities cannot be long concealed from those who have any discernment. What we are speaks so loudly that nobody can hear what we vociferously lay claim to being.

Genuineness of character and humility of spirit are to be regarded as pearls of great price whose possession makes a person really noble. Be open-minded and teachable! Do not pose as all-wise and all-knowing! Keep a genuine feeling of humility! The happy person is the humble one, rarely the arrogant one.

Developing imagination. This is, after all, a prosaic world, with its humdrum, day-by-day working and eating and sleeping. Even much of our so-called entertainment is mechanical and commonplace. We move about in conventionalized grooves; we fall into unescapable ruts in the sameness of our experience; we are in danger of becoming automatons, robots, cogs in the wheels of a machine civilization. Under such circumstances, the importance of a temporary escape from the world of mechanical things, of confining walls, of monotonous routine, cannot be overestimated, nor can its joy be discounted.

We are creatures not merely of muscle and bone and sinew; we are creatures also of spirit, of mind, of fancy and imagination. "The life is more than meat, and the body is more than raiment." Life at its fullest embraces mental and spiritual adventuring, imagining, creating. To be well adjusted to life, we need on occasion to be able to soar above its monotony and to enjoy the upper air of poetry, of music, of art, of literature, of drama.

No life can be quite satisfying unless the individual can find time to develop an interest in the things of the imagination. If you can tuck your foot into Cinderella's slipper or step through Alice's looking glass; if you can go in fancy to Lilliput and to Brobdingnag; if you can adventure with the magic carpet and Aladdin's lamp; if you can live again in King Arthur's England or in William Tell's Switzerland or in Cooper's America; if you can stand with Columbus on the bridge of the *Niña;* if you can journey with Ponce de León to Bimini in search of the magic Fountain of Youth; if you can go in a covered wagon across the prairies to a great new land; if you can throw off the restraining bounds of the here and now and fare forth for an hour now and again into the glorious yesterday, or into the beckoning mystery of tomorrow —then you may well understand what it means to develop fancy and to find joy in the land of the imagination. Thus you can live with yourself most agreeably and be surprisingly happy.

List on a form like that on page 463 some of the most stirringly imaginative books or tales you have ever read.

HOW PSYCHOLOGISTS WORK

Psychologists have found it interesting and illuminating to inquire into the factors that make for leadership among children and adolescents. It must be apparent to the most casual of observers that some boys and girls appear to be born leaders, while others never aspire to such a status in their groups.

HIGHLY IMAGINATIVE STORIES I HAVE READ

Author	Title
1. Edgar Allan Poe	"The Pit and the Pendulum"
2.	
3.	
4.	
5. etc.	

(Stories like these equip us with seven-league boots with which we may in fancy travel fast and far!)

Observers of the social play of very young children have found that even at the pre-kindergarten level unmistakable signs of future leadership are in evidence among the members of the group. Some three-year-olds and four-year-olds already dominate the play scene, making decisions for the rest and assigning roles to them; others either stand aloof or else follow willingly the example and the directions of the leaders.

Working from this observed contrast between very young children, psychologists have concluded that there are two fundamental patterns of social behavior: the *ascendance pattern* and the *submission pattern*. People who fit into the first of these categories—the ascendant individuals—are those who have tended from very earliest childhood to dominate their fellows, to outsmart them, to control them, even to coerce them into conformity with their will. The opposite sort of people—the submissive individuals—tend to submerge their own personalities, to permit their wishes to be overridden, to let somebody else take the initiative and determine what is to be done.

In the pre-kindergarten group these two fundamental personality patterns are clearly distinguishable. There are those children who make most of the noise, who ride roughshod over the rest, who are most talkative, who do most of the initiating and planning, who are the most apt to be surrounded by the others. On the other hand, there are the children who are shy and reserved, who are rarely if ever stimulated into even a momentary role of leadership, who copy slavishly the activities begun by the ascendants, who are always assigned, placed, labeled, bandied about by their more dominating fellows, who shrink from the limelight and sit on the side lines of action.

It has been observed by child psychologists working in this field of dominance-submission that future strong and commanding adult personalities can be discerned in the dominant behavior of two-year-old children, and that the reserved, apologetic, hesitant men and women of tomorrow can be foreseen in the submissive, reticent children in any nursery school. Coming personalities, it appears, like coming events, "cast their shadows before"!

An interesting question arises out of these observations of the child psychologists: How does a child start out in the first place to show dominance or submissiveness? From what essentially different backgrounds do the very young children that attend any nursery school come, which might be presumed to account for their contrasting ascendant-submissive behavior?

While it is unquestionably true that hereditary structures and predispositions play a part in determining the nature of the behavior pattern in a given child, it is also true that home and family training and experience contribute largely to it. Students of childhood are agreed that whatever in a child's early training endangers or destroys his self-confidence becomes a powerful factor in making him a submissive creature; and conversely, that whatever in the experiences of a child's earliest years contributes to his sense of adequacy and his faith in himself is an equally powerful factor in making him a dominant individual.

By the time he reaches the nursery school age, a child has had enough home training for his general pattern of behavior to have been cast in a definite mold. Thus, observers find that the submissive type of child shows fear of incurring the displeasure of the ascendant children; that he relies far more than the latter upon the help and favor of adults, often clinging to them or ambushing himself behind them for protection; that he is hesitant about initiating and continuing any activity of his own choosing; that he laughs excessively or shows defensive overenthusiasm; that he blushes, wilts at the first signs of criticism, and tends to retreat within himself.

Looking back of these evidences of timidity and self-distrust, psychologists find much in the early home training and environment of the retiring child to account for his submissiveness when he gets to nursery school and kindergarten. Spoiled or babied by his family, never taught or required to stand upon his own feet, excused for his mistakes and his failures, petted and fondled, shielded from the give-and-take experiences of normal association with other children, championed and overpraised by all—such a child learns in his own home during his earliest years to be submissive by failing to develop a normal degree of self-confidence and assurance.

No wonder that by the time he reaches nursery school or kindergarten, he is already cast in the fixed mold of submissiveness and insecurity. Such a child, torn from the shelter of an oversolicitous home, is ill prepared to assume any role of leadership or dominance, either in school or, in all probability, in the life beyond the school.

TO HELP YOU LEARN

Some Questions to Answer

1. Do you believe it is really possible for anybody in the occupational world to so submerge himself as to be content to remain a follower all his life? In other words, doesn't everybody—even the most lowly worker—aspire to some sort of leadership?

2. Why should the present be any more restless an age than any that has preceded it?

3. Do you think you personally are ever so strongly influenced by the excitement and rush of modern life that you find it hard to let down and relax? Explain.

4. Isn't happiness a rather unworthy, selfish goal for us to strive after? Can you accept it as a worthy goal, and at the same time reconcile it with such goals as duty, service, and the like?

5. Do you suppose an arrogant person might be just as happy as a humble one? Explain your reasoning.

Working with Psychology

1. Make the following series of observations. Spend half an hour or so in some local department store and inoffensively study the faces of several of the clerks. Select particularly those who are waiting on customers at the moment when you observe them. Adopt the viewpoint of an official of the company who is taking this opportunity to familiarize himself with some of the more obvious traits of the employees as indicated in their facial expressions and general attitudes. Make some sort of record of your findings, such as the number whom you find satisfactory in their demeanor and the number who show irritation or boredom.

2. Appoint some member of your class to talk with the superintendent or some other official of a large store or office in order to find out what characteristics and traits his company looks particularly for in its employees. Prepare in advance two or three leading questions to ask, like the following:

What do you consider the best single characteristic of an employee in your organization?

What have been the principal causes that have led you to dismiss any employee or employees?

Other students may be appointed to visit other establishments, and notes may be compared later in class.

3. Try this experiment soon in some friendly social group in which you spend an hour or two. Refrain from the customary give-and-take of conversation in order to test out your own capacity for listening. Instead of initiating topics for discussion, and instead of contributing personally to them as they come along, without, of course, being absolutely silent, do your best to be stimulating to the other conversationalists in your immediate group by the maintenance of an air of deep interest in what is being said, by adopting the attitude of keen attention, by smiling engagingly and appreciatively, and by encouraging others to participate actively. Ask leading questions to keep the conversation from sagging. Try not to be artificial in your attempt to get into the spirit of this experiment, but try your hardest to *feel* interested in what is said.

4. Self-confidence, as has been pointed out in this chapter, is quite different from conceit and vanity, principally because the self-confident person possesses a fund of inner strength and control that sustains him in his work and in any crises that may present themselves before him. The vain person, on the other hand, is extremely likely to be unresourceful, using his assumed superiority to conceal his real incompetence. Bearing these facts in mind, make a mental survey of some of the notable (or notorious) characters in history and literature and classify them as follows:

SELF-CONFIDENCE *VERSUS* CONCEIT

These Were Calmly Self-Confident	These Were Colossally Conceited
1.	1.
2.	2.
3.	3.
4.	4.
5. etc.	5. etc.

What Others Say

1. In Popular Psychology:

How to Win Friends and Influence People by Dale Carnegie. An interesting, easily read book which has as its main theme the contention that by convincing people of their own importance one is readily accepted by them as a desirable person to have about.

Man, the Unknown by Alexis Carrel. This "profoundest, wisest, and most valuable book in the American literature of our century" (Will Durant) explores the vastness of the individual's inner life and personality. An unsurpassed guide book for those who would understand themselves better.

2. In Biography:

The Life and Letters of Emily Dickinson by Martha D. Bianchi. A fascinating story of one of our great poets who lived a life of solitude and reflection, yet who was at the same time a beautiful character who never thought of herself.

Alone by Richard E. Byrd. One of the most intensely moving stories of heroism and courage. Only one who could live harmoniously with himself could undergo the trials of this undaunted Antarctic explorer.

3. In Fiction:

The Good Companions by J. B. Priestley. An amusing story indicating how a number of individuals—complete strangers at the outset—can be thrown together by chance and can get on famously with one another.

4. In Drama:

R. U. R. by Karel Capek. A fantastic melodrama showing what an impossible world this would be to live in if all the people in it were robots that knew how to work but were totally lacking in all the social attributes.

5. In Poetry:

Alastor; or the Spirit of Solitude by Percy Bysshe Shelley. An allegorical poem in which self-centered seclusion is avenged by the ultimate and speedy ruin of the character portrayed. The poem represents the outpouring of Shelley's own emotions.

WHAT'S AHEAD IN CHAPTER 18

Are You Self-Centered or Social-Minded?

Oscar Wilde, the well-known English author (1856-1900), was undoubtedly one of the outstanding egoists of his day. He adopted an effeminate pose and a lackadaisical manner, scorning sports and the athletic life for flowing hair, extremely affected dress, and a sunflower in his buttonhole! In college, he decorated his room with brilliant flowers, blue china, and peacock feathers, and languidly followed the life of an aesthete.

So unpopular did he make himself among his fellow students that he suffered many an indignity from them. On one occasion they stormed into his room and all but wrecked its contents. On another occasion they seized young Wilde and gave him a thorough ducking in a pond. They could neither understand nor accept a youth so obviously egotistical and artificial.

Later on, adopting as his slogan the popular "Art for art's sake!" he became the leader of a new movement in London, called the Aesthetic Movement. Throughout his brilliant but rather short life, he continued to display a self-centered and affected personality.

Another Englishman—Sir Wilfred Grenfell—was a personality of quite a different sort. Feeling a strong attraction toward people and a keen desire to be of service to them, he fitted out his first hospital ship immediately after finishing his medical course, and began a career of service to humanity that lasted throughout his long life. (See the frontispiece.)

Cruising for three years in the North Sea, he devoted himself as a medical missionary to the North Sea fishermen. Subsequently he went to Labrador, where there was not a single physician within six hundred miles, and there for nearly fifty years he ministered to the needs of the poor people in the subarctic. Many a perilous voyage he made, often in unseaworthy ships, often by dog and sledge, to visit his patients on the rim of the sea. Even after his enterprise had grown so much that he had at his disposal well-equipped hospital ships, and dispensaries and hospitals on shore, he continued to make thrillingly unselfish trips through storms and blizzards and over hazardous ice fields to reach those in need.

Not only did he serve the people of Labrador as a physician, but he organized schools for their children, medical centers and dispensaries for those requiring hospitalization, and new industries to afford employment for the poor natives living so desperately near to the bare subsistence level.

Grenfell was a man who found his happiness in helping others. His memory is revered today throughout the world, and he is regarded as one of the great servants of mankind.

Ted Bassett had just been voted by his classmates the most popular member of the senior class.

"That's one vote that was a hundred per cent!" exclaimed Joe Staples, approvingly, as he and "Tubby" Coleman were walking home together after school. "Ted's the finest fellow in Cooper High!"

"Right-o!" agreed Tubby. "Ted's one grand fellow! Just think of Ted Bassett and then think of that little stronghold of conceit—Philip Appleby!"

"Philip Appleby!" snorted Joe. "Why bring *him* up?"

"Oh, just in contrast to Ted!" persisted Tubby. "It's hard to see how two fellows *could* be so opposite!"

"*I'll* tell you how they could!" exclaimed Joe. "Ted Bassett is always joining in in whatever we do; Appleby—never! Ted's a good mixer; Appleby's sufficient unto himself! Ted's always in good humor and everybody likes to have him around; old sour Apple-by never cracks a smile and never fits in with the crowd. Ted's always thinking about the other fellow and doing something helpful for him; Sour-Face never thinks of anybody but Appleby!"

"I guess you're right," Tubby said. "I hadn't ever tried to think it out before and put it in words."

Attractive Personalities Are Unselfish

Here are specimens of two very different kinds of personalities. Grenfell's is the outflowing sort that wins and serves other people; so, obviously, is Ted Bassett's. Wilde's, on the other hand, is the inflowing sort that focuses attention and concern upon itself; so, too, is Philip Appleby's. Wilde-Appleby personalities are self-centered, vain, egotistical; Grenfell-Bassett personalities are altruistic, unselfish, genuine, and hence winsome and attractive to others. Which kind do you think you have?

✓ ✓ ✓

In this chapter you will learn something about personality and what makes it interesting and attractive—or the reverse. You will find out that almost everybody possesses a dominant pattern or style, tending toward either egoism or altruism. You will meet two new terms, *introversion* and *extroversion,* and will learn what they mean in terms of personality. You will also find some suggestions for developing your own personality along desirable patterns.

Photos by A. Armstrong Roberts and Keystone View Company

Fig. 68. Which of these seniors would you pick for the most happy-go-lucky, the most studious, the prettiest, the most humorous, the most popular, the most likely to succeed? Do you think you might change your judgment if you knew the people?

18. PERSONALITY

Before beginning work on the chapter, take a few minutes to enumerate all the things you can think of that characterize individuals with pleasing personalities. Use the form below for recording your ideas:

THE PEOPLE I KNOW WHO HAVE THE BEST PERSONALITIES

1. Have open, frank faces, alight with animation.
2.
3.
4.
5. etc.

Think about the most engaging persons you know and try to determine what it is about them that makes their personalities striking.

PERSONALITY—A MAGIC WORD

Loose meanings. The English language has many words that people use loosely to convey various meanings. Among such words, *personality* is conspicuous for its indefiniteness and elusiveness. We hear it said, for example, that Brown has "a wonderful personality," that Black has "a forbidding personality," that White "just has no personality at all!" Advertisers who promote "systems" of "personality culture" profess to be able to make "weak personalities" over into "strong" ones; to aid their clients to develop "dominant, aggressive personalities"; to impart to them the secrets of "winsomeness," of "popularity," of "making friends and influencing people."

Popular writers and lecturers refer to personality as though it were some tangible, material thing, as objective as one's face or hand or foot.

Personality for sale! Advertisers of patent "remedies" and "beautifiers" guarantee "pep" variously by the use of laxatives, vitamins, or breakfast foods (take your choice!); they assure "date-appeal to debs" and to their escorts by the use of the right hair oil; they prescribe for "smartness" the use of their special deodorants; they would fill their customers with energy and make them "go-getters" by feeding them pills to "wake up their liver bile."

And so it goes! Everybody wants "personality," in the form of "pep," "date-appeal," and "smartness." Examination of the advertising pages of most of the poorer magazines will convince almost anybody in short order that these qualities may be purchased like so much sugar, or flour, or lard. The recipes for providing us with "personality" are innumerable! "Success" books are found on every counter.

WHAT PERSONALITY REALLY IS

How ridiculous! All of these things may perhaps be included within the meaning of personality. To suppose, however, that personality is comprised *merely* of "pep" and appeal and energy is greatly to oversimplify a very complex matter.

Far from being limited to such glaring traits as we have just mentioned, *personality* must be defined as the sum total of all an individual's characteristics and traits woven into a pattern that gives him a particular *style* (characteristic manner or distinctiveness) as an individual. This style affects both himself and everybody who is thrown into contact with him.

Personal factors. From the standpoint of his own *ego,* or self, one's personality is manifest in the degree of his success in satisfying the fundamental motives of life; of his capacity for adjustment to the situations of life without undue friction; of his skill in achieving personal recognition and success; of his ability to perceive right and wrong; of his power to conquer inferiorities, conflicts, and negative emotions; and of his capacity so to order his life that he may know happiness and be acquainted with serenity.

Social factors. From the standpoint of the social group which judges and evaluates him, one's personality is shown in the degree of his sympathy with others and of his effort to aid them in satisfying the fundamental motives of life; of his willingness to expend a part of his energy in advancing the social welfare; of his active desire to make his ideals of right and wrong something more than a mere armchair philosophy; and of his capacity to make others feel serenity, courage, and faith by reason of their contact with him.

These two factors not irreconcilable. It might appear on first thought that these two components of personality—the personalized and the socialized—are irreconcilable, that it is impossible for the individual to satisfy his own personal drives for success and happiness and at the same time be zealous to help his family, his friends, his associates, and beyond them, the whole of society, so far as he influences it, to achieve similar satisfactions.

Herein, however, lies the acid test of character. If the individual is completely self-centered and possesses no wish to influence others favorably, his whole personality is badly out of focus. From such self-centeredness spring all kinds of negative emotions, including jealousy, fear, and anger; from it issue unscrupulousness, conceit, indifference, cruelty; from it also arise conflict and neurosis. Unquestionably much of the bitterness and strife and mental breakdown in the world have their origins in the selfishness and unsocialized motives of men who sell out everything to the advancement of their own personal ends. Such monstrous ideals as these reflect themselves in monstrously one-sided personalities. The world suffers perennially from the chaos wrought in society by individuals of this order.

Maintaining a sensible balance. On the other hand, the *good* personality reflects a concern for social ideals and purposes, along with the will to achieve personal satisfaction and happiness. Indeed, the latter is in part at least an outcome of the former. The thing that will best determine whether you or I have a good personality is the balance which we have been able to achieve and to maintain between the personal and the social motives.

If a man can gain happiness for himself and be at the same time possessed of a vigorous will to increase the happiness of others; if he can feel the thrill of personal success and yet is able both to enjoy and to increase the success of others; if he can divide his values between his own welfare and the improvement of his fellow men; if he can maintain his own freedom of spirit, of effort, of thinking, and at the same time cultivate and defend the same freedom in those around him— then his personality tends to be a good one.

Seen in relief against the puny, limited concept of personality proclaimed by the "success books," by the "personality culture systems," and by the popular advertisers in their myriad recipes for "smartness," "date-appeal," and "pep," this real concept of personality as we have just described it is infinitely more complex and significant for us all.

JUDGING PERSONALITY

How we "size up" people. Each of us is called upon frequently to "size up" the personality of somebody with whom we are thrown into contact. In this naïve evaluation of the other fellow we do not, at least until we have come to know him very thoroughly, discern necessarily the complete, long-time style or pattern of his personality.

We are influenced in our casual judgment of him by many of the superficial, easily detected traits that are most apparent; for instance, we take note of his physical stature, his personal appearance, his facial expression, his gait, his conversation, and his general bearing. We look for the light in his eye, the ring in his voice, the confidence in his face—or the opposites or partials of these. We notice his poise, his posture, the "cut of his jib," his features, the condition of his health, his complexion, and his motor control, and from our observation of these and other external traits we arrive at some sort of working idea of his total personality.

First impressions are often wrong. Casual observation of this sort does not, of course, penetrate far into the real personality of the individual being appraised. First impressions may be lasting, but they are frequently misleading or actually wrong. All of us will do well to postpone forming judgments about those with whom we rub elbows until we have been associated with them long enough to learn the fundamental drives and purposes that characterize them.

The dominant pattern in personality. The particular style of an individual is, in other words, determined only in part by these observable externals. The central fact about personality is that it is organized or built around one or more central motives which give it its peculiar style. To the creation of this style the physical traits contribute somewhat, as, for example, height to impressiveness, shortness to unimpressiveness, beauty to conceit, plainness to inferiority, deformity to seclusiveness. Over and above the contribution of these and other physical traits to the pattern of one's personality, however, are the motives and purposes which dominate an individual's attitudes and reactions.

Generosity or self-interest. However we may subdivide these dominating motives, there are but two in the last analysis, and they are all-inclusive: the first is the pattern of generosity and interest in other people; the second is the pattern of egoism and self-interest. Everybody in the world presents in his personality either one or the other of these two dominant pat-

Photo by Brown Brothers

Fig. 69. Which was the dominating pattern of Napoleon Bonaparte's personality—generosity or self-interest?

terns, or some combination of them. To the continuance of this pattern consistently in a given individual, all his physical traits either contribute naturally or must be compelled to contribute by discipline or neglect.

It is unquestionably true also that a person's internal physiological make-up and organization have a part in the original formation and in the consistent furthering of the pattern or style. About these latter, however, we have little dependable information.

A complex matter. Before we can intelligently evaluate the personality of an individual, in other words, we shall need to take into account his external physical features and appearance, his internal physiological and hereditary organization, and his acquired or accumulating life purposes, goals, and values. The sum total of all these material and immaterial forces makes up the personality of an individual. And even then, after we have arrived at some adequate analysis of these factors, we can judge the adequacy of his personality only as we find it affecting and influencing other personalities.

Make a list of the twenty-five strongest personalities you can think of in world history, and indicate what was the dominant pattern in the life and work of each individual you list:

MY TWENTY-FIVE STRONGEST PERSONALITIES

Individuals	Dominant Life Patterns
1. Napoleon Bonaparte	To advance himself and his own interests
2.	
3.	
4.	
5. etc.	

(If you find it difficult to identify as many as twenty-five powerful personalities, set your own number. Do not "pad" your list: make each entry an intelligent one that you can easily defend.)

PERSONALITY TYPES—PRO AND CON

Attempts to classify men. There are two kinds of people in the world, someone has satirically remarked: those who divide people into types and those who do not! For thousands of years there have been all kinds of attempts to catalogue people into types or groups, such as, the sane and the insane, the good and the bad, the bright and the dull, the ambitious and the lazy.

The ancient astrologers (and certain modern ones) found in the stars the index to human character and proceeded to classify everybody into astrological pigeonholes. Hippocrates typed men on the basis of body fluids. Phrenologists of later days discovered in the peculiar formation of an individual's skull the key to his character and aptitudes and were allegedly able to type men on the basis of cranial "bumps." Palmists have been able to "read" in the wrinkles and shape of the hands the characters and drives of those who have sought their counsel, and they have typed their clients on this basis.

Small basis for classification. Modern scientific research is inclined to look decidedly askance upon all efforts of this sort. There seems to be little reliable evidence, in the first place, that types exist, and still less evidence that if they did exist they could be distinguished by divination or soothsaying or phrenology or by any other of the devices commonly employed by quacks to enrich themselves at the expense of the credulity of their victims.

No two people are alike. It is idle to suppose that people can be classified into two opposite personality types, any more than that they can be divided into two intellectual types, or two moral types. The probabilities are that no two people in the world are completely alike. Instead of supposing that they all fall into two hard and fast categories, it is more reasonable

—and certainly more scientific—to suppose that there are all degrees of capacities and traits, and that one degree merges almost indistinguishably into the next. Thus, on a horizontal line which might represent intelligence, we shall find at one end of the line the genius, at the other end the idiot, and all other degrees of intelligence spaced between these two extremes.

So with personality. There are not the pessimists and the optimists, but all degrees of pessimism and optimism among people; there are not the ambitious and the lazy, the selfish and the altruistic, the irascible and the even-tempered, the nervous and the calm, but all stages and degrees between. Moreover, in the same individual there are varying degrees of most traits under different conditions and at different stages of development.

The extrovert and the introvert. A noted Swiss thinker—Jung (pronounced yŏong)—has proposed a very interesting classification of people into types called *extroverts* and *introverts*. This classification is widely known and popularly recognized as having some obvious basis in fact.

People who look outward. Extroverts, according to Jung, look outward rather than inward; they are interested in things, events, people, activities. The extroverted individual enjoys being with people, makes a good mixer, is a good leader, inspires confidence, is a realist, an affable individual, a hail-fellow-well-met type. He makes a good salesman, politician, foreman, leader of men. All of us know plenty of people who fall within this general pattern.

People who look inward. Introverts, on the other hand, tend to look inward rather than outward. They turn their attention and their interests chiefly upon themselves and are less concerned with things, events, people, activities. The introverted individual lives in an inner world of ideas, feelings, values; he shuns social experience; he prefers to read, to deal with ideas, to introspect. He tends to be idealistic rather than realistic; he speculates much, is uneasy with people and inclined to be critical of them. He succeeds best in an occupation like bookkeeping, drafting, writing, or in other fields in which he can spend much of his working time with himself and his own ideas. All of us know many introverts, or at least people who tend toward introversion.

All degrees of extroverts and introverts. We should be careful, however, to avoid the conclusion that there are only these two extreme patterns of extroversion-introversion. Not only are there extroverts: there are all degrees and types of extroverts, from the completely extroverted person to the near-introvert. By the same taken, not only are there introverts: there are all degrees and types of introverts, from the completely introverted person to the near-extrovert. As a matter of fact, Jung himself distinguished no fewer than eight different degrees or types of introversion-extroversion. There are undoubtedly many more than these.

To avoid the appearance of seeming to classify people into the two groups of extroverts and introverts, we shall be wise if we speak of them and think of them as possessing *some* of the traits of the introvert or of the extrovert. Those well-adjusted people who fall somewhere between the two extremes are sometimes called *ambiverts*. A happy blend of introversion and extroversion is always to be preferred. Neither the extreme introvert nor the extreme extrovert is well adjusted to his environment.

Select two persons whom you know well, one of them possessing traits strongly suggestive of introversion, the other possessing those suggestive of extroversion. On the form below note down the prominent characteristics of each individual, concealing, of course, the identity of both:

TRAITS OF AN INTROVERT AND OF AN EXTROVERT I KNOW

The Introvert—	The Extrovert—
1. Is characteristically uneasy in the presence of others.	1. Is always the "life of the party."
2.	2.
3.	3.
4.	4.
5. etc.	5. etc.

(We rub elbows every day with these contrasting types of personality. It is fascinating to study the behavior and interests of both.)

INFLUENCE OF HEREDITY AND ENVIRONMENT

Glands and genes influence personality. While types as such do not exist, we should not suppose that one's inheritance has nothing to do with his personality. Whether because of the subtle influence of the inherited glandular system, or because of other little-known and little-understood vehicles of heredity, the fact remains that temperaments differ. This fact can be observed even in earliest infancy, before the effects of training and environment have been exerted. Several experiments carried on with children under one or two years of age have shown conclusively that some of them are characteristically jolly and gay, while others of identical environment are somber and fretful.

Consistency of the hereditary pattern. Moreover, it develops that the original pattern remains consistent throughout the early years: the happy, smiling baby continues true to form in subsequent months and years, as does also the serious and fretful individual. If you and I are today characteristically jovial and optimistic, we must thank in part our inherited organization; if we are the reverse, the blame must lie equally in part at the door of heredity.

The environmental pattern within a race. When we come to *racial* differences, it is more difficult to establish definite traits that can be attributed to racial heredity. The probabilities are that the cultural, geographic, and climatic factors exert great influence over peoples, and that Scandinavians and Mediterraneans, Eskimos and Malaysians, Americans and Chinamen are in considerable measure products of their respective cultures quite as much as they are of their respective ancestries.

The cultural pattern and the individual. Social factors within the same race and the same local culture and family affect personality strikingly. The influence of parental attitudes upon any child is a strong factor in determining his personality. If the parents spoil him, if they shelter him unduly from the give-and-take of normal play life with other children, if they neglect the proper training of his body and mind, if they thrust him forth too early or if they restrain him too long, if they do not help him to feel security and loyalty, if they nag and scold him excessively, if they belittle him and his ambitions, if they overstimulate him, if they allow him just to grow, like Topsy—it is inevitable that his personality when he reaches maturity will bear the marks of this childhood training, or lack of it.

On the other hand, if the parental influence and example have been such as to encourage the child to be self-reliant, to form good habits and attitudes, to have ideas of his own and stand up for them, to outgrow the natural childish selfishness and grow into an adult pattern of altruism and of concern for all that is noble and high in the world, to "dare do all that may become a man"—then it is equally inevitable that all this parental care and solicitude will be revealed in his adult character and personality.

Factors in the child's environment. There are, of course, many other influences that make their impress upon the personality of the child and youth besides home training. Among

these forces we may list the following as of prime importance
in helping to shape the child's personality:

(1) The school, which trains the mind and fosters the social
attitudes;

(2) The church, which introduces the individual to the higher
realms of the spiritual;

(3) The playground and the playmates, prominent sources of the
cultivation of loyalties, social consciousness, and group spirit;

(4) The community, which provides opportunities for the ex·
pression of co-operativeness, sympathy, and good citizenship;

(5) The books, reading materials, amusements, sports, and interests that fill leisure hours and impress the individual dramati-
cally with the thinking, the feeling, and the willing of the race.

Every one of these and all other social agencies that play
upon the growing individual must be regarded as helping to
weave the complex pattern of personality and to determine
the general style and pattern of the individual.

HOW CAN ONE'S PERSONALITY BE DEVELOPED?

In a broad sense every chapter in this book has been concerned with the question of personality and how to develop
and perfect it. We shall take the time here only to add a few
suggestions for improving the personality. For of course one's
personality *can* be improved and developed.

By maintaining a proper balance. Everybody knows people
who are one-sided in their interests and emotional behavior;
for example, the recluse, the social butterfly, the person gnawed
by envy or jealousy, the fanatic, or the extremist in any area
of experience.

The integrated individual is not overbalanced in any direction, but presents to the world a harmonious, well-unified
personality. If you would be such an individual, you should

strive to conquer disappointments and regrets over unattainable goals and endeavor to find satisfaction in working toward the attainable ones; to avoid being at cross-purposes with yourself; to eliminate emotional conflicts from your life; to rule out fears, misgivings, and resentments; in short, to unify all your energies and purposes toward the achieving of the style or pattern you have set for yourself.

By cultivating a saving sense of humor. Good humor often saves the day. By cultivating a sense of humor one provides himself with a powerful ally that will help him over many a difficult obstacle. It is a mistake for anybody to take himself too seriously all the time. Unless he can relax and laugh—yes, even laugh sometimes at himself—he is lacking in one of the essential traits of a strong personality. Learn to look on the lighter side of life, at least on occasion; learn to break with a smile or a laugh the tension that builds up within you in times of effort and stress.

"People who do not know how to laugh," remarked Thackeray, "are always pompous and self-conceited." Ill humor, rather than good humor, goes with pompousness and conceit. The well-adjusted person shuns self-importance as he would the plague. If he learns to laugh and to be of good cheer, he will find that his outlook on life will keep much sweeter and saner. Far from being pompous and conceited, he has a chance of achieving that friendliness and geniality without which no personality is ever charming.

By keeping worry at a distance. Do you know anybody who is apprehensive of tomorrow, fearful of what it may bring, troubled about many things? Do you know any member of that unhappy and unblest class of people who are chronic worriers? Consultants in psychology and psychiatry probably deal with more patients who fall in this general fear-category than with all others put together.

Some people look for worries! It must, of course, be admitted that all of us have circumstances in our lives that are not to our liking, and that even give promise of becoming more vexatious rather than less so. Still, the well-integrated personality does not allow worry to sour or to paralyze him. He tries to do whatever comes to his hand to the best of his ability, and to leave the outcome with fate or with a kind Providence. He does not enshroud himself in a cloak of presentiment; neither does he anticipate the bad or the unfortunate. His traits are *balanced:* no one of them—like worry —is thrown up into a peak that casts shadows on the surrounding areas of experience. If there is any real and sufficient cause for worry, he can be as anxious as the next man, but he does not go about looking for something to get worked up about. He endeavors to keep worry at a distance; and by filling his life with determined action, confidence, and a clear purpose, he succeeds famously.

Neurotics have a bad influence. Nervous people and worriers not only are enemies to their own serenity and well-being, but also destroy the happiness and peace of those about them. "The neurotic never dies young, but his friends always do!" is a saying that is frequently valid. For the sake of their relatives and associates, if for no other reason, "nervous" people ought to mend their ways. This is, of course, far easier said than done, for many such individuals find themselves perennially in the grip of a paralyzing force that they cannot conquer. This is especially true of people who have allowed themselves to grow up into adulthood the victims of fears and forebodings. Youth is the time in which to learn to master your fears and conquer your "nerves." It is quite as important to cultivate serenity and faith and confidence as it is to learn to be truthful and co-operative.

Record on the form below the principal things that you

personally have worried about. That is to say, without trying to think up situations or conditions that you think might trouble you, note down only the real things that have bothered you and caused you uneasiness and apprehensiveness:

THINGS THAT WORRY ME

1. I worry a lot for fear something may happen to my father and mother.
2.
3.
4.
5. etc.

(You may have only one or two things to record. If you have *none,* you are fortunate!)

By avoiding oversensitiveness! The oversensitive person finds plenty to hurt his feelings! Like the eavesdropper who is always spying to overhear what others may be saying about him, the oversensitive individual is rarely at a loss to find criticism and belittlement of himself. It is easy for him to twist, to his own humiliation, harmless remarks that reach his ears even though they have only the remotest—if any—intended reference to him. His feelings are easily hurt by the ordinary give-and-take of social experience; he seems almost to be set to find a slight, or a criticism; he invariably "puts the coat on" when some casual remark strikes him in what he feels to be a vulnerable spot. He is too thin-skinned to bear the gentlest disapproval, and if actual reprimand or censure were to come his way, he would never recover!

Some people have to be handled gingerly! No doubt you know such people. One always has to regard them out of the corner of his eye to note when their feelings are hurt or their pride piqued. They require a different kind of handling from that which we accord ordinary folks. They must be safeguarded from all reproach and all blame. So long as their associates "handle them with gloves on" and go out of their way to reassure them frequently of their indulgence and appreciation, they get on well enough in the social group. But let admonition or chiding be directed upon them, and they forthwith become hopelessly upset and may even withdraw themselves from circulation! To win them back requires a good deal of wooing and protesting of better faith in the future.

It is well for all of us to watch our inner behavior to see whether we are foolishly sensitive and morbidly susceptible to slights and disparagements. If we find ourselves to be so, now is the appointed time and today the appointed hour for us to set our faces against such socially unhealthy attitudes and begin to learn to be thicker-skinned. There is scant satisfaction to be had by the oversensitive individual as he rubs elbows with his matter-of-fact fellows.

HOW PSYCHOLOGISTS WORK

Certain ancient philosophers, notably Hippocrates, seeking to account for the differences among personalities, believed that a person's dominant mood or temperament was determined by the peculiar condition and interrelationship of the body fluids. Four different fluids were differentiated: blood, phlegm, yellow bile, and black bile. The sanguine individual was the man in whom the first of these fluids or "humors"—blood—was dominant. He was optimistic and enthusiastic, and perhaps also quick-acting but weak-willed, by virtue of the fact that his blood dominated the other humors. Phlegm dominated the second type of individual—the phlegmatic—and made him sluggish, slow, indifferent, and rather weak. Yellow bile, when dominant, caused a man to be choleric: that is, easily aroused to anger and rage, and quick and strong in his responses. Black bile made the individual melancholic, pessimistic, and cynical.

Modern scientific research has, of course, failed to substantiate any such connection between the four "humors" and the four temperaments enumerated. Personality is no longer believed to depend upon the chemistry of blood and bile.

Still, there is no question about there being an important relationship between personality and body chemistry. The modern researcher finds this relationship in studying the secretions of the *ductless glands,* or *endocrines.* Tucked away in various corners of our bodies, this system of glands manufactures powerful chemical substances which are absorbed into the blood and have been shown to exert a profound influence over both the physical structure and the emotional setup of the individual. We must be content here merely to refer briefly to some of the principal ones of these glands.

The *thyroid gland,* lying at the base of the neck, exerts a marked influence over growth and the rate of oxygen combustion in the body. If the gland is underactive in childhood, the body becomes misshapen, the head becomes enlarged, the mind fails to develop, and the individual remains all his life, unless early treatment is available, lazy, dull, and indifferent. If the gland becomes underactive after childhood, the individual becomes abnormally fat and lazy. Overactivity of the thyroid, on the other hand, causes the person to become restless, excitable, fretful and high-strung, sleepless and nervous.

The *pituitary gland,* in the skull at the base of the brain, exerts a profound influence over the physical growth of the body. The pygmies and dwarfs we sometimes see in the circus and on the vaudeville circuit were victims of an underactive pituitary in childhood. Frequently such persons are subnormal in mentality and are subject to occasional outbursts of temper. They are often irritable and "ornery."

At the other end of the scale are the giants—the Brobding-nagians—whose great height and size are due to an over-activity of the pituitary during childhood and youth. Thus, Robert Wadlow, an Illinois youth, at nineteen years of age weighed 435 pounds and measured eight feet six inches in height—the tallest man on record. His parents and four brothers and sisters were of normal size. Sometimes it happens that the pituitary begins to overfunction after youth has passed, in which case various isolated parts of the body—such as the hands, the feet, the jaws—start growing again, and grotesque features are produced.

The gonads are glands that make for femininity in the woman and masculinity in the man. If the gonads do not function in the girl, the individual remains childish and un-derdeveloped and fails to build those subtle traits which are ordinarily associated with the loveliness of womanhood. Failure of gonad function in the boy is associated with a weak or feminine voice, with the arresting of development, and with a lack of strength and dominance ordinarily connected with masculinity.

These and the other ductless glands are all co-ordinated into a system which is interacting, and whenever one of them secretes abnormally it tends to interfere with the smooth functioning of the others. Profoundly disturbed emotional conditions and personality changes occur in individuals whose glands become thus unbalanced and unco-ordinated. Unquestionably the ductless glands, when working properly, influence favorably the physical growth of the body and supply at least the background for normal and wholesome personalities. Underactive, overactive, or mutually unadjusted, they work in opposite directions, causing abnormal physical growth and development and supplying the basis for abnormal and un-wholesome personalities.

Thus the modern "humors" are not greatly different in their functional influence from the "humors" of the ancients: the latter recognized and the former establish the importance of the internal chemistry of the body as casting the individual in this, that, or the other mold. The difference lies in the nature of the chemical substances themselves.

TO HELP YOU LEARN

SOME QUESTIONS TO ANSWER

1. How does the popular understanding of *personality* differ from the scientific concept?

2. What mistakes do people make when they judge somebody's personality from casual or naïve observation? What traits are likely to figure prominently in influencing their judgment? What ones may be ignored completely?

3. If all the people in the world cannot be satisfactorily classified into the good and the bad, what classification, if any, *can* be made of them?

4. How can one distinguish between sensible worry and foolish worry? Do you consider yourself to be a worrier, or are you a rather confident individual?

5. What experience have you had with oversensitive people? Why are they hard to get along with and hard to handle?

WORKING WITH PSYCHOLOGY

1. Find in the advertising pages of a popular magazine a specimen advertisement of a "personality culture" system. Clip it and analyze it impartially from the standpoint of its probable merit as a means of developing or of improving the personalities of those who might give it a trial. Approach your conclusions with an open

mind, trying to be fair in your evaluation both to the advertiser and to the potential customer.

2. Do the following bit of research. Find out everything you can about phrenology and phrenologists in the encyclopedias and books of reference available in your library. Study a little of the work and influence of Francis Joseph Gall, who was probably the founder of modern phrenology (about 150 years ago). If possible, locate either an original or a copy of a phrenological chart and note its principal features. See what criticism you can find in reference books or in psychological texts regarding phrenology as a system of personality appraisal.

3. Review your study of the normal curve of distribution, which you learned about in an earlier chapter (see Chapter 13), and relate it to the discussion of personality types in the present chapter. Actually construct a curve of this sort, indicating within it the proportion of people who are possessed of an average personality, a stronger than average one, a notably dominant one, a weaker than average one, and a completely weak one. Construct similar distribution curves for the sanity of people, the goodness of people, the ambitiousness of people, and the altruism of people.

4. Do the following experiment. Clip from illustrated magazines or tabloids, pictures of ten different persons not generally known. Number each, from 1 to 10, and mount them side by side on a large sheet of cardboard or tough paper. Each member of the class is then, working independently, to estimate the personality traits of each person pictured, noting down the three most obvious characteristics he observes. After all the judgments have been made, compare the results obtained and draw conclusions relative to the ability of people to judge personality offhand. The experiment will be more interesting if each student attempts to rate on a scale of 100 the amount of each of the three traits he thinks he sees in the people studied. Thus, one might get this result from studying a picture of an unknown person:

(1) Kindness 75%
(2) Ambition 50%
(3) Fearlessness 40%

(Do not, of course, use these suggested characteristics in just this same way.)

494 INTRODUCTORY PSYCHOLOGY

WHAT OTHERS SAY

1. In Fiction:

The Strange Case of Dr. Jekyll and Mr. Hyde by Robert L. Stevenson. A classic story of dual personality, symbolizing the conflict between the selfish and the unselfish in a man's nature.

The Magic Bow by M. Komroff. A fascinating tale of Paganini, the famous violinist, whose strange personality led some of his contemporaries to think that he was in league with the devil.

Ethan Frome by Edith N. Wharton. In the character of Zenobia, Ethan's whining wife, who enjoys numerous imaginary ailments, will be found an excellent portrayal of the self-centered personality.

2. In Biography:

Margaret Ogilvy by James M. Barrie. One of the most touching of biographies, revealing the splendid personality of Barrie's own mother, and representing a beautiful tribute to her.

Memoirs of a Midget by Walter de la Mare. A strongly appealing account of the profound influence exerted by physical dwarfishness upon personality. An intimate portrayal of the reactions of Miss M. to her peculiar defect.

3. In Drama:

Mary of Scotland by Maxwell Anderson. A great play, depicting the strong, almost brutal personality of Elizabeth, in contrast with the equally strong but more gentle personality of Mary. A poetic drama of unusual power.

4. In Poetry:

Flammonde by Edwin A. Robinson. The portrait of a personality which, though "banished from better days," was dominated by the general pattern of altruism and charm.

WHAT'S AHEAD IN CHAPTER 19

How Can Delinquency Be Controlled?

On one occasion, after J. Edgar Hoover had addressed a club in a Southern city, he was a bit amazed to find a twelve-year-old boy making his way toward him, and still more amazed when he listened to the lad's very earnest request.

"I want to be a G-Man!" he announced. "I want to serve my country by fighting crime the way you are doing!"

The director of the F. B. I. was impressed with the seriousness of this boy, and, although the minimum age for joining the G-Men is twenty-five years, he sat down with him and mapped out a course of study that would make him eligible when he became old enough. The boy's application for appointment as a special agent in Mr. Hoover's bureau is on file, and in the meantime he is actually proceeding with the studies which the director outlined for him.

For the hundreds of agents of the F. B. I., the underworld has come to have a most healthy respect. Every one of them is a specially picked individual, clean-living, intelligent, and highly trained for his job. Since the F. B. I. has a record of some 95% of convictions in the cases brought to the courts, it is no wonder criminals and would-be criminals are jittery! One way to diminish crime and delinquency is to make "shady" characters more respectful of law.

Back in 1904, in New York City, forty boys had been brought into the Children's Court for various kinds of delinquencies and misdemeanors. The logical thing to do with

495

them would have been to send them to reform school, even though more than half of the children so sentenced "graduate" into major crime when they leave.

A man named Coulter thought there was a better way. He enlisted forty business men, each of whom was to assume a friendly interest in a boy, take him to the ball game, invite him home with him, and win his confidence. That was the beginning of the Big Brother Movement and the Big Sister Movement. Today there are hundreds of these organizations in our large cities, with thousands of Big Brothers and Big Sisters befriending and influencing for the good tens of thousands of boys and girls each year. Boys and girls who steal, who commit acts of malicious mischief, and who walk perilously close to the shadow land of crime are thus brought under new influences and persuaded to adopt new standards. More than 95% of them turn their backs permanently upon crime.

Another way to diminish crime and delinquency, then, is to provide children with sympathy, understanding, and a chance to go straight and to be loyal.

Tom Solomon was unhappy a great deal, as a young boy. His father and mother did not get on well together, and Tom worried about it. Home wasn't a very cheerful and attractive place because his parents were always angry at each other.

By the time he was sixteen, Tom could stand it no longer, and to find a means of forgetting his troubles, he joined a gang of young desperadoes. For a time his identity was not revealed, but when, one dark night, he participated in a spectacular "holdup," in which one member of his gang was killed and a policeman wounded, Tom was caught and put in jail. At the trial his guilt was established; indeed, he admitted being an accomplice in the holdup. He admitted further that there had been for several years a great upheaval in his mind over his family situation, and that once he had embarked upon a career of lawbreaking, he had been unable to stop. Tom was given a sentence aggregating twenty years in state's prison.

A third way to diminish crime and delinquency would be, it seems, to provide happy homes for children to grow up in.

Happy Homes More Important Than G-Men

In this last anecdote we come to the real point of the whole matter of crime and delinquency. Mr. Hoover's G-Men may deter many from crime; Big Brother and Big Sister Movements may redeem hordes of young delinquents from becoming real criminals later on; but crime would be pretty well wiped out of any country if only one hundred per cent of its homes were happy, interesting places in which boys and girls could grow up amid good influences.

✓ ✓ ✓

In this chapter you will learn much about the nation's greatest disease—crime. You will understand why it is that a career of lawbreaking appeals to some individuals more than it does to others. You will find out what conditions are ordinarily found associated with crime, and what are the commonest misdemeanors committed by the younger delinquents. You will learn, too, that crime is no respecter of persons. You will be introduced to some wholesome suggestions for nondelinquents to follow if they would make their lives count most.

Fig. 70. *How do slum clearance projects like this help to prevent crime?*

19. CRIME AND DELINQUENCY

Before you begin, note down on a form like the one below some points of contrast between the type of home that might be expected to produce youthful lawbreakers and the type that would probably produce boys and girls who would find their happiness in going straight:

TWO PRODUCTS OF THE AMERICAN HOME

The Law-Abiding Young Citizen	The Lawbreaking Young Delinquent
Why?	Why?
1. Because his family is a happy one.	1. Because life at home is un-happy.
2.	2.
3.	3.
4.	4.
5. etc.	5. etc.

It will be a good plan for you to bear in mind, as you think about this problem, a number of actual homes in your neighborhood and community that you know or have heard about. Base your entries upon existing conditions, good and bad.

CRIME: THE NATION'S GREATEST DISEASE

In newspapers and magazines you read a good deal about cancer and heart disease and tuberculosis and the other great modern plagues that afflict the human race. Bad, indeed, they are—these maimers and killers of men, and scientists in laboratories and hospitals and clinics are searching constantly to find means of overcoming them.

A plague that attacks all ages.   Still, the most destructive and widespread of all diseases is crime. Like most other plagues, it attacks both the young and the old, the white and the black, the country-dweller and the city-dweller. The shameful admission has to be made, too, that in our own United States the crime disease stalks more boldly and brazenly than it does in any other civilized country.

Our unenviable national record!   The Federal Bureau of Investigation of the Department of Justice lists very nearly one and one-half million major crimes (1,484,554 in 1939) as occurring in this country each year, and these figures take no account of the far greater number of lesser crimes. Furthermore, in proportion to our total population we have the greatest prison population of any country in the world. One person in every thirty-seven, according to the Law Enforcement Committee of the American Bar Association, is a criminal. The total cost of crime in the United States reaches the staggering annual figure of fifteen billions of dollars, a sum equivalent to one third of the total value of all the manufactured goods produced in industrial America.

The heaviest toll of crime at nineteen.   A generation or so ago, most criminals were adults somewhere between forty and fifty years of age. For the past quarter of a century and more, however, the peak age of the criminal has been declining, until at the present time the Federal Bureau of Investigation finds nineteen to be the age at which the greatest number of arrests are made. Indeed, during a recent year, 34.8% of all the arrests made for all causes in the United States were of young people under twenty-five; 31% of all the arrests made for crimes against property were of persons under twenty-one.

These facts are disconcerting enough, but they are all the more disheartening when one finds that the number of arrests of young people between sixteen and twenty is distinctly on the increase, and that no fewer than one hundred thousand boys and girls under sixteen years of age pass through our juvenile courts every year.

Why nineteen? Dr. Sanford Bates, formerly director of the United States Bureau of Prisons, thus accounts for the fact that the highest frequency of arrest and imprisonment comes at nineteen years of age:

> It is not difficult to picture the youth of nineteen as at the most restive and critical age in his whole life. He has outgrown the restraints of the schoolroom and the control of his family. He has not yet been steadied by the assumption of business or marital responsibilities. Many writers have pointed out that there has been a loosening of the ties which have kept the younger generation in the paths of rectitude in the past. . . . And so we find the average boy at nineteen at the maximum of his strength and physical power and under a minimum of restraint. He undergoes a sudden transition from the control of school life to the complete liberty of an adult man. His nineteenth year, therefore, is a season when crime takes its heaviest toll. Year by year thereafter it decreases. As the boy grows older he tires of adventure. He assumes responsibilities that divert his energies. He is, perhaps, arrested and confined and learns that crime does not pay.

—"The Young Criminal: A Sharp Challenge,"
New York Times Magazine, August 4, 1935.

JUVENILE DELINQUENCY A STRONG CHALLENGE

Seeking the best corrective treatment. To those youthful lawbreakers whose age is sixteen or under, society applies the term "juvenile delinquent," and establishes the juvenile court to sit in judgment over them and determine what will be the best corrective treatment to redeem them and make them over into good citizens. The whole problem of juvenile delinquency is one of the most challenging ones confronting sociologists and psychologists at the present day. Quite apart from the heavy financial burden involved in detecting delinquency and in handling it in the courts and beyond the courts, there is the infinitely more important matter of helping the rising generation to avoid conduct that inevitably brings disappointment and often remorse, suffering, and loss of freedom.

Efforts to solve the problem. Few problems of the age are receiving more attention on the part of expert investigators than is this problem of delinquency. Books, articles, and news features are being written about it; surveys to determine its prevalence and the types of delinquency are being conducted in many centers; state departments and commissions as well as federal bureaus are expending huge sums of money in endeavoring to discover and remove its causes so far as possible; various foundations and social organizations are devoting themselves to crime research; and recently a Presidential Crime Commission made a country-wide investigation of all forms of criminal conduct and their effects upon the nation.

THE COMMONEST CRIMES AMONG YOUNG PEOPLE

Why children are haled into court. A recent publication of the Children's Bureau of the United States Department of Labor lists the delinquency cases of boys and girls in 291 courts during a single year as shown at the top of page 503.

It will be seen from this table that, among boys, appropriation of the property of others accounts for half of all the crimes committed, and that mischievousness or carelessness accounts for half of the remainder; among girls, the table indicates that some form of running away, truancy, and unruliness accounts for well over half of all the cases. Most of these offenses could be said to be expressions either of disregard for others or of discontent with the surroundings.

It's easy to get started as a criminal. We shall inquire shortly into some of the prominent causes associated with

Reasons for Court Referral	Boys	Girls
Automobile stealing	3%	Less than 1%
Burglary	14%	1%
Holdup	1%	Less than 1%
Other stealing	31%	11%
Carelessness or mischief	26%	10%
Traffic violation	3%	1%
Truancy	5%	11%
Running away	6%	16%
Unruliness	6%	28%
Sex offense	2%	17%
Injury to person	2%	2%
Liquor or drugs (use, possession, sale)	1%	1%
Other reasons	0%	1%
Total	100%	100%

juvenile crime. But first, a quotation from Commissioner Mc-Cormick of the city of New York, which appeared in the *New York Herald Tribune* for March 13, 1936, will prove interesting as showing how easy and natural it sometimes is for a boy in a great city to embark upon a career of delinquency and crime:

You have heard discussions of the slums, those miasmic swamps that menace lives, not only of those who dwell in them, but also of those who dwell beyond their borders. Picture yourself a restless, growing boy in your teens, living in one of the cold-water tenements, the American-born son of poor immigrant parents, for example. The family flat is poorly furnished, overcrowded, cold in winter and stifling-hot in summer. There are three kids for every bed and two adults for every chair. Your parents are worn out with insufficient food and long hours of work. They find solace in a scuttle or two of beer every evening, and relief from tension in the quarrels which the beer engenders. They talk their native tongue and understand hardly a word of English. You are American, proudly so. You do not know the language of the old country and are contemptuous of it, and of your parents who speak it.

Evening comes—you don't worry about your homework because you plan to play truant tomorrow. You go out into the streets, your playground. The public school in your neighborhood is dark: it costs too much to pay an evening janitor to keep it open. The gymnasium is dark—the auditorium with its movie machine is dark—the shop where you were developing an interest in electricity is dark.

But the Elite Bar, on the corner, is not dark. Through the window you can see Limpy Louis, who has just beaten the rap on a burglary charge for the twentieth time, setting up the drinks for the house. In the place across the street Big Charlie, the policy-slip racketeer, is talking business at a corner table—his Packard roadster stands outside. Down the block a cellar club caters to a clientele that never earned an honest dollar.

Your wants are simple, but there is no money at home to satisfy them. Even the ten-cent "movie" is out—there are no extra dimes in your house. You meet Jimmie on the corner, and he suggests that you both hook a ride on the rear of a truck up to Blank Street. There you meet some of the boys you were swimming with off an East River dock last Saturday—and you go to their clubhouse—a cellar room in a vacated tenement—and hear the plans for a foray on a store that closes early. You are so far from home that all the cops seem strangers to you, and you go in on it. The job is pulled off successfully, the petty loot is disposed of to a fence, the proceeds are divided, and you go home with $2—untold wealth—in your pocket, and on your lips the ready excuse that you have been over at Hymie's house. Your father beats you, because his father beat him when he was a boy, but he doesn't learn about the $2.

And thus—as naturally as that—is the boy started on the road to juvenile delinquency and adult crime.

Do you think many boys who lived in similar circumstances would have the desire and the will power to go straight?

THE PRINCIPAL CAUSES OF DELINQUENCY

Various causes have been proposed. Though crime is our chief disease, the causes back of it are not easy to point out. In the past many people have been inclined to assert that there is only one cause of crime, but they have disagreed as to the one cause. If a person was a hereditarian, he referred to poor heredity and criminal ancestors as the one cause. If he was an environmentalist (*euthenist*), he laid all crime at the door of the slum or otherwise inadequate surroundings in which the individual child grew up. If he was an educational philosopher, he deemed a weak and clumsy system of schooling to be at fault in the production of delinquency. If he was a religionist, he blamed crime and delinquency upon irreligion and a decadent morality. And so it has gone!

But there is no single cause. If there is any one thing we do know now about the origin of delinquent behavior in any young person, it is that there is *no single cause.* Just as in a physical disease like tuberculosis, in which the presence of active tubercle bacilli, *plus* a lowered resistance power of the individual's body, *plus* an inherited constitutional weakness, *plus* inadequate diet and other unhygienic practices, must all be blamed for its actual appearance in the individual—so delinquent or criminal behavior is always found to be associated with many contributing causes.

In the following paragraphs we shall discuss some of the most commonly found conditions that are associated with delinquency in young people. As you think about them, you will find it interesting to notice how each one of them was operating in the imaginary case quoted from Commissioner McCormick.

Insecurity in the home. There is no more essential single influence for good in the life of anybody—be he child or adult

—than a pleasant and comfortable home in which he feels faith and security and to which he tends to be strongly loyal. Nearly every sharer of such a home has a sense of membership, of responsibility, of appreciation. Let that security be destroyed, and not only is the pleasurableness of home eliminated, but the feeling of loyalty and obligation to it is also reduced sharply or actually destroyed completely. As a matter of fact, there has been no study yet reported by responsible investigators in this country that has not found delinquent behavior more often associated with insecure homes than with any other single factor.

The earmarks of an inadequate home. What is an insecure home? It is not necessarily the home over which hangs constantly the grim fear of poverty, although poverty may contribute to a sense of insecurity, as we shall see. It may be a home in which death has taken away one or both of the parents and so deprived the children of normal care. It may be a home in which there has been parental separation or divorce, which reduces sharply the feeling of comfort and security of those who are left in it. It may be an inharmonious home, in which the members constantly quarrel, and in which there is little to attract and nothing to command loyalty and respect. It may be any of these sorts of homes, for none of them is secure; none of them calls forth strong sentiments of devotion and comradeship in its juvenile members; none of them can impress children with a confidence in the unvariableness of home and love and understanding.

Seeking excitement and satisfaction. Can you detect, in the home described by Commissioner McCormick, some of the earmarks of the insecure home? Can you see why, on the strength of these factors, the boy could hardly be expected to find in his home security and peace of mind? And can you understand, too, why it is that boys from such unfortunate

home environments find a false kind of excitement and satisfaction and a comforting sense of group spirit by fleeing from
them and allying themselves with other companions for adventures into delinquency?

The comradeship in crime supplies an extremely satisfying loyalty
to a pal or a gang that should have found expression in the family
circle. The community of planning, sharing, storing, keeping secret,
and the like, gives some measure of security to the young delinquent,
some feeling of identification with the life and welfare of others,
some flattering notion of his importance and indispensableness in
the gang group. Thus the gang comes to . . . provide persons to
whom to be loyal, and a milieu in which one feels himself indispensable and hence secure.
                    —Lawrence A. Averill, *Adolescence,* p. 140.

Poverty. Poverty, too, is very commonly found associated
with delinquency on the part of the boy or girl. It is easy to
understand how the very poor home is lacking in many of
the comforts and all of the luxuries that appeal strongly to
young people. Such a home is a pretty drab place for the
youngster who comes in contact elsewhere—notably in the
movies—with "advanced" standards of living and with the
amazing wealth of other people.

Associated with poverty in the home are, of course, tired and
worn-out elders, complaining and grumbling older brothers
and sisters, plainness and bareness of walls and furnishings,
physical discomforts and inconveniences, overcrowding, and a
host of other unattractive conditions and experiences.

An easy step from drab home to crime. To spend much
time in such surroundings is likely to be distasteful; to think
of bringing pals and friends home for an evening is out of the
picture completely. Abandoning the home for as many of the
waking hours as possible and seeking various sorts of sham

happiness and excitement in whatever channels happen to offer, becomes a powerful motive to the restless young person. Thrills, adventure, and gaiety outside the walls of home beckon alluringly, and many a boy is thus attracted to street corners and "hangouts" and cheap forms of entertainment from which it is but a step to lawlessness and crime.

Can you understand why the boy in the quotation from Commissioner McCormick was being attracted into criminal gang behavior by the poverty-stricken condition of the family setting in which he was placed? Small wonder that he took to the streets in the evening and became an easy victim of circumstances. A counterfeit sort of happiness was to be found beyond the bare walls of home: adventure, spending money, thrills—all were there. What did the beating he suffered at the hands of his father matter, save to confirm him still more in the newly beckoning, glamorous way of life!

Maintaining "honor" with the group.   Solitary delinquency is somewhat rare. Especially is this the case with the major, the more serious forms of delinquent behavior. Misery is not the only thing that loves company; crime, too, flourishes in partnerships of two or more connivers. A recent study of first offenders in New York City showed that about 75% were involved with one or more companions when they were arrested. Sometimes the degree of involvement is limited to keeping watch while others do the robbing or burglarizing; sometimes it is limited to planning the details of the crime; sometimes it involves active participation.

The law does not excuse any who are concerned with a delinquent act, whether they are in the front line or in the rear. All are guilty and all are answerable to society.

One of youth's best characteristics.   One of the strongest and best characteristics of adolescents is their loyalty to their own group, to their own companions and mates. Young people are customarily reliable, faithful, co-operative. They stick together with a splendid group spirit. They court their comrades' approval and favor and will do nothing to bring disfavor or contempt upon one another. They will not disclose "gang" secrets, and they dread above everything else getting the reputation of being "tattletales," or "squealers."

These traits are just as conspicuous among delinquent or near-delinquent gangs as they are among more orderly groups. Consequently, once a young person has been a participant in a lawbreaking escapade, he will maintain the greatest loyalty to the others involved with him, shielding them with the most complete alibis and maintaining attitudes of utter and perfect ignorance of both the whereabouts and the actions of the gang members. To turn "yellow" is about the worst trick any young person could possibly play.

We may be very sure that McCormick's imaginary boy would, if he were cornered by his father or by any other adult—police or otherwise—shield his fellow thieves and remain faithful to them through thick and thin. This is a noble trait in anybody. The pity of it is that the deeds into which youngsters drift are at times unworthy. In a better cause, this group loyalty and co-operation would be the strongest kind of asset.

Living in a delinquency area. Every social worker and every socially-minded person knows that some sections of our great cities, and indeed of smaller cities and towns, are worse breeders of crime than other sections in the same community. In cities like New York, Chicago, Omaha, and San Jose, California, it has been possible to study this problem carefully, and the results show that certain sections lying about the industrial district produce more crime than other districts outlying. These districts have been appropriately called "delinquency areas." They are characterized by dense population and overcrowding, by poor housing, by poverty, by lack of play-grounds and parks, and by underworld "dives."

Gambling dens and other hangouts. Children and young people who live in poor surroundings will almost inevitably be driven to the streets and too often will find their way into the gambling dens and the hangouts of crooks and underworld characters. Because of their at first innocent and entirely natural efforts to find a place to play and something interesting to do with themselves, these youngsters are thrown into contact with bad influence, bad example, and bad companions. There is no place in the slums where they can play safely, no place where they can amuse themselves and give expression to their drives for social experience and comradeship under wholesome conditions.

Importance of slum clearance. One of the great sociological advances which our country is making at the present time lies in the clearance of slums and in the building of new homes to accommodate those who have been forced to live in the tenement areas, where sunshine, fresh air, and playgrounds have been practically unknown.

What conditions savoring of delinquency areas and slum environment did you observe in the neighborhood surroundings of Commissioner McCormick's boy?

Do some more thinking about delinquency areas before you proceed to the next section of this chapter. On a form like that on page 511 list what seem to you to be the principal features or characteristics of such a crime-breeding area.

DELINQUENCY IS NO RESPECTER OF PERSONS

Both rich and poor become its victims. While it is true that most of the factors we have enumerated as being associated with delinquency are found more commonly among poverty-stricken groups, we must not jump to the conclusion that there

1. Lack of any playgrounds.
2.
3.
4.
5. etc.

(Consider the worst parts of your own town or city for suggestions in handling this problem.)

is no delinquency among the children of the middle class and of the well-to-do. Notwithstanding the fact that these more fortunate children grow up in environments rich with stimulating opportunity, and notwithstanding the fact that they go longer to school and are somewhat better taken care of from the health point of view, nevertheless, they occasionally become delinquent.

Sometimes because they are spoiled, sometimes because they are pampered and overprotected, sometimes because they are held to overstrict standards of conduct, sometimes because they are given too much attention and subjected to too much stimulation and too much budgeting of their time and activities—for all these and other related reasons it may happen that the children from better economic environments become easy victims of the lure of the streets. It makes little relative difference whether a young person accustomed to poor treatment at home lives in the slums or on the avenue: he finds it easy to cast off the restrictions that surround him and to embark upon an intriguing career outside of the family setting.

There is no immunity. Delinquency is, in other words, no respecter of persons, regardless of their economic status. Neither is the degree of intelligence of a young person necessarily any defense against delinquent behavior. In fact, as high as 70% of delinquents have been found to fall within the normal range of intelligence. Nor is race any deterrent to antisocial conduct. All racial and national extractions are ordinarily included in the delinquents passing through any metropolitan juvenile court on any day. Neither is knowledge of right and wrong, by itself, any guarantee that a young person's conduct will be satisfactory before the law. Both delinquents and nondelinquents have been found to score equally high on ethical-knowledge tests that have been administered to both groups. To repeat a remark made earlier in this chapter: crime is a disease, and from it nobody can be regarded as safely immune.

DESIRE FOR ADVENTURE IS STRONG IN YOUTH

Experience, adventure, thrill! Regardless of where the youth lives, or of how well adjusted he may be in his home life, or of whether he is white or black, bright or dull, in school or out of school, it is characteristic of him that he will have a strong craving for adventure and for the limelight. Because the limitations of his childhood are past and he finds himself possessed of newly unfolded powers of mind and body, the young person feels a strong and insistent call to add experience to experience, adventure to adventure, knowledge to knowledge, thrill to thrill. His whole being is alive to the opportunities for self-expression that his environment offers, and it is to be expected that he will seek to take full advantage of them.

Forgetting the consequences. If his earlier home training has been inadequate, or if his thirst for adventure is particularly keen, or if he has not learned the valuable lessons of self-control and of respect for law and authority, or if he chances to drift into the company of companions whose ideals and standards are somewhat off-color, it will be easy—desperately easy—for him to throw caution to the winds and join in some foray or adventure that may bring him disaster or shame or sorrow. In the innocent excitement of the moment, he may be quite unable to stop to think of consequences. Once opportunity has presented itself, the suggestion of seizing it has been made, and quick acquiescence in the plan has been manifested by all, he is swept off his feet and plunged on the spur of the moment into what seems to him at first blush to be capital adventure.

WHY YOUTH IS OFTEN IRKED BY THE LAW

Universal chafing against the law. Throughout their childhood and early adolescent years, young people are exposed to a great deal of adult faultfinding with the laws as they exist in the community. They hear their elders, for example, complaining about the income tax laws, the traffic laws, the real estate tax laws, the gasoline tax laws, the regulations against liquor and against certain drugs and narcotics, the game laws, the Sunday closing laws; and they find it easy to adopt prejudiced or out-and-out hostile attitudes toward law and toward the constituted authority which is charged with its enforcement.

It is surprising to notice how many people one rubs elbows with in the course of a day who devote a part of their conversation to criticism or strong condemnation of the law against this, or the law requiring that, or the law regulating the other thing.

A strange inconsistency! With that strange but very human inconsistency characteristic of most of us, these same adult critics and denouncers of the law as it affects them personally are overzealous to preach to their children the importance of obeying all sorts of spoken rules of conduct set forth by themselves, and all sorts of laws, human and divine, written and unwritten, by which society is regulated.

Since their earliest play life, children may have been warned that the policeman will come and take them away if they are naughty; from their earliest school days they may have been cautioned that the law requires them to attend sessions regularly and that they will be arrested if they don't. They have doubtless been advised early and late to walk "in the straight and narrow" at all times and under all circumstances. They have been assured that wrong does not pay, and that sooner or later the law always catches up with those who defy it. They have been warned against getting in with bad gangs or companions, against being mischievous and rowdyish, against coasting on forbidden streets, against riding their bicycles in the park or on the sidewalks, always with the moral plainly pointed out—that acts such as these are against the law and certain to lead to trouble with the police.

Matching wits with the police!　All in all, it is understandable why young people sometimes come to feel that the law is something that interferes and limits, and that police and other officials are to be regarded with a weather eye. When they entertain ideas and opinions like these, they may easily come to feel that matching their wits with those of policemen and other constituted authorities holds great possibilities in the way of thrills and excitement. They engage in delinquent or near-delinquent behavior, not with a desire to break laws or to be bad, but rather as a means of using their mental and physical resources to the maximum.

A little success in such gambling is most exhilarating, and tempts the mischief-makers on to further repetitions in order to continue the exhilaration. The inevitable, of course, ordinarily happens and they are almost certain to come to grief shortly.

Collect from newspapers several accounts of delinquent acts committed by adolescents, and attempt to assign to each deed its probable contributing causes. Use this form for recording the items and your reactions to them:

DELINQUENT ACTS REPORTED IN THE PRESS

Delinquency or Crime	Probable Contributing Causes
1. Setting a fire	Lack of interesting things to do Bad companionship
2.	
3.	
4.	
5. etc.	

(You cannot, of course, be sure that the reasons you assign are the real ones in each case, but the chances are excellent that they will have something to do with it.)

IMPORTANT ATTITUDES FOR NONDELINQUENTS

Be loyal, but be sure of your group! In this chapter we seem to have been more concerned with delinquent than with law-respecting and law-abiding young people. Let us close on a note of wholesome, nondelinquent behavior, which is, after all, the experience and the ambition of most of the youth in our schools.

Loyalty to the group is the first requisite to happy associations with others—loyalty to its standards, its leaders, its program. The only safeguard the young person should insist upon is that the group in which he moves shall be a worthy one, with worthy aims and ideals. If this be true, then, any young person ought always to be a faithful and loyal member of his group, eager to participate wholeheartedly in its activities and its program.

Enjoy adventure but know when to stop. We live in an exciting age and an exciting world. Youth's natural quest after adventure and thrill certainly has any number of channels through which to find satisfaction. Both delinquents and nondelinquents have this strong desire for dash and excitement; the only distinction between the two groups is that the former are either willing or are easily persuaded to go too far in finding their thrills, whereas the latter understand where the limits are beyond which legitimate behavior cannot be extended. The drive in itself is a good one; like most other strong wants, however, it has to be held in proper control.

Photo by Black Star

Fig. 71. Do you regard the policeman as your friend? What would your community be like without any enforcement of the law?

Remember that the law is our friend. Generations of experience have taught the race the necessity of checks and control upon personal freedom, both for society's own best good and for the best interests of the individuals that make it up. No matter how primitive a race of people may be, it recognizes some sort of law, often personified in the chieftain or in the elders of the tribe. As civilization has become more complex, laws have multiplied and the people themselves have taken over their formation and their enforcement. Consequently the ordinances and regulations that exist upon our statute books today are there because they have the support or the consent of the people.

Looked at from this point of view, laws are seen to be friendly, not hostile; they safeguard and protect us, and guarantee us as much independence of action as is compatible with the comfort and welfare of our neighbors. The good citizen—whether he be a junior citizen or an adult citizen—has a wholesome respect for the laws of his country and of his community, and does not willingly set them aside to indulge his own personal desires or abnormalities.

HOW PSYCHOLOGISTS WORK

Much research upon the problem of juvenile delinquency and waywardness has been carried on in recent years. Alarmed by the fact that commitments to our prisons reach their peak at about the age of nineteen (it was forty a generation ago), psychologists and sociologists have attempted to identify those physical and social conditions that may be presumed to share the responsibility for delinquent conduct in children.

Obviously, if a person can grow up through his childhood and adolescent years without straying into wayward or near-criminal behavior, the chances are excellent that he will continue to be a law-abiding member of society. It is those people who are drawn into unlawful conduct in the early, formative years of life who are likely to become our criminals later on. Like Tom Solomon, whose brief story was told at the beginning of this chapter, once an individual is embarked upon a career of crime, he is hardly ever able to stop.

We have already referred to the relationship between an insecure or an inadequate home, on the one hand, and delinquent conduct on the other. One investigator, after a careful study of 330 children who were victims of some sort of misconduct, reached the conclusion that 90% of them came from sociologically poor homes. While this percentage is somewhat higher than other studies have revealed, it is strikingly true that no major investigation of delinquency has yet been reported, either in this country or in Europe, that does not suggest a very high correlation between children's homes and children's conduct.

Delinquency areas have also been mentioned in our previous discussion as producing a highly disproportionate share of delinquents and criminals. These areas are likely to be located close to the center of population in a city, where housing is poorest and congestion most marked, and where recreational facilities are limited or lacking altogether. One interesting study pin-mapped the neighborhoods in five large cities where delinquent boys between ten and fifteen years of age lived. In this piece of investigation it was found that without exception the number of delinquent boys increased sharply as the center of the city was approached. As many as 18% to 20% of all the delinquent boys in two of these cities were discovered to live within one mile of the center. At two miles out, in all five cities, the rate had dropped to 10% or lower.

Many studies have also been made of physical health, intelligence, personality traits, and emotional adjustment as these may relate to delinquent conduct. While the evidence is not without occasional exceptions, most of the studies show that the wayward, misbehaving child and youth are somewhat below par in one or more of these catagories. One investigator, for example, found more visual and auditory defects among delinquents than among nondelinquents. Some studies have revealed physical defects of the more serious type in from one third to three fourths or more of the delinquents investigated.

There is good agreement among the researchers that low-grade intelligence characterizes the delinquent population to a greater degree than it does the nondelinquent group. One study of nearly 2,000 prisoners in a penitentiary revealed that more than three fourths of them were dull-normal or lower, while another study of more than 500 people arrested and tried in police court showed about one third of them to be actually feeble-minded in some degree.

There is similar agreement among students of crime and delinquency that emotional and personality abnormalities appear very much more commonly among criminal groups than among the general population. One investigator, after summarizing reports of studies made in European cities as well as in American communities, concluded that "most criminals are psychoneurotics or otherwise mentally sick."

On page 520 is a table of seven significant studies in delinquency as it is related to physical, mental, and personality disorders. It indicates the sort of findings research men are reporting.

All research men hasten to point out, however, that while abnormalities of a physical, mental, or emotional sort are more prevalent among lawbreakers than among nondelinquents, there are plenty of delinquent and wayward individuals who possess superb physical health, keen minds, and reasonably good emotional adjustment. Thus, it is all very well to say (as Anderson and Leonard report) that 34.2% of court delinquents are found to have physical defects of some sort or other; the fact remains, however, that there must be 63.8% of them who are in the pink of health! Or to say (as Anderson reports), that 31.4% of police court cases are feeble-minded, and so not intelligent enough to be responsible for

STUDIES OF DELINQUENCY

Name of Investigator	Source of Study	Per Cent Found Physically, Emotionally, or Mentally Defective
1. Anderson and Leonard	1,000 court delinquents	34.2% physically defective
2. Brigham	500 delinquent girls	Total of 527 physical defects
3. Fernald	562 annual admissions to a reformatory	79% physically defective
4. Montague	743 children's court cases and inmates of reformatories, training schools, workhouses, and penitentiaries	79% physically defective
5. Anderson	502 police court cases	31.4% feeble-minded 58% nervously or mentally abnormal
6. Bassett	1,000 Boston Municipal Court cases	45.6% with some degree of mental abnormality
7. Root	1,916 prisoners in a penitentiary	81.1% with intelligence ranging from imbecile and moron to dull-normal

their acts; there still remain 68.6% of court cases whose intelligence is normal or above. Undoubtedly some of the keenest minds in the underworld are actual geniuses!

Let us conclude the whole matter: Crime and delinquency are not primarily the expression of handicapped bodies, nor of sluggish minds, nor yet perhaps, of neurotic traits; instead, they indicate the reasoned or unreasoned behavior of thoroughly normal people, for the most part—people who are physically sound, mentally bright, nervously stable. Crime will never be eliminated by programs for the correction of physical defects, for *eugenic* births (those in which heredity is controlled), for the cure of neurotics. Crime will be elim-

inated when homes, communities, schools, and all other sociological agencies co-operate to help us all to live satisfying lives
in childhood, in youth, and in adulthood.

TO HELP YOU LEARN

SOME QUESTIONS TO ANSWER

1. What is the aptness of calling crime a disease? What are some
of the points of similarity between the two? Are there some striking
points of difference?

2. Why is it that sociologists are all agreed that the home is such
an important agency in promoting desirable attitudes and conduct
in youth?

3. Should one conclude from the discussion of poverty as a condition often found associated with delinquent behavior, that the
children of the poor are certain to find their way into crime? Or
may an economically poor home be a sociologically excellent one?
Explain.

4. Since delinquency appears not to be related particularly to the
economic, or the intellectual, or the racial, or the ethical-knowledge
status of an individual, what is it that prompts one adolescent to go
wrong while another one goes right?

5. Have you heard people express themselves as feeling restricted
or hampered by the law? In what respects? What do you think of
this attitude?

WORKING WITH PSYCHOLOGY

1. Do the following piece of research: Consult available sources
in your school or town library for an analysis of crime and delinquency statistics in your own state. Find the chief crimes committed,
the age and status of those who commit them, and the economic
cost of crime to the community. Study similar statistics for your
state as of a decade ago, and construct curves to indicate trends in

(1) the volume of crime committed; (2) the ages of the criminals; and (3) the economic costs of crime.

2. Invite a representative from some law enforcement agency in your community to talk to your class, either on the general subject of crime and delinquency or on some particular phase of the problem with which he happens to be directly concerned. Such an individual might be a police official, a member of the district attorney's staff, a judge, a local representative of the Federal Bureau of Investigation, and so on.

3. Evaluate in class all the adolescent organizations and all the older groups in which adolescents have membership in your community that arouse strong loyalties in their members and exert upon them influences that make for law and order rather than for questionable adventure and delinquency. List the organizations on the blackboard and talk over the contributions which each of them is making to the welfare and adjustment of their young members. One such group might be an athletic club; another, a camera club.

4. Suppose, for the purpose of this problem, that you were given the job of reorganizing your entire community along the lines of promoting the highest welfare and satisfactions of its youth. Suppose also that unlimited funds for the purpose were placed at your disposal, and that the adult population was ready to co-operate with your plans wholeheartedly. Determine upon the specific changes in the present community setup which you would probably introduce, such as new parks, playgrounds, community houses, clubs, social centers, libraries, gymnasiums.

WHAT OTHERS SAY

1. In Social Research:

Marijuana—Assassin of Youth by H. F. Anslinger, *American Magazine,* July 1937. The U. S. Commissioner of Narcotics paints a gruesome picture of the delinquencies and crime to which those who are crazed by the use of this particular weed are driven.

Youth in Hell by Albert Bein. Personal reminiscences of the author's vivid experiences while serving, at fifteen, a term in a southwestern reform school. The brutality and demoralization are almost unbelievable.

Farewell, Mr. Gangster! by Herbert Corey. An intimate picture of the activities and achievements of Mr. J. Edgar Hoover and the Federal Bureau of Investigation in combating crime in the United States.

2. In Fiction:

Little Dorrit by Charles Dickens. A highly appealing story of a girl born in England's old debtors' prison, Marshalsea in Southwark, and brought up within its walls. Some of the best traits in prisoners are revealed.

The Varmint by Owen M. Johnson. The story of an impudent boy, deemed a "dangerous criminal" in school, and a center of disaffection among the other boys. Yet Humperdink Stover was afterwards reclaimed by rigorous training at Lawrenceville.

3. In Drama:

Dead End by Stanley Kingsley. An absorbing story of gangsters and police set against a background of New York tenements. Pleasure and vice, wealth and poverty, love and crime are all intermingled.

4. In Poetry:

Scum o' the Earth by Robert H. Schauffler. An excellent appreciation of the contributions made to America by humble immigrants. A refreshing poem, when one considers the too commonly accepted notion that from the immigrants come our criminals. They do not!

WHAT'S AHEAD IN CHAPTER 20

What is Good Mental Health—and Poor?

Ferdinand Magellan, "conqueror of the seas," had one burning wish. It was to reach by water the rich spice islands of the East and discover safe water routes along which the precious ginger and cinnamon and pepper could be transported to Europe. More tenaciously than most of the heroes of history, Magellan kept to his task, even though harassed by mutiny among the captains of his five ships and discouraged by his failure to find any waterway through the western continent.

Southward along the coast of hospitable Brazil he sailed, into the ice and snows of the antarctic winter. Undaunted by shipwreck, by fierce storms, by near-starvation, by bitter denunciations and the actual desertion of some of his captains and crews, he kept at his task. At last he came to the intricate channel which posterity was to call the Straits of Magellan.

Beyond the Straits, with only three ships left and with provisions reduced to crumbled, maggoty bread and to the very rats from the hold, this man of indomitable courage and will pushed ever westward across the south Pacific. His eyes sunken in their sockets, his face haggard, and his comrades starving and dying around him, he still kept the prows of his vessels headed toward the west.

At last—the Ladrones, the Philippines, Cebu—and death for the brave commander in a battle with the islanders of Mactan. Magellan never reached the Moluccas—the spice islands. But he left the record of a "heroic, simple man who dared greatly, fought desperately, and succeeded in the grand manner."

Vincent Van Gogh, the Dutch painter, was eccentric all his life, from the time when at twenty-one, he was earning five pounds a month as a clerk in Goupil's London Gallery, to the day when, at forty-six, he pressed a revolver into his side and pulled the trigger.

Dissatisfied with his first job as an art salesman, he became a curate in London's slums. After a time he left England for Belgium, where he devoted himself to missionary work among the poor miners of the Borinage. Here, consumed by the passion for sketching, he discovered what his life work was to be. He went to The Hague to become a pupil of Mauve. He was somewhat spasmodically kept in funds by his brother and by a rich uncle, who was nevertheless scandalized by his nephew's unconventional conduct.

Proceeding to Arles, France, he recorded on canvas after canvas the incredibly beautiful colorings of skies and fields and orchards. On one occasion—penniless—he lived four days on twenty-three cups of coffee and a loaf of bread. In a last fit of insanity, from which he had suffered violent seizures that had required periodic confinement in an institution, he arose from his easel in a cornfield and, turning his face to the sun, blotted out his life forever.

Joe Illing: I've decided to go into politics. That's about the easiest job I know! Tom Barson's uncle is a member of the city government, and Tom says he makes a lot of money on the side!

Perry Sanders: What do you mean, Joe—"on the side"?

Joe: Oh, you know politics is honeycombed with graft, and there's money in it!

Perry: Yes, but I don't see—

Joe: You don't *see?* Well, *I* see! What do you suppose it costs to run this city, anyway, for a year?

Perry: I don't know. Thousands of dollars, I guess.

Joe: Millions! And who do you think gets a rake-off when contracts are let for this and that? The politicians! They know how to steer things their way. I'm going in for it as a career!

Perry: What do you have to do to get started?

Joe: Oh, you've got to have some kind of a "pull," of course —a "friend at court," as the saying goes. That's the only way. Tom's uncle has told me all about it. He'll get me in.

Mental Health Is Vital to Success

In these three situations we have a striking contrast between people who tackle their tasks with sound, healthy minds and those who tackle them with unhealthy ones. Magellan throws himself and all that he has unreservedly into his life work; Van Gogh sets himself at length a splendid task but is lacking in the necessary mental health to see it through; Joe Illing selects a task that needs the best and finest in a man's character, but he brings to it a purpose and an outlook that are the reverse of sound and healthy.

✓ ✓ ✓

This final chapter will introduce to you some specific principles of mental health. You will learn what the mental hygienist understands by a "task"; how dreamed-of tasks are to be achieved; why the only permanent thing in the world is change; how necessary to mental health is a saving faith in God and in one's fellow men. You will learn also what is meant by psychological "weaning." You will find some wise rules, too, for preserving mental health in the family circle, and some suggestions looking toward the time when you will be choosing a mate and setting up your own family circle.

Fig. 72. The healthy-minded person has a task which he takes pride
in doing well. Does this commercial artist enjoy his work?

20. DEVELOPING A HEALTHY MIND

Before you begin the chapter, see what your own present ideas are about healthy minds and unhealthy ones. List on the form below the ideas which you have:

TWO KINDS OF MINDS

These Are Healthy, Sane, Well Adjusted	These Are Unhealthy, Sick, Poorly Adjusted
1. Minds that stick to the task	1. Minds that neglect the task
2.	2.
3.	3.
4.	4.
5. etc.	5. etc.

There are, of course, all degrees of mental health and mental illness. Try to think of some of the most sane people you know, and of some of the least sane ones, and then extract from both types the qualities that account for good and for poor mental adjustment.

THE IMPORTANCE OF HAVING A HEALTHY MIND

Inmates of feeble-minded institutions. No matter how healthy a person's body may be, it will profit him little if he does not possess a healthy and sound mind to direct it. Indeed, you would find in many a feeble-minded institution, if you were to make a canvass, people in considerable numbers whose physical health is good enough. Yet these same individuals are so low in their mentality that they have to spend much if not most of their lives under detention, where they can do no harm either to themselves or to others.

Save for the bare fact that they are not physically uncomfortable, the inmates of these institutions are, of course, totally unable to derive any real benefits from their physical soundness. They cannot use it as a basis upon which to project themselves into a stimulating business or professional or occupational career; nor can they use it as a springboard into sports, or social service, or any of the altruistic fields of expression—all because, though their bodies are sound and well, their minds are the minds of babes.

Inmates of hospitals for the insane. Still another sort of institution where we might find people with good bodies but with minds helpless to manage them would be the mental hospital. Here are people who once had sound minds, but who have lost them, and who are now mentally diseased.

If you could see George Crestley today, for example, as he broods away his life in such a hospital, you would realize vividly how much a sound mind means.

George is twenty-two years old. Less than two years ago he was a popular, active, intelligent youth, interested in a score of things, including school, sports, and sociability.

Today he is only a shadow of himself as he sits, silent, detached, somber, with no interest left in anything or anybody, himself included. His splendid physical health is sharply reduced, because of his inactivity. If he speaks at all, it is only in monosyllables. Never a smile lights his face; never a regret flitters across his darkened consciousness that he can no longer swing a bat, play his accordion, mingle with his set; never, apparently, a yearning for the things that were. He sits in a darkened inner world, and there is slim likelihood that any light will again penetrate it for many long months and perhaps years to come.

Less extreme forms of mental ill health. The feeble-minded and the insane are, of course, extremes of the mentally unsound, and as such often have to be confined to institutions. In a less extreme form, we come upon unhealthy minds in the people with whom we are thrown into contact every day. They are neither feeble-minded nor demented. They may even pass for ordinary persons; actually, however, their mental health is insecure.

Here are a few of the mentally unhealthy types:

People who live an aimless, purposeless existence, unfired by ambition and a goal;

People who are lazy and slothful, allowing others to assume their proper responsibilities and fight their battles for them;

People who permit their emotions rather than their intelligence to govern them, and who rush blindly ahead to grief;

People who allow themselves to grow mentally indolent and to lose contact with the forward movement of civilization;

People who lose their bearings easily, who become panicky and frightened, who withdraw before the combat starts;

People who take themselves too seriously, who overemphasize their own opinions and plans, who cannot smile and see the humorous side;

People who are handicapped by fears, inadequacies, and slinking inferiorities, who are afraid of life and face it dubiously;

People who have never grown up but who have remained infantile in their outlooks and values.

People who have forgotten, if they ever knew, how to play.

These types of persons are as unsound mentally as are the feeble-minded and the insane. The difference is only one of degree, and it is sometimes but a step from these unfortunate mental attitudes to the more insidious and difficult ones manifested by the inmates of institutions. It behooves us all, then, to inquire rather carefully into our own personal viewpoints and behavior patterns in order to see wherein our own mental health may be improved. We shall endeavor in the remaining pages of this book to suggest some of the simpler ways in which we may all strive for that priceless boon of sound mental health.

THE HEALTHY-MINDED PERSON HAS A TASK

A job makes for sanity. There is nothing so likely to keep a man sane as the awareness that he has a task to perform, a job to do in the world. Give a man a job and you have largely provided him with the keys to sanity and self-respect. Take away his job—or worse still, put him into a mood that makes him resent having a job—and you have set his feet on the high road to mental illness. It is amazing how many people there are in the world who complain of the work they have to do, who seek actively for ways to reduce it or to avoid it altogether. Fortunately there is also that vast majority of people who accept their jobs as inevitable responsibilities, as points of departure for comfort, happiness, and self-respect.

The first pay envelope! Almost everybody looks forward eagerly as a child and youth to the time when he will be old enough to get a job and "be on his own." The prospect is a fascinating one. There is a great thrill attached to the first pay envelope or the first regular pay, and rightly so, for the recipient has shown by his industry and self-investment that he is now an integral part of the great, far-flung workaday enterprise to which untold millions of people in the world are committed. Awareness of this fact, and of his embarkation upon a task that identifies him with the mass of responsible employed people, is decidedly a sobering and stabilizing force in the life of the young person.

Pride in the task is essential. The nature of the job itself is of little consequence, assuming that it is some type of legitimate enterprise. It may be manual or head work; it may be skilled or unskilled, in factory or on farm: the important and only essential thing is that it be accepted as one's *task*, and that he shall discharge it faithfully and even with some degree of pride.

A janitress in a large public building, with which the author is familiar, feels her part in the upkeep and comfort of the building to be so important that there is always a subdued glow of satisfaction on her face as she busies herself with cleaning walls and furnishings and floors. And a gardener whom the author sees often at work is as proud of his early blooms and neatly trimmed hedges and cropped grass and well-edged lawns as though he were really the owner of the estate rather than the gardener.

Such faithful and industrious workers as these merit everybody's respect and admiration. And they themselves always have the inner satisfaction that goes with unswerving commitment to a task. Contrast their mental health and sanity with that of the idler, the loafer, and the parasite who identify themselves with nothing constructive.

SOUND-MINDED PEOPLE FULFILL THEIR DREAMS

Push is better to rely upon than pull. Some individuals are more concerned about "pull" than they are about "push." They are of the opinion that nobody ever "gets there" without some "pull," and unless a person knows somebody with influence, he cannot hope to achieve much of anything worth while. Some other individuals are convinced that the world owes them a living, and that all they can be expected to do is sit back and let somebody else discharge their obligations. They remind one of the unthrifty farmer who, being too lazy to bother himself with the confining spring and summer task of raising a pig, waited until autumn and then rolled his pork barrel out of the cellar and prayed that the good Lord would fill it with pork against the coming long winter.

The healthy-minded person may and should be a dreamer, but he ought to have the foresight and industry to make his dreams come true. The healthy-minded person may be aware of the fact that some people have "pull," but he does not cast about to find leverage for his *own* ascent; he has faith in his own integrity and in his own capacity to achieve his goal by honest and sustained efforts. His faith in the future is not beclouded by speculation regarding the influence that he might be able to muster. Others may line up their "friends" as they will, but he proceeds confidently to make his plans for achieving his objective, and to hew his way to it under his own power and by his own determined efforts. If his friends really amount to anything, they will rally to his aid, anyway, and give him all the honest help they can. There should be no recourse to "pull" among people who have something to offer to the occupational world.

THE HEALTHY-MINDED PERSON EXPECTS CHANGE

You can't hold back the clock! How gratifying it might be if the mother could hold back the hands of time and keep her child always her child; or if the child could perpetuate those golden days in which he is a child, protected and championed by his parents, shielded from the harshness of the world, and revered as the central actor in the sheltered drama of home! But life is not like that. The world is not static. Everything moves on. Everything changes and becomes something else. Childhood with its limitations merges into youth, with its greater opportunities and its greater capacities and responsibilities. Youth broadens out into adulthood, with its infinitely more complex potentialities and programs for achievement. And in due time adult powers begin to decline and old age creeps over the former man of affairs.

Not only does the physical body change; so does everything

else. The physical environment changes; the earth changes; human relationships change; neighborhoods and homes change; attitudes and ideals change; values and traditions change. The well-adjusted, healthy-minded individual realizes that the things of today are but transient, and that tomorrow is bound to bring different situations, different problems, different ways of thinking and feeling and doing. "The old order changeth," indeed, and nobody can entirely anticipate what lies beyond today.

If we take it for granted that "only change is permanent," and try our best to develop self-reliance, broad interests, tolerant attitudes of mind, and the cheerful expectation of change, we shall meet whatever new problems and situations may arise in the years ahead of us with confidence and even with anticipation.

Think over this matter of change as you yourself are aware of it in your own continuing experience as an individual. On the form below suggest some of its manifestations:

AREAS OF LIFE IN WHICH I AM CONSCIOUS OF CHANGE

Change Occurs in These Areas:	Physical	Intellectual	Family	Social
As shown by the fact that:	1. My size has increased as I have grown older. 2. 3. 4. 5. etc.	I have better judgment to-day than I had last year.	Two of my near relatives have recently died.	I am more confident in my-self than I used to be.

(Add any other areas of experience you wish, of course.)

THE HEALTHY-MINDED PERSON KEEPS COOL

Cool heads are better than hot ones. In the stepped-up age we live in, crises are bound to arise more frequently than in a more static kind of civilization. These crises may be in the nature of "jams" into which our machines get us, as for example in industrial accidents, traffic accidents, and the like. Or the crises may be in the nature of personal, or family, or political or social, or vocational, or professional difficulties, as for example when a person finds himself maladjusted in his home or school, or unsuited to his job, or confronted by a change of boss or of party in power.

Regardless of the nature of the crisis with which we are confronted, it is important that we shall "keep our heads," remain cool and poised, keep our tempers, refrain from blaming others. The man who, panic-stricken because of an accident, flees the scene without making himself known is temporarily, at least, out of control; so is the man who "walks out on" his wife or his employer; so is the man who flies into a passion when his side is defeated, or when his candidate is unsuccessful, or when his competence is called into question. Cool heads are at a premium in an exciting and "jittery" age. The mob may be counted upon to be hotheaded; it is upon you and me, and all the other folks who are intelligent and disciplined, that the responsibility of providing an example of intelligent and rational behavior in times of crisis must fall.

HEALTHY-MINDED PEOPLE KNOW HOW TO PLAY

A safety valve. Play and the capacity to play are as essential to our mental health as are work and the capacity to work. Play is a safety valve through which we rid ourselves of too much steam and step down our nerves from the throbbing pulsation of active work. Play is a temporary way of escape from the baffling, the vexing, the unsolvable, and we all need regularly this release from the constant strain of the age. Play is a great stabilizer, helping us to forget the trying and consuming things of everyday life and to engross ourselves **for**

the time being in what is pleasing and recreating. Play is the great protector of our sanity, withdrawing us all now and again from our preoccupation with the trying and the confusing and the exhausting, and engulfing us in periodic moments of distraction and release.

An antidote to the poisons of the age. When a person forgets how to play, how to let down and relax and find enjoyment in simple avocations and fads and whimsies, he is in a bad way indeed. It is a mistake for anybody, however ambitious and eager he may be to drive toward his goals, to take himself too seriously on all occasions. He needs plenty of opportunity to laugh—at himself and at his fellows; to indulge his lighter fancies; to venture into the fascinating realms of hobby; to joke and chat with his associates; to relax and let the world go by for a season; to romp with children, with youth, with grown-ups; to sing, dance, paint, sketch, read, hike, go to the theater or the movies, lie on the beach, watch the clouds drifting and the sunset fading.

To do these things now and then, and to find delight in them, is to furnish any of us with a powerful antidote to the poisons that cling about our body-machine when it is geared to the rapid tempo of the modern age.

HEALTHY-MINDED PEOPLE USE MONEY WISELY

Every dollar has one hundred cents. Some people are born with silver spoons in their mouths. They never have to earn money, but fall heir to it by the fortunes of birth. Other people there are who must earn their money by the sweat of their brow. The latter usually understand far better the value of money than do the former. So many dollars represent to them the expenditure of so many hours of their energy, strength, or brain power. Naturally they, too, are the people who think twice before they "blow in" their hard-earned dollars; they are much more careful in their expenditures than the rich-born; they are much less likely to be extravagant or wasteful. They have had to learn the often painful lesson that a dollar means one hundred cents, each one of which is a definite product of their active brain, or brawn, or both.

Using money for self-improvement. He is a wise individual who knows the value of money and knows also how to expend it wisely, so that it will bring him the greatest amount of happiness and satisfaction—happiness and satisfaction, not merely in the number and extent of his material possessions, but in the immaterial acquisitions he may get for himself and in the good he can do for others. To see a bit of the world; to patronize concerts and exhibits; to attend lectures; to improve oneself generally—these are ends to be secured through the wise expenditure of money quite as much as the acquisition of material goods and luxuries.

"For he owed not any man." The well-adjusted individual learns to live within his means, to pay his debts and his bills promptly, to shun installment buying, to put aside some portion of his earnings regularly in the form of savings. Nothing can contribute more to a personal feeling of security and well-being than the awareness that one has money in the bank, that he owes no man anything, and that he can look the world unflinchingly in the eye. On the other hand, nothing can be a source of greater discouragement and perhaps apprehensiveness than the awareness that one's creditors are ever on his trail, that he is improvident and careless in the use of his money, and that he is always only one jump ahead of financial disaster.

Self-sufficient folks. The extreme which is just the opposite of spendthriftiness and improvidence is stinginess. Most penurious people are selfish or indifferent to the call of need and of philanthropy. They feel no impulse to relieve suffering, or to give to this, that, and the other cause. Their values are principally self-centered. Everything revolves about themselves and their immediate families. They "hang on to" their money; they "salt it down"; they "never spend a cent"; they are "snug as the bark of a tree"; they are close-fisted; they are skinflints and Shylocks. These are among the popular expressions commonly applied to such people.

A pretty good rule for the intelligent use of money was laid down many generations ago by a noted English religionist, who advised people to "Give all you can, spend all you can, and save all you can!" Undoubtedly the most serene individuals are those who both earn and save, store up and give. Money thus becomes to anybody a splendid medium for the all-around development of character and of enduring satisfactions if it is made to take its proper place in the pattern of our lives.

Is money the root of all evil—or may it be the root of much good? On the form below suggest some positive uses to which money is put which enhance the social good:

SOME SOCIALLY VALUABLE THINGS MONEY CAN DO

The Thing Under-taken	Example	Results
1. Research in medicine	The work done in the Mayo Clinic	Diseased people are made well.
2.		
3.		
4.		
5. etc.		

(Money ought to have tremendous power for good in every area of human experience.)

HEALTHY-MINDED PEOPLE HAVE FAITH IN GOD

Man's preoccupation with his machines. Devoting himself and his energies to the production and management of his machines, man has grown overconfident of himself and his skill. Flattered by his success in achieving domination over the material things of his environment, he has become conceited, vain, self-sufficient. Master of the physical universe, he has seen no need or place for God; indeed, he tends almost to regard himself as God. Is not he himself creator, discoverer? Does he not himself pull the strings and see his handiwork perform for him? Bold, arrogant, he finds it easy to forget his lowly estate. Tremendously occupied and preoccupied with his machines, he has neither the time nor the inclination to be humble and reverent. Humility and reverence are not becoming to creators.

Man has thus far been too inclined to place his faith in himself and in his own competence to solve his own and the world's problems. By leaving out God, man has neglected to put his own strength and will in touch with the great Source of all strength and will, and in consequence has failed in redeeming society and the world. Man has been so captivated and inflated by the amazing control which he has gained over the material world and its forces that he has all but overlooked the creative and regulative power of God. He is like a Roman governor, who, bloated with power and importance, has forgotten Caesar.

Why faith and reverence are essential. Faith in God and reverence for His illimitable might and for His eternal laws are essential traits in us all. Through them, men experience the greatest ennobling and refining of character that is possible to human achievement; through them they are led to an awesome comprehension of the sweep and majesty of divine power; through them they attain to that state of spiritual wonder without which life is limited to dull and prosaic materialism; through them they develop an admiration for a universe that is boundless and limitless; through them they achieve a sobering conviction of the timelessness of time and of the space-lessness of space; through them they are able to get a proper perspective of themselves in relation to the whole created order.

More and more one finds serious people turning to the power of religious faith as the one infallible means of salvation for a world that has plunged itself dangerously out of control. More and more they are beginning to sense the importance of faith in God as the Great Arbiter of the universe and to understand that only as men observe and practice it can they discipline themselves and live amicably and helpfully with their fellow men.

HEALTHY-MINDED PEOPLE BELIEVE IN OTHERS

Faith on lower levels than religious faith is also essential in the modern world. You have faith in your parents, that they will continue to provide for you a home and the necessities of life; you have faith in your teachers that they will continue to help you to prepare as well as possible for life tomorrow; you have faith in your friends and mates that they will be loyal to you through thick and thin. We all have faith in the grocer that he will sell us only healthful food; in the banker that he will protect our deposits and return them to us, with interest, when we demand them; in the engineer that he will construct a skyscraper or a suspension bridge or a tunnel that will be safe for those who make use of it; in the pilot that he will bring us to the desired port; in our representatives that they will attend to the best interests of the people; in government, that it will be stable and secure. Faith in these people and agencies is taken as a matter of course, and our faith is ordinarily justified.

This same principle of faith governs the conception, the creation, and the operation of even machines. The inventor has faith in his ideas, the artisan in his skill to objectify the ideas

of the inventor, and the operator in the reliability of the handiwork of the artisan. All along the line modern civilization depends on the mutual faith which men have in one another,
and on the respect which they have for each other's contribution to the social welfare.

On the form below enumerate a large number of individuals
and institutions in which you have complete faith that they
will fulfill their obligations or promises:

MY FAITH IN OTHER PEOPLE AND IN INSTITUTIONS

I have faith that:
  1. The bank will pay me dividends on my savings.
  2.
  3.
  4.
  5. etc.
(Mutual faith is what makes the world go round for us all.)

SOUND-MINDED PEOPLE ARE COURTEOUS AT HOME

Dr. Jekyll and Mr. Hyde. When we are at home among
those we know best, we sometimes forget to be courteous and
agreeable. "Familiarity breeds contempt," as the saying goes,
and so indeed it often does. It is easy to criticize, easy to find
fault, easy to contradict, to fly into a passion, to speak un-
kindly or impolitely when in the bosom of one's own family.
Outside, on the other hand, one tends to be on guard and on
his good behavior. When he is with other people he may be
the soul of courtesy and consideration—a pattern of good conduct, speech, dress, carriage, and deportment. To those whom
he meets and with whom he associates he appears to be somebody well worth while.

A well-bred person is consistent in his personality. He is not
Mr. Hyde at home and Dr. Jekyll away from home; he maintains the same courteous and cordial attitudes and the same

character traits under both conditions. He strives consciously to be as attractive and interesting when with his own people and under his own roof as when he goes out among others. Somehow, unless he is thus consistent, he does not ring quite true, and his personality gives off a false note that is usually not too hard to detect.

Faultfinding and peevishness. Nothing strikes the casual visitor in any family circle more powerfully than does the mutual respect, or lack of it, in which the two generations hold each other. Living within the four narrow walls of a home, it is desperately easy for all concerned to fall into the habit of faultfinding and peevishness. It is particularly easy for the young adolescents to do so. Naturally critical and impatient, they tend, unless they exercise eternal vigilance, to develop highly unfortunate mental attitudes toward their elders. Peevishness is a vice just as much as lying or trickery are; it can make any personality unlovely, and can mar the happiness of any home.

It may sometimes happen, of course, that your parents, tired and perplexed with the cares of the day, and worried over tomorrow, grow irritable, both toward one another and toward you. We all need to put forth special effort in the family circle to pardon the occasional moodiness we find, to be particularly sympathetic toward those who carry the burdens of the day, and to keep serene and sweet so that they may find peacefulness and understanding. Weary fathers and mothers will be able to maintain happier attitudes themselves if they realize that their adolescent children are trying hard to keep sunny and agreeable.

Forgotten parents. In the thrill of new-found companionships and the ardor of exciting adolescent adventure in school and club and set, it is sometimes easy to forget the kindness and the faithfulness of parents and to drift apart from them emotionally. Under such circumstances one may come to exaggerate shortcomings and defects and to grow actually indifferent to his parents or even scornful of them. While this is likely to be but a passing phase of growing up, it is a most regrettable one and should be eliminated as much as possible.

Appreciate your parents. Take them into your confidence and follow their advice. Show them by little acts of kindness and thoughtfulness that you love them and are proud of them. Don't make the mistake of waiting until they are no longer with you to realize what you owe them. As Nixon Waterman puts it:

> A rose to the living is more
> Than sumptuous wreaths to the dead;
> In filling love's infinite store,
> A rose to the living is more
> If graciously given before
> The hungering spirit is fled—
> A rose to the living is more
> Than sumptuous wreaths to the dead.

Your parents may be old and worn; they may be poor; they may be illiterate or may bear slight marks of culture; they may speak broken English and may seem foreign in many of their ways. Such things as these make no difference. A child's parents are his *parents,* and as such they deserve all his love and respect. Often they have sacrificed nobly and given of themselves more than they should in order that they might provide their children with better opportunities and a better education than they themselves enjoyed. These things are never to be forgotten and ought to endear them to their children regardless of surroundings or circumstances.

Bring your friends home! Most parents are interested in the friends and associates of their children and are glad to meet them and to know who they are. Sometimes young adolescents neglect to give their elders this opportunity and have their social good times elsewhere than at home. At school parties, at dances, at young people's meetings, at the movies, at soda fountains they mingle with their friends, but they neglect to entertain them at home. While it is true, of course, that a few parents do not welcome visiting youngsters and discourage their children from bringing them home, most parents are apt to feel decidedly hurt at this lack of thoughtfulness, and are saddened by the neglect implied.

It is a decided wrench, anyway, for most adults when their adolescent boys and girls begin to drift away from them a bit and to form comradeships outside. This natural wrench may be greatly eased if the young people introduce their new friends to them and display a gratifying pride in their home and parents. It must be remembered also that parents are often clever at discerning the innermost traits of their children's companions, and sometimes, if they are permitted to know them, are able to give helpful advice regarding them.

HEALTHY-MINDED PEOPLE ARE MENTALLY WEANED

Growing up is more than growing big. Growing up into adulthood is something infinitely more complex than the mere adding of height and weight. It is more than long trousers and a beard, more than dancing slippers and evening gowns. Becoming an adult involves, along with physical maturing, emotional and social maturing to a degree only faintly realized by the child who looks forward to "being big," or even by many adolescents, who likewise look forward to "coming out parties" and "being their own boss."

The first essential in the process of growing up into healthy-minded adulthood is psychological weaning. That is to say, before an individual ever achieves true maturity, he must become emotionally independent of his family, able to stand on his own feet and to make his way without the continued solicitude and guidance of his parents. Some people never reach the stage in their evolution where they become self-regulating and self-reliant.

Consider, for example, the case of H. W., who had dreamed for years of going to a particular college some three hundred fifty miles from where he lived. Throughout childhood and earlier adolescence he had worked hard at his studies so that there would be no question of his being admitted unconditionally. At last the time came when he said good-by to his father and mother and sisters and left his home environment to go away to college.

Having arrived at the college city, H. W. was from the very first hour homesick and miserable. Classes from day to day passed almost as though they were unreal, for his thoughts kept running away from the present and carrying him back to the family rooftree which he had recently left. Within a fortnight he began to lose weight and even developed a hacking cough which he was convinced meant tuberculosis. The college doctor could find nothing wrong with him, but he continued to cough—if anything, more hackingly than ever. The only bright spots in his days were those when he received letters from home, or when he sat at his table replying to them. He could not get into his studies, and he dreaded every classroom.

Finally, after "sticking it out" for a scant three weeks, H. W. packed his bag and hied him back to his home. There he was received with undisguised joy by parents and sisters—who had apparently been as homesick for a sight of H. W. as H. W. had been for a sight of them. Needless to add, his hacking cough cleared up within a few hours, and within a month he had gained back all the pounds lost. But he did not return to college that year. Nor any other year!

Grown-up infants! Here is a not uncommon case of a psychologically unweaned individual. He was grown up in the physical sense—indeed, he was quite a strapping young fellow; but from the standpoint of emotional and social maturity, he was almost as much an infant as the day he was born!

True, leaving home is often a considerable shock to anybody, when he is doing it for the first time, and he may suffer pangs of homesickness that almost floor him. But when the nostalgia is so keen that one resorts to a hacking cough, or has a nervous breakdown, or develops a paralysis of arms or legs or speech muscles in order to win sympathy, or in order to convince himself that he is trying to do the impossible and so avoid his obligations (all of which *escape mechanisms* are commonly indulged in by psychologically unweaned people when they attempt to be on their own), then the persistence of his truly infantile nature becomes perfectly apparent to anybody and everybody, excepting usually himself.

It is doubtful whether H. W. understood that his cough and his loss of weight and failing health were not genuine, but were his unconscious means of escaping the responsibilities of adulthood and reverting to the old family circle from which he could not tear himself loose. To the outsider, however, or to any keen observer of human nature, the real reason why H. W. returned home was quite obvious.

Building new loyalties. What does psychological weaning mean, then? It means learning to journey far across the threshold of one's childhood home, when the time comes, and daring to face life with some show of confidence. It means learning to find satisfactions that are not limited to the original family circle. It means, without lessening one iota the loyalties to father and mother, the building of other loyalties to oneself, to his chance of a job and of success, and later to his mate and his new family circle. It means the building of a feeling of security, of self-confidence, of self-reliance. True adulthood is never achieved by people like H. W. unless and until they

Fig. 73. Becoming an adult requires that one shall conquer homesickness and learn to be independent. Does any one of these college boys appear to be psychologically unweaned?

take themselves in hand, learn to see through the trickeries of escape mechanisms, and discipline themselves to stand up alone and fight.

Building self-confidence. The goal of psychological weaning, as we have intimated, is the establishment of independence. Theoretically, it is possible for a person to wean himself from his childhood circle and still fail to establish complete independence. Plenty of people who are emancipated from the family circle live an aimless, ineffective sort of existence, with little decisiveness, and with no strong purposes and no stimulating objectives.

Independence implies more than that one is independent of his parents: it implies that he has learned to look to himself for the driving power and the regulative power necessary for adjusting himself to a modern world. It implies that, while understanding the significance of interdependence and social co-operativeness, he is yet conscious of the fact that character in an individual is forged out upon the anvil of self-confidence and of faith in his own abilities and possibilities.

Think over a considerable number of people whom you know personally, and decide who of them are psychologically weaned and who of them have remained overdependent upon their family or friends. Record on a form like that on the next page some of the earmarks of both sorts of individuals.

THE SOUND-MINDED PERSON WANTS HIS OWN HOME

New loyalties and old. Every normal young person looks forward to the day when he can establish his own home circle. It is not too soon now to begin to wean yourself emotionally from your present family circle in anticipation of the day when new loyalties will have to be established. The setting up of these new loyalties will not, of course, necessitate destroying the present ones. The wife and the husband can and ought

PSYCHOLOGICALLY WEANED AND UNWEANED PEOPLE I KNOW

These Individuals Are Emotionally and Socially Mature	As Indicated by This Sort of Conduct	These Individuals Are Emotionally and Socially Infantile	As Indicated by This Sort of Conduct
1. J. M.	Always faces his problems fairly and squarely.	1. P. N.	Has to be coddled and shielded from life.
2.		2.	
3.		3.	
4.		4.	
5. etc.		5. etc.	

(It is to be hoped that the mature people you know will exceed the infantile!)

to remain every whit as devoted to their parents and their original family circles as they were before they ever met each other. But without weakening the ties of the childhood group, room has to be made for the building of the new hearthstone and the development of new loyalties to it.

Look forward, not back! Some people, when they marry, still look back regretfully upon the passing of the old circle; their heartstrings still cling tenaciously to their parents; and their parents more or less actively resent the intrusion of a mate into the life of their offspring. Many a new home "goes on the rocks" because of this infantile holdover of childhood loyalties and their blighting effects upon the married pair. Such individuals have failed to learn the lesson that it is natural and normal for new homes to be established, and that their stability and endurance must rest in large measure upon the wholehearted consecration of the husband and wife to the bond which they have established, and upon the willingness and even eagerness of the older generation to keep "hands off" and give the new partnership a chance to succeed.

Choosing a mate.   Some day you will make the most important decision of your life: the choice of a mate and companion.
When that time comes you will have passed completely out of
the period of preparation for life into life itself. You will take
upon yourself the full name of man or woman. Heretofore,
even though you have had satisfying companionship with
friends and comrades, you have in a sense walked alone; hereafter you will walk with a lover. Be sure it is with a lifelong
lover. Be sure that he whom you choose, or she whom you
choose, is, in the first instance, healthy and clean like yourself,
and in the second instance somebody in whom you can put
your trust and your faith and your hope of happiness.

It may be that you already know rather definitely who the
individual is with whose life you are likely to ally your own;
it may be that you have already met the individual but are
unaware that his or her future lot is to be cast with your own;
it may be that it will be somebody whom you will meet and
learn to love some years hence. It matters little, so long as when
you are ready to make the decision, you satisfy yourself that
here is a man or a woman whom you can love and trust and in
whose presence you can feel a continuing joy and stimulation.

Romantic love still exists.   Enduring conjugal love is not
yet dead in the world; it did not go out with the troubadours
and the knights-errant of Arthur's court. Enduring love is still
possible between a man and a woman, and is able not only to
bring joy and comradeship during the honeymoon season but
to continue to enrich and ennoble life throughout all its vicis-
situdes and all its perplexities. Choosing a mate is no easy task
if the choice is to be a happy one; it requires something more
than a passing infatuation, or a fleeting passion, or an attack
of puppy love. It is not to be successfully accomplished by a
romantic elopement or a sudden ecstatic moment of thrill and
glamour. Altogether too many marriages fail because the part-

ners made the silly mistake of confusing a fleeting physical attraction with a lifelong and satisfying association.

HOW PSYCHOLOGISTS WORK

For people whose mental health has become completely broken, society maintains mental hospitals. These institutions are ordinarily state-controlled and bear the same relationship to mental disease as do general hospitals to physical disease.

Until within the last two centuries, the plight of mentally ill people was most unfortunate and pitiable. Throughout all of early history, and most of modern, demented persons were thought to be possessed of devils, and hence were often driven from the haunts of men and compelled to live in caves and forests, utterly isolated from their fellows and deprived of every form of human ministration. As late as the last century, the insane in many parts of enlightened America were herded into almshouses, jails, and "lunatic asylums," where not infrequently they were confined in damp basements, in iron cages, and in strait jackets, and were most cruelly neglected by everybody.

It seems unbelievable that human society, which has been for many centuries solicitous for the welfare and recovery of its physically sick members, should have been so negligent of its mentally sick. After all, disease is disease, whether it attacks a man's stomach or whether it attacks his brain. The only sensible and human thing is to study it and search out means of controlling and conquering it, regardless of whether it has lodged in the circulatory system or in the nervous system. The fact, however, that the mentally sick people are likely to show erratic outward behavior has served to single them out as persons to be pointed at in merriment. Let an individual's liver or lungs behave abnormally, and society is all sympathy; let, however, his brain misbehave, and—save for some of his immediate family circle—he is likely to be regarded with raised eyebrows and subjected to ridicule.

Society has gone far, though, from the detention house in which, not very long ago, the mentally sick were confined behind barred doors and windows and were left to die or get well as chance might decree, to the modern State Hospital, with its skilled staff and its competent medical service. Manned by highly trained *psychiatrists* (specialists in mental disorders), administered by state officers, and recognized everywhere as centers for research into the problems and forms of mental disease, these institutions have taken their place prominently among the great and beneficent projects of the race.

There are many contributing causes of mental illness. Among them psychiatrists ordinarily distinguish prominently the following:

Defective heredity
Unstable nervous system
Lesions (injuries) in the brain
Poisons or toxins from physical disease
Toxins from prolonged fatigue, overwork, and exhaustion
Physical deprivation, such as famine or solitude
Great fear, worry, or shock.

Like physical disease, mental disease also occurs in many forms and varieties, each one of which is recognized by the psychiatrists by means of its peculiar or characteristic symptoms. Here are some of the more common classifications of *psychosis* (the psychiatrist's term for mental disease):

(1) *Dementia praecox (schizophrenia)*, occurring often in early life and characterized by a gradual withdrawal from reality into a confused dream world which it is difficult for the psychiatrist to penetrate.

(2) *Manic-depressive psychosis (circular insanity)*, charac-

terized by successive periods of great excitability alternating with extreme depression and withdrawal.

(3) *Paranoia,* in which the patient commonly experiences great delusions regarding himself. These delusions are sometimes *delusions of grandeur (grandiose delusions),* in which the patient identifies himself with some notable historical personage; sometimes they are *delusions of persecution (persecutory delusions),* in which he believes somebody—it may be his closest friend or relative—is plotting his disgrace or his actual destruction; sometimes they are *Messianic delusions,* in which he is obsessed with the idea that he is called upon to save the world or bring in Utopia.

(4) *General paresis,* in which the victim is gradually bereft of all sense of honor and decency, deteriorating rapidly to complete paralysis both of body and of mind.

(5) *Alcoholic psychosis.*

(6) *Acute cocaine intoxication.*

(7) *Morphinomania.*

These three are similar in basis, in that each is a mental condition resulting from brain destruction by poisons—in the first case (alcoholic psychosis) from the excessive use of alcohol; in the second (acute cocaine intoxication) from use of some form of cocaine; and in the last (morphinomania) from habituation to morphine. Foolish people often resort to these three forms of intoxication in order to escape from the drabness or the harshness of their ordinary surroundings, and to find exhilaration and joy in abnormally stimulated ideas and fancies. Their doom is inevitable as the poisons eat their way into the nervous system and ultimately destroy it.

The attitude of all intelligent, socially minded people toward those unfortunates in their midst who are mentally sick ought to be one of sympathy and understanding. To joke about them, to laugh at or about them, to submit them to indignities of any sort is to betray in one's character a distinct absence of intelligence and a stunted sense of fitness and propriety. These people are sick, and they need to be so regarded and so treated by every thinking person.

TO HELP YOU LEARN

Some Questions to Answer

1. What have been some of the prominent effects of man's absorption in his machines upon his sense of values and upon his character? Have these effects all been destructive, or can you think of some that have been unquestionably constructive?

2. Do you think you can discern a progression in the idea of God from the primitive conceptions of the aborigines, through the classic conceptions of the Greeks and Romans, to the conception of faithful men and women of today? Explain.

3. Why is the habit of being overdependent on one's parents an undesirable one from the standpoint of one's own ultimate social and emotional maturing?

4. Do you know any broken home? Was it broken by death, or by the separation of the parents? Or is it broken by conflict and friction between them?

5. What does it mean to be an adult? When does one start becoming an adult in the social and emotional sense? How long does it take him to achieve adulthood?

Working with Psychology

1. A notable study of the aims of high school education, made by the National Education Association, lists as one of the principal objectives the promotion of "worthy home membership," the idea being that no person is truly educated who fails to become a worthy and attractive individual in his own family circle.

Draw up the human specifications, as you see them, of a stable and happy family in which, in addition to the father and mother, are a boy and a girl in high school, a younger brother in the grades, and an aging grandparent. Limit the items in your specifications to "Contributions of the father and mother to the happiness of the family," and "Contributions of the high school children to its happiness." Keep your family an ordinary one, and make your specifications ideal without being impossible. Avoid, for example, such Utopian specifications as "The parents never chide or scold"; "Tom is the soul of courtesy and thoughtfulness toward his aged grandfather," and the like. Compare results in class, and from them construct master specifications for such a home.

2. Arrange with the superintendent of a local or near-by mental hospital for some member of his staff to visit your class and talk to it on the general subject of mental health. In the question-and-answer period following, have brought out as clearly as possible the principal causes of mental disease, its means of prevention, its cost to the state, its extent in the community, and the informed attitude toward the whole problem which intelligent citizens and voters ought to take.

3. One of the causes of home conflicts and misunderstandings is the commonly observed circumstance that the older generation— the parents and grandparents—tends to have become conservative in its outlooks and values, while the younger generation—the boys and girls in the home—tends to be strongly liberal and even radical. What evidences can you find contradictory or confirmatory of these tendencies? If the latter is the case, suggest ways in which the two viewpoints may be reconciled with one another.

4. "Only change is permanent." Now that you have completed this introductory excursion into the fascinating realm of psychology, take an hour or so of time to think over what changes you seem to have experienced in your own values and viewpoints as the course has gone forward. Some of these changes in your outlook and adjustment will have come about because of the indisputable fact that you have grown a bit older and more mature; others of them will have been achieved because you have done a lot of thinking about life and about yourself in this study of psychology. Summarize your conclusions in an oral evaluation of the results of your adventuring into the field of psychology.

What Others Say

1. In Psychology:

Letters to Susan by Margaret C. Banning. An excellent and interesting book dealing with most of the problems girls encounter in the process of growing up into womanhood. A sympathetic and helpful treatment of the achieving of mental health.

The Art of Thinking by Abbé Ernest Dimnet. The noted Canon of Cambrai Cathedral provides in this volume sound and stimulating advice for those who would be mentally healthy in their adjustment to the demands which life makes upon us all.

Keeping a Sound Mind by John J. B. Morgan. One of the most helpful books of all those dealing with mental health. Written by a prominent psychologist, it is packed full of challenging discussions of the ways and means of keeping ourselves sane and wholesome personalities. It is attractively written and fascinating to read.

What We Live By by Abbé Ernest Dimnet. A most delightful book on the general theme of satisfying and adventuresome living on the higher plane.

2. In Religious Essay:

Return to Religion by Henry C. Link. A noteworthy presentation of the contributions which faith in God has to make to happy and successful living in the modern age.

3. In Fiction:

Big Family by B. Partridge. A very amusing portrayal of some of the problems of family living, presented by five boys and three girls who tell their troubles, their adventures, and their romances.

4. In Drama:

The Goose Hangs High by Lewis Beach. An entertaining comedy dealing with the efforts of a modern family to adjust themselves to difficult circumstances.

5. In Poetry:

Abou Ben Adhem by Leigh Hunt. The vision of Abou, who saw an angel in his chamber writing in a book of gold, listing the names of all those who loved their fellow men. "And lo! Ben Adhem's name led all the rest."

INDEX

Accidents, in industrial plants, 235

Activity, mental: as a want, 16-18; essential in study, 91-93; essential in thinking, 286

Adjustment (*see* Harmonious living, Mental health, Obstacles); poor, 366-78; good, 363-66, 445-47, 450-52, 459-62, 531-51

Adrenal glands, defined, 263

Amnesia, 176

Anger: universality of, 249-50; good and bad in, 250-51; conquest of, 261-62

Animals: wants of (*see* Wants, Animal); training of, 183, 185, 199-201; our similarity to, 249

Appreciation: vocational importance of, 401-402; as an ideal of character, 430-31; essential to leadership, 449

Aptitude testing, 397-98

Association, law of, 188-94

Associations: learning to form, 166-68; in learning, 183-85, 188-94; in conditioning, 199-201, 205-208

Astrologers: medieval, 298; as propagandists, 305-307

Attention, 127-54; importance of paying, 127-29, 144, 164-66; continuous bombardment of, 131-32; purpose of, 132-36; power to focus, 132-33; as paving the way for perception, 133-36; importance of experience in, 134-36; involuntary, 136-38; voluntary, 139-40, 146; fluctuation of, 141-44, 150; attitude of, 145; rules for improving, 145-47; importance of sense organs in, 147-51; and illusions, 150; in learning, 195

Attitudes, 106-126; in study, 90-91, 91-93, 95-96, 144, 145, 169-70, 198; permanence of, 106-107; of optimism or pessimism, 106-107; our dominate, 109-18; toward work, 109-10, 216-17, 225-26; toward perseverance, 110; toward thrift, 110-11; toward custom,

111-12; toward country, 113-14; toward other peoples, 114-16; toward morality and religion, 116-18; toward ourselves, 118; sources of, 118-21; strong feeling connected with, 121-22; importance of changing, 122; investigations of the effect of movies on, 122-24; in learning, 193; in vocations, 383, 392-93, 450-52; for nondelinquents, 515-17; toward insanity, 551-52, 553-54

Averill, Lawrence A., 82, 507

Aviation: as a vocational field, 384; in high school curriculums, 406

Balance: organ of, 63; in personality, 476, 485-86

Benzedrine sulfate, harmful effects of, 310-11

Boredom: relation to fatigue, 212-14; and pseudo fatigue, 223-25

Brain, human: importance of, 53-54; as seat of consciousness, 64; parts of, 65-67; areas in, 65-66; diagram of, 66; investigation of areas in, 76-79

Brain response: 70-71; diagram of, 70

Bridgman, Laura: examination of brain of, 76-79; diagram of brain of, 78

Cannon, W. B., 248

Case histories: showing difficulty of breaking bad habits, 43-44; showing conditioned fear, 252-53; showing poor adjustment to conflict, 360; showing insanity, 529; showing lack of psychological weaning, 545

Cerebellum, 65, 67

Cerebrum, 65-67

Character: vocational importance of, 399-402; examples of good, 411-14; definition of, 415-16; stability of, 416-17; good, as leading to good acts, 417-18; conflicting influences shaping, 418-21; importance of emotion in, 422-24;

Escape mechanisms, 375-78

Excitement: universal craving for, 457-58; youthful search for, 506-507, 512-13, 515-16

Exercise, law of, in learning, 194-96

Experience: and perception, 134-36; building up, 135-36, 145-46

Experimentation, as a psychological method, 74, 263

Experiments, psychological: on animal drives, 19-21; on habit formation, 45-48; on the effect of distractions on work, 100-103; on the rate and amount of forgetting, 176-79; on conditioned learning, 205-208; on fatigue, 234-36; on the effect of emotion, 263-66; on measurement of intelligence, 342-49; on measurement of honesty, 434-36; on ductless glands, 490-91

Extrovert, 481-82

Eye: as gateway to brain, 59-60; diagram of, 148

Failure (*see* Conflict, Obstacles)

Faith: in oneself, 367, 459-60, 548; in God, 538-40; in others, 540-41

Family: security through the, 11; resemblance in the same, 327-28 (*see* Home)

Fatigue: and work (*see* Work); defined, 218-20; toxins, 219-20; pseudo, 223-25; experimentation in, 234-36; as a cause of insanity, 552

Fear: as a deterrent, 251; children's, 251-52; conditioned, 252-53; worry a form of, 254; conquest of, 262; as a cause of insanity, 552

Feeble-mindedness, 528-29

Feelings: and emotions, 240-69 (*see* Emotions); pleasant and unpleasant, 244-47; physical side of, 245; higher, 245-46; as different from emotions, 247

Focus of attention, 133

Followership: need of, 447-48; in vocations, 450-52

Forgetting: reasons for, 171-75; principle of, 178; curve of, 178

Fortunetellers, as propagandists, 304-307

Frequency, principle of, in learning, 191

Freud, Sigmund, 376

Friendship: security through, 11; as a source of attitudes, 119; reasons for, 422-23; meaning of, 454-55

Galvanometer, 264

Generosity, as a personality pattern, 478 (*see* Social-mindedness)

Genes: in heredity, 325; influence of, on personality, 483

Geneticists, defined, 325

Genius: of Pasteur, 323; unpredictability of, 329

Getting along, with others and oneself (*see* Harmonious living)

Glands: adrenal, 263; sweat, 264; influence of, on personality, 483, 490-92; ductless, 490-92

Gonads, 491

Graphs: showing speed in learning new habit, 47; showing rate of forgetting, 178; showing daily production in industrial plant, 235

Group living, importance of, 445

Habits, 25-50; good and bad, 25-27; our slavery to, 29-32; inevitability of, 32; formation of good, 32-33; ease in forming, 34-36; possibility of breaking, 36-37; as time savers, 37-38; as the basis of skills, 38; as conservers of energy, 38-39; as mind freers, 39, 147; as impeders of progress, 40-41; James's laws for forming, 41-42; quotation from James concerning, 42-43; case histories concerning, 43-44; experimentation on, 45-48

Happiness: a universal goal, 458-59; ways of achieving, 459-62

Harmonious living, 440-68; leadership and followership in, 440-42, 447-50; with others, 444-55; in a social world, 444-47; with superiors and co-workers, 450-52; by being a good listener, 452-54; by being a friend, 454-55; with oneself, 455-62; by achieving happiness, 458-62

Heredity, 320-52; importance of both environment and, 320-25, 334-35; in Jukes and Bach families, 320-21; determined by genes, 325; of like traits by all, 326; of family traits, 327-28;

Leadership, 447-50: need of, 449; need for appreciation in, 449; need for capacity for, 449-50; among children and adolescents, 462-65

Learning: attitudes in, 90-91, 91-93, 95-96, 144, 145, 169-70; method of recall in, 93-94; by rote, 160-62; logical method of, 163-71; whole and part methods of, 172; principle of distributed practice in, 173; law of use in, 174, 194-96; emotions in, 175; experimentation in, 176-79; some rules of, 183-211; associations in, 166-68, 183-85, 188-90, 199-201, 205-208; importance of laws of, 187-88; principle of frequency in, 191; principle of recency in, 191-92; principle of primacy in, 192; principle of vividness or intensity in, 192-93; principle of mood in, 193; law of exercise in, 194-96; law of effect in, 196-98; principle of conditioning in, 199-201, 205-208; principle of transfer in, 202-204; experiments on conditioned, 205-208

Leisure time, use of, 232-34

Lie detector (see Polygraph)

Light wave: as stimulus to eye, 59-60; diagram of, 60

Listening, art of, 452-54

Living, with others and oneself (see Harmonious living)

Love: as an emotion, 255; romantic, 550-51

Loyalty: as an ideal of character, 428-30; as a cause of crime, 508-509; to the right kind of group, 515; building new, 546, 548-49

Malingering, mechanism of, 376

Manic-depressive psychosis, 552

Margin of attention, 133

Marriage, looking forward to, 548-51

Martyr complex, 375

Mate, choosing a, 550

Medicines, patent, 307-309

Medulla oblongata, 65, 67

Memory, 155-182; good and poor, 155-57; rote vs. logical, 159-61; limitations of rote, 161-62; advantages of logical, 163-64; how to develop a logical, 164-71; reasons for a poor, 171-75;

peculiarities of, 175-76; experimentation in, 176-79; tests of, 159, 180-82

Mental age, 345

Mental health: in solving conflicts, 363-66, 373-74; development of, 524-56; vital to success, 524-26; importance of, 528-31; people who lack, 530, 551-54; need of a task for, 531-32; fulfilling dreams makes for, 532-33; expecting change makes for, 533-34; keeping cool makes for, 534-35; need of play for, 535-36; using money wisely makes for, 536-38; faith in God makes for, 538-40; courtesy at home makes for, 541-44; need of psychological weaning for, 544-48; wanting one's own home makes for, 548-51

Mind, active (see Activity, mental)

Mind, healthy (see Mental health)

Mnemonics, use of, 170-71

Money, use of, 536-38

Mood: principle of, in learning, 193; Hippocrates on, 489

Morality: attitudes toward, 116-18; active and passive, 426 (see Character)

Movies, as a source of attitudes, 120; investigations of the effect of, on attitudes, 122-24

Muscular strain, organs of, 63

Nationalism, 113-16

Nerves: sensory or afferent, 67, 69, 70; motor or efferent, 67, 69, 70

Nervous system: plasticity of, 35-36; modifiability of, 36-37; central, 64-71; auxiliary, or autonomic, 71-73; unstable, 552

Neurologist, defined, 76

Neurosis: as an escape mechanism, 377-78; bad influence of, 487

Nonsense syllables, 179

Notetaking, in study, 98

Observation: as a psychological method, 73, 263; importance of, 285

Obstacles: meeting, 353-80; attacking or running away from, 353-55, 366-67; conflicts in meeting, 357-62 (see Conflict, Failure); solving conflicts when meeting, 363-73; protecting one's ego

Recall: usefulness in study, 93-94; method of, in memory experiments, 176-77; thinking is more than, 274-76

Receiving mechanism: importance of, 53-54; use of, 59-68

Recency, principle of, in learning, 191

Receptors, defined, 62

Recognition, method of, in memory experiments, 176, 177

Reflex action or response, 68-69; diagram of, 69

Regression, mechanism of, 376

Relearning, method of, 176, 177-78

Reliability, as ideal of character, 427-28

Religion: attitudes toward, 116-18; essential to mental health, 538-40

Repression, mechanism of, 376-77

Responding mechanism: importance of, 53-54; description of, 68; kinds of, 68-71

Response: reflex, 68-69; brain, 70-71; conditioned, 199-201, 205-208

Reverie, thinking is more than, 275-76

Reviews, proper spacing of, 173-74; importance of, 191-92

Rivalry: social, 13; economic, 13-14; political and professional, 14

Scientific basis of psychology, 51-82; receiving, comprehending, responding, 51-54; objective and subjective worlds, 56-59; sense organs as gateways to brain, 59-63; eye, 59-60; ear, 60-61; skin sense organs, 61-62; taste organs, 62; olfactory organ, 62; organs of muscular strain, 63; organ of balance, 63; organs indicating pain and comfort, 63; limitations of sense organs, 64; central nervous system, 64-71; brain, 64-67; cerebrum, 65-67; cerebellum and medulla, 67; spinal cord, 67-68; responding mechanism, 68-71; reflex response, 68-69; brain response, 71; auxiliary nervous system, 71-73; psychological methods, 73-74; fields of psychology, 74-76; scientific investigation of brain areas, 76-79

Security, as a want, 9-11

Self-centeredness: as preventing friendship, 454-55; as a personality trait, 469-71, 475, 478

Self-confidence, need for, 548

Self-control, emotional, 260-62; as an ideal of character, 432

Self-expression, as a want, 7-19

Self-interest, as a personality pattern, 478 (see Self-centeredness)

Selfishness (see Personality, Self-centeredness)

Semicircular canals, 63

Sense organs, 59-64 (see Scientific basis of psychology); importance of, in attention, 147-50

Sincerity, importance of emotional, 422

Skill, manual, in vocations, 396

Skin sense organs: as gateways to brain, 61-62; diagrams of principal, 61

Sleep, and rest, importance of, 222-23

Smell (see Olfactory organ)

Social-mindedness: indispensability of, 445-47; as a personality trait, 469-71, 475, 478

Sound wave, as stimulus to ear, 60-61

Sour grapes mechanism, 368-69

Spastics: defined, 52; Dr. Earl Carlson's clinics for, 53

Sphygmograph, 263

Sphygmomanometer, use in studying emotion, 263

Spinal cord, 67

Sportsmanship, as an ideal of character, 432

Stanford-Binet intelligence test, 343-46; photograph of materials used in, 344; setup of, 345

Stimuli: defined, 60, 132; external and internal, 132-33; arousing involuntary attention, 138; adequate and inadequate, 199-201, 205-208

Studying, 83-105; ease or difficulty in, 83-85; importance of efficiency in, 87-88; in school, 88-90; hints for, 90-96; making outlines in, 96-97; taking notes in, 98; using knowledge acquired in, 98-99; physical conditions in, 99-100; effects of distractions on, 100-103; satisfaction from, 197; attitudes in (see Attitudes)

Submissiveness, as a childhood trait, 463-65

Substitution: as emotional transfer, 259-60; solving conflict by, 364-65